Ius Comparatum – Global Studies in Comparative Law

Volume 58

As globalization proceeds, the significance of the comparative approach in legal scholarship increases. The IACL / AIDC with almost 800 members is the major universal organization promoting comparative research in law and organizing congresses with hundreds of participants in all parts of the world. The results of those congresses should be disseminated and be available for legal scholars in a single book series which would make both the Academy and its contribution to comparative law more visible. The series aims to publish the scholarship emerging from the congresses of IACL / AIDC, including: 1. of the General Congresses of Comparative Law, which take place every 4 years (Brisbane 2002; Utrecht 2006, Washington 2010, Vienna 2014, Fukuoka 2018 etc.) and which generate (a) one volume of General Reports edited by the local organizers of the Congress; (b) up to 30 volumes of selected thematic reports dealing with the topics of the single sections of the congress and containing the General Report as well as the National Reports of that section; these volumes would be edited by the General Reporters of the respective sections; 2. the volumes containing selected contributions to the smaller (2-3 days) thematic congresses which take place between the International Congresses (Mexico 2008; Taipei 2012; Montevideo 2016 etc.); these congresses have a general theme such as "Codification" or "The Enforcement of Law" and will be edited by the local organizers of the respective Congress. All publications may contain contributions in English and French, the official languages of the Academy.

More information about this series at http://www.springer.com/series/11943

Académie Internationale de Droit Comparé
International Academy of Comparative Law

Nicolás Etcheverry Estrázulas
Editor

Bilingual Study and Research

The Need and the Challenges

Springer

Editor
Nicolás Etcheverry Estrázulas
School of Law
University of Montevideo
Montevideo, Uruguay

ISSN 2214-6881 ISSN 2214-689X (electronic)
Ius Comparatum – Global Studies in Comparative Law
ISBN 978-3-030-84549-0 ISBN 978-3-030-84550-6 (eBook)
https://doi.org/10.1007/978-3-030-84550-6

This Springer imprint is published by the registered company Springer Nature Switzerland AG.
The registered company address is: Gewerbestrasse 11, 6330 Cham, Switzerland

Contents

Bilingual Study and Research: The Need and Challenges

Nicolás Etcheverry Estrázulas and Sofía Cairo

1 Introduction

To begin with, my most sincere gratitude to the extraordinary group of National Reporters that have so well responded to our requests, with dedication, commitment and excellence during the last months and throughout almost one year.

It would be unfair if I would not also give a big thank you to my Uruguayan collaborator Sofia Cairo, as well as to Alexandre Segenackic for his permanent dedication towards this academic event. And finally to our moderator, Dominique Custos, who was so diligent in helping us to organize the oral session of our topic in the last weeks before the Congress.

How many hours per semester should be required in legal courses so that such education may be considered and become bilingual? This is a difficult and even impossible answer to respond because it may vary significantly from country to country. Especially if you have in mind that in several of the National Reports we received, those countries or regions are already bilingual or even multilingual. If you add the amount of dialects or sub-languages that are spoken in some of them, the answer is even harder. Take for example China, Italy, Finland or Belgium and we will find the huge difficulty to establish what a bilingual or multilingual legal education should be considered as such.

This General Report will be also published, together with the National Reports from each jurisdiction, by Springer Nature Switzerland in a thematic volume.

N. Etcheverry Estrázulas (✉)
School of Law, Universidad de Montevideo, Montevideo, Uruguay
e-mail: netcheverry@um.edu.uy

S. Cairo
Hughes & Hughes, Montevideo, Uruguay
e-mail: scairo@hughes.com.uy

N. Etcheverry Estrázulas (ed.), *Bilingual Study and Research*, Ius Comparatum – Global Studies in Comparative Law 58,
https://doi.org/10.1007/978-3-030-84550-6_1

On the other hand, it has been a significant coincidence that all the Reports agree on one issue: Learning a second or even sometimes a third language in order to be skillful as a lawyer, judge,, or whatever legal profession you may practice, is much more than simply use the correct words and pronounce them properly. Much more important than this, Bi-lingualism aims at something higher and tougher at the same time. It is supposed to achieve a fair—if not complete—understanding and comprehension of the culture you are dealing with. Consequently, the way the questions are asked, the emphasis employed in such and such sentences or phrases, or the way the questions are responded when everyday issues and problems arise, may reflect a deeper or lighter knowledge of that culture.

Needless to say, it is in my opinion actually outdated and even absurd to focus the debate of bilingual legal education in terms of nationalism versus internationalism, because both need to co-habitate and complement each other in order to survive, expand and look towards the future.

Donc, une veritable et profonde education juridique Bi-lingue doit se fournir d' une nourriture assez variée, qui comprend non seule et exclusivement la langue, mais aussi l' historie, la geographie, les coutumes, l' ethique et meme encore la psicologhie du pays ou le juriste va travailler. Tout cela n' est pas facile a acquerir pendant seulement quelques mois. Si le but est vraiment d' obtenir une vraie et intégrale education juridique Bi—lingue, élèves et professeurs doivent se proposer un difícile—mais au meme temps appassionant—defi: celui de comprehendre une differente culture non seulement par sa langue, mais par sa vie, ses gens et son historie.

Comme citoyens d' un monde de plus en plus interdependant, nous avons, je crois et suis meme convaincu, une urgente necessité de trouver les moyens d' accepter ce defi et d' obtenir cette education et comprehension le plus vite et le plus largement possible. C' est n' est pas simplement pour des raisons académiques ou bien culturelles; c' est sourtout pour des raisons de survivance, de justice et de fraternité que le monde entier a besoin d' accepter ce defi et d' obtenir ce but. C' est serait vraiment tragique d' oublier notre histoire et une fois de plus, renouveller la chute de la Tour de Babel...

Nowadays it seems almost mandatory to support not only a bilingual education, but rather a trilingual education, if the circumstances allow it. Globalization and increasingly growing cultural interdependence not only require it, but they practically impose it. We refer to an education in general, which before targeting the legal field, focuses on learning and mastering more than one language, that is, one's own language properly read, spoken and written and one or two foreign languages, if possible.

In other words, perhaps quite frankly, having the possibility of learning foreign languages and not doing so by choice, out of laziness or simple disinterest, is equivalent to opting for educational atrophy, or what is more, a cultural suicide. It is clear that we are not referring to other types of circumstances that actually and objectively prevent reaching those goals. We do criticize those cases of mental fatigue, or contempt for what is foreign or different that leads to having certain persons or social groups culturally isolated, who only pay respect to what is theirs, being content with a well-defined territory, fair and small from the cultural point of view, however broad and extensive it is territorially speaking. This becomes even more serious when such indifferent or contemptuous attitude becomes clearly aggressive and combative of everything that is different to their way of life; escalating from defending to attacking and destroying any other way of thinking and believing.

Therefore, thinking about the need to target, extend and strengthen bilingual and multilingual educational systems is a priority. Common sense, interdependence and shared convenience require it.

If we deem that the aforementioned is important in terms of languages in general, more so it will be if we focus on legal education specifically. We do not intend to exhaust the reasons and arguments in defense of this point of view; we will simply mention a few that we consider most relevant:

1. Unless a Law Firm is managed in a very local and insular working and professional context, nowadays being proficient in a second language is "a must" for any professional seeking to join such Firm.
2. Knowing and mastering (which are not the same) one or more foreign languages broadens our way of thinking, our willingness to comprehend (which is not exactly the same as understand) different cultures and this eventually improves the chances of obtaining better remuneration for any professional work.
3. Learning about the origin, roots and etymology of different words or expressions allows us to learn in greater extent and depth the history, geography and culture of the countries. Consequently, the advantage of a bilingual or if possible, multilingual legal education, broadens the horizon of any professional.

Not only will professionals know "more about the law", but they will also have a better understanding of the world, of different societies in general, as well as their different ways of learning, thinking and acting in very different life circumstances. In the case of jurists, having the possibility of learning to read and speak a specific language which they usually foresee that they will be using for work, study or research reasons, is acquiring a tool or key that may open many doors. Not acquiring such tool or key when one has the possibility of doing so, is as already said, a professional and cultural atrophy.

Two examples can better illustrate this point: (a) In several Latin countries it is common to find expressions that begin with a negative form such as "*¿no le gustaría otro café?*" ("*wouldn't you like another coffee?*"); or "*¿no es verdad que este paisaje es muy agradable?*" ("*Isn't it true that this landscape is very nice?*"*);* or "*¿no me haría el favor de decirme la hora?*" ("*Wouldn't you do me the favor of telling me what time it is*?"). In different cultures those negative forms may seem shocking or contradictory, while in other places they convey courtesy. (b) Really learning a language implies understanding not only words and their meaning, but also the intonation of phrases or sentences. The same phrase or sentence can have very different meanings and interpretations according to the intonation. As an example: "*¿Qué quiere insinuar con su pregunta?*" ("*What do you seek to imply with your question?*"), or "*Esto puede llevarnos por caminos insospechados…*" ("*This can* *take us through unsuspected paths . . ."), or "¿Qué está sucediendo aquí?" ("What is going on here?"*) or "*No sabes lo que te espera. . ." ("You don't know what is waiting for you. . .*"). Failure to properly perceive the intonation used can lead to misunderstandings and unrepairable flaws in the communication of the subjects involved. A final example: asking "*¿Qué es la verdad?*" ("*What is the truth*?") can be done with the actual intention of discovering it or in an indifferent, haughty and ironic manner, without having the least interest of finding out.

If Latin was once the universal tool that allowed people to approach and interact, in this twenty-first century the key has been atomized into an almost essential bunch of keys that includes English, Spanish and Chinese, but also others such as French, German, Russian and Portuguese. These are not so universal from the quantitative perspective, but do have an enormous qualitative efficiency. Being proficient in all seven is a utopia but learning and mastering three of them is an achievable goal, with discipline and dedication. Undoubtedly, having an educated ear is a great advantage which is not achieved by everyone. Nonetheless, without a good ear, one may learn to read and speak a language, especially if there is a chance to live for some time in the country where it is spoken. The opportunity offered through the academic exchange agreements between the universities of places as distant and different as Uruguay and China, Brazil and Canada, London and Moscow, Berlin and Buenos Aires is a tremendous kick-off to start acquiring or polish those skills. Experience indicates that the intellectual and cultural enrichment of students, teachers and researchers who are part of these exchanges is invaluable.

Learning and becoming proficient in a foreign language involves a lot more than knowing and being able to convey foreign words and expressions. It implies learning about the cultural context, the way of life and the idiosyncrasy underlying that language. In short, it is not only about understanding the language, but also learning it in a more comprehensive manner.

I would like to recall some ideas expressed by S.I. Strong in the ***Review Essay – Bilingual Education in the United States***—when she quotes two books written by Xabier Arzos,

> "**Bilingual Higher Education in the Legal Context**. . ." and Katia Fach Gómez, "**El Derecho en Español: Terminología y Habilidades Jurídicas para un Ejercicio Legal Exitoso**. . .": In that review he says "While no one would dispute that English should be the primary language of instruction in U.S. law schools, the failure of the U.S. legal academy to consider issues relating to secondary instruction in other languages fails to take into account the significant and potentially growing number of U.S. citizens, residents and visitors who have limited proficiency in English. . . As various commentators have recognized, the shortage of U.S. lawyers with foreign-language skills increases the risk that certain segments of society will be unable to obtain useful legal advice and assistance. Shortcomings in law schools' foreign-language offerings have also injured U.S. law students' ability to function in a globalized world. . ."[1]

Further ahead she adds:

[1] Strong (2014), p. 356.

> Some people believe that conversational fluency, supplemented by a good bilingual legal dictionary, is all that is needed to provide legal advice across linguistic barriers. In fact, nothing could be more dangerous. Law is intimately bound up in a particular cultural and legal context, and bilingual lawyers must do more than simply acquire a specialized vocabulary. Instead, a lawyer functioning in a foreign language must be able to understand how certain concepts are interpreted and applied within a foreign legal system or by a client with limited English proficiency. Therefore, specialized coursework concerning bilingual lawyering is necessary if U.S. law students are to learn how to practice in multiple languages. (...) There are numerous ways to approach multilingual legal education, and the United States needs to adopt a system that is tailored to U.S. legal, historical and cultural norms. (...) Some readers might look at the English-instruction efforts of European law faculties as evidence that English is currently operating as an international lingua franca, which would subsequently suggest that there is little need for bilingual legal education in the United States. However, closer analysis of international legal practice indicates that lawyers working in certain regions often need to know languages other than English... Furthermore, U.S. law schools still need to address problems associated with domestic clients who have limited English proficiency...[2]

I fully agree with Professor Strong. Her comments reflect some of the more important issues and challenges we have for the following years in the field of bilingual education.

Having made this introduction, we will now try to develop the topic of bilingual legal education in a more objective and academic framework, thanks to the generous contributions of the national reporters from different countries who have seriously and dedicatedly collaborated with us. My most sincere thanks to our colleagues Bert Demarsin, Sébastien Van Drooghenbroeck, Nicholas Léger-Riopel, Xiangshun Ding, Marcus Noorgård, Alicia Nylund, Anne Brunon-Ernst, Stefan Grundmann, Elena Ioriatti, Mark Fenwik, Efrén Chávez-Hernández, Ramona Popescu, Carmen Achimescu, Alan K. Koh, Andrew Jen-Guang Lin, Mathias Reimann, as well as to Sofía Cairo Duaso, my assistant during these months, who with great patience and very good humor has helped me significantly in building up this General Report.

2 Bilingual Legal Education in Belgium

Belgium has three official languages: Dutch, French and German. The Kingdom's territory is divided into four linguistic areas: the monolingual Dutch-speaking area, the monolingual French-speaking area, the monolingual German-speaking area and the bilingual area (French-Dutch) around the nation's capital, Brussels. About 60% of the Belgian citizens speak Dutch, slightly over 38% speak French and the remaining 1% speak German.

Besides, the use of English is undoubtedly on the rise, due to Brussels' role on the international political scene. Given the city's role as the capital of the European Union and the home to many international institutions, Brussels is commonly

[2] Id, pp. 358–359.

referred to as *World Decision Center II*, after Washington DC. Considering the multilingual Belgian society, as the Reporters point out, it is hard to imagine how the legal education provided at university—both bachelor (180 credits) and master (120 credits)—could not take into account that context and remain merely monolingual. There are several reasons why the bilingualism or multilingualism is promoted in Belgium. First of all, the openness to foreign languages is essential for academic reasons. In addition, there is also a professional and cultural need for multilingualism in Belgium, as clear communication between the country's communities should remain possible at all times.

Hence, it is not surprising that languages courses (general or legal) in at least two target languages other than the program's main language are a compulsory part of the curriculum of all bachelors in law organized at Belgian law schools. In addition, in most bachelor programs and even all master programs numerous legal courses are taught in a foreign language.

However, the amount of language courses offered as part of the curriculum at Belgian law schools is subject to some important restrictions. In particular, all programs have to comply both with the maximum limits laid down by the decrees of the Communities, and the potential minimum threshold set forth in interuniversity agreements. Consequently, both the foreign language courses and the legal courses thought in a foreign language may take different forms even independent from the Erasmus system. As a result, the landscape is very heterogeneous, ranging from the inclusion of some foreign language courses in the curriculum, to the creation of master programs entirely taught in a foreign language.

The National Reporters focused on the bilingual (and even trilingual) programs of two universities: Université Saint-Louis – Bruxelles and KU Leuven.

Belgium is a federal State composed of Communities and Regions (art. 1 of the Constitution). Belgium comprises three Communities: the Flemish, the French and the German-speaking Community.

According to Article 127 of the Constitution, education—including university education—falls within the competence of the Communities and their decrees. The decrees of the Flemish Community apply to universities located in the unilingual Dutch-speaking area, as well as universities located in the Brussels bilingual area, which—because of their activities—are said to belong exclusively to the Flemish Community. On the other hand, the decrees of the French Community not only apply to the universities located in the unilingual French speaking area, but also to the universities located in the bilingual area which are said to belong exclusively to the French Community. There is currently no university in Belgium's unilingual German-speaking area.

According to Article 129 of the Constitution, the Communities regulate by decree the use of languages in the field of education as far as the unilingual areas are concerned. In Brussels, however, the use of languages is regulated by the federal state. The Community determines in particular whether, under what conditions, and to what extent the education provided by the francophone Brussels universities may be in a language other than French. The same goes, mutatis mutandis, for the

Flemish Community as far as the Dutch-speaking universities in Brussels are concerned.

The Flemish Parliament has regulated the use of language at institutions of higher education, for both administrative and educational matters.

According to Article II.260 Codex Hoger Onderwijs (*Flemish Code on Higher Education*) institutions for higher education are supposed to function in Dutch, since it is the language that should be used for administrative purposes. Article 261 of the same body requires the education itself to be in Dutch too. In this way the legislature tries to preserve Dutch as the prime language for education at universities that fall under the authority of the Flemish Community. At the same time, the Flemish authorities recognized the importance of foreign languages as a sensible and justified means of communication in certain scientific fields, as a facilitator for foreign exchanges and a boost of international professional mobility.

At Flemish universities, education is supposed to be in Dutch, as a matter of principle. However, at bachelor and master level, there are four exceptions to the above principle: (1) foreign language courses should be taught in that language; (2) Visiting professors from abroad; (3) Non-Dutch courses that students at their own initiative follow at another institution of higher education; and (4) Courses can be taught in a foreign language, provided that the institution explicitly motivates why a change of language is functional for the course and beneficial.

In addition, courses taught in Dutch may have some foreign language component. For example, course material may include a reader which is partly composed of English or French articles. According to Article 261, a bachelor program is Dutch-spoken as long as the number of courses taught in a foreign language is below 18.33% of the entire program. For master programs, that threshold is 50%.

The Flemish Legislature obliges institutions that offer the same program to determine in close collaboration the program's "domain-specific learning outcomes".

In the French Community, university education is organized by the decree of 7 November 2013 defining the landscape and organization of higher education. Article 75 of this decree provides that all educational institutions, without any exception have to use French for administrative purposes. However, some exceptions are possible here as well, taking into consideration if there are enrolled in undergraduate or graduate studies some number of credits can be organized in other languages. Other exceptions are made for Advances Masters and PhDs.

The Université Saint-Louis – Bruxelles is active in a number of disciplines in the field of humanities and social sciences, including Law. Of the 3978 students enrolled in the university, 1712 are in the Faculty of Law: 1566 in the bachelor program, 136 in the Advanced Masters, and 10 in the PhD program. The 1566 bachelor students either signed up for the daytime program or the off-schedule program for those who are already professionally active.

At the Université Saint-Louis – Bruxelles 15.52% of the law students do not have the Belgian citizenship, or have two nationalities, one of which is not Belgian.

Among the Academic staff (187 members), 10% is not Belgian. 13% of the teaching staff and the senior researchers obtained their PhD abroad. Every year, the

Université Saint-Louis – Bruxelles hosts about 10 foreign researchers during their sabbatical leave.

KU Leuven is an institution for research and education with international appeal. It is a comprehensive university, offering top-level study programs in almost every scientific domain. Currently, KU Leuven offers some 240 programs in Dutch, 86 in English, 2 in French and 1 in Spanish.

In 2017–2018, KU Leuven had a total of 57,335 students. Among them 9784 are international students. The foreign countries with the largest student populations are, in descending order, the Netherlands, China, Italy and Spain.

The Law school is one of the biggest faculties at KU Leuven. Some 70 law professors work at the Faculty of law among whom 10% are foreigners. Additionally, over 50 visiting professors teach in various programs. Hence they significantly contribute to the multilingual environment at the KU Leuven law school. Currently (year 2017–2018) the Faculty of law is home to 5455 students spread over 3 campuses: Leuven, Brussels and Kortrijk. At the Brussels campus, law students can either choose for the unilingual bachelor in law (taught in Dutch) or the bilingual program set up in collaboration with the Université Saint-Louis – Bruxelles, its partner university.

The advanced master in IP-ICT law is multilingual per se, as courses are taught in English, French and Dutch.

Bilingual (and trilingual) bachelors in law at the Université Saint-Louis – Bruxelles and the KU Leuven – Campus Brussels

Twenty-six years ago, the former Facultés Universitaires Saint-Louis *(now Université Saint-Louis – Bruxelles)* and the former Katholieke Universiteit Brussel *(now KU Leuven – Campus Brussels)* blazed a trail by **creating a bilingual (French-Dutch) undergraduate program in law for their respective students**. The following year, they continued along that path by setting up the bilingual French-English and the trilingual programs in French-Dutch-English.

The motives underlying the creation of bi- and trilingual programs were diverse. One of the reasons was the ambition to arm students with the linguistic skills required for legal practice, in particular in a multilingual work environment such as Brussels. A report entitled "Horizon 2025" approved by both the French and German-speaking Bar Association and the Flemish Bar Association, emphasized that, at the end of curriculum any lawyer should master her/his mother tongue, but should also have studied English and the country's other dominant official language. Another reason to implement this programs was the wish to allow students to conduct research as wide as possible, and to increase their ability to consult source material in a foreign language. Furthermore, the desire to promote student mobility between the undergraduate and graduate level. Finally, another reason was the ambition to promote cultural openness to the other community.

Neither the students nor the teaching staff or the academic authorities opposed to the implementation of these bi-/trilingual programs.

All students get basic language training, yet the more intense bilingual (or trilingual) program is fully optional. Indeed, students are free to sign up for this language-wise more challenging type of legal education. These programs are growing in popularity from the Reporters view. In particular they attract an increasing number of students who grew up in linguistically mixed families or who passed through content and language integrated learning.

Overall bilingual education tends to be quite challenging for teachers, as these programs normally require them to fully master the foreign language too. However, this problem does not arise with regard to the bilingual program co-organized by the above mentioned universities, since all teachers are native speakers.

In respect with the profile of students following a bilingual program, it must be said that neither at the Université Saint-Louis – Bruxelles, nor at KU Leuven, Campus Brussels enrollment in the bilingual program is dependent upon an entrance exam.

The joint bilingual bachelor program of KU Leuven-Campus Brussels and Université Saint-Louis – Bruxelles is essentially based on a system of exchanged courses. Students in this program who enrolled at Université Saint-Louis will take a number of courses taught in Dutch at KU Leuven – Campus Brussels while being exempted from the corresponding courses in French (and the other way around, for the students enrolled at KU Leuven – Campus Brussels). In practice, these exchanges are very easy, as the walking distance between both universities is not even 10 min. Since both universities teach "Belgian law", in theory all courses are eligible for exchange. Accordingly, the partner universities agreed to exchange the following courses: *Introduction to Law, Constitutional Law, Law of Obligations, Property Law, Family Law, Administrative Law and the Law of Contracts & Torts.*

The evaluation methods used in the courses that are taught in a foreign language are quite diverse. They might consist in written exams with open questions or multiple choice questions, oral examinations, written assignments, taking part in a bilingual moot court (e.g. Moot Court in constitutional law, in which all Belgian universities participate).

At the Université Saint-Louis – Bruxelles law students can also choose to sign up for the bilingual bachelor program taught in French and English. In this program, a number of courses that are taught in French in the standard (monolingual) program, will instead be offered in English. The program is exclusively run by the Université Saint-Louis – Bruxelles and its staff. All teachers are Saint-Louis faculty. Some of these courses concern "non-legal" topics, such as *Introduction to the culture of the English speaking world*, *Economics* or *Political Science*. In legal courses the language is altered to English whenever this seemed relevant. That is obviously the case for courses concerning foreign law (e.g. Introduction to the Common Law), but also for courses that are highly comparative in nature (e.g. Introduction to comparative law).

At the Université Saint-Louis – Bruxelles, in both bilingual programs (French-Dutch or French-English), USL students may choose to add a third language (English or Dutch) and thus render their bachelor program truly trilingual. In this case, over 50% of their program will be taught in a foreign language.

Related to the materials the Reporters pointed out that they use the course material (book, syllabus, slides, and exercises) that they developed themselves in Dutch.

Documentary resources (legislation, doctrine, case law) are easily available in their language, since both Dutch and French are official languages in Belgium. Legislation is enacted in both French and Dutch; case law is produced in either French or Dutch; some court decisions are entirely and systematic translated.

The command of English required to teach at university is quite high. Indeed, in article 270 Codez Hoger Onderwijs, the Flemish Community set several requirements in order to guarantee the quality of the language used for teaching. The Decree states that the teaching staff has to have a language proficiency at level ERK C1 for the language in which the course is organized.

It is worth mention, that KU Leuven has an impressive list of ERASMUS destinations.

From the Reporters view, it could be said that both at the Université Saint-Louis – Bruxelles and the KU Leuven, law schools undeniably promote the bi- or even trilingual curriculum. Moreover, these programs have expand and intensified over the years. This tendency towards multilingualism seems to exist at all Belgian universities, as they all have recently intensified the language training in their curriculum. Some new initiatives are the English master programs the law schools of KU Leuven (in collaboration with the University of Zurich) and the University of Antwerp which were recently set up. Without any doubt, other universities will follow these examples in the near future and will establish new kinds of bilingual programs as both students and employers cheer the above evolutions with joy.

Overall, neither the students, nor the public authorities perceive the above development towards multilingualism as a threat to the cultural/national identity.

3 Bilingual Legal Education in Canada

The Canadian reporter delivers a particular, specific and original vision concerning Bilingual Legal Education. His approach tends to explain the differences between two ways of understanding legal positivism; the Rule—paradigm and the realist epistemology. To better explain and understand what the main cornerstone of his essay is, here are some hints of what le Cas de L'Acadie means. To do this we rely on the work of Annette Boudreau, a member of the Université de Moncton, from which the author of this report is also a professor:

> Ce texte traite de la construction des représentations linguistiques en Acadie en partant de l'analyse des articles de presse publiés dans deux journaux importants, soit L'Évangéline (1887–1982) et le Moniteur Acadien (1867–1926). L'accent est placé sur trois périodes clés de l'histoire acadienne, la première s'étalant de 1880 à 1910, la deuxième de 1950 à 1967, et la troisième de 1970 à 1973, périodes choisies en fonction de leur importance à illustrer les moments forts de la construction de l'espace social acadien. L'article décrit d'abord les principales idéologies linguistiques trouvées dans les éditoriaux et les lettres d'opinions du lecteur, puis s'attarde à la période contemporaine et montre comment les discours sur les pratiques linguistiques se sont diversifiés. Les différentes stratégies mises de l'avant par les artistes sont présentées. Ceux-ci participent à la construction de nouvelles façons d'appréhender les pratiques linguistiques qu'ils voient plurielles et polivalentes.

> Un langue n'est jamais trop riche. Mais notre langue est assez riche de son propre fonds sans que nous soyons obligés d'aller si souvent faire des emprunts à l'étranger. Quelle nécessité y a-t-il de dire "club" au lieu de cercle, la "season" pour la saison, le "hall" qui vient de notre halle, à nous, est "lunch" et "luncher" pour collation ou goûter? (Parlons français, L'Évangeline, 29 mai 1890)

> Si vous êtes descendants acadiens le sang français coule encore dans vos veines, conservez le français ainsi que votre langue. N'ayez pas peur d'une langue que des génies n'ont pasée honte de parler avant vous. (Le Moniteur acadien, 20 novembre 1884)

> Depuis la fin de années 1970, des sociolinguistes ont souligné l'importance du recours aux représentations dans l'analyse des situations linguistiques pour expliquer le maintien, le développement ou la disparition des langues...

Having established this, we will go on to analyze the National Reporters essay. The Faculty of Law of the *Université de Moncton* "...is host to a variety of - sometimes unique and surprising - events that could be could considered "phenomena" of transystemism in a multilingual context of legal education..." The Faculty of Law, which offers a unique training of common law taught exclusively in French, was founded in 1978 in the City of Moncton, in the Province of New-Brunswick, Canada:

> The University of Moncton was founded by integrating three colleges: College Saint-Louis, College du Sacre-Coeur and College Saint-Joseph. Undergraduate degrees in adult education had been founded by the university in the year 1989. Students get admission in this school on the basis of their extracurricular activities, GPA, letter of reference, as well as interview questionnaire. As all the classes of this school are conducted fully in French, student who are seeking admission must have a strong command on French language. University of Moncton doesn't require its students to take the LSAT (Law School Admission Test) as it considers the score of LSAT, if provided.

> University of Moncton Faculty of Law offers the basic LL.B. and also the graduate LL.M. Besides this, the university also offers degrees such as: the LLB-MEE (Masters of Environmental Studies), LLB-MAP (Masters in Public Administration) and LLB-MBA (Masters of Business). Moreover, students who have a degree of B.C.L or LL.L. (Civil law degree) from any Canadian school have the permission to enroll their names in the school for two semesters and complete a J.D. For international students who are willing to understand the common law tradition, the faculty offers a D.E.C.L (Degree in Common Law) as well.[3]

> ...Transsystemic teaching of law, as is also often found in multilingual contexts of legal education, can and have been celebrated as powerful remedies to the dominant paradigm of legal education, rooted in a legal positivistic ("LP") view...

As the National Reporter sharply remarks this view is generally accepted[4] as the dominant model of teaching, reasoning, and adjudicating legal matters.[5] The limits

---

[3] See the interesting presentation offered by the Canada Law Schools resources, available online at http://www.canadalawschools.ca/atlantic-canada/new-brunswick-universities/13-university-of-moncton-faculty-of-law.

[4] Generally, see: Samuel (2003).

[5] This is not to be understood as meaning that the notion of Legal Positivism *itself* is non-contentious. Many myths exist *about* what Legal Positivism is or is not, as a variety of authors

of such a model are, perhaps incidentally, made more visible in a transsystemic or multilinguistic contexts of teaching, as those are the conditions in which they train legal minds at the *Université de Moncton*. In the author words "...may these short iterations be of use to many who face the challenges of multilingual, or multisystemic, contexts of legal education..."

A First Dogma of Legal Positivism: The Rule-Paradigm[6]

The National Reporter states that the multilingual and transsystemic education, be it through the generally available mean of comparative law, unravel the deeply rooted polysemy inherent to even the most casual legal concepts to be encountered. "...Multiple explanations to this un-fixedness of the meaning of legal concepts are offered by the legal literature; this polysemy is perhaps one the first "terrors" to be faced by legal students. How tragic it is to be facing norms purporting to be just and universal, which are also modeled using that profoundly imprecise medium of language! This finding, in itself, as stemmed a whole field of legal studies gravitating around the now classic *themata* of the hartian open texture of the (legal) language..."

Further on the author addresses a crucial repercussion of this issue, pointing out "...One of the many consequences of this relative imprecision of legal language, as most eloquently revealed to a lawyer endeavoring a transsystemic reflexion, is to reveal the relative unvavailability of the rule-paradigm as the only method of resolving legal matters. The "canonic" syllogism, as a means of resolving legal problems was developed, and possibly meant to be applied, to premises that are fixed, and objective.[7] How can the syllogism as a tool retains its centrality when the major premise, the enunciation of the Rule, be it enshrined in common law judgments or in a piece of legislation, is often times irremediably mobile?..."

The National Reporter explains that this aftermath of legal interpretation, rendered highly vibrant through the problems of transsystemism, has led some scholar to offer a variety of means to understand "...what is *really* happening when one speaks of *legal method* or *legal reasoning*. A now well-documented[8] field of legal research covers the means by which legal solutions take place, especially in the context of transsystemism. For some of these scholars, it is unavoidable to take into account the profoundly cultural dimension of legal institutions, as to avoid the risk of "faux amis": similarly phrased concepts buttressed by different cultural context accounts for sometimes very different legal solutions or means of enforcing what seemingly may be the same notions..." In order to see the true nature of legal

---

have suggested such as Norberto Bobbio, John Gardner. For the finality of this short note, we are concentrating on myths conveyed by LP itself and not the myths *about* LP.

[6]For Samuels, the success of Legal positivism is in part due to two fundamental assumptions: "The first is that legal knowledge consists of legal rules; the second is that these legal rules are identifiable in terms of their particular sources and independent of all other social norms arising from other, non-legal sources". Samuel (2003).

[7]See: Huhn (2002), p. 813.

[8]As a seminal source, see: Teubner (1989), pp. 727–757.

reasoning the National Reporter encourages us to engage in a multidisciplinary approach, approaching different perspectives such as law and economics, law and literature, law and society.

The author establishes that "...As any fiction, the Rule paradigm has roots in reality and reflects the *habitus* and in many cases the actual practices of legal problem solving. May it be only noted that this method is relative to the complexity of the legal problems at hand, which in some case need to be addressed through a richer matrix, especially in the case of transsystemic or multilinguistic questions of law. In such circumstances, law perhaps cease to be a matter of rules, and students, lawyers and judges alike encounter law-as-a-social-fact, a living, and forever context-bound content-matter that it would be of disservice to treat only through the lens of a rule paradigm meant for much simpler matters.... than human ones..."

A Second Dogma of Legal Positivism: A "Realist" Epistemology

The National Reporter explains that a recent field of legal methodology and legal epistemology covers a ground that remained relatively un-touched up until the recent years: that is, the role of **facts** in the legal reasoning, as opposed to the role of rules. Likewise to rules, facts themselves have long held a status of undisputable objectivity, but this status has often been put into question through the works of comparative law, and transsystemic contexts.

> ...It may very well, according to prominent legal epistemologists such as Geoffrey Samuel, Christian Atias or Theodor Ivainer, that facts themselves are an object of construction and interpretation and: "the idea that legal science is a discourse that has its objet actual factual situation is to misunderstand, fundamentally, legal thought."...[9]

Un important apport des travaux récents en épistémologie juridique concerne précisément l'étude des modalités particulières de traitement des faits par le droit. Il n'est pas ici question uniquement d'une étude des règles de preuve et de procédure, mais plutôt de l'adoption d'un regard apte à révéler les principes et les présupposés qui président au passage des faits à la norme, c'est-à-dire des modes par lesquels le droit construit l'intelligence de son objet.[10] Le professeur Samuel reconnaît même dans l'étude du modèle par lequel le droit « construit » les faits qui sont appelés à interagir avec la normativité juridique l'objet premier de la science juridique et le thème central de son épistémologie.

Pour cet auteur, soucieux de faire bénéficier aux juristes des acquis issus du champ de recherche de l'épistémologie des sciences, l'objet de l'épistémologie juridique est plus précisément la structure par laquelle le droit procède d'opérations de médiation entre la réalité empirique (les faits) et le domaine des normes :

> [Legal science is to be envisaged through a constructive form]. That is to say it has to be envisaged through a structure which mediates between facts and science (law), allowing the legal scientist both to make sense of the facts and to discover solutions from transformation within the structure. Such a structure is what one calls a "model". What, then, is the basis for

[9] Samuel (2004), p. 74.

[10] L'expression est de Berthelot (2008), p. 124.

such a legal model? This, of course, is the fundamental question that should motivate and direct any work on legal epistemology.[11]

À ce titre, l'épistémologie invite à reconnaître que la factualité juridique est un construit : le juriste sélectionne des éléments de la réalité empirique, en disqualifie d'autres. Ainsi, un « point de vue » sur le fait opère une transition chez ce dernier de phénomène en objet du savoir juridique. Le fait est ainsi naturalisé[12] aux besoins du savoir juridique, s'y incorpore. Astolfi ajouterait que les faits n'ont aucune existence a priori : ils ne prennent tout leur sens qu'en relation avec un système de pensée, une théorie, bref en passant par le filtre d'une vision des choses ; nous pourrions penser qu'il s'agit là de la conception juridique du monde.[13]

Que se passe-t-il alors? Le « fait » cesse d'être le rempart que l'on a toujours bien voulu reconnaître contre l'évolutive et changeante règle de droit. Le fait cesse de lutter contre l'arbitraire, mais est dès lors tout entier devenu lui aussi objet d'*arbitration*, de *méditation* tant par les parties que par la raison juridique, construit de part en part par le droit et ses (méta)méthodes, et non à l'extérieur de celle-ci. Or comme l'a à si juste titre posé Gilles-Gaston Granger, que Samuels trouve tout à fait applicable au droit, l'objet d'une discipline justement n'est pas le « monde » dans sa phénoménalité observable, mais plutôt :

> This epistemological thesis is [. . .] applicable to law since this is a discourse or « science » (*intellectus*) which does not operate directly on the facts (*res*). What the lawyer does is to construct a model of the social world and it is, arguably, this model which acts as the bridge between the social and the legal worlds. That model is both the *res* (object of knowledge) and the *intellectus* (knowing subect).[14]

Il est maintenant clair que le traitement des faits par le droit n'est que superficiellement[15] capté par les règles de preuve et de procédures dont se dote un système juridique donné. Dans sa structure profonde, le traitement de la factualité par le droit est le produit de présupposés tacites qui échappent à l'étude des seules règles de preuve et de procédure : certains auteurs nous invitent par ailleurs à

---

[11] Samuel (2004), p. 19.

[12] Thomas (1973), pp. 103–125. Voir plus généralement, Teubner, "Pour une épistémologie constructiviste du droit".

[13] Astolfi and Develay (1996), p. 25. Il est possible de trouver une autre formulation de cette idée chez Hanson (1958).

[14] Samuel (2003), p. 2.

[15] Ce mot n'étant pas utilisé dans son sens péjoratif. Comme le souligne Dubouchet, certains problèmes simples ne requièrent que l'application du syllogisme juridique et pourraient être entièrement régis par une intelligence non nécessairement réflexive : (1) une raison formelle. Là où les problèmes deviennent plus complexes, là où les faits présentent une moins grande isomorphie avec le droit statutaire et jurisprudentiel applicable, rend nécessaire l'application de la (2) raison dialectique. Pour Dubouchet, s'appuyant sur les travaux de Carl Schmitt, certaines situations factuelles peuvent émerger qui ne soient tout simplement pas régies ou visées par le droit applicable et exigent alors l'expression de l'autorité confiée au juge, qui usera alors de raison réthorique. As cite in Nicholas Léger-Riopel, "Transsystemic and Multilingual Contexts of Legal education: le Cas de L'Acadie", p. 4.

découvrir la *véritable* méthode d'un savoir disciplinaire par l'étude de ses paradoxes, de ses controverses, plutôt que de ses apparentes unités, réussites et succès techniques. À ce titre, comme l'a souligné l'auteure Hammer, les fictions juridiques et l'imagination juridique auxquels président ces présupposés tacites font par moment « disparaître » les faits.[16] La fiction juridique et la « tendance de toute fiction à se substituer purement et simplement à la réalité »[17] devient alors par l'alchimie toute particulière de la raison juridique la seule vérité juridiquement officiellement reçue.[18] La méthode d'interprétation des faits par le juge, si elle ne trouve pas son explication dans des règles juridiques muettes à ce sujet, devient dès lors un objet pressant de l'épistémologie juridique. La voie pour une épistémologie constructiviste du droit est dès lors tracée.

4 Bilingual Legal Education in China

The first thing to bear in mind when it comes to this immense country, as the Chinese Reporters remind us, is that bilingual legal education in other languages in China is rare. The reason for this is that few teachers know other languages. Furthermore, due to China's primary and secondary education system, students who understand other languages are accounted as a relatively small proportion. A second aspect to take in consideration is that China is a multi-ethnic, multi-lingual, multi-dialect, and multi-character country, which includes 56 ethnic groups, many of which have their own languages.

Nevertheless, in the last 20 years this country has experienced enormous changes in terms of going global and taking the One Belt and one Road initiative which promotes international multidisciplinary exchanges; legal affairs and legal knowledge are not an exception.

[16] Gail Hammer, "Transparent: when legal fictions and judicial imagination make facts disappear, they enforce transphobic discrimination". As cite in Nicholas Léger-Riopel, "Transsystemic and Multilingual Contexts of Legal education: le Cas de L'Acadie", p. 5, note 13.

[17] Ch. Atias, précité, note 1, à la p. 21.

[18] "Competent judges should be able to prioritize facts over legal fictions. Judges should not be so distracted by difference that they fail to recognize facts. "The politics of control and domination are interrupted when we embrace our own fears and anxieties to transcend them." Competent judges should be able to notice, recognize, acknowledge, evaluate, and then set aside their own discomfort and emotional reactions. Those reactions are a source of information, but just one of the sources of information available to judges. They are not the guiding principles. Even if courts do not love transgender people, they are tasked with working justice and, at a minimum, tolerating difference. In courts' decisions, love, or the lack of it, should not determine whether the result is justice." Gail Hammer, "Transparent: when legal fictions and judicial imagination make facts disappear, they enforce transphobic discrimination", précité, note 12, à la p. 161 et suiv. As cite in Nicholas Léger-Riopel, "Transsystemic and Multilingual Contexts of Legal education: le Cas de L'Acadie", p. 5, note 14.

As stated by the National Reporters, Bilingual Legal Education can be divided into two kinds from the perspective of subject and object: (1) One is based on Chinese students as the object of acceptance; teachers of this type are mostly domestic teachers who have good foreign languages ability or foreign teachers invited from other countries as the subjects of teaching; (2) The other is to recruit foreign students as the object of education, such as the "Chinese Law" program. Therefore, the expression "bilingual" for Chinese students does not only focus on Chinese and one foreign language; it may also mean Chinese and one of the ethnic minorities' languages for those students (i.e. Mongolian). This is what offers Inner Mongolia University School of Law since 1988 in order to train its students in the acquisition of skills to deal with legal matters both in Chinese and Mongolian.

Besides this, the most common form of bilingualism is the combination of Chinese and English such as the Program offered by ***Renmin University*** in Comparative Law since 2009; it has different courses such as the Comparative Law Academic Seminar, the International Business Course (that combines litigation, arbitration, contracts and corporate business planning), American Law courses mainly taught by American professors, or EU law courses mainly taught by teachers from Sweden, the Netherlands and France, focused in the EU constitution, EU trade, tort and intellectual property law.

At the same time, the Comparative Law Program uses the international resources of Renmin University to hire first-rate scholars from the universities of Geneva, Tokyo University and Waseda University to teach courses such as "Comparative Contract Law", "Comparative Trust Law between China and Japan" "Comparative Contract Law between China and Japan".

According to the National Reporters,

> **Peking University School of Transnational Law (STL)** is the only law school in the world that combines an American-style Juris Doctor degree (J.D.) with a China law Juris Master degree (J.M.) and enroll students from China and other countries in the world. STL provides an academically rigorous, bilingual four-year program of legal education that prepares students for the mixture of common law, civil law, and Chinese legal traditions increasingly characteristic of the global economy…

The ***China-EU School of Law (ECSL) at the China University of Political Law and Science (CUPL)*** was co-sponsored by the Chinese government and the European Union in 2008. It is a unique institution for educating law students; for conducting and facilitating legal research and consultancy; for professional training of judges, prosecutors, lawyers, and other legal professionals; and a platform for China-EU research, teaching, legal academic and professional exchanges and collaboration. It aims at

> (…) "implementing a qualification program leading to a Chinese post-graduate qualification and/or a European post-graduate qualification (the "Master Program"), an exhaustive program of professional training (the "Professional Training"), and engaging in research and consultancy activities, including joint training for Ph.D. students (the "Research and Consultancy Activities".
>
> The "Double Degree Program" consisting of the "Juris Master of Chinese Law" (JM) and the "European Law Master Program" (LL.M.), is the central program of ECSL. As an

integrated part of the Double Degree Program which will last for 3 consecutive academic years/6 consecutive semesters, the duration of "Juris Master of Chinese Law" can be technically identified as for 3 semesters. (...) Upon graduation, these students receive both a graduate diploma and a master's degree certificate from China University of Political Science and Law and a master's degree certificate from the University of Hamburg (the European partner of ECSL).

Courses of the European Law Master program should be taught in English and courses of the Chinese Juris Master program should be taught in Chinese (...) If necessary, ECSL will provide for the translation of lectures and class materials in order to meet the audience's needs. (...) ECSL has also developed a Chinese Law Program (LL.M in Chinese Law) in English teaching for foreign students. All the courses of this program are taught by Chinese professors in English, the content mainly focus on China's laws (...)

The College of Comparative Law of CUPL, founded in 2009, integrates the Institute of Comparative Law, the School of Sino-German Law and the School of Sino-American Law.

It is the only comparative law teaching and research institution in the Chinese higher education and research sector. The College comprises 42 staff members, including 30 academic staff. Among the academic staff, 29 of them hold doctoral degrees, accounting for 97%. The College boasts high qualifications of its academic staff and distinctive features of internationalization, as 16 academic staff have attained their degrees from world-known overseas universities, making up 53% of the total. The academic staff are proficient in the world's major languages like English, German, Italy, Russian, French and Japanese...

Shanghai Jiao Tong University adopts the "three plus three years system" legal education model to break the traditional curriculum system to cultivate undergraduate and master's law school students. It emphasizes the integration of foreign languages and law major during the curriculum. The undergraduate education finishes at the end of the third year, and as from the fourth year to diversion in order to select a few outstanding undergraduate students to accept three consecutive years of high-level legal education, and eventually receive a master's degree. This project calls for mastery of two UN languages and mastering the knowledge of economic, financial, trade, business management and international relations.

Southwest University of Political Science & Law, School of International Law has developed the "Foreign Legal Talents Education Program". Its general object is to cultivate a host of foreign legal talents who are well-versed in international rules, competent in dealing with transnational legal affair. Through the admission process, the School of International Law will select 10 people to implement the 3 + 2 + 1 year mode: 3 semesters to learn professional knowledge that focus on case study and are supplemented by practice. They carry out the activities for legal negotiations, debates and other legal skills competitions that target at cultivating foreign legal capabilities through the course practices in addition to foreign legal expertise knowledge. After those courses, there are two semesters practice training, which includes 3 months foreign law practices or overseas short-term study and one semester graduation thesis writing (WTO cases and foreign laws practice cases) and career choosing and planning. The program is bilingual. Bilingual courses cover one-fourth of the whole courses which focus on the WTO cases and other foreign-related cases. There are also many kinds of legal English activities like Legal English

Debate Competition, Legal English Writing Competition or other forms of competition, so as to develop students' professional English ability.

Shanghai University of Finance and Economics sets up a training program for senior legal personnel in the free trade area through the integration of specialization and localization. 75% of the courses (international financial law, international trade law, international investment law) are taught in English. The project is also served as an elective course. After finishing the course, students can obtain a certificate of "Free Trade Zone Senior Legal Person Training Program"

Law School of Shandong University has an original program because it uses not only the combination of Chinese and English selected by most of the colleges, but also set the "Chinese-Japanese Economic and Trade Law Class" for undergraduates.

> (. . .) It is the first university in China that uses Japanese as a professional foreign language for Legal undergraduate education which aims to cultivate legal professionals with a high level of Japanese proficiency and familiarity with the economic and trade laws in China and Japan. Students in this class should not only need study English and Chinese law like general undergraduate classes in law school, but also have to study most Japanese language courses and the Introduction of Japanese law, Japanese civil law, Japanese criminal law and other courses such as Comparative Law between China and Japan (. . .) The law school also sends students to law schools in Japan for exchange study. . .

The National Reporters highlight some aspects that need to be taken in consideration: (a) In China bilingual teachers are relatively weak and unevenly distributed (b) In many national famous law schools, mostly teachers have overseas exchanged experiences and most of them are Doctor returnees. (c) However, undergraduate colleges are unable to attract Doctor returnees because they are located in remote areas (d) Although in those undergraduate colleges there is no problem in their English abilities, they are still not able to realize the goal of bilingual legal education very well because of their poor understanding of professional legal knowledge. (e) The use of textbooks is relatively scarce, there are very few. One exception can be the "Introduction to Law", edited by Jiang Dong, which makes some changes that are more suitable for Chinese students on the basis of another original textbook. It chooses ten chapters of the original twenty-four, which are more suitable for Chinese students to learn, divided into two parts—Chinese and English. The English part still uses of the original textbook, the Chinese part is added by "basic vocabulary definitions" "key words" "key legal knowledge analysis" and so on. The textbook takes into account the integrity of English textbooks and students' English level, from a practical point of view to make it easier to promote.

Concerning Bilingual Legal Education for Foreign Students, the Chinese Law Program was first launched by ***Tsinghua University*** as a Master's Program on Chinese Law Education in 2005. Hence, it has developed to eight universities including Peking University, Renmin University of China, China University of Political Science and Law and Beijing Normal University. The Ministry of Education has no special regulations on the enrollment of Chinese law masters and the teaching methods, therefore, as the Program follows the general requirements of an LLM American Law but adapted to set up a Master's program in Chinese Law for foreign students (LL.M Program in Chinese Law, hereinafter referred to as Master of

Chinese Law Project). Teaching all in English has facilitated the study of Chinese law by foreign students and has expanded the student community with great potential for development. The Chinese Law Program takes generally 2 years. Most of the legal systems involved in these courses are similar to Anglo-American law because they transplant American laws or are based on international conventions and treaties. *"They are less affected by the differences in legal cultures and traditions..."*

Besides this, and as it usually happens in other countries, obtaining the Chinese lawyer qualification requires passing the national bar examination. One of the qualifications for joining the bar examination is that students need the citizenship of the People's Republic of China. This means that foreigners are currently unable to obtain the Chinese lawyer qualification. According to the law of our country, foreign law firms and foreign lawyers are also not allowed to engage in legal affairs in China.

In many cases, the Master of Chinese Law program not only teaches Chinese language knowledge, but also Chinese culture knowledge. Law is more of a "local knowledge," legal education, so it must be combined with China's special national conditions, traditional culture and values to carry out. Many colleges and universities have opened "Chinese traditional law" and "Chinese society and law" or "Chinese language" courses in Chinese Laws programs. Representative examples of this tendency are the courses recently offered by ***Peking University, Tsinghua U., Fudan U., China University of Political Science and Law, Xiamen U., University of International Business & Economics, and Renmin University***. The latter offers an LLM Program in Chinese Law fully in English (2 years) that is of special interest for students from abroad such as Hong Kong, Macau and Taiwan. As the National Reporters affirm,

> (...) The teaching faculty in the LL.M Program have extraordinary academic credentials. Most professors have experience studying and/or teaching in leading law schools in the most prestigious universities, such as Harvard, Yale, Oxford and Cambridge. They all have deep understandings of both Western law and Chinese Law. At the same time, Renmin Law School offers valuable internship opportunities in top law firms and other institutions for students to achieve their career planning...

5 Bilingual Legal Education in Czechia

It is significant to begin this summary by saying that this National Report was submitted because of the interesting contributions of other national reports and lively debate that took place during the 20th Congress of the IACL in Fukuoka—Japan. In the words of the Czech reporter, those contributions and debates "inspired his asking for an opportunity to join subsequently and deliver the report", which was consulted in due time and authorized.

In his view, the process of "Anglicisation" in Czechia has been growing steadily in the recent years, especially among the new and young generations, but at the same time some resistance has been appearing, supported by reasonable arguments. Pressures for further Anglicisation have found complications because of the protection of minorities and their own specific languages as well as the recent growth of immigration. Although monolingualism is still very strong and obvious in this country (and the Constitution of the Czech Republic did not find necessary to proclaim Czech as the national or state language) there is no doubt that English has become the complementary second language for communication with foreigners in international trade, investment, modernisation, culture and tourism.

Nevertheless, the question whether this process of Anglicisation is in a point of no return or finding stronger resistances and will recede is very difficult to answer. Some politicians, entrepreneurs, journalists and officials began to question Anglicisation as a different form of "language imperialism" and even proposed a discussion about compensation or taxation to this new procedure of obtaining great benefits and profits.

As shown, the tendency to use the English language more and more often is either seen with sympathy and practicality or with discomfort and disgust.

Some intents to find alternative second universal languages such as Esperanto, Latin, German, French (gradually fading especially in academia), Russian (especially strong during the 1948–1968 period), Polish and Spanish have not been successful insofar. Even Slovak—which is a mutual intelligible language with Czech—is becoming less and less useful, especially because of the diversity of laws that emerged after the dissolution of Czechoslovaquia.

So all in all, English remains the most accepted global *lingua franca* in the country. It has many academic advantages, especially for Universities and not so much for primary and secondary education. As the national reporter explains

> This dominance of English has apparent advantages. Academicians and students need not master several languages for understanding in international settings. Translations of scientific and expert literature decreased significantly. Interpretation at conferences disappeared. (...)
>
> Many politicians, officials, journalists, professors and students think that any international exchange and cooperation is beneficiary if not essential for excellence. Universities become mentally xenophile. Internationalisation has become slogan and mantra. Anglicisation seems to ease this internationalisation. Education in English can attract more international students than education in other languages. It also eases recruitment of professors and lecturers. Unsurprisingly, internationalisation overlaps with Anglicisation...

The information obtained by this General Reporter is that there are four Schools of Law in Czechia (Charles University in Prague, University of New York, Masaryk University and Cevro Institute that also has a School of Political Studies). These four offer the top LLM Programs in Czech Republic.

Despite some attempts to strengthen the Anglicisation process, such as the one pursued by the **Masaryk University in Brno and its Faculty of Law**, not everything is in favour of this tendency, because of several reasons explained by the national reporter: as Czechia is a welfare state, public money to finance tertiary education is scarce, there are no study fees, underfinancing is chronic, governance of universities and their faculties is problematic and there is weak patriotism, (at least in what is concerned with preserving a national language and culture). On the other hand, a rising patriotism and disgust towards Anglo-American models of society, government and law could result into hostility, which is also dangerous and inefficient for the Czech population, especially if we consider legal practitioners that always find English as a pragmatic, strong and useful weapon to use and perform when international issues and problems arise.

An interesting comment and advice from this national reporter is that until now,

> (...) few evaluate the quality of English in mentioned activities. Support for its enhancement is perfunctory if not absent at all (...) we should expect misunderstandings resulting from imperfect translations and be cautious towards eventual misuse of shortcomings. On the contrary, national administration and judiciary is rigid, it usually requires translation...

He reminds the readers of his report that it is not so common and easy to master both foreign law and language and also, if we consider law as a science and lawyers,

> ascertain legality of human behaviour (required/allowed/prohibited) when interpreting statutes. They formulate pros and cons and rebut their opponents. Attorneys and in-house counsels argue in favour of their clients, enterprises and institutions. Officials and judges balance legal argumentation in their decisions and judgments. Legal scholars analyse law in academic treatises for education of students and information of legal practitioners.

Bluntly Said, Law Is Enacted, Interpreted and Applied in Particular National Language

Therefore, meaning of words in this language is crucial. National discourse is primary in law. It has thus little sense to write and publish texts about national law in any foreign language. Even argumentation with international review is unconvincing. Respectable foreign reviewers would argue with unfamiliarity with Czech law.

Ultimately, international communication of legal scholars is also specific. Comparative studies rely on national reports written by authors from particular countries, while their initiators and organisers summarize findings in general reports. Despite huge effort spent by reporters, we frequently read summary of national law and its practice together with outline of political, social and economic aspects. Necessary unifying set of questions contorts results, while selection of topics usually reflects interest of leading professors from elite countries.

Ultimately, legal practice is comparable. Attorneys and in-house counsels hesitate to provide advice on foreign law, not talking about representation of their clients and employers at offices and before courts of other country even if allowed. Few master both foreign law and language. Instead it, they contact local lawyers. Many law firms establish international networks for this purpose.

An example given by the national reporter is that the Masaryk University has also mandated that **theses** submitted within so-called habilitation shall be in English since 2020.

> (...) Habilitation consists of an evaluation of pedagogic and scientific performance of an academician. Czech academicians become docents at various ages. The procedure is lengthy, demanding, cumbersome, and its results unpredictable. Success generally enhances individual position and usually results into an indefinite labour contract (tenure). Professors are the supreme rank. Many academicians do not achieve this rank altogether. Supporters justified this requirement principally with extended pool of reviewers...

The national reporter finds this initiative unsatisfactory and he would be pleased if the University could be more flexible in relation to this exigence prepared for next year. The arguments that support his point of view are strong: such praising in further Anglicisation could become a short way to undermine Czech nationality, especially when it refers to core law studies that should not be de-nationalized.

What we observe in this national report and his prudent comments is the following: As in any other country, the use of a second international legal language must always be considered useful and even necessary; but it should never become an abusive way of losing or forgetting the national roots of its own history and transform the specific culture and way of life of its population.

6 Bilingual Legal Education in Finland

Finland has two constitutionally recognized national languages Finnish and Swedish, which means that bilingualism is a national cornerstone.

Finland's judicial system is a civil law system and the primary source of law is the codified laws and statues. The court system has two branches: courts with civil and criminal jurisdiction (District Courts—Courts of Appeal—Supreme Court) and courts with jurisdiction in administrative matters (Administrative Courts—Supreme Administrative Court).

The official languages of Finland are Finnish and Swedish, which is stated in the Constitution. However on the Åland Islands which is an autonomous and demilitarized region, the official language is Swedish only. The Constitution further states that everyone has the right to use either Finnish or Swedish in communication with the national authorities. Finnish is spoken by approximately 90% of the population and Swedish by little over 5%. The Swedish-speaking Finns live mostly in the coastal areas of Finland and on the Åland Islands.

Children permanently residing in Finland must attend compulsory schooling, which stars in the year the child turns seven (7 years old). Finland does not have compulsory school attendance since a child can be given instructions at home on the condition that the instructions correspond to the basic education. Basic Education is free of charge and encompasses nine years from the age of seven to sixteen years (7–16 years).

Section 12 of the Basic Education Act (628/1998) states that, in keeping with the instruction language of the school, the pupils shall be taught Finnish, Swedish or Saami as a mother tongue, alternatively the Roma language, Sign language or some other language which is the pupil's native language. The instruction in mother tongue stars in the 1st form.

In schools which the instruction language is Swedish, the instruction in Finnish as the second national language normally stars in the lower forms (1st and 2nd form), while in Finnish schools the instruction in Swedish as the second national language generally stars later in the 6th or 7th form.

In the Upper Secondary Education (optional after the completion of the basic education), there are also compulsory as well as optional (advanced) courses in the second national language. *Since 2005, the only compulsory test is the one in the mother tongue. English is normally taught as the first foreign language in the basic education as well as in the upper secondary education.*

The higher education in Finland is divided into universities and polytechnics. Most of the universities have as their administrative language Finnish. These universities also do not, generally, have any of the teaching in Swedish. Courses given in English are nowadays, however, prevalent at all Finnish universities. Hanken School of Economics (with campuses in Helsinki and Vaasa) and Åbo Akademi University (with campuses in Turku and Vaasa) are the only two universities that are Swedish-speaking. The University of Helsinki is bilingual (Finnish/ Swedish), which makes it a bit peculiar.

Bilingual Legal Education in the University of Helsinki The University of Helsinki was established in 1640 and is the oldest and largest university in Finland. The total number of the students at all level is little over 32,000.

The University of Helsinki is the only bilingual university in Finland. The language of instruction and examination are Finnish, Swedish or English. The University of Helsinki is the only university in Finland that offers academic education in Swedish in the fields of law, medicine, social work, social psychology, veterinary medicine, agronomy, geography and journalism. According to section 74 of the Universities Act (558/2009), there shall be at least 28 professorships with Swedish being the teaching language at the University of Helsinki. Services and student counseling are provided in Finnish, Swedish and in English. There are also education programmes and courses in English in some fields at the university.

There are eleven faculties at the University of Helsinki. The Faculty of Law is the leading institute of legal education and research in Finland. The Faculty employs about 140 teachers and researchers.

About 2300 students are pursuing degrees in Finnish, Swedish and in English at the Faculty of Law. In addition, the Faculty hosts on a yearly basis around 140 exchange students from all over the world. Doctoral studies can be completed in any of the three languages as well. Studying abroad for a period is also a popular choice among law students. **Since 1991, there is a Master of Laws diploma programme fully taught in English at the Faculty**. This particular Master's programme is focusing on International Business Law (IBL). Including: contract law, company law, intellectual property law, competition law and commercial disputes resolution.

There are separate tests and quotas for Finnish-speaking and Swedish-speaking applicants; therefore the applicants must, when applying, choose which of the two national languages will be the main language of their law degree. About 200 Finnish-speaking and 22 Swedish-speaking applicants are annually admitted to the education programme in Helsinki.

The Bachelor of Laws Degree comprises 180 ECTS credits, which is equivalent to 3 years of full time studies. The Bachelor's programme includes a variety of studies and examination in compulsory as well as optional disciplines. It is possible to complete the Bachelor's degree as a bilingual degree, this implies that the student completes at least one third of the Bachelor's programme in the national language (Finnish or Swedish), that is not the student main language of the degree. The student will then get a specific mention of the bilingualism in the degree diploma.

The legal studies include courses and examinations, which generally require a lot of individual reading of textbooks. Lectures series are held annually in every compulsory discipline. And normally the lecture series end with a minor exam, an essay or a study diary. The final exams are usually in the form of book exams or take-home exams.

The teaching language depends on the teacher, in some disciplines, there are parallel lectures in Finnish and in Swedish, and in other disciplines the lectures are given in one language only. Sometimes there are also lectures in English if the teacher does not speak either of the two national languages or if the subject is very international such as public international law or energy law. The students are, however, always entitled to write their exams and course work in Finnish or in Swedish regardless of the language of the lectures. In exceptional cases, though, where the teacher is foreign the students may be asked to do the lecture exam or the written assignment in English, but then the students are allowed to use dictionaries.

The course material is usually in the language of the lectures or the language of the course. However, the literature relating to the specific disciplines, i.e. the exam literature, is mainly, in Finnish. There is a shortage of Swedish legal literature dealing with Finnish law, which puts the students who are pursuing a degree in Swedish at a disadvantage.

There are compulsory seminars in specific disciplines, where the students train in academic legal writing and in acting as an opponent of another student's text'; hence the seminar courses comprise of both writing and discussions. These seminars are held in Finnish, Swedish and/or English.

The Vaasa Unit of Legal Studies Since 1991, the Faculty of Law at the University of Helsinki has maintained a unit of legal studies in Vaasa. The population of Vaasa is about 67,000, 70% of whom have Finnish, 23% Swedish and 7% other languages as their mother tongue.

The Main Reason Behind the Establishment of a Campus in Vaasa, Was the Need for Bilingual Legal Practitioners in the Region The city has a District Court, a Court of Appeal and Administrative Court with special competence in environmental matters, a prosecutor's office, a Regional State Administrative Agency, a Center for Economic Development, Transport and the Environment, a Tax Office and many solicitor's officers. In addition to this, the Vaasa region is the home of the largest energy technology cluster of the Nordic Countries and many international enterprises. Due to this there is a growing need for multilingual legal expertise in these business fields.

In the late 1980s it was felt that there was a clear shortage of lawyers competent in both national languages in the Vaasa region. Thus, the Faculty of Law at the University of Helsinki established a campus in Vaasa.

The aim at the Vaasa Unit is to ensure that equal instruction proportions are given in Finnish and in Swedish. The study environment in Vaasa is truly bilingual; both students and teachers use Finnish and Swedish interchangeably. The students are not required to become fully fluent in both national languages, but they must be able to understand instruction and study materials in Finnish, Swedish and also in English to some extent.

It is essential for a country with two national languages and where the citizens have the right to communicate with either one of them, that their Faculty of Law is able to educate lawyers with sufficient skills in both national languages.

The language policy of the Vaasa Unit is a bit peculiar; it could be characterized as extremely liberal: everybody—teachers, students, and administrative staff—can use either Finnish or Swedish of their own choosing and the recipient must accept that choice and be prepared to understand the speaker.

The discussion on bilingualism is, at least in Finland, **actually more a question of multilingualism**. The University of Helsinki has a great national responsibility regarding the legal education in Finland, since it is the only provider of a full law degree in both national languages.

Over the years, the legal education has been permeated with an international perspective. In addition to the International Master's programme, the Faculty of Law is involved in several international projects. Collaboration with researchers outside Finland is also very common. Furthermore, the main publication language in some of the more international fields English. Companies and thus also legal counsel work increasingly in an English-speaking environment with all communication (including contracts) being drawn up in English. Thus, **legal education programmes are today in fact tri- or multilingual, albeit that officially degrees are still only mono or bilingual**.

7 Bilingual Legal Education in France

The national French Reporter, Anne Brunon-Ernst begins her work with argumentative considerations that are important to quote:

> Language has always been key to the building of nation-states in Europe, thus explaining the prevalence of monolingual States. Their promotion was justified on grounds that the territory of a State ought to be defined by common linguistic and cultural boundaries. Conversely, this gave rise to independence movements and greater demands for minority-language recognition, thus paving the way for the first bilingual higher education institutions as early as the nineteenth century. Nowadays, the preservation of national and regional language has been given supra-national legal support by France's membership of the European Union (EU). Bilingual education thus has a long-standing history, which predates the EU integration, and which cannot be isolated from the social, political and institutional contexts of its creation and continued existence. Because of the relative decline of the nation-

> state models in the Post War era and globalised higher-education and employment markets, it is reasonable to assume that bilingual education is bound to be on the rise. The case of "bilingual legal education" (BLE) is unique in more ways than one. Law cannot exist outside language. Law is drafted, enforced and administered through acts of language. Moreover, legal concepts take meaning within their own legal system, thus they are highly dependent on the frame of reference set by the legal order. To a more limited extent, this can also be true of trans-national legal subjects such as EU law. Far more than in any bilingual programme involving any other discipline, BLE has always entailed more than simply using a different language as a teaching medium, as the very content of the law is system-bound. Some concepts might not have any equivalent in another legal system (e.g.: there is no translation for the English legal concept of trust in French law), or might describe a particular position in the justice system which has no equivalent in another (e.g.: there is no equivalent in the common law of the French juge d'instruction). Thus, BLE has to teach also skills which are not legal per se, but linguistic, such as, but not restricted to, the ability to translate, switch languages and design information bilingually…(…) France has one official language, French (…)The present report therefore considers the use of BLE as referring to the teaching of a law programme in two different languages, one of which would be French, and the other a foreign language (referred to for the purpose of the report as the target language (…)The report excludes from its scope any programme which might be taught exclusively in an institution outside France. It thus considers only programmes taught either in France, or part in France and part abroad …

Further on she adds an interesting and difficult question:

> Does a law programme require a minimum number of hours taught in the target language to qualify as "bilingual"? Is one module (18 to 37,5 hours of teaching per year) sufficient to fulfil the "bilingual programme" requirement, or should a more substantial proportion of the teaching be taught in the target language to meet the standard?(…)

The answer to this is not simple as there are no universal standards that may establish when a bilingual legal programme is considered as such. Especially when each country and each university, throughout different guidelines and controls, may have very different perspectives and commitments in terms of what may be or not considered a BLP (Bilingual Legal Programme).

The French report indicates that in 2015–2016 there were around 210,000 students enrolled in law and political sciences programmes at university, with 14% of foreign students, half of them coming from the African continent. 125,000 of those students were undergraduates, 78,000 studied postgraduate courses and around 7000 were taking PhD programmes. As she points out,

> There is no legal obligation to teach a foreign language at undergraduate level. Each university is free to make it a mandatory requirement for the award of a bachelor's degree. In practice, very few programmes do not offer either optional or mandatory language classes at undergraduate level…(…) The heterogeneous audiences for which standard-track or specific-track programmes are designed might have a direct or indirect impact on which subjects are taught, how, by whom and when.

Anne Brunon-Ernst identifies four categories of BLE: (1) Exchange programmes (2) Double and joint-degrees (3) Degrees partially taught in a foreign language (4) Degrees exclusively taught in a foreign language. As it generally happens in most countries, the French public university system is fully or partially State-funded.

Certification of programmes for the award of national degrees is granted exclusively by the State.

> The same procedure applies also to private higher education institutions which are allowed to award standard French undergraduate and post-graduate degrees (licence (LLB), master (LLM), doctorat (doctorate)) if their legal programme complies with the standards set by the French Ministry of Higher Education and Research. Although over the past decade, there has been a drive towards more autonomous management of French universities, which has not always been successful, the certification system has not evolved significantly. Thus the French State has sufficient leverage to create effective incentives for universities to comply with any education policy. However, it stands in a double-bind. On the one hand, it seeks to encourage foreign student enrolments and French student mobility, but on the other hand, it imposes French as the compulsory language of teaching. Only a certain number of exceptions to the **Loi Toubon** make it possible for French universities to teach their programmes in another language than French. In practice, law faculties have been able to make use of the exceptions provided in the **Loi Fioraso** to develop the wide range of BLE ... Nonetheless the official language requirement might slow down the growth of BLE in the future.

Also, as in several other countries, as said by A. Tsu and J.W.Tollefson in the paper "The Centrality of Medium of Instruction Policy in Social-Political Processes",

> behind the educational agenda are political, social, and economic agendas that serve to protect the interests of particular political and social groups.

The National Reporter quotes another research paper written by L. Purser that sustains

> (...) linguistic policies are "never simply an accident, but rather results of deliberate decisions involving more than simply the academic community".

In conclusion to these reflections Anne Brunon—Ernst affirms that

> (...) among the other players which have a stake in legal education policies, students and employers have a key role in creating a demand-led market for BLE.

This General Reporter is inclined to say that these players will have a major and increased role in the near-by future.

> (...) The increase in global business makes graduates who have bilingual legal skills extremely attractive. However, as of yet BLE does not train fully competent jurists in two legal systems (except for the notable exception of joint-degrees, which still require additional qualification). BLE skills are nonetheless adequate for most workplace tasks. BLE skills are not expert skills in another legal system but rather comparative legal and language skills which allow jurists to find their way around the institutional setting, legal rules and procedures of another legal system, translate and design information bilingually in their own system for jurists from other systems and to negotiate efficiently with target country lawyers.
>
> If French jurists want to meet employment demands in a global economy, they need to master the legal and linguistic tools of comparative communication. Only BLE trains jurists for these skills... "

The challenges still to face in BLE accordingly to the French report are multiple and complementary: skills in listening, reading, writing, in oral communication as well as in oral interaction and interpretation. Because "*language is embedded in culture*" those skills need to combine language and legal issues. That is why the national French Reporter mentions the importance of disciplines such as Language for Specific Purposes (LSP) as well as the use of English in a particular domain (ESP) an approach to language learning based on the needs of the learner. These kind of programmes will be more and more helpful

> (. . .) to identify ways in which the target language is embedded in the legal and professional culture of a given community. What is the specific terminology in the field? What are the recurrent language structures student will use in the different tasks they will be asked to carry out in the workplace? How does language reflect the professional culture of the target country? Research is carried out in these fields to bring answers to these questions, and help devise programmes that are tailored to the professional needs of students . . .

Finally, another tool that is more and more on request in France are the Specific English Courses (Anglais de specialité or ASP) that help its students to identify relevant features of communication (terminology, phraseology, genres, communicative situations, culture, etc.) in a specialized domain such as law.

8 Bilingual Legal Education in Germany

In a similar way, the German Report written by Stefan Grundmann points out the relevance of plurilingualism in actual times, which should be seen as a powerful tool instead of an obstacle for communication:

> (. . .) "reduction to one global language carries the risk to impoverish law, namely its pluralism that conveys as well the idea and the essence of a pluralism in societal models. . ." (. . .) La langue – c'est une arme, et en me référant en ceci librement aussi à Foucault, je soutiens dans cet article que le **plurilinguisme**, en droit, de nos jours, est considéré surtout comme un obstacle où il devrait en vérité être entendu comme **un des plus grands pouvoirs**. . . (. . .) language informs or influences formation of thought and language – strongly, very strongly, perhaps even as the major factor of all (. . .) language forms thought, thought about legal and societal models. Hence, reduction to one language is completely at odds with a world of multiple legal and societal models and even more at odds with a world in which pluralism of societal models – a form of individualism – is seen as being paramount and foundational also from a normative perspective. One may point to the fact that pluralism in legal and societal models and believes is even seen as a foundational value enshrined in constitutions (at least in the Western world). One may even go so far to say that the global legal community, if it does not want to betray to some extent the foundational value of pluralism, has a moral duty to foster (much more vigorously and actively) a form of discourse that is based on a variety of languages".

When writing his report Grundmann frankly shares some of the objections he had to face with some of his colleagues at Humboldt University who are strongly in favour of the Europeanization of private law and consequently upholding the flag of German language as an instrument to enhance the practice of law "made in Austria, Germany and Switzerland". Additionally, he explains

> (. . .) Indeed, while this may not be of similar importance for small countries or less important universities, it may be paramount for leading universities in jurisdictions that really

substantially have shaped and still shape legal thought – other than that in the Anglo-American world...

Some academic adversaries at Humboldt therefore blamed him for having accepted and indeed proposed the name of **'European Law School'** for the network he describes further on in his report and the title of **'Juriste Européen'** for those who have successfully completed its curriculum and the Master exams in three European countries.

It did not help that I insisted on the fact that this institution and curriculum is, in its essence, about multiplicity of languages ('plurilinguism'), of styles and of models – more than any other offer and model existing before. Similarly, he will blame me for writing this account in English and perhaps not even 'forgive' me for the mere fact that, at the end, I add a shorter variant of this text in German (and also in French), containing all major arguments (...)

The German Reporter agrees with his opponents when they argue that

reduction of the global discussion to one language, a lingua franca, carries the risk that a good number or even most of the ideas developed in the larger part of the world, in their native languages, is de facto excluded from the discourse or strongly reduced in importance. This risk is exacerbated by a dominant attitude in the global discussion of law to see a diversity of languages mainly as an obstacle to a common discourse and much less as a chance for richer, more nuanced, more pluralist discussion of legal and societal models. This implies that poverty in languages is seen as constituting the most efficient arrangement of discussion while it could also well be perceived as an intellectual shortcoming – reducing knowledge and diversity in the global discourse(s). (...)

The German report then highlights the increasing relationship between law and economics as well as how both influence on the evaluation and the development of legal solutions. This phenomena, which was for a long period of time neglected, is nowadays seriously taken into account and develops two different approaches in terms of understanding and trying to resolve economical and legal issues and problems: a more economic approach instead of the ordo-liberal school approach. Both approaches differ in substance and methods at the time of finding better regulations and solutions to those issues and problems. This has—in his view—three major consequences:

(1) The difference between both approaches is enormous, the law and economics approach having the main advantage of being so readily 'applicable', but also the main shortcoming of basing its results on assumptions that often abstract (strongly) from real world settings and often fail to have plausibility checks. One could speak in the one case of an approach more rigorously based on a formalisation and calculus, in the other of a value based approach that is more reality oriented and inspired and fuzzy. (2) Despite the importance of the difference, the latter is relatively little discussed and therefore we are relatively little aware of the comparative advantages and disadvantages of the two approaches either. We do not really discuss whether dependence on models and calculus does not exclude large parts of lawyers' communities from the discourse to a larger extent than an approach that is more principle and value oriented. (3) This lack of discussion is by no means limited to the Anglo-American world, but would seem to be influenced by the virtual lack of a pluri-linguist global discussion platform. This lack of pluri-linguist global discussion would seem to have different outcomes on both sides of the Atlantic – namely that an alternative approach is more easily neglected in the Anglo-American world, but also that, in jurisdictions such as those of continental Europe, the law and economics approach as shaped in the U.S. is either 'followed' or rather rebutted, not discussed, modified and transformed...

An interesting example of these distinctions is presented by Grundmann when he asks

> (...) If a calculus and model oriented approach to transnational economic transactions was not able to detect the flaws of a process bundling masses of sub-prime loans via securitization and outsourcing into SPVs, manufactured into CDO/CDS under the guidance of global rating agencies and then rated by them, with an investor community relying collectively and in a uniform way on the correctness of such models, might not the existence of alternative approaches in a global discourse have been helpful to cast doubt? Approaches that favour more robustness and plausibility checks instead of 'exact' calculus.
>
> These considerations pose the question of who has responsibilities in maintaining enough linguistic diversity, and they explain as well why (academics such as Alex Flessner) are right at least in categorical terms when insisting on German as a tool for explaining a whole legal world of thought...

Cautiously, the National Reporter adds that this universal and plurilingual view of issues and problems which in one hand could diminish the **personal or national navel focus of them**, should by the other hand be limited to a certain amount of languages:

> (...) This plea for more diversity – in languages and hence in societal models – can remain realistic only if one admits that the circle of languages consistently participating in a global discourse will (and must) remain relatively restricted even in a global discourse community more adequately shaped than that based on English only...

In his opinion, English, French, German, Spanish, Chinese, Arabic and Portuguese should probably be sufficient for this purpose. Philosophically speaking he adds a defiant and interesting challenge:

> (...) If law is about fairness and social sciences discussion should be shaped such that it can most adequately further the common understanding and welfare, responsibilities for a more diversified discourse environment are probably just as much and perhaps even more with the Anglo-American world itself. This may sound counter-intuitive, but **it could well be still more convincing if the impetus for a discourse rich in languages and hence in legal and societal models came as well – and very prominently from key institutions and key players in the Anglo-American world**. The role of the U.S. may even be paramount in this as it is not renowned for taking in ideas and diversity views from other parts of the world very easily (some even speak of 'academic imperialism'). Opting for diversity, formulating a plea of diversity would seem particularly convincing if formulated based on the particular strong position of those who start from the dominant language...

In this General Reporter point of view, this could and should be very necessary as well as revolutionary, but it seems that we shall need some time to see it happen, especially while the actual American Presidency is governing the USA...

After these considerations, the report presents a survey on the German Universities that offer pluri-linguist legal education. Basically there are three options: (a) Courses taught in other languages than German are often required in the German general final law exam, the so-called State's exam ('Staatsexamen'); these kind of foreign language courses apply to all lawyers leaving German universities with the regular law degree (close to 100%). (b) Curricula and study courses for foreign students (more accurately: requiring a law degree other than the German State Exam) leading to Master degree at German universities. These courses can be found in

German, but as well in other languages, mostly English. (c) Genuine double degree programmes, with integration of genuine university leaving exams both in a German *and* in a foreign university.

Separately, and as something that this General Reporter finds especially attractive and innovative, is the offer which goes well beyond such double degree Programmes. This is the **European Law School network (Berlin/London/Paris/Rome/Amsterdam).**

As said, many Universities in Germany have extended Programmes of Foreign Law taught in Mother Tongue; the report explains that in a good number of cases, the foreign language taught courses in foreign law are also part of the (more extended) double degree programmes—if those universities have such a scheme—i.e. are used in both contexts. Other Universities as well allow a year of specialisation to be passed abroad, but this is discretional; if so they develop a regime which allows for substitution of some requirements and courses by a parallel curriculum at a university abroad.

In other cases, Universities have developed Master Programmes (L.L.M.) in German and foreign languages; large number of those curricula are on business law designed for students and practicing lawyers from Germany or abroad. The most common foreign language used is English. Other Master Programmes (L.L.M.) are focused on German Law or EU Law, as well as on Large or Targeted Subject Areas or Regional Contexts.

The Double Degree Programmes is a third alternative in which many German Universities have become more and more involved. The list of the foreign Universities participating in these DDP is too long to mention them.

Apart from the funding and scholarship issues that are common to most European Universities, the survey mentions some interesting aspects when it comes to **the Educational and Policy** considerations.

As it is common in several other countries, legal education in two or more languages is absorbed between a 10 and a 15% of the graduates. The arguments that support it are similar everywhere: it develops open-mindedness, enhances professional and labour initiatives and different skills, promotes cultural exchange and integration, etc. As said before, this diversity instead of being seen as an obstacle should be considered as a powerful weapon to encourage those same arguments.

Let us quote Prof. Grundmann once again:

> (. . .) "In law, the comparative law method would probably first come to mind when differences of language and of legal styles are at stake. It forms the natural key discipline for questions of diversity. Looking at this discipline and also comparing it to parallel strands of theoretical approach(es) in the social sciences, may not really be conclusive with respect to questions of pluralism, but still be telling to some extent. In a nutshell: German and French were the languages of comparative law. The founding fathers were writing in French and German – translated into English. . ." These remarks may not be shared by everyone, but this General Reporter strongly agrees with them. Further on he adds another shared remark: (. . .) "the endeavour of developing uniform rules or principles has completely dominated the comparative law world in Europe in the last two or three decades. Would this not imply that diversity was rather seen as an obstacle than as richness in the European main stream discourse..?"

As a way to conclude these interrogations the National Reporter makes a final challenge:

> (. . .) In a comparative law approach, one trend which would perhaps come closest to such a 'varieties' approach could be called **'comparative legal foundations' approach'**. Instead of looking at single solutions for concrete problems, it would focus on the interplay of the main structures and determinants of the legal architecture, for instance which role plays the **constitution, namely fundamental rights,** in the development of private law (direct/indirect/no application), which **court** develops these ideas, how do other social sciences influence the development of the legal academic discourse, how practice and which social sciences, etc. etc., and relate this to the institutional structure of this jurisdiction, including the question of **who are the main law authorities**. Such a comparative legal foundations' approach acknowledges these varieties, it also does not follow an approach of—in principle—the 'superior model'. It could even add foundations to an approach in which a pluralism of models is positively seen, at least in principle. While there is in my view no equally seminal piece in legal scholarship to the 'varieties of capitalism' work by Hall and Soskice yet, a prominent and parallel line of thinking could clearly be developed on this basis and this could be the basis of a broad, innovative research agenda. . .

As a good example of entailment and commitment towards this kind of legal education, the report describes the labour of the European Law School. Created in 2007, the purpose of ELS is that graduates must study and sit exams in three languages and in three countries with three major "styles" of legal thinking and practice, doing a full domestic exam in their home country and passing two LLM curricula in two other different countries, all three purposefully aligned. The first three Universities that developed this Programme were Humboldt—Berlin, King's College—London and Paris 2—Pantheon-Assas. As from 2013, Rome, Amsterdam, Athens, Lisbon, Madrid and Warzaw joined the ELS, which means, as said by the German Reporter, a sufficient example of different legal styles and problems that may be found in actual Europe. This broad representation is strengthened by the fact that the full majority of the students that are taking these international courses and sit for the exams have better overall performances and results in comparison with the national law students. Creativity, team work, networking activities, coordinated curricula, joint summer schools, and even more fluence in their own mother tongues are some of the aspects reflected in their students after the first 10 years of the ELS. The German Reporter concludes:

> (. . .) The European Law School is designed to give life to a 'narrative' of Europe in which diversity of languages and styles is seen as opening up the realm pluralist thought, and not mainly as an obstacle to one global approach on the basis of English. . .

9 Bilingual Legal Education in Italy

The Italian Reporter Prof. Elena Ioriatti describes a complex and very sui generis situation in her country. Although foreign languages and particularly English is increasing in Italy's Academia, there are some special characteristics that need to be taken in consideration:

> Italy is not a monolingual State and its regional dimension offers evidence as to the presence of protected minority languages and cultures. However, even if ethno-linguistic groups have gained not only political and linguistic autonomy, but even independence in the recruitment of the key legal professions (notably lawyers and judges), legal education remains monolingual in those areas. Bilingual legal education in Italy is much more linked to a trend of favoring the spread of English as a lingua franca, facilitating mobility in the European area, as well as to become a differentiating feature for universities in a competitive context. The core of these changes lies in the academic autonomies of the Italian universities – most of them are state universities – but this trend to a more multilingual academic model as opposed to the one of linguistic homogeneity is facing some forms of resistance on the governmental level. (...)

Until early sixteenth century Latin was the most used language for the educated population; the development of vernacular languages such as Florentine (a type of Tuscan language) was afterwards completed with what is now referred as Italian, a recent phenomenon that spread over the last quarter of the twentieth century, mostly due to the pressure of the media and the Fascist policy of linguistic unification. From then onwards,

> (...) a very complex language system developed, in which people often tend to use the Italian language to read, write or speak for the purposes of elevated discourse, and at the same time use a local dialect when dealing with more domestic/local kinds of conversation... (...)

The Reporter explains that there are two important bilingual regions in Italy which are that are Valle d'Aosta and the South Tyrol, the first with the obligation to draft laws in Italian and French, the second to do so in Italian and German, sometimes Ladin as well. This third option is an officially recognized Romance language spoken in the provinces of Trentino, South Tyrol and a small part in the Veneto region.

In Valle d'Aosta the full bilingualism is well established in primary and secondary school but is not so strong in advanced education, especially in the field of law. The main University (Aosta) does not offer a full curriculum in law and all the legal classes taught in the other curriculums are held exclusively in Italian.

The other interesting region where normative bilingualism can be found is the Province of Bolzano (Bozen) that, along with Trento, is part of the autonomous Region of Trentino Alto-Alto Adige (South Tyrol). Here, the most common spoken language is German, almost a 70% of the population speaks it, 25% speak Italian and 5% Ladin.

> (...) Today South Tyrol enjoys a broad administrative and legislative autonomy and is known as the territory in which the linguistic minorities have been recognized the greatest degree of protection and widest range of rights. The institutional setting of the province is specifically designed to permit the cooperation of the two main linguistics groups (German and Italian speakers), and every person has the right to use either language when relating to both the judiciary and the organs/offices of the public administration. As a consequence, documents directed to the public are also usually bilingual and the civil servants who work in the judicial and administrative fields are required to speak both languages. Furthermore, all laws and normative acts have to be drafted in both languages, and, when involving interests of the Ladin community, in this third language too (...) In both regions bilingual law drafting concerns institutions – and therefore concepts – of Italian law, which are applied

> within one single legal system, namely the Italian one, and are merely expressed both in Italian and in a second legal language which is not only Italian, but German. A special organ has been founded to address this specific set of problems: in South Tyrol the **Joint Terminology Commission**, composed by both Italian and German speaking experts, with the scope of creating, developing and expressing the terminology of the Italian legal systems in German. In Valle d'Aosta laws are drafted predominantly in Italian and subsequently translated by translators working within the **Service de promotion de la langue française.** Therefore, particularly in South – Tyrol, the legal professions – lawyers, judges, notaries – but civil servants too, even having a predominant language skill, are required to understand the translation and the correspondence of legal terminology adopted in both languages (...)

As for University legal education in these bilingual regions, the difficulties that arise are similar to many other countries. As said by the National Reporter,

> To be able to enforce law and administrative justice in the two languages, the system should be able to count on a sufficient number of legally educated bilingual legal professionals and bilingual law graduates in general (...)

Consequently, until now Italian is still the ruling language in tertiary education, although several courses are offered in other residual languages such as English, German or French.

This characteristic also applies to post graduate legal education in those bilingual regions. Graduates who like to enter the classical legal professions such as lawyer, judge or notary are not really trained in two languages; the responsibility for this specific need relies more in the respective Law Bar Association rather than in the Universities.

> The Bolzano school for the legal profession ensures that post-graduate legal education complies with the requirements for access to the Bar exams, also with regards to bilingualism. Students may attend classes in either Italian or German, but not all the programs in all disciplines are available in both languages. This depends mostly on the availability of the German speaking professors more than on the subject of the lecture, even if experimental double language classes have been recently introduced. This model is based on a co-teaching method of the same legal subject by two teachers, each being bilingual, but prevalent in one of the two languages. However, these bilingual classes are part of the general program of the school the aim of which is not to train young jurists in bilingual legal terminology or legal translation. As a consequence, in most case readings and pedagogical material are not available in the two languages...

Similarly, at the French speaking area of Valle d'Aosta, students are not especially motivated to study law in a language other than Italian. Moreover, this also is due to the fact that the regulation of legal language in Valle d'Aosta is a lot less incisive compared to South Tyrol, where all citizens have the right to use their language when dealing with legal offices and court cases. Consequently, decrees and sentences must be translated in the chosen language. On the other hand, in Valle d'Aosta, translation is foreseen only for specific legal deeds.

> (...) For the time being, the nearest universities which offer a full law curriculum in law are the **University of Trento (Italy) and the University of Innsbruck (Austria)**; it is interesting to notice how the latter that is located in the Austrian region of Tyrol, offers an integrated curriculum in Italian law, which covers both the Austrian and Italian legal systems and in which the classes are taught in German as well as in Italian.

> Finally, and strange enough, the only University offering a bilingual German-Italian training course for lawyers (avvocato/Rechtsanwalt) is the **University of Florence,** offering a program in which Italian students interested in the legal profession in Germany attend part of the courses in Köln (Germany) (. . .)

As for the vast majority of the cases, what concerns the degree of internationalization of high education in the legal fields depends of the State. The State is the exclusive authority to regulate the development and recognition of the legal degrees and titles to access the legal professions (lawyer, judge, notary). This is what is known as the **Laurea Magistrale in Giurisprudenza** obtained after a 5 year legal study program. The program is mostly mono-linguistic (Italian) due to technical, cultural and linguistic reasons rather than because of other nationalist or protective measures implemented by the State. As from 1933, Italian is the official language of teaching and of the examinations in all university structures.

> (. . .) Actually, the foreign language of teaching – any language other than Italian – is the only requirement which is necessary to qualify a University program as "international". The internationalization process of legal education is a complex phenomenon that has gradually interested all the European educational systems, responding to the need of the state to be competitive in a global market, as well as with the neo-liberal idea that universities "produce" services of economic values, that have to be competitive and attractive, as all the other economic activities. Within this complexity, aspects such as competition among law schools, convergence of academic curricula, student attraction, mobility of researchers and students are the ingredients of a successful educational system in the legal fields. Like many other European educational systems, internationalization has been the "engine" of the recent development of bilingual education in Italy. It is therefore not surprising that the language of instruction in bilingual programs is English, and legal education is no exception. . .

As shown in other reports, the process of internationalization in Italy has been centered more in Europeanization, especially after the implementation of the protocol signed in Bologna in 1988. In this "Bologna Process" this country was one of the first European countries to enforce the necessary reforms in order to harmonize the university systems. This was done by introducing the 3 plus 2 system that complete and finishes the Laura Specialistica. This has shaped two different models of graduate legal training: one more traditional and cultural, the other mostly operational and variegated that aims more to the business world and the labor market; the first is more theoretical (listen and learn) the second is more practical, where students have to develop more creative and participative skills. Although not bilingual per se, the use of other languages apart from Italian is much valued (especially English, German, French and Spanish) in order to achieve better training skills and better jobs in the nearby future. The recent European economic crisis also played a significant role, especially in the last 10 years, forcing many young students to migrate, searching new labor opportunities in foreign countries. The knowledge of other languages in addition to the native one, is more and more recognized as a powerful weapon to succeed outside national frontiers.

The Italian Reporter describes a recent and very relevant example of the new Bologna Process of aiming at a wider and more global vision in education, by explaining the model established at the Faculty of Law of Trento where she helds a teaching post and where she created and coordinated the Program described below: the first law bachelor entirely offered in English; a "cultural mission" with the main goal of training students in comparative and transnational law; as she relates,

> the Faculty of Law of Trento has always been cultivating the language skills of its students through International mobility programs, double degree projects, as well as by offering a good number of elective courses in other languages besides Italian. With the passing of time, these choices in legal education have been reinforced with the introduction in the students' curricula of legal language courses as well as with the launch of a "Law and Language program".
>
> Thus, it is no surprise that the very first law course entirely offered in English in Italy – and the fourth in Europe – was established in this environment. The program **Comparative European and International Legal Studies (CEILS)** is, at present, the only law three year English bachelor in Italy, as well as one of the very few established in Europe.
>
> This three-year school is included within an overview in which courses offered in English are developing progressively.

Afterwards, the interested students may continue and finish the post-graduate or double degree programmes offered in various languages, and mainly taught by guest visiting professors or professionals who are experts on a certain topic. As the Reporter admits,

> (…) The Faculty's professors were involved in the difficult challenge of teaching their subjects in a new language. The Author of this report also took part in this new teaching approach and was able to directly experience the tight relation between language and teaching methodology. As regards some experimental teachings, as in the case of the Author, with a course in Comparative Legal Systems, language is not just a means to communicate comparative knowledge. This choice for bilingualism is due to the need to take steps in the direction of the Europeanisation of the law curriculum: in these terms, language is method, as "the law practitioners need to be capable of crossing national borders not only physically but also intellectually and English, as according to the Eurobarometer, at present is the most spoken foreign language in Europe (…) Given the positive result of this teaching experiment, the law bachelor Comparative European and International Legal Studies CEILS (three years) was launched in 2017 and it is now offered alongside the traditional program in Italian of the Faculty of Law (five years).
>
> The students enrolled in the Italian five year program have also the possibility to join the Law and language program and so attending language courses, legal language courses and other training activities in French, German, Spanish and English language.

The challenges and difficulties that lie ahead for the Italian academic international law culture are still strong. The protection policy enforced by national institutions to preserve Italian language will not diminish for the moment. To achieve the 5 year degree Laurea in Giurisprudenza or the Master degree in Law, Italian will continue to be mandatory. And this was recently confirmed in November 2017 when the Consiglio de Stato applied a principle that had already been laid down by the Constitutional Court: judgement No 42/2017 which guarantees that the overall teaching of universities must respect the primacy of the Italian language, along with the principle of equality, the right to education and academic freedom.

For many Italian academics the application of this principle is a good way of preserving the Italian culture and language. For others, this is only a draw back and a way of cooling down the emergent need of legal internationalization. In between these two radical positions we may find the ones who ponder how much foreign languages, and especially English, should be reasonable and required in the legal academia in the years to come.

10 Bilingual Legal Education in Japan

Japan's situation regarding BLE is, at least in the National Reporter's point of view, quite original because of its complexities and somehow contradictions.

To begin with, two different stages must be taken into account: before and after 2004. That year was a "key" one to introduce and develop a new educational system more alike with the US-style of the law schools. In reality, Japan has experienced two different and competing institutional pressures in the context of BLE. (a) One pushing to a more diverse form of legal education but aiming to reinforce and enhance better Japanese lawyers inside the country, (b) the other one, with the commitment of the Ministry of Education, to internationalize Japanese universities and undergraduate law faculties in view of globalization and commerce.

The results of the new plan have not been—until now—the ones expected. The reformers and builders of the first current or pressure, hoped for a significant rise in the pass rates for the bar examination in Japan and this did not occur: it still remains low, currently between 20% and 25%. Consequently, law schools and law school students actually have focused their limited study time on "core" examination subjects, leaving little time or reason to pursue more diverse and creative course offerings, including courses taught in languages other than Japanese or courses making extensive use of foreign language materials.

On the other extreme, the interest of the Ministry of Education to internationalize its education has obtained some new developments, although it is still uncertain which of these two tendencies shall prevail in the nearby future. The National Report reflects some of the innovations and challenges taken by the University in which the reporter is based, that is Kyushu University, which clearly is not following the traditional educational trends, but rather a much more actualized and modern view of the issues at hand.

A little bit of history: "*Prior to 2004, the only pre-condition to take the national bar examination was high school graduation. A university law degree of any kind was not necessary. The bar examination was, however, notoriously difficult, with a pass rate fluctuating between 2-3%. This meant that by the year 2000, Japan had less than 30,000 lawyers for a country with a population of over 120 million.*" *(. . .) In order to assist candidates taking the bar examination, a network of private, specialized "cram" schools emerged independent of the universities. For those talented enough to pass, the bar examination was a gateway to, rather than the end-point of, professional legal training. A special institution run by the Supreme Court, the Legal Research and Training Institute would enroll those who had passed the bar examination and train them for a two-year period. In this way, future* *prosecutors, judges, and practicing lawyers would be trained together, before entering into the work force...*"

The National Reporter adds a clarifying aspect:

> This does mean that Japan had no university-level legal education. Quite the contrary. Rather, the vast majority of students who enrolled on an undergraduate law degree at one of the many (90+) law faculties (hougakubu) **had no intention or prospect of pursuing a career in legal practice**. Rather, **there was a clear separation – at least, in comparison with other jurisdictions – between university legal education and the legal profession.** Instead, an undergraduate law degree **was seen as providing a general education, ideally suited to a career in the public sector – as a national or local government official – or in a private company.** As such, a law degree from a good university was seen as a ticket to a stable career in the life-long employment system that functioned so effectively in the post-war development of Japan. (The underlying is General Reporter's responsibility).

As a consequence, this way of understanding legal education, so separated from the finalities pursued in the legal profession, the "encyclopedian" or generalist culture provided by Universities such as the undergraduate law faculty of Tokyo had one main objective: to produce and form the elite of the Japanese—level bureaucrats as well as the new leaders in the fields of finance and commerce. In this process, academic performance at university was accorded much less weight than the particular university one attended. High school students were placed under enormous pressure to get into the best university possible (such as the mentioned above), in order to secure their future employment prospects.

> (...) As such, pre-2004 undergraduate university legal education in Japan was a high status, generalist training, rather than a specialized, graduate, or professional style of legal education. Undergraduate legal education was certainly not designed with a view to produce practicing lawyers or other legal professionals...

Complementary, previous to 2004 the main Universities both public or private, had graduate schools of law that offered Master's and Doctoral level courses mainly oriented on comparative law, but again, with one main and specific target: to prepare its students for a career as university teachers and researchers (not as legal practitioners) with a certain mastery of a foreign language and the law of that country in a special field. The two main preferences in terms of language, due to historical reasons, were German or French.

Hence,

> "pre-2004 "legal education" in Japan could be divided into several different components: (i) university legal education, comprising a generalist undergraduate program; (ii) research-oriented graduate schools with a strong focus on comparative law; (iii) a series of specialized "cram" schools which would prepare candidates to pass the bar; and, (iv) a professionalized legal education, which came **after** passing the Bar examination and served as the only real practical legal training one would receive before entry into the three main legal professions of lawyer, prosecutor or judge..."

In 2004 the Educational Japanese Authorities enhanced what was meant to be a sort of radical change in terms of Legal Education: the introduction of Law Schools with a US JD style education in a 2 or 3 years—program, depending on whether students had studied law as undergraduates. Completing law school became a pre-condition for taking the new national bar examination. Significantly, the new law school system was added "**on top**" of the undergraduate and graduate level legal education described before. This means that—contrary to what other countries such as Korea did a few years later—Japan did not close down the undergraduate law faculties or the research-oriented graduate schools of law. The origin of this reform was the general dissatisfaction with the state of the legal profession by the mid 90ties:

> (...) it was often difficult to obtain legal services and much of the supposed "non-litigiousness" of the Japanese could be better explained by the difficulties and costs of finding a reliable lawyer. Most lawyers tended to be concentrated in the big cities of Tokyo and Osaka, creating an uneven geographical distribution. Many people also criticized the quality of legal professionals, as the lack of genuine competition created little incentive for legal professionals to offer a better standard of service (...) after the Japanese economy fell into recession, pressure emerged to reform the system. The pressure came from several sources. The Ministry of Justice and Supreme Court in Japan wanted to increase the number of prosecutors and judges. Big business began to complain about the lack of quality in the legal profession. And, as the economy declined, more disputes emerged. The trend towards de-regulation meant that government control over the economy was decreasing. The capacity of government to manage conflict was diminishing...

As one can observe, this is just another example of how economic issues may impose legal, social and cultural reforms; on the other hand, many legal, social and cultural changes have played a significant role and had tremendous impact in the economy of certain countries and regions.

In any case,

> the key event in the reform of legal education was the creation of a Justice System Reform Council in June 1999. After two years of deliberations, the Council's recommendations were released in June 2001. These recommendations were to the have a profound impact on legal education of Japan and provided the template for the new post-2004 system.
>
> The primary aim of the Council's recommendations was to reform the justice system and increase reliance on the law as a means of social ordering. A key element of the transition towards a "law-governed society" was the call for an expansion in the number of lawyers, judges and prosecutors...

There was great optimism and confidence in the creation of these new law schools. The market would determine the number of the new and well prepared lawyers, which in an average of 70–80% would be admitted to the legal profession after passing the bar examination. To support the newly created law schools, it was proposed that (at least, until 2011) only those who graduated from a law school could be eligible to sit the new examination, which would still have to be passed to qualify as a lawyer, public prosecutor or judge. Two programs would be offered: a 2-year program for those who had studied law as an undergraduate and a 3-year program for those who hadn't. The expectations were to have around 3000 lawyers graduating every year. The bet was to increase the quantity but also the quality and diversity of the new lawyers. The new law schools would move away from the narrow focus of private cram schools that had emerged to support students competing to pass the old-style bar examination. In order to accomplish this the Council recommended recruiting law school applicants from a wide range of academic and professional backgrounds:

> A lawyer with a degree in medicine, for instance, would be better placed to assist a client in the context of medical malpractice suite. Or, a lawyer with experience of the creative industries would be more effective in handling a copyright dispute...

Another aim was to enlarge and cover the gaps of geographic diversity in order diminish the centered influence of urban cities such as Tokyo and Osaka. And finally, to frame "internationalized lawyers" experts in business and international exchange.

Curiously enough, and maybe because of the pressure and resistance of the stakeholders of the traditional legal education system, the undergraduate law departments or faculties were maintained as a source of employees for government and internal business. As already mentioned, Korea did not follow the same path and many undergraduate law programs and departments were closed down when they opened the new law schools, as it happened in Seoul National University.

Therefore, as from 2004 the majority of law faculties in Japan offered: (1) the traditional general undergraduate legal education; (2) a research-focused graduate school; and (3) a new professional Law School, responsible for preparing students for the bar examination.

Sixty-six new law schools opened in that year and the competition to attract the best students was fierce. But the first results of launching and recruiting the new model of lawyers in the new era were not the ones expected. The number of students allowed to pass the bar examination increased much more slowly than originally envisaged. The government had to accept that instead of 3000 graduations per year, only half was reaching that goal. Not only this, but also the percentage pass rates began to drop to disappointing figures: from 48% in 2007 to around 25% in the period 2009–2015. The government's officials tried a feeble excuse: all in all, Japan should not become a litigious society, so 1500 new lawyers per year was enough, especially to avoid unnecessary competition and also to promote quality instead of quantity.

The introduction of an alternative way to pass the bar exam in 2011—a preliminary qualifying bar examination centered in six basic subjects—didn't obtain satisfactory results and simply supposed a return to the basic and traditional roots: the new kind of lawyers were not meant to be so necessary and the new generation of students would focus again in becoming well trained administrative officers, bureaucrats or researchers. The five more distinguished Universities in producing the best pass rates have been Keio, Tokyo, Chuo, Kyoto and Waseda in that order.

Another issue that has to be taken in consideration is the economic cost of attending to private law schools in relation to public ones. In average, it implies a 50% higher and not many students can afford that difference, especially if the light at the end of the academic tunnel seems so distant, dim, and ineffective. A logical consequence of all this is that applications to Law Schools are down from a decade ago, and some schools have been forced to merge or even close down. The persistent declining pass rate for the bar examination—25% on average—forced law school students again to focus on core examination subjects, leaving little time or incentive to pursue courses offered in other languages.

A different path to reimplement the new type of internationalized lawyers in some universities has been the introduction of programs mainly or exclusively taught in English. This can be a way of considering and accepting the term "*Bilingual Education*" in Japan in the last 10 years. It was the path, as the National Reporter explains, to "re-invent" the graduate education by offering in some universities Master's and Doctoral programs taught mainly or exclusively in that language.

In order to better understand the trends that have been followed in Japan's BLE the reporter separates three different kinds of programs: (a) the ones offered by professional law schools (b) undergraduate programs with general legal education (c) graduate-level programs. Finally, the reporter signals the personal experience of Kyushu University where he is based, which offers all the three programs mentioned above.

(a) **Law Schools**: As said before, these new institutions experienced an optimistic start that collapsed a few years later. An article written by Dan Rosen—from Chuo University Law School in Tokyo—reflects both stages. From his point of view, many of the subjects taught at the beginning of the new Law Schools never appeared in the future bar exams. At first, they were accepted and chosen by the students as a way to expand their general culture and obtain some level of legal diversity. But things changed radically when the bar exams began to prove that only some core and traditional topics were frequently and persistently asked. What was required to pass the exams was memory and repetition; no need to intertwine knowledge or compare systems. The result? The students learned the lesson: forget the idea and hopes of diversity and internationalization; disregard all subjects and courses that are complementary such as law & economics or law & sociology, legal ethics, Roman or German law. Stick to the only courses and subjects required to approve the bar examination and if that is achieved, afterwards say goodbye to the law schools altogether. Dan Rosen, like many other professors are wondering how many students per year shall be attending courses that are considered a luxury and a waste of time for the new generation of students. As stated by the National reporter,

> (...) No matter how much the government may have emphasized the need for broadly trained lawyers, by maintaining a strict bottleneck on entrance to the profession, students are pushed into focusing on the bar-exam related subjects and away from other courses that can quickly come to be seen as a distraction from the core task. This includes courses with a strong foreign language component...

In view of this situation two alternatives may rise. Adopt the Korean model that limited the number of law schools but also required some universities with accredited law faculties to stop their undergraduate legal education, or increase the bet on internationalization, such as Luke Nottage's proposition that shows the case of the University of Sydney as a good example of cooperation between Australia and China, by promoting a 3 plus 2 double degree program (see page 19 of the report). Whether any of these alternatives shall be adopted remains doubtful in the National reporter's point of view.

(b) **Undergraduate Law Faculties:** These institutions have been "pushed" towards a different direction, especially by several governmental Ministries: internationalization of undergraduate teaching, learning and research. A example of this tendency was the 2009 Global 30 project that offered English only undergraduate courses and programs, or the Top Global University Initiative which began in 2014 and finishes in 2023. Funded by the Japanese government that approved US$77 million to attract more foreign faculty and students in the main Japanese Universities classifying them in two categories, A and B and accordingly giving more or less funds per year to each of them. Kyushu University, rated A, receives US$4.2 million annually because of its potential to be ranked among the top 100 in world university rankings. Type B universities receive US$1.7 per year. Two main "pushers" of this initiative have been Prime Minister Shinzo Abe and several Japanese companies that need to re-shape and re-invent the new professionals in order to compete in the global race where Japan has been losing presence and markets.

In 2013 the government launched Japan's Revitalization Strategy that aims to double the number of Japanese students studying abroad by 2020 (from 60,000 to 120,000). This was complemented with

> the "Tobitate (Leap for Tomorrow) Study Abroad Initiative". This scheme which hopes to make Japan a nation in which "ambitious young people are given the opportunity to go global" offers various chances for students to study abroad. A standout among these opportunities is the so-called "Young Ambassador Program". This program provides scholarships and other aid with the help of private-sector contributions aiming to collect 20 billion yen. The goal is to help 10,000 of these young "ambassadors" by 2020…

It is still very soon to predict and evaluate the results of all these strategies and initiatives. At least ten more years will be needed to reap what has been sown.

As already mentioned, Japanese legal education has not followed the usual standards of launching skilled and specialized professionals in such and such area of expertise. On the contrary, it has developed the encyclopedian, general approach helpful to work afterwards in different levels of the government or local companies. Hence, one can find two different and parallel trends or paths in Japanese education: (1) the scientific-research (2) the practice—oriented. Until recently, the comparative legal education was mainly or exclusively taught in Japanese, although German or French law was the target of the comparative investigation. The finality of such education was to have a better knowledge and understanding of the Western World, but mainly as a mere intellectual curiosity or search for diversity. And there were no urges from up-ward companies or administrations to receive new well practiced and skilled professionals.

But something began to change since the last end of the twentieth century and beginning of the twenty-first century: (a) the realization that English would still be the lingua-franca necessary to move in commerce, business and politics (b) the realization that the Asian region (and particularly China) was beginning to acquire more and more economic and political influence in the Western world. Kyushu University was one of the first to understand these changes and began to do something about it by hiring more and more foreign academic professors. Consequently, as the National reporter explains,

> there has been the creation of new four-year undergraduate programs that can be described as genuinely bilingual in the narrow sense that it involves a combination of law courses that are taught in both Japanese and English with the stated aim of producing "global lawyers" or, at least, those with the necessary language and legal skills to become global lawyers. An example of this type of bilingual law program is the so-called "Global Vantage" program (GV) launched in Kyushu University in 2015. This program is only open to 10 students per year and involves a separate English-language entrance examination from the traditional undergraduate program, but students are offered a genuinely bilingual program that aims to build language skills in English, as well as legal knowledge in both Japanese and English...

To put this in Samuel Huntington words, in China the slogan was "Ti-Yong" (Chinese knowledge for basic principles, Western knowledge for practical skills) and in Japan the slogan was "Wakon Osey" (Japanese spirit for Western techniques). (**) Samuel Huntington—The clash of civilizations and the remaking of world order.—Ed. Paidós SAICF—1997—page 86—Spanish edition.

Some of the aims of the GV program are to foster expertise in the fields of law and political science, to develop creative and flexible problem solving, proactive leadership roles both nationally and internationally. Again it is too soon to evaluate the results of this program, especially because of the low number of students that are involved each year. Nevertheless, employers are optimistic with GV in the long term.

Graduate Schools The establishment of the new law school system in 2004 reduced the number of students wishing to enter the research-oriented post-graduate law programs offered at a Master's or Doctoral level. The reasons for this decline of interest in a more research oriented graduate level legal education may vary, but one logical one to extract is that the new students have a more practical and very "consumer" way of understanding education. If it is useful and provide skills in the short term, they will take it; if it is a long term and therefore uncertain way to obtain a future employment, they will not. This may explain why several law faculties have broadened their recruitment to bring in former lawyers, prosecutors and judges (i.e. those with practical experience) to teach as professors in the new law schools. The national reporter finds also another reason for this change of orientation:

> ...Of course, this "opening up" legal academia to those with more experience of the realities of legal practice makes a lot of sense given the demands of the law school system. One of the design issues with the new law school system was that **the overwhelming majority of the faculty members responsible for preparing students for the new bar examination had not passed the bar examination themselves, nor did they have any experience of legal practice. They were researchers and not practitioners. "Opening up" of faculty recruitment has been a logical response to the law school system...**

Consequently, the role of graduate schools after the reform in 2004 remains with a big question mark. The Japan example is another of many which reflects what usually happens when reforms and new programs are designed by persons who may have great theoretical ideas that confront and clash with the practical realities that appear in the short or long term.

The intermediate key that may open new doors in BLE is again internationalization. This is the big focus of Universities such as Kyushu that is more and more providing graduate programs taught either entirely, or substantially, in English at both a Master's and Doctoral level:

> The such first program, the LL.M. in International Economic and Business Law (IEBL) was established in 1994. At the time, it was the only Master's course taught entirely in English within Japan and was designed to overcome the main obstacle to studying law in Japan, namely the Japanese language. Kyushu University's IEBL program focuses on international and comparative trade and business law. An LL.D. program allowing students to complete a doctoral dissertation in English was added in 2000...

Other universities such as Keio, Kobe, Nagoya and Waseda followed the path opened by Kyushu. The bilingualism of the programs is quite peculiar, because in strict sense one cannot say they are taught both in English and Japanese; in reality Japanese is offered as an option, but in general, legal education is proposed and taken in English. The advantage of the "*relative*" *l*ow cost of graduate school tuition fees in Japan compared to the US, makes it attractive for Asian students to choose a Master's law degree in English geographically situated in the Eastern region.

Another initiative from Kyushu was to host a new program, the **Young Leaders Program (*YLP in Law*)**. The Ministry of Education designated Kyushu to host and develop

> (...) this Master's level graduate program (that) targets young legal professionals and government officials from designated emerging economy countries. Initially the geographical focus of the program was North East and South East Asian countries but recently a number of other countries have been added including India, South Africa and Turkey. Students on the YLP are integrated into the IEBL program where they study legal issues with a particular focus on international and comparative trade and business law. Again, these programs are taught entirely in English...

Kyushu University's Bilingual Master's (*LL.M.)* degree program in Law (*BiP*) is another attempt and innovation to offer bilingual legal education. It offers overseas graduates of Japanese language undergraduate programs or those with a legal background and a strong background in the Japanese language, the opportunity to take a Master's degree in law in a bilingual environment:

> The program is designed for students who already have a solid foundation in the Japanese language. (...) As such, the program is principally intended for Japanologists or lawyers with strong Japanese interested in (i) Obtaining a deeper understanding of Japanese culture and society through the study of historical or contemporary issues in Japanese law & politics; or (ii) Preparing for a legal career in Japan or connected to Japan by studying Japanese and international business law...

As a part of the Program students have to do a Master's thesis under the supervision of two faculty members. It can be on any legal topic and must be written in either English or Japanese. They are also expected to complete a 20 page's summary of the thesis in the other language. Finally, students are offered the opportunity to participate in an internship of 2–4 weeks at either a Tokyo-based international law firm, company or government agency. The *BiP* program is still very small, with only 2–3 international students per year enrolling.

The conclusion that arises after this panorama of Japanese education is somehow enigmatic: Is Japan striving for still a traditional and "core subjects" education, towards new and original forms of internationalization, or thirdly, to somehow a middle-road kind of legal education that remains modern and open to the Western world while keeping faithful to its own culture? The three kinds or types of students found in Japan nowadays do not give us yet a conclusive answer. As it usually happens in the Eastern World, much more time is required to see the result of these tendencies...

11 Bilingual Legal Education in Mexico

The official languages in Mexico are Spanish (Castilian) and 68 indigenous languages called "linguistic groupings". It is estimated that in 2015 there were 7,382,785 people aged 3 years and over who speak an indigenous language. The languages with the highest number of speakers are: Nahuatl, Maya and Tseltal.

Regarding the number of people who speak English in Mexico, according to estimates from the National Institute of Statistics and Geography (INEGI), the population over 18 who speak English is approximately 9.4% of the population.

The Teaching of Law In Mexico there are 1770 Higher Education Institutions (universities) that offer a degree in Law. The number of students of the law degree in 2016 was 354,753 of which 176,232 are males and 178,521 women.

The **main educational institution in Mexico is the National Autonomous University of Mexico (UNAM)**, whose enrollment of law students in 2016 was: 11,603 students. In 2017, the Law School of the UNAM has a population of 11,856 undergraduate students and 1002 postgraduate students (Masters and PhD).

The Reporter addressed the proportion of foreign students to local students pointing out that in 2016, 101 foreign exchange students were received, who studied a semester at the UNAM. This indicates that the proportion of foreign students is just 1.14%.

In the Postgraduate Studies, the proportion is 99.6% of national students and 0.4% of foreign students in the Master of Law; and of 95.7% of national students and 4.3% of foreign students, in the Doctorate in Law.

Furthermore, it is important to underline the proportion of foreign professors to local professors. There are 40,184 academics throughout the UNAM, and in 2015, 300 foreign visiting professors were received (that means approximately 0.74%). Regarding the Faculty of Law, the proportion is similar (less than 1%).

Regarding the nationalities represented in the student body, the main foreign nationalities represented in the student body are Colombians, as well as Spaniards, Peruvians, Canadians and Americans.

In the **School of Law of the UNAM there is no bilingual legal education program** because the number of foreign students and professors is still limited.

However, in the field of Postgraduate Studies in Law, the Institute of Legal Research of the UNAM has a "Master's Degree in American Law" which is taught in four semesters, whose content is equivalent to the Juris Doctor taught in the United States, but offered in Mexico. This program is aimed at Mexican students who want to be more than bilingual lawyers: "bi-legal" lawyers.

Number of visiting professors per year. In 2006, there were 1293 visiting professors from abroad at the UNAM (3.22%).

In the area of undergraduate education, no attempt was made to initiate perhaps because the number of foreign students, or nationals who are fluent in English or another foreign language, is even lower.

However, in populations where there is an indigenous majority, so-called "**intercultural universities**" have been implemented, **which teach classes in Spanish (Castilian), but incorporate some indigenous languages into the substantive functions, becoming bilingual schools**. According to information from the Ministry of Public Education there are eleven intercultural universities located in eleven states of the Republic, whit 14,008 students enrolled in 2015–2016. Among them, the Intercultural Universities of Chiapas, of the State of Tabasco, of the State of Puebla and the Veracruzana Intercultural University have a degree program in Law with an intercultural approach.

There is **the "Master's Degree in American Law"** taught by **the Institute of Legal Research of the National Autonomous University of Mexico** (national public university), the **Illustrious and National Bar Association of Mexico** (national association of Mexican lawyers), as well as **the School of Law of Sinaloa** (private university of local character), **a postgraduate program that is an example of bilingual legal education in Mexico**.

All the teachers engaged in this Master's Degree in American Law are local and they teach the classes in both languages, but the own and specific institutions of the American common law are taught in English. There is only one American professor that is the coordinator of the Master's Degree.

The program began in 2011 as an initiative of the law doctors Hector Fix-Fierro (at the time director of the Institute of Legal Research of the UNAM) and Oscar Cruz Barney (at that time president of the illustrious ad National Bar Association of Mexico); with the idea of studying the legal system of the United States of America. The objective of the Master's Program is to train Mexican jurists to advise companies, offices and organizations in the United States, which carry out activities in Mexico or Latin America.

As the Reporter sharply pointed out there has been no resistance from students, faculty or authorities. However, **it is clarified to the students that the Master's degree does not accredit them to practice law in the United States, nor to present the Exam before the Bar of that country**.

There are many areas of law taught in a foreign language: Private Law, Commercial Law, History of Law, Constitutional Law, Administrative Law, Procedural Law, Legal Methodology, Legal Deontology, and International Commercial Law.

One of the main positive effects of this Master is that the students are more competitive in the work force because they can be hired by companies, associations or other foreign institution that carry out activities in Mexico and Latin America, since the students are experts in Mexican Law (Civil Law) and United States Law (Common Law) in a globalized world.

The methods for evaluating students used in the United States are followed for the students in the American Law, that is, the case method for teaching, and the evaluation through written exams, under the system of "encrypted name".

The selection of professors has been carried out among researchers from the Institute of Legal Research of the UNAM. The textbooks (casebooks) of the subjects have been purchased directly from the publishers of the United States. The same texts are used, as if they were studied in the United States,

All students are Mexican, who speak and understand English language very well.

From the Reporter's perspective it can be said that there has been an improvement in the last 5 years regarding BLE in Mexico. There is a plan to teach the Master in other States of the Mexican Republic.

There is coherence between BLE offered from the academic point of view and the vision of the Law Firms in Mexico, since the Master in American Law is oriented to solve the needs of the law firms, especially those that deal with foreign and international entities.

The National Reporter believes that the interest in BLE will grow in the country due to the fact that more offers of education will arise. Furthermore, the Law Firms will have more interest in hiring "bi-legal" lawyers.

The main language as an option for bilingual legal education is English. Once again, as we have seen throughout the report, English is the first choice since it is the most common worldwide. Other languages that could be chosen as part of bilingual legal education are French or German. The bilingual legal education is conceived as an opportunity to compete better in the international order.

12 Bilingual Legal Education in Romania

Taking as leading example the Faculty of Law of the University of Bucharest, Romanian National Reporters Ramona Popescu and Carmen Achimescu, as so do other Reporters, mention the Constitutional duty to impart all levels of education at their respective national language, also providing the right to minorities to receive education in their own language. Therefore, it is commonplace to discover in all the submitted reports a mixture of self-preservation of the native language combined with a flexible acceptance of foreign languages either to protect minorities or to promote bi-lingual or even tri-lingual education in view of the growing demands of the students, the future employers of these students, as well as internal and external reasons linked with political, cultural or commercial needs.

Recurrently, the increase of migration in several countries has played a major role in the foundation and development of Bilingual Legal Education.

Apart from the traditional courses that can be found at the University of Bucharest offered to 3200 undergraduates, 600 postgraduates and 180 doctorates, the Romanian Reporters mention the original **College juridique franco-roumain d'etudes europeennes**. It is a part of the School of Law which offers a bilingual course that may take 3–5 years with specialization on European Law. Several French Universities are entwined to offer this course together with the University of Bucharest. Among them, Paris 1 Pantheon-Sorbonne. An average of 250 students take this course every year. The College Juridique was created in the 1990s after the fall of the Romanian communist regime and was enhanced by the strong cultural influences of the French law in Romania as from the nineteenth century. The principal purpose of its foundation was to open Romania to the Western World and to promote a new generation of young jurists with the skills to exercise the law beyond Romanian boundaries.

Another project in the nearby future is a double degree course Spanish-Romanian in partnership with Universidad de Valencia, also aiming at European Law but taught in Spanish.

Programs such as Erasmus have been very helpful to expand student's international mobility not only in Europe, but throughout the different continents.

Yet, in several European countries BLE courses strongly depend of the material and financial resources of each university. This occurs due to the lack of professors who are able to teach courses in other languages rather their own native one. Romanian Reporters confirm this view when they sustain that, although the need for universities to adopt a broader international scope is understood, this goal can hardly be met due to the fact that the organization of BLE courses is still very difficult since there is a shortage of technical, economic and human resources. As a result of these difficulties, only between 10% and 15% of Romanian students are actually focusing their careers with an international perspective.

Another important reason for this, as the National Reporters point out, is that **Law Faculties are generally less able to attract foreign students because of the specificity of their subjects, an issue that can be more easily overcomed in other Faculties with a more technical profile.**

13 Bilingual Legal Education in Singapore

Singapore is officially a multi-ethnic, multi-religious, multi-language nation-state with four official languages (English, Mandarin Chinese, Bahasa Melayu, and Tamil) to be used in Parliament or the provision of essential government services. Although, Bahasa Melayu is a national language, as the National Reporter states, apart from the Malay ethnic community in Singapore, relatively few other citizens are conversant in Malay at any serious level. There is a government-run programme under which middle-school students who are not classified "Malay" may enroll in Malay language classes, but the take-up rate is low.

Singapore citizens are classified for official purposes into four racial categories: "Chinese", "Malay", "Indian" and "Others". A person classified into a particular racial category is required to be taught the language(s) ("Second Language") corresponding to that racial category i.e. Mandarin Chinese for "Chinese", Bahasa Melayu for "Malay", Tamil, Hindi, or another Indian language for "Indian", and the closest relative or a foreign language (French, German, or Japanese) for "Others".

As local university admissions—and especially for law faculties which are the most selective faculties next to medicine—generally require a good grade on the Second Language subject on school-leaving examinations/qualifications, it can be assumed that most local law students in Singapore have some working knowledge of at least their Second Language on top of high proficiency in English.

However, legal proceedings must be conducted in English (with interpretation possible) and all documents not in English translated into English. There is no right, whether at civil or criminal law, to legal proceedings in any of the three official languages other than English.

Hence, for legal purposes, Singapore is **de *facto* a monolingual jurisdiction**, using only **the English language**.

For education purposes as well, save for language or language-related special subjects, all education—whether at pre-university or university level—is conducted in the **English language**.

The **National University of Singapore**, Faculty of Law (NUS Law) admits approximately 220–240 students every year for its 4-year LL.B programme. Over 100 students are admitted to its LL.M programme per year, and 3–5 candidates are admitted to the Ph.D. programme each year.

The vast majority of students (90–95%) enrolled in the NUS Law LL.B. programme are local students (Singapore citizens). The bulk of foreign students enrolled as undergraduates typically have received a substantial part of their pre-university education, ranging from 2 (high school) to 6 years (middle and high school), in Singapore, and usually under an established government scholarship scheme. However the proportion is reversed for the graduate programmes. LL.M. programmes are dominated by foreign students, with only a handful of local students enrolled each year (of whom a number are on generous scholarship terms), and there have, to the best of the Reporter's knowledge, only been 2 local students who have graduated from Ph.D. programme in the last 10 years or so.

Relating to the proportion of foreign professors to local professors, as of 23 of March 2017, counting full-time (excluding emerita), tenured, tenure-track and untenured positions at the rank of lecturer of above, foreign faculty represent 47.6% (30 out of 63). This does not include a number of special contract full-time positions created primarily for locals (for which 10 out of 11 are locals). The count does not include a considerable body of research staff based at the research centers or postdoctoral fellows.

As a matter of impression, NUS Law has a relatively diverse student population at the graduate level and in terms of incoming undergraduate exchange students, but official data on the composition of the student body is not available. As the National Reporter affirms, as a matter of impression, students from Malaysia, China and India are the most numerous (after local students).

There is no comprehensive or systematic bilingual legal education programme NUS Law, and only 1 course is taught in a language other than English ("Chinese Legal Tradition and Legal Chinese"). This is an elective course read by third-and fourth-year undergraduate, and is not compulsory except for students who are planning to go on students exchange at law faculties in the People's Republic of China. From the Reporter's personal recollection, less than ten students were enrolled in his year (AY 2012–2013).

For the academic year 2017–2018, NUS Law welcomed a total of 25 visiting professors based in Canada (1), Japan (1), England (9), Australia (8), United States of America (7). This figure only includes visitors who taught at least one intensive course over 3 weeks.

From the Singapore Reporter's view it is unlikely that a comprehensive bilingual legal education programme was seriously considered for implementation at NUS Law, despite a considerable and long-standing interest on the part of Associate Professor Gary Bell, who is on the Singapore's National Committee for IACL.

However, in light of the fact that there is one course that is taught in Mandarin Chinese (and also involves an English-language component), the Reporter considers this enters in the category of a bilingual legal education programme.

Historically there is no importance whatsoever attached to bilingual legal education except for the purpose of outgoing students exchange to exchange partners in the People's Republic of China. Students participating in this programme are expected to read and pass the sole bilingual course above mentioned as a condition of their exchange programme.

The only professor to teach courses in two languages was born in China (People's Republic of China) and educated in China (Bachelor's, Master's), England (Master's), and the United States (LL.M., J.S.D.).

To the best of the Reporter's knowledge, only two local professors can be said to teach in the Chinese language, but only in the context of students' consultations. One professor, was involved for many years in teaching a small group (tutorial) graduates students from China enrolled in the LL.M. in Corporate & Financial Services Law programme, for whom Company Law was a required subject for their degree.

Another professor is naturalized Singapore citizen, but was born and raised in the People's Republic of China, and received her first law degree there. She taught Company Law on a special LL.M. programme co-organized with the East China University of Political Science and Law (based in Shanghai, People's Republic of China), with classes spread over bot the NUS Law's campus in Singapore, and ECUPL's in Shanghai.

14 Bilingual Legal Education in Taiwan

In 2016, the total number of law students at **National Taiwan University College of Law** was 1526 (including students in the undergraduate, master and Ph.D. programs).

For the purpose of comparison, in 2016, there are 35 universities having the department, college or school of law or having a bachelor or advanced legal studies program. There were 119 legal studies programs, including 40 undergraduate programs, 66 master programs, and 13 Ph.D. programs.

In 2016, the total number of law students in Taiwan was 19,662, including 13,503 students in undergraduate programs (bachelor of laws), 5845 students in master of laws programs and 314 Ph.D. students.

Relating to the proportion of foreign students, a distinction must be made. There are two types of foreign students at NTU College of Law. The first type is "degree students" pursuing a degree, such as a bachelor of law degree (LL.B.), master of law degree (LL.M.) or doctoral degree (Ph.D.), who must comply with the same requirements in order to obtain the respective degree. The other type of foreign students is coming as exchange students who usually stay for one or two semesters and enroll in courses they select.

As for the **degree students, the number of foreign students at NTU College of Law has maintained at the range of 77 to 82 during 2007 and 2016**. The proportion of foreign students to local students at NTU College of Law was 5.6 to 100 in 2016 and 6.6 to 100 in 2007. In other words, **foreign students constitute 5.3% if the student body at NTU College of Law in 2016 and 6.19% in 2007**.

With regard to the Exchange students (foreign students not seeking for degrees) coming to NTU College of Law, there has been an upward trend in the number of exchange students over the last 18 years. The number was in the single digit by 2008, crossed 10 in 2009, and exceeded 100 in 2016.

In relation to the proportion of foreign professors to local professors, at the College of Law, National Taiwan University, 100% of full-time faculties are the nationals of Taiwan. However, there are visiting professors who are paid to teach a course (in a regular semester or complete teaching intensively in less than a month) and visiting scholars who are unpaid and come to conduct short-term research.

Many different nationalities are represented in the student's body, there were many international students enrolled in undergraduate, master and doctoral programs at NTU College of Law during the period from Academic Year 2000–2017. The top 5 foreign countries in terms of number of degree students at NTU College of Law during that period are China, Japan, Korea, Mongolia and Thailand.

The majority of courses are conducted in Mandarin at NTU College of Law. However, they do provide English courses and some conducted in German and Japanese for local and international students to enroll. In the last 10 years, there were 12 English courses offered in Academic Year 2009 (the fewest offered year), while there were 39 English courses offered in Academic Year 2015 (the most offered year).

The number of visiting professors in 2016 was 344 constituting 8.2% of the faculty at NTU.

The Reporter sharply addresses from his view what means bilingual legal education. What courses can be considered as bilingual legal education courses is, as mentioned by the National Reporter, an issue itself.

> (...) By the definition of bilingual education, we usually refer to courses that are conducted in the native language and another language. In Taiwan, a bilingual legal education course is a legal course that is taught in Mandarin (or Taiwanese), the native language of Taiwan, and English (or other foreign language). From personal observation, there may be very few courses that are considered to be bilingual legal education courses according the strictest definition...

As the National Reporter points out, the importance of bilingual legal education courses is that it provides students many benefits in learning the legal regimes. Firstly, students learn how to read foreign legal material in foreign languages, particularly in English. Secondly, they learn how a legal concept is expressed in other foreign jurisdictions. Furthermore, local students may interact with international student in the courses. Finally, students may learn the comparative approach in learning law.

In the National Taiwan University College of Law there are professors that teach courses in both languages. English courses are offered in line with the policy of NTU to accommodate more and more international students who have not yet been able to attend the courses conducted in Taiwan's language. Another type of English courses is designed to train the local students to learn in English environment. These courses are usually related to foreign law, Anglo-American laws and international law. Occasionally, local professors co-teach a course with foreign professors who come for the full semester or for only a few weeks. For example, during 2008 to 2012, Professor Ming-cheng Tsai, former Dean of NTU College of Law, **initiated a Comparative Law Course held in several semesters, inviting guest speakers from universities of different countries**.

Some of the aims for boosting bilingual legal education is to provide local students opportunities to learn directly from foreign scholars, to access to foreign legal regime, to get familiar with foreign legal materials, and partly to accommodate more and more international students, particularly exchange students, professors are encouraged to start a bilingual legal education course.

The first reason to start a bilingual legal education course from the Reporter's perspective is to correctly introduce foreign law and legal terminologies to local students. The second reason is to benefit local students to access to different sources of foreign legal materials so that they learn where to find foreign law and legal materials. The third reason is to accommodate the increasing international students who have not been able to attend courses conducted in local language. For this purpose, English courses have become the policy of several top universities to encourage professors to run English taught courses. Most English taught legal courses are in the master program and mainly in comparative legal studies in nature.

From several universities' point of view, to offer more English taught courses is in response to the trend of globalization and internationalization and to allow students to get used to the English learning environment.

In practice and in reality, from the National Reporter's perspective, there are, and I quote

> (...) several obstacles in carrying out the bilingual legal education program or in running English legal courses in Taiwan...

First, it takes more time to prepare an English taught legal course and there are not many incentives for local professors to conduct legal education courses in English. It is crucial to mention though, as the reporter later expressed, that he has not seen many objections or resistance against bilingual legal education directly, "these objections are mainly against university's policy requiring faculties to offer English taught courses". Professors offering BLE courses do not receive any additional financial concessions comparing with offering regular courses conducted in local language. The criticisms are mainly against the compulsory policy itself.

Another obstacle is that English taught courses are not popular among local students. A course not conducted in local language is not popular if it is not a required course to be taken.

The areas that they have decided to teach in a foreign language are the mentioned below. Firstly, a popular option is Comparative law or for the purpose of comparative studies. Secondly, it is also commonplace to find courses related to International Law. Thirdly, they may also offer courses to study Anglo American Laws. Furthermore, other topics of law that have caught attention of international society such as Arbitration and Intellectual Property Law, International Human Rights Law, International Disability Rights Law.

The majority of students who have received bilingual legal education or attended English taught courses have been able to outperform in terms of having better chances to getting into the top law firms and more internationalized listed companies as in-house counsels. Many top law firms look for lawyers with proficiencies in foreign languages, particularly in English.

Speaking of the evaluation methods, it can be agreed as the Reporter says that different professors evaluate students differently. In most bilingual or foreign language taught courses, students are evaluated by their performance in the class and the final exam or term paper.

Professors teaching bilingual legal education courses usually choose the area of law they specialize. Therefore, they usually are familiar with and able to obtain the necessary resources. Textbooks in some courses are used, such as Anglo-American Contract Law. Legislative materials, statutes, case law, scholarly writing, etc. are easily accessed from online legal research services, such as Westlaw and Lexis. Once again, one has to bear in mind that different professors design their reaching and materials differently.

Students enrolled in bilingual legal education courses are usually having different levels of proficiencies in the foreign language used in the courses. In order to encourage students with lower proficiency in English, it is a policy for many professors to explain, in the course description, that English is not the major element for evaluating the students.

For BLE courses or English taught courses, the National Reporter states that the number has increased gradually or at least maintained the same level in the past 5 years. The number of BLE courses is related with the number of visiting professors.

Most professors offer BLE courses mainly from the academic point of view. However, professors have noticed and encouraged students pointing out the advantage that BLE students have when applying for a job in comparison with the rest of students who have not enroll in a BLE course. Law firms, particularly those with international businesses, will recruit students having received bilingual legal education.

The main language chosen as an option for bilingual legal education is, once again, English. The reason the National Reporter refers to English is because most of the literatures in the areas of law are in English.

If another language had to be chosen, due to the fact that Taiwan is a civil law country, they will chose German and Japanese laws, since many areas of law are patterned after those laws.

Finally, it must be underlined that from the National Reporter's perspective Bilingual Legal Education is not perceived by students, faculty members, State authorities or Law Firms as a threat to national roots or culture.

15 Bilingual Legal Education in the United States

The American Problem with English as a Global Legal Language
On a global level, English is the most predominant language. Since the late twentieth century, US-American and British law firms have shaped global legal practice. For US-American lawyers, this creates a peculiar situation. On the one hand, the global predominance of legal English gives them a significant professional advantage: their native language is the lingua franca of the world today. On the other hand, it dramatically diminishes their need to master any other tongue since they can get away with English most of the time.

Therefore, most Americans make little investment in acquiring even a reading knowledge of a foreign language. Efforts to train students in foreign legal languages play decidedly marginal role.

The Status Quo: The Marginal Role of Foreign Language Training The status quo of foreign language teaching in US-American legal education is difficult because comprehensive data are hard to come by. This report is based on the information obtained primarily from the individual law schools and websites by the research staff of the University of Michigan Law School. Although there are two nationwide organizations the American Bar Association (ABA) and the Association of American Law School (AALS), none of them collect information on the matter since foreign language teaching is not a requirement.

The picture shows that foreign language teaching in US law is currently quite rare. Nevertheless, a development has been made, since over twenty years ago Gloria Sanchez pointed out that there were no foreign languages courses at all. Today, there are a variety of curricular offerings introducing US law students to law in a foreign language, and a few law schools have made serious efforts in that direction.

The existing offerings can be divided into three groups: dual degree programs (1); individual foreign language courses at US law schools (2); and opportunities to study or work abroad (3).

More than 30 law schools claim to offer joint degree programs with foreign institutions. In most of these programs, US law students obtain the basic law degree in the respective foreign jurisdiction in addition to their home institution's JD; in some, they spent a year abroad and receive the more limited LLM degree. The total number of these law schools looks more impressive than it really is in the context of foreign language teaching. While almost all these joint programs are with institutions in non-English speaking countries, many do not require full fluency in, and some not even significant command of, the partner country's vernacular. In addition only a very small number of students actually pursue a joint degree with foreign language.

Still, where they do require fluency, they provide significant exposure to the law of another country in the vernacular. This does not necessarily lead to full-fledged bilingualism in the sense that the students become as capable in the foreign tongue as they are in English, especially in the legal and business context. But they can be expected to reach a level of proficiency that enables them to perform professional work in at least one foreign language.

Foreign language courses in US law schools have a long history. Today, of the accredited law schools in the United States, more than 40 claim on their websites to offer courses in one or more foreign languages. It is still a distinct 20% minority, also it is unclear how many of these courses advertised are actually taught on a regular basis and the number of participating students seems to be quite small. On the whole, it is fair to assume that, at the very most, a few hundred out of more than 100,000 US law students in the United States ever take a course in a foreign legal language.

The design and coverage of the courses varies. Most of them focus directly on foreign (legal) language training for American lawyers. Where they introduce students also to aspects of the respective foreign legal systems, they do so more or less incidentally and in order to provide cultural context. A few courses however are designed as introductions to the basic features of foreign legal systems in a foreign language.

Many US law schools run summer programs abroad, usually in attractive locations and often in non-English speaking environments, sometimes providing more touristic than educational value.

A large number of American law schools also offer semester abroad programs in partnership with foreign universities, often in multiple venues, some with different requirements of fluency in the local language.

The scope of languages covered by courses in US law schools remains somewhat Euro-centric but there is a trend towards a more global range. By far the most frequently foreign (legal) language in US law schools and programs is Spanish –a global language in its own right –. By now, Hispanics comprise nearly one fifth of the US population.

Language instruction is also offered in the other two most prominent Western European languages, i.e., French and German, and sometimes in Italian.

The published teaching materials fortify the primacy of Spanish in the language programs of US law schools. In recent years, three books were published for use by teachers of Spanish as a foreign legal language.

The advantage that most immediately comes to mind when listing the reasons to teach law in a foreign language is directly professional; a lawyer who can work in a foreign language can better attract and communicate with non-English speaking clients. In fact, lawyers with foreign language skills appear to be in growing demand. It is especially great in international practice, as well as in immigration and other public interest work.

Beyond that learning law in a foreign language is an opportunity to acquire sensitivity to foreign cultures—an important professional asset in its own right, particularly in a global environment.

Moreover, there is reason to believe that studying foreign languages is generally good brain training. To begin with, bilingual persons are particularly apt at "divergent thinking". Bilingualism opens the lawyer's mind to multiple options and solutions. Furthermore, bilingual individuals are often better at "executive control" of information. There are strong reasons to believe that studying law in a foreign language enhances a lawyer's "social intelligence" and "imaginative capacities" as well.

Finally, American scholars have also justly pointed out that communicating with a client in his or her own (native) language creates a human connection and avoids degradation. It is a sign of "respect for the individuality of the interlocutor and an acknowledgment of her basic human dignity".

Conclusion: A Question of Commitment

American law schools currently proffer very limited training in foreign (legal) languages. This is true even though such training generates multiple professional and educational benefits which are generally recognized in the literature. The potential for expanding such foreign language training is stronger than the American reputation for monolingualism intimates. Yet, a realistic assessment of the possibilities and a sober cost-benefit analysis suggest that courses in foreign languages neither will nor should be offered by all law schools or taken by a majority of students.

Still, the current situation is deficient. The vast majority of American law schools offer virtually no opportunities to experience law in a language other than English. Not offering a class even in Spanish is difficult to justify for any major US law school today. In light of the American law schools' virtually ubiquitous claims to promote diversity and to train students for practice in a globalized society, such disregard of the language dimension is actually somewhat embarrassing.

How can American law schools move towards offering instruction in foreign languages more broadly? From the National Reporters eyes, it would probably help if the American Bar Association as their accrediting body and the Association of American Law Schools as their professional organization pushed in that direction. Ultimately, however, offering foreign language instruction on a more regular basis is a question of every law school's institutional commitment. Such commitment needs to be based on a wider appreciation of the professional and educational advantages of studying law in a foreign tongue.

In conclusion, it must be admitted that the current political climate in the United States is not so supportive of foreign language study as it was years ago. Nationalism is resurgent and hostility towards immigration and immigrants is a renewed widespread phenomenon.

References

Astolfi J-P, Develay M (1996) La didactique des sciences, 4e édition. PUF, Paris, p 25

Berthelot J-M (2008) La construction de la sociologie, 6e édition. PUF, Paris, p 124

Hanson NR (1958) Patterns of discovery: an inquiry into the conceptual foundations of science. Cambridge University Press

Huhn WR (2002) Use and limits of syllogistic reasoning in briefing cases. Santa Clara Law Rev 42:813

Samuel G (2003) Epistemology and method in law. Ashgate

Samuel G (2004) Epistemology and comparative law. In: Van Hoecke M (Dir) Epistemology and methodology of comparative law. Hart, Bruxelles, p 74

Strong SI (2014) Review essay – bilingual education in the United States. J Leg Educ 64:356

Teubner G (1989) How the law thinks: toward a constructivist epistemology of law. Law Soc Rev 23(5):727–757. https://doi.org/10.2307/3053760

Thomas Y (1973) La langue du droit romain. Archives de Philosophie du Droit, pp:103–125

Multilinguism in Legal Practice and Legal Education: The Case of Belgium

Bert Demarsin and Sébastien Van Drooghenbroeck

1 Introduction

Belgium has three official languages: Dutch, French and German. The Kingdom's territory is divided into four linguistic areas: the monolingual Dutch-speaking area, the monolingual French-speaking area, the monolingual German-speaking area and the bilingual area (French-Dutch) around the nation's capital, Brussels. Based on the population figures of the three monolingual areas, and the estimated breakdown of the capital's population between French and Dutch speakers, about 60% of the Belgian citizens speak Dutch, slightly over 38% speak French, and the remaining 1% speak German (Fig. 1).

Besides, the use of English is undoubtedly on the rise, due to Brussels' role on the international political scene. Given the city's role as the capital of the European Union and the home to many international institutions, Brussels is commonly referred to as *World Decision Center II*, after Washington DC.

Considering the multilingual Belgian society, it is hard to imagine how the legal education provided at university—both at bachelor (180 credits) and master level (120 credits)—could not take into account that context and remain merely monolingual. First of all, the openness—at least passive—to foreign languages (two or even three) is essential for academic reasons. After all, legal training is document-based,

This contribution was finalized in July 2018. The factual and legal data presented in this contribution are up to date until that moment.

B. Demarsin (✉)
Faculty of Law, Leuven, Belgium
e-mail: bert.demarsin@kuleuven.be

S. Van Drooghenbroeck
Université Saint-Louis, Faculty of Law, Brussels, Belgium
e-mail: sebastien.vandrooghenbroeck@usaintlouis.be

N. Etcheverry Estrázulas (ed.), *Bilingual Study and Research*, Ius Comparatum – Global Studies in Comparative Law 58,
https://doi.org/10.1007/978-3-030-84550-6_2

Fig. 1 Language areas in Belgium

and most often, these case decisions and scholarly writings are just dressed up in one language, without being translated. In addition, there is also a professional and cultural need for multilinguism in Belgium, as clear communication between the country's communities should remain possible at all times.

Hence, it is not surprising that language courses (general or legal) in at least two target languages other than the program's main language are a compulsory part of the curriculum of all bachelors in law organized at Belgian law schools (there are 6 in the French Community[1] and 7 in the Flemish Community[2]). In addition, in most bachelor programs and even all master programs (there are 3 in the French Community[3] and 5 in the Flemish Community[4]) numerous legal courses are taught in a foreign language.

However, the amount of language courses offered as part of the curriculum at Belgian law schools is subject to some important restrictions. In particular, all programs have to comply both with the maximum limits laid down by the decrees of the Communities, and the potential minimum threshold set forth in interuniversity agreements (**II**). Within these limits and thresholds, the universities are largely free to fill in the curriculum either individually or based on agreements concluded between them. Consequently, both the foreign language courses and the legal courses thought in a foreign language may take different forms—even independent

[1]Université Saint-Louis—Bruxelles, Université Catholique de Louvain, Université de Liège, Université libre de Bruxelles (both at the Brussels and Mons campus), Université de Namur.

[2]Universiteit Antwerpen, Vrije Universiteit Brussel, Universiteit Gent, Universiteit Hasselt, *KU Leuven* (at 3 locations: Leuven, Brussels and Kortrijk).

[3]Université catholique de Louvain, Université de Liège and Université libre de Bruxelles (at its Brussels campus).

[4]Universiteit Antwerpen, Vrije Universiteit Brussel, Universiteit Gent, Universiteit Hasselt and *KU Leuven* (at its Leuven Campus).

from the Erasmus system. The landscape is indeed very heterogeneous, ranging from the inclusion of some foreign language courses in the curriculum, to the creation of master programs entirely taught in a foreign language.[5] At all Belgian law schools, both types of language education are generally on the rise. Since it is impossible to discuss in detail the wide variety of programs offered by all Belgian law schools, we will consequently focus on the bilingual (and even trilingual) programs that our two universities (*Université Saint-Louis-Bruxelles* and *KU Leuven*) have set up for 26 years. However, before exploring the actual content of this program (**IV**), we will recall some factual data concerning these two universities (**III**).

2 Regulatory Framework

2.1 Overview of the Distribution of Competences in the Field of Education and the Use of Languages for Educational Purposes

Belgium is a federal State composed of Communities and Regions (art. 1 of the Constitution). Belgium comprises three Communities: the Flemish Community, the French Community and the German-speaking Community (art. 2 of the Constitution).

According to Article 127 of the Constitution, education—including university education—falls within the competence of the Communities and their decrees. The decrees of the Flemish Community apply to universities located in the unilingual Dutch-speaking area (the *Universiteit Antwerpen*, the *Universiteit Gent*, the *Universiteit Hasselt* and the *KU Leuven* (Campus Leuven and Campus Kortrijk)), as well as universities located in the Brussels bilingual area, which—because of their activities—are said to belong exclusively to the Flemish Community. The *Vrije Universiteit Brussel* and the Brussels Campus of the *KU Leuven* operate mainly in Dutch (both for education and administration). Accordingly, the above decrees of the Flemish community also apply to these institutions. On the other hand, the decrees of the French Community not only apply to the universities located in the unilingual French-speaking area (the *Université de Namur*, the *Université de Liège*, the *Université Catholique de Louvain* and the Mons Campus of the *Université libre de Bruxelles*), but also to the universities located in the bilingual area which—because of their activities—are said to belong exclusively to the French Community (*i.e.* the *Université Saint-Louis-Bruxelles*, the *Université libre de Bruxelles* (Brussels Campus) and the Brussels Campus for medicine and pharmacy of the *Université Catholique de Louvain*).

[5]This is the case at the University of Antwerp (since 2016) and at the *KU Leuven* (at its Leuven Campus, in collaboration with the University of Zürich, since 2014).

There is currently no university in Belgium's unilingual German-speaking area. Moreover, if an entirely bilingual (French-Dutch) university (both administration and education) were to be founded in Brussels, it would fall under the authority of the Belgian Federal State. After all, such bilingual university could not be said to belong exclusively to the Flemish nor the French Community.

According to Article 129 of the Constitution, the Communities regulate by decree the use of languages in the field of education, as far as the unilingual areas are concerned. In Brussels, however, the use of languages is regulated by the Federal State. However, according to the Constitutional Court (judgment 44/2005, 23 February 2005, B.11.2 *et seq.*), this federal competence does not keep the Communities from regulating the language in which education is organized and dispensed. Accordingly, the French Community is competent to regulate the use of languages for educational purposes in the francophone Brussels universities. The Community determines in particular whether, under what conditions, and to what extent the education provided by the francophone Brussels universities may be in a language other than French. The same goes, *mutatis mutandis*, for the Flemish Community as far as the Dutch-speaking universities in Brussels are concerned.

Finally, without going into detail, we stress the fact that in order to exercise a regulated legal profession in Belgium (bar, judiciary, notary, bailiff) a solid knowledge of a number of fundamental topics of Belgian law is required. Candidates either proof to have passed through law school at a Belgian university, or, for holders of a foreign diploma, to have subsequently recognized its equivalence through a university program or by sitting a test of competence organized by the Bar, and covering, among other things, civil law, civil procedure, criminal law, criminal procedure, etc.

Both in the Flemish and the French Community, the above fundamental topics of Belgian law are taught at bachelor level. This explains why it is very difficult to organize an Erasmus exchange in the course of the bachelor program. Obviously, an exchange within Belgium, a so-called *Erasmus Belgica*, allows to by-pass this obstacle. Later on, we will discuss these *Erasmus-Belgica* exchanges in greater detail, as the bilingual bachelor program of *KU Leuven* and the *Université Saint-Louis—Bruxelles* fits within that framework (see *infra* IV.4.).

2.2 Language Education and Education in a Foreign Language: The Regulatory Framework Applicable in the Flemish Community to Universities in General, and Law Schools in Particular

2.2.1 Maximum Limits Imposed by or Pursuant to the Decrees of the Flemish Community

The Flemish Parliament has regulated the use of language at institutions of higher education, for both administrative and educational matters.

According to Article II.260 Codex Hoger Onderwijs (Flemish Code on Higher Education) institutions for higher education are supposed to *function* in Dutch, as this is the language that should be used for administrative purposes.

Article 261 Codex Hoger Onderwijs requires the *education* itself to be in Dutch too. In this way the legislature tries to preserve Dutch as the prime language for education at universities that fall under the authority of the Flemish Community. At the same time, the Flemish authorities recognized the importance of foreign languages as a sensible and justified means of communication in certain scientific fields, as a facilitator for foreign exchanges and a boost for international professional mobility. The end result is a complex set of rules on the use of languages for educational purposes, with many parameters that determine the limits of the universities' policy margin.

As said, at Flemish universities, education is supposed to be in Dutch, as a matter of principle. However, at bachelor and master level, there are 4 exceptions to the above principle:

1. Foreign language courses should be taught in that language;
2. Visiting professors from abroad are not obliged to teach in Dutch;
3. Non-Dutch courses that students, at their own initiative and with the consent of their home institution, follow at another institution for higher education;
4. Courses can be taught in a foreign language, provided that the institution explicitly motivates why a change of language is functional for the course and beneficial to the student and the professional field.

In addition, courses taught in Dutch may have some foreign language component. For example, course material may include a reader which is partly composed of English or French articles, or a foreign guest-speaker can be invited in a course that is taught in Dutch.

According to Article 261, §3 Codex Hoger Onderwijs, a bachelor program is Dutch-spoken as long as the number of courses taught in a foreign language is below 18,33% of the entire program (in ECTS and not including the exceptions 1 and 3 mentioned above). For master programs, that threshold is 50%. A university can only set up a program that exceeds the above language limitations, if there is an equivalent Dutch program in place in Flanders. In addition the university has to establish why the wider use of a foreign language is functional for the program and beneficial to the student and the professional field.

In addition, article 266 Codex Hoger Onderwijs imposes quota on the number of non-Dutch spoken programs: at least 94% of the bachelor programs and 65% of the master programs should be Dutch-spoken. Every year, the Flemish government verifies whether the above thresholds are met and reports the results to the Flemish parliament.[6] Students in Dutch-spoken program have the right to take their exams in Dutch. That is also true for courses taught in a foreign language.

[6] Art. 268 Codex Hoger Onderwijs.

2.2.2 The curriculum's Agreed Minimum Content with Regard to Language Skills

The Flemish Legislature obliges institutions that offer the same program to determine in close collaboration the program's "domain-specific learning outcomes". In 2014 the Flemish universities jointly did so for the bachelor and master of law programs. The "domain-specific learning outcomes" of these programs specify the set of competences/skills all bachelor (*c.q.* master) students in law should acquire at law schools under the authority of the Flemish Community. The NVAO[7] validates domain-specific learning outcomes for all master, bachelor and graduate programs in Flanders after they have been established by the Flemish Universities.

The domain-specific learning outcomes of the bachelor of law do not *as such* impose specific foreign language skills. However, according to the program's domain-specific learning outcomes all masters of law should be able to find, evaluate and use legal source material in both Dutch and French ("*Rechtsbronnen in het Nederlands en in het Frans vinden, naar waarde schatten en gebruiken op academisch-wetenschappelijk verantwoorde wijze*").

2.3 *Language Education and Education in a Foreign Language: The Regulatory Framework Applicable in the French Community to Universities in General, and Law Schools in Particular*

2.3.1 Maximum Limits Imposed by or Pursuant to the Decrees of the French Community

In the French Community, university education is organized by the decree of 7 November 2013 'defining the landscape and organization of higher education.[8] Article 75, § 1 of this decree provides that all educational institutions, without any exception have to use French for *administrative* purposes. In its §2, the same article requires the *education* itself, including the examination, to be in French too. However, some exceptions are possible here.

- For undergraduate studies (bachelor), a quarter of all credits (*i.e.* 45 credits) can be organized in another language;

[7]The Accreditation Organization of the Netherlands and Flanders NVAO was established by the Dutch and Flemish governments as an independent accreditation organization tasked with providing an expert and objective assessment of the quality of higher education in the Netherlands and Flanders.

[8]Décret du 7 novembre 2013 'définissant le paysage de l'enseignement supérieur et l'organisation académique des études', *Belgian Official Gazette* 18th December 2013.

- For graduate studies (master), half of the credits (i.e. 60 credits) can be organized in another language. Upon governmental approval and under the condition that « *les études visées [aient] un caractère international dérivant de l'excellence du champ scientifique ou artistique, ou de sa nature particulière* » it is possible to go beyond this threshold of 60 credits, and to organize the entire master program in a foreign language;
- For programs organized in collaboration with another educational institution which does not belong to the French Community;
- For *Advances Masters* and PhDs, which can be entirely in another language, such as English.

It is also possible to deviate from the above rules, when students are offered the choice of taking a particular topic either in French or in a foreign language. Indeed, according to article 75, §2, paragraph 2 of the decree: « *de manière générale, toute activité d'apprentissage d'un cursus de premier ou deuxième cycle peut être organisée et évaluée dans une autre langue si elle est organisée également en français* ». Hence, universities that fall under the authority of the French Community can set up bachelor programs that are mainly taught in a foreign language, provided that students can always choose to take these courses in French. It is on the basis of this general exception that the *Université Saint-Louis—Bruxelles* is able to organize its bilingual and trilingual programs.

2.3.2 The Curriculum's Agreed Minimum Content with Regard to Language Skills

In order to ensure undergraduate (bachelor) students to move up to the second cycle (master) within the French Community, the bachelor program is subject to some minimum harmonization. According to the decree of November 7, 2013, at least 60% of the bachelor curriculum (*i.e.* 108 credits) should be harmonized (article 125, § 2). The law schools jointly define the minimum content and submit it to the *Académie de Recherche et d'Enseignement Supérieur* (ARES) for approval.

The latest harmonization agreement (April 14, 2014) provides that in the Bachelor of Law program (180 credits) a minimum of 10 credits should be devoted to foreign language learning (general language training or legal terminology). The language training can be in English, Dutch or German. On the other hand, universities are not obliged to include in the curriculum a number of (legal) courses that are taught in a foreign language. Nor do these agreements oblige the universities to impose such courses on their students.

On November 28, 2015, the deans of the five francophone law faculties jointly defined the learning outcomes in terms of skills and competences of the bachelor program: according to this document, all bachelors of law should display "*specific linguistic knowledge in two other languages, at least passively*".

The above requirements are a strict minimum: as long as they respect the "maximum requirements" of the decree, all universities can push their language policy much further.

3 Some Facts and Figures

3.1 The Université Saint-Louis: Bruxelles

The *Université Saint-Louis—Bruxelles* was founded in 1858. The university is active in a limited number of disciplines in the field of humanities and social sciences, including Law. Except for European Studies, all programs offered at *Université Saint-Louis* are at bachelor level. However, together with the *Université de Namur* and the *Université Catholique de Louvain*, the *Université Saint-Louis* co-organizes an Advanced Master in Human Rights Law and another Advanced Master in Environmental Law and Public Real Estate Law (second cycle of specialization). The *Université Saint-Louis—Bruxelles* can also award Doctoral degrees in Law (third cycle).

Of the 3978 students enrolled at Saint-Louis University in the year 2017–2018, 1712 are in the Faculty of Law: 1566 in the bachelor program, 136 in the Advanced Masters, and 10 in the PhD program. The 1566 bachelor students either signed up for the daytime program (1407) or the off-schedule program for those who are already professionally active (159). At the end of the academic year 2016–2017, 235 students were awarded a bachelor's degree in Law at the *Université Saint-Louis—Bruxelles*.

At the *Université Saint-Louis—Bruxelles*, 15,52% of the law students do not have the Belgian citizenship, or have two nationalities, one of which is not Belgian.

Among the academic staff (187 members), 10% is not Belgian. 13% of the teaching staff and the senior researchers obtained their PhD abroad. Every year, the *Université Saint-Louis—Bruxelles* hosts about 10 foreign researchers during their sabbatical leave.

3.2 KU Leuven

KU Leuven is an institution for research and education with international appeal. It is a comprehensive university, offering top-level study programs in almost every scientific domain. Currently (year 2017–2018), *KU Leuven* offers some 240 programs in Dutch; 86 in English; 2 in French and 1 in Spanish. *KU Leuven's* 15 faculties are organized into three groups: Humanities & social sciences group, Biomedical sciences group and Science, engineering and technology group. Each group has a doctoral school. Since October 1, 2013, *KU Leuven* boasts 15 campuses spread across Brussels and 10 cities in Flanders. In 2017–2018, *KU Leuven* had a total of 57.335 students. Among them 9784 are international students. Students from approximately 150 countries study at *KU Leuven*. The foreign countries with the largest student populations are, in descending order, the Netherlands (1905), China (888), Italy (677), Spain (539).

The law school is one of the biggest faculties at *KU Leuven*. Some 70 law professors work at the Faculty of law among whom ca. 10% are foreigners. In addition over 50 visiting professors teach in the various programs. Here the share of foreigners is significantly higher (ca. 30%). Moreover, numerous visiting professors are Belgian, yet from the southern (francophone) part of the county. Hence they significantly contribute to the multilingual environment at the *KU Leuven* law school. Currently (year 2017–2018) the Faculty of law is home to 5455 students, spread over 3 campuses: Leuven, Brussels and Kortrijk. The Leuven Campus is the main one, offering bachelor, master and advanced master programs in law. The Kortrijk and Brussels campuses are smaller and mainly focus on bachelor education, although the Brussels Campus also hosts 2 very large advanced master programs, one in IP-ICT law and another in company law. At the Brussels Campus, law students can either choose for the unilingual bachelor in law (taught in Dutch) or the bilingual program set up in collaboration with the *Université Saint-Louis—Bruxelles*, its partner university.

The advanced master in IP-ICT law is multilingual *per se*, as courses are taught in English, French and Dutch. There are 2 possible tracks. The first one focuses on Intellectual Property Law. Here, the majority of the courses are taught in *either* Dutch *or* French. Students in the second track focus on ICT Law and follow all courses in English. However, students are largely free to swap courses which often results in a program that *de facto* comprises courses in Dutch, French and English. In addition, the program includes a master's dissertation, which again can be in Dutch, French or English.

4 Bilingual (and Trilingual) Bachelors in Law at the *Université Saint-Louis—Bruxelles* and the *KU Leuven—Campus Brussels*

Twenty-six years ago, the former *Facultés Universitaires Saint-Louis* (now *Université Saint-Louis—Bruxelles*) and the former Katholieke Universiteit Brussel (now *KU Leuven*—Campus Brussels) blazed a trail by creating a bilingual (French-Dutch) undergraduate program in law for their respective students. The following year, the *Université Saint-Louis—Bruxelles* continued along that path by setting up the bilingual program in French-English and the trilingual program in French-Dutch-English.

4.1 The Underlying Motives

The motives underlying the creation of bi- and trilingual programs were rather diverse. The following reasons undoubtedly all were at play:

- the ambition to arm students with the linguistic skills required for legal practice, in particular in a multilingual work environment such as Brussels. A report entitled "*Horizon 2025*", approved by both the French- and German-speaking Bar Association (AVOCATS.BE) and the Flemish Bar Association (OVB), emphasized that, at the end of curriculum any lawyer should master her/his mother tongue, but should also have studied English and the country's other dominant official language (page 34).[9] Especially in Brussels, many positions within the judiciary require true bilingualism, or at least a thorough command of both French and Dutch (see the Law of 15 June 1935 on the use of languages in judicial matters).
- the wish to allow students, in the course of their studies, to conduct research as wide as possible, and to increase their ability to consult source material (scholarly writing and case law) in a foreign language. In most fields, such source material is just indispensable to any research worthy of that name;
- the desire to promote student mobility between the undergraduate and graduate level: obtain a bachelor degree in a university belonging to one Community (French or Flemish), and subsequently pursue their master in a university belonging to the other Community (Flemish or French) and possibly a second Advanced Master abroad;
- the ambition to promote cultural openness to the other community, through personal encounters in a classroom setting with a mixed audience of francophone and Dutch-speaking students.

Neither the students nor the teaching staff or the academic authorities opposed to the implementation of these bi–/trilingual programs.

All students get basic language training (see *infra* IV.3.1), yet the more intense bilingual (or trilingual) program is fully optional. Indeed, students are free to sign up for this language-wise more challenging type of legal education. However, in case the program turns out to be too demanding, they can always revert to the unilingual program in the course of the first year or at the end of it (if difficulties persist). Among students these bilingual and (trilingual) programs are growing in popularity. In particular they attract an increasing number of students who grew up in linguistically mixed families or who passed through content and language integrated learning (so-called immersion education) either at elementary or secondary school, or ran school at an institution belonging to the other Community (*e.g.* francophone child going to a Flemish school), which is common in Brussels. For the same

[9] http://agissons.avocats.be/wp-content/uploads/2015/03/22.05.2015-rapport-final-horizon-2025-FR.pdf (last accessed 23th February 2018).

reasons, the bi- and trilingual programs are popular among students who graduated from a European or international school.

Overall bilingual education tends to be quite challenging for teachers, as these programs normally require them to fully master the foreign language too. However, this problem does not arise with regard to the bilingual program co-organized by *KU Leuven*-Campus Brussels and the *Université Saint-Louis*, since all teachers are native speakers on both sides. They all exclusively teach in their mother tongue, while only students swap classrooms, when they join their classmates at the receiving institution.

4.2 The Multilingual Bachelors in Law at the Université Saint-Louis—Bruxelles *and* KU Leuven*, Campus Brussels: Facts and Figures*

4.2.1 History

The bilingual French-Dutch bachelor program co-organized by the *Université Saint-Louis—Bruxelles* and *KU Leuven—Campus Brussels* exists since the academic year 1991–1992. Its content evolved organically over the past 25 years. Major reforms were implemented in 2011.

The bilingual French-English program that Saint Louis University organizes alone exists since the academic year 1992–1993. The trilingual programs (French, English, Dutch) were established at the same time. Here again, these programs evolved organically. In 2016–2017, however, they underwent a major reform.

4.2.2 Evolution of the Number of Students

In recent years, the total number of bachelor students in the bilingual or trilingual program (all 3 years) at the *Université Saint-Louis—Bruxelles* has been constantly on the rise (Table 1).

At the start of the academic year 2017–2018, at USL-B 78 students (out of 766) had enrolled in the first year of the bilingual French-Dutch program, while 304 students had enrolled in the first year of the bilingual French-English program. About 46% of the bachelor students who graduated in 2016–2017 completed a bilingual or trilingual bachelor program.

Also on the *KU Leuven*-side the bilingual program (Dutch-French), organized at the Brussels campus in collaboration with the *Université Saint-Louis—Bruxelles*, is clearly on the rise. The table below shows the number of students in the first phase of

Table 1 Number of bachelor students of University Saint-Louis-Brussels enrolled in a monolingual/bilingual/trilingual program

Bachelor students	2013–2014	2014–2015	2015–2016	2016–2017
Ordinary program (in French)	638	644	635	705
Bilingual program (French-English)	250	277	389	413
Trilingual program (French-English-Dutch)	18	24	43	56
Bilingual program with KU Leuven (French-Dutch)	64	77	76	53
Trilingual program with KU Leuven (French-Dutch-English)	18	22	42	65
Total	988	1044	1085	1292

Table 2 Number of bachelor students of KULeuven-Campus Brussel enrolled in a monolingual/bilingual program

"Starters" at KU Leuven—Campus Brussels	2013–2014	2014–2015	2015–2016	2016–2017	2017–2018
Ordinary program (in Dutch)	112	141	100	71	98
Bilingual program with USL-B (Dutch-French)	62	68	77	98	123
Total	174	209	177	169	217

the bachelor in law (so-called "starters"[10]) in both the ordinary (*i.e.* monolingual) bachelor and the bilingual bachelor program (Table 2).

4.2.3 Language Proficiency for Admission: The Profile of Students Following a Bilingual Program

Neither at the *Université Saint-Louis—Bruxelles*, nor at *KU Leuven* enrollment in the bilingual program is dependent upon an entrance exam.

At the *Université Saint-Louis—Bruxelles*, however, all new students sit an exam (*test d'orientation)* to map their language skills. Since the bilingual program is not mandatory, a student who experiences serious difficulties in keeping up can always decide to abandon the bilingual program and revert to the unilingual track. In addition, students in a bilingual program who failed to obtain at least 14/20 at the above test, are required to take an additional 60 h of language training in the target language.

Saint-Louis students who choose the bilingual French-Dutch track tend to have a fairly good level of Dutch. However, most often students—like the rest of the population . . .—seem to "overestimate" their command of English.

A 2016 survey into the profile of students enrolling in a bilingual program at the *Université Saint-Louis—Bruxelles* led to the following conclusions:

[10] A student is a starter as long as he did not obtain a minimum of 60 ECTS in his bachelor program.

- the majority of *Saint-Louis* students in the Dutch-French bilingual program organized together with *KU Leuven* graduated from a Flemish secondary school or a school under the authority of the French Community that applies content and language integrated learning (so-called "immersion education"). Accordingly they all had, at least a part of their education in Dutch);
- 20% of *Saint-Louis* students in the bilingual French-English program had previously graduated from an international school or one of the four European schools located in Belgium

During the summer, the *Université Saint-Louis* organizes preparatory classes in order to allow students to strengthen their language skills. The university also awards financial support to language internships and preparatory tracks for a number of standardized language tests, such as TOEFL, IELTS or Cambridge.

Also *KU Leuven*—Campus Brussels organizes an number of tests at the beginning of the academic year in order to assess the language skills of the new bachelor students. Research pointed out the strong connection between a student's academic command of his mother tongue (*i.c.* Dutch) and his study success at university in general and law school in particular. Therefore, *KU Leuven* attaches great importance to the students' results at the test "*Academic Dutch*". Students who failed the test are offered a number of language workshops to improve their academic language skills (*e.g.* reading comprehension). Although the majority of the students at the Brussels campus clearly have Dutch as their mother tongue, in September 2017 some 29% of the new bachelor students did not give proof of sufficient language skills in Dutch to allow a smooth start at university. This high percentage clearly underscores the (increased) need to invest in Dutch language training.

In addition to the Dutch language exam, *KU Leuven* law school assesses the level of French of its new students at all three campuses. The students at the Brussels campus (where the bilingual program is organized) score significantly better for French than their fellow-students at the Leuven or Kortrijk campus. At the same time they score significantly lower for Dutch. That is quite understandable. After all, at the Brussels campus the ratio of students with a non-Dutch speaking background (either home situation and/or secondary school) is clearly higher. In addition, as far as the command of French is concerned, there is an important gap between the results of the students from the bilingual program and the unilingual program in Brussels. In 2017, 38% (30% in 2016) of the students from the unilingual program failed to pass the test, whereas only 9% (only 3% in 2016!!!) of the students of bilingual program. The results at the French test are often used to urge students to reorient, in case they somewhat overconfidently chose for the bilingual program. For nearly all law students (both from the unilingual and the bilingual program), the results on the French test serve as an open invitation for further language training in French.

4.3 Content of the Various Bilingual Bachelor Programs

4.3.1 Overview of the Monolingual Bachelor Programs

Both at *KU Leuven* and the *Université Saint-Louis* all bachelor programs impose language training on their students. In the monolingual programs the share of language courses or courses taught in a foreign language is obviously less important than in the bilingual programs. It is a sort of "minimum package". Nevertheless these "minimum packages" still devote quite some attention to language training.

At the *Université Saint-Louis,* this "minimum package" includes:

- In the first bachelor year: 60 h (7 credits) of general language training either in Dutch or in English (student's choice). Exceptionally, English or Dutch can be replaced by German;
- In the bachelor second year: students who choose English in the first year will take a 45-hours course of legal English and 30 h course on reading legal text material in Dutch; students who choose Dutch in the first year will take a 45 h course of legal Dutch and 30 h course on reading legal text material in English. Exceptionally, students may change the language of the reading course to German or Spanish.
- In the third bachelor year: all students should take at least one course in a foreign language (English or Dutch): *e.g. EU Law: Foundations* instead of *Fondements institutionnels du droit européen or* Intellectual property law/Intellectueel Eigendomsrecht instead of *Droit de la propriété intellectuelle.*
- Occasionally, there are guest speakers who contribute (in English or Dutch) to courses taught in French. These interventions generally last 2 to 4 h.

At KU Leuven this "minimum package" includes:

- In the first bachelor year: a 26 h course (3 ECTS) on *Français juridique* and a 26 h course (3 ECTS) on Legal English;
- In the second bachelor year: The course *Public law II. International and European Law* (54 h – 8 ECTS) is taught in English. In the course and tutorial on *Legal Methodology* (10 ECTS) all students will have to work with source material (legislation, preparatory documents, case law and scholarly writings) in both Dutch and French. For their assignments, students will equally draw from source material in both languages. In order to improve the students' ability to draft legal texts in Dutch, the tutorial on *Drafing legal texts* is a mandatory part of each student's curriculum (even though the majority of the students are native Dutch speakers).
- In the third bachelor year: The course *Fondements du droit* is taught in French. In addition, students have to choose 6 ECTS from a list of optional courses. Some of these courses are taught in English (*e.g.* Introduction to common law) of French (*e.g. Introduction en droit français*).
- Throughout the entire bachelor program, *KU Leuven* has a strong tradition of inviting guest speakers from all over the globe. Their contributions are in English, French or Dutch and generally last 2 to 4 h.

4.3.2 The Bilingual Bachelor Program, Jointly Organized by *KU Leuven*—Campus Brussels and the *Université Saint-Louis—Bruxelles*

The joint bilingual bachelor program of *KU Leuven*-Campus Brussels and *Université Saint-Louis—Bruxelles* is essentially based on a system of *exchanged courses.* Students in this program who enrolled at *Université Saint-Louis* will take a number of courses taught in Dutch at *KU Leuven*—Campus Brussels while being exempted from the corresponding courses in French. The other way around, students enrolled in the bilingual bachelor program at *KU Leuven* join their francophone classmates at the *Université Saint-Louis—Bruxelles* for a number of courses. They are obviously excused for the corresponding courses in Dutch, taught at *KU Leuven.*

In practice, these exchanges are very easy, as the walking distance between both universities is not even 10 min. Since both universities teach "Belgian law", in theory all courses are eligible for exchange. Accordingly, the partner universities agreed to exchange the following courses: *Introduction to Law, Constitutional Law, Law of Obligations, Property Law, Family Law, Administrative Law and the Law of Contracts & Torts.* On the other hand, the students of *Saint-Louis* take in the bilingual track some more general courses in Dutch, such as *Sociology* and *Legal History* which are taught at *KU Leuven* Campus Brussels.

In addition to "exchanged" courses, the bilingual program also comprises some specific courses organized in the target language within each of the partner universities. For example, the *Université Saint-Louis—Bruxelles* organizes courses in Intellectual Property Law, Media Law and Economic Law in Dutch, as well as a seminar in Legal theory. In the same way, the third year course *Fondements de droit* is taught in French at the *KU Leuven* for those who are in the bilingual program (Table 3).

The evaluation methods used in courses that are taught in a foreign language are quite diverse:

- a written exam with open questions or (on some rare occasions) multiple choice questions
- oral examinations;
- a written assignment (*e.g.* solve a legal case, research assignment);
- take part in a bilingual moot court (*e.g. Moot Court in constitutional law*, in which all Belgian universities participate)

4.3.3 The Bilingual French-English Bachelor Program at the *Université Saint-Louis-Bruxelles*

At the *Université Saint-Louis—Bruxelles* law students can also choose to sign up for the bilingual bachelor program taught in French and English.

In this program, a number of courses that are taught in French in the standard (monolingual) program, will instead be offered in English. The program is

Table 3 Overview of the bilingual Dutch-French bachelor program for students enrolled at KU Leuven—Campus Brussel

Taught in Dutch
Taught in French
Taught in English

First Year

Course	**Credits**
Legal history	7
Sociology	3
Ethics	6
Economics	7
Philosophy	6
Logic reasoning	3
Introduction to law (at the *Université Saint-Louis - Bruxelles*)	8
Law of obligations (at the *Université Saint-Louis - Bruxelles*)	6
Constitutional law I (at the *Université Saint-Louis - Bruxelles*)	5
Legal French	3
Legal English	3

Second Year

Taught in Dutch
Taught in French
Taught in English

Course	**Credits**
Commercial, company & economic law	10
Legal methodology (including internship)	10
Drafting legal texts	5
Public law II. International and European Law	8

(continued)

Table 3 (continued)

Family law (at the *Université Saint-Louis - Bruxelles*)	8
Property law (at the *Université Saint-Louis - Bruxelles*)	3
Constitutional law II (at the *Université Saint-Louis - Bruxelles*)	6
Administrative law (at the *Université Saint-Louis - Bruxelles*)	6
Law of contracts and torts (at the *Université Saint-Louis - Bruxelles*)	8

Third Year

Taught in Dutch
Taught in French
Taught in English

Course	**Credits**
Civil procedure	6
Criminal law & criminal procedure	9
Labour law and social security law	8
Tax law	5
Legal Psychology	5
Comparative law	3
Comparative law (tutotial)	3
Legal tutorial 1	3
Legal tutorial 2	3
Bachelor thesis	4
Optional courses	6
Foundations of the law	6

Overview of the bilingual French-Dutch bachelor program for students enrolled at the *Université Saint-Louis - Bruxelles*

Taught in French
Taught in Dutch

(continued)

Table 3 (continued)

First Year

Course	Credits
Dutch (general language course)	4
Sociology (at KU Leuven – Campus Brussels)	3
Introduction to law (at KU Leuven – Campus Brussels)	9
Introduction to law (tutorial classes)	4
Psychology	5
History	4
Philosophy	8
Roman law	8
Constitutional law (I)	5
Legal methodology	4
Critical analysis of information (and tutorial classes in History)	3

Second Year

Taught in Dutch
Taught in French
Taught in English

Course	Credits
Criminal Law	6
Legal Theory	4
Moral Philosophy	4
Property law	3
Criminal procedure (and tutorial classes)	4
Constitutional Law II (and tutorial classes)	6
Economics (in french) or Economics (in English)	5
Legal English	4

(continued)

Table 3 (continued)

Legal History (at KU Leuven – Campus Brussels)	7
Law of obligations (at KU Leuven – Campus Brussels) (and tutorial classes)	8
Media Law	5

Third Year

Taught in Dutch
Taught in French

Course	Credits
Law of contracts and torts (and tutorial classes)	6
Labour Law	4
Administrative Law (and tutorial classes)	6
EU Law : Foundations	5
Civil procedure	**5**
Optional course	**5**
Natural Law or Law, Ethics and Politics	4
Commercial, company & economic law	**5**
Intellectual Property Law	4
Family Law (at KU Leuven – Campus Brussels)	9
Bachelor thesis in Legal Theory	7

exclusively run by the *Université Saint-Louis—Bruxelles* and its staff. All teachers are *Saint-Louis* faculty. They are not necessarily native speakers.

Some of these courses concern "non-legal" topics, such as *Introduction to the culture of the English speaking world*, *Economics* or *Political Science*. In legal courses the language is altered to English whenever this seemed relevant. That is obviously the case for courses concerning foreign law (e.g. *Introduction to the Common Law*), but also for courses that are highly comparative in nature (*e.g.*

Introduction to comparative law), or that present a strong international, European, transnational or "meta" dimension (*e.g.* EU Law: Foundations, Intellectual Property Law, Law and Religion, Legal History, Legal Theory, Natural Law).

On the other hand, courses on local "Belgian" law (*e.g.* Constitutional law, *Administrative law*, ...) continue to be taught in French. In these cases, it would not make any sense to swap language. It would rather do more harm and cause difficulties.

The evaluation methods used in the courses that are taught in English are the same as those referred to above.

4.3.4 The Trilingual French-Dutch-English Bachelor Program at the *Université Saint-Louis-Bruxelles*

In both bilingual programs (French-Dutch or French-English), USL students may choose to add a third language (English or Dutch) and thus render their bachelor program truly trilingual. In this case, over 50% of their program will be taught in a foreign language.

The evaluation methods used in the courses taught in Dutch/English are the same as those referred to above.

4.4 Resources

The bilingual program (Dutch-French) jointly organized by *KU Leuven* (Brussels Campus) and the *Université Saint-Louis—Bruxelles* is essentially exchange-based: francophone students from the *Université Saint-Louis—Bruxelles* take classes in Dutch at the Brussels campus of *KU Leuven*. All *KU Leuven* professors are native speakers. They use the course material (book, syllabus, slides, exercises,...) they developed themselves in Dutch. The other way around, Dutch-speaking students of *KU Leuven* (Brussels Campus) go to the *Université Saint-Louis* for courses taught in French, based on course material dressed up in French. Documentary resources (legislation, doctrine, case law) are easily available in the other language, since both Dutch and French are official languages in Belgium. Legislation is enacted in both French and Dutch; case law is produced in either French or Dutch; some court decisions are entirely and systematic translated.

Overall, neither *KU Leuven*, nor the *Université Saint-Louis—Bruxelles* are in a position to attract many native speakers for courses taught in English. This is due to numerous reasons, yet in particular the fact that in Belgium university positions are not as financially rewarding as in the UK of the US. Therefore it is often hard for Belgian universities to recruit professors from an Anglo-Saxon background.

The command of English required to teach at university is nevertheless quite high. In the French Cummunity, the universities verify the linguistic skills during the recruitment process. In Flanders, on the other hand, Parliament intervened explicitly.

Indeed, in article 270 Codex Hoger Onderwijs, the Flemish Community set several requirements in order to guarantee the quality of the language used for teaching. The Decree states that the teaching staff has to have a language proficiency at level ERK C1 for the language in which the course is organized. All members of teaching and academic staff that do not teach in Dutch, have to achieve a language proficiency for Dutch at level ERK B2 within 3 years upon appointment.

The courses taught in English do not concern the "local (*i.e.* Belgian) law" (*supra*), yet either internationally oriented matters (*e.g.* European law, international law, human rights law, common law, legal theory, natural law) or non-legal topics (*e.g.*. political science, economics, ...). In these fields prime source material in English is abundantly available.

4.5 The Outcome

Both at the *Université Saint-Louis-Bruxelles* and *KU Leuven*—Campus Brussels, the (bilingual) programs offered only concern the undergraduate (bachelor) level. Since none of the above campuses hosts a master program in law, there are no precise data on the inflow of their respective students on the job market.

Students from the multilingual programs of Saint Louis seem to turn more easily towards a Flemish university for their master. About 46% of the 235 students who graduated from the *Université Saint-Louis-Bruxelles* in 2016–2017 stemmed from a multilingual bachelor program. In 2017–2018, 24 of these students enrolled for the master of law taught in Dutch at either *KU Leuven* or Ghent University. In the same year, 6 students chose for a master program taught in English at the University of Antwerp.

Over the past years, the interest among students in a master at a Flemish law school is clearly on the rise. The chart shows how the *KU Leuven* master of law (taught at the Leuven Campus) attracts an increasing number of students from the *Université Saint-Louis—Bruxelles* (Table 4).

As far the students of the bilingual track at *KU Leuven*—Campus Brussels are concerned, there is not really an increased outflow to master programs at the universities of the French Community. This is mainly due to the fact that, unlike the *Université Saint Louis—Bruxelles*, *KU Leuven* itself offers both bachelor *and* master programs (not at Campus Brussels, yet definitely so at the Leuven Campus, where the bachelor students of all three campuses spend their third bachelor year).

Table 4 Number of former students of University Saint-Louis-Brussels pursuing the Master program at the KULeuven

2011–2012	2 students
2012–2013	6 students
2013–2014	8 students
2014–2015	5 students
2015–2016	5 students
2016–2017	16 students

Consequently, most students just remain at *KU Leuven* (Campus Leuven) upon graduation from the bachelor program. However, this does not mean that they are no longer exposed to multilingualism during their academic training. Quite on the contrary! After all, the master of law at *KU Leuven* offers students numerous ways to include in their curriculum a set of (legal) courses that are taught in a foreign language. In addition, *KU Leuven* has an impressive list of ERASMUS destinations. As a consequence, any master student who want to go abroad for an ERASMUS experience, can do so. Therefore, it is fair to say that multilinguism is easily achieved within the master program.

4.6 The Future

Both at the *Université Saint-Louis-Bruxelles* and the *KU Leuven*, the law school undeniably promotes the bi- or even trilingual curriculum. Moreover, these programs have been expanded and intensified over the years. This tendency towards multilinguism seems to exist at all Belgian universities, as they all have recently intensified the language training in their curriculum. The *Université Catholique de Louvain* is a good example as in 2017 it set up a program in Dutch, in close collaboration with the *KU Leuven*. Other new initiatives are the English master programs the law schools of *KU Leuven* (in collaboration with the University of Zurich) (2014) and the University of Antwerp (2016) recently set up. Without any doubt, other universities will follow these examples in the near future and will establish new kinds of bilingual programs, as both students and employers cheer the above evolutions with joy.

Overall, neither the students, nor the public authorities perceive the above development towards multilinguism as a threat to the cultural/national identity.

Transsystemic and Multilingual Contexts of Legal Education: *Short Iterations on Two Dogmas of Legal Positivism*

Nicholas Léger-Riopel

1 Introduction

As a point of origin of this brief note, be it said that the institution in which the author holds the status of professor, the Faculty of Law of the *Université de Moncton* is host to a variety of—sometimes unique and surprising—events that could be could considered "phenomena" of transystemism in a multilingual context of legal education. The Faculty of Law, which offers a unique training of common law taught exclusively in French, was founded in 1978 in the City of Moncton, in the Province of New-Brunwsick, Canada:

> The University of Moncton was founded by integrating three colleges: College Saint-Louis, College du Sacre-Coeur and College Saint-Joseph. Undergraduate degrees in adult education had been founded by the university in the year 1989. Students get admission in this school on the basis of their extracurricular activities, GPA, letter of reference, as well as interview questionnaire. As all the classes of this school are conducted fully in French, student who are seeking admission must have a strong command on French language. University of Moncton doesn't require its students to take the LSAT (Law School Admission Test) as it considers the score of LSAT, if provided.
>
> University of Moncton Faculty of Law offers the basic LL.B. and also the graduate LL.M. Besides this, the university also offers degrees such as: the LLB-MEE (Masters of Environmental Studies), LLB-MAP (Masters in Public Administration) and LLB-MBA (Masters of Business). Moreover, students who have a degree of B.C.L or LL.L. (Civil law degree) from any Canadian school have the permission to enroll their names in the school for two

N. Léger-Riopel (✉)
Université de Moncton, Law Faculty, Moncton, Canada
e-mail: Nicholas.leger-riopel@umoncton.ca

N. Etcheverry Estrázulas (ed.), *Bilingual Study and Research*, Ius Comparatum – Global Studies in Comparative Law 58,
https://doi.org/10.1007/978-3-030-84550-6_3

semesters and complete a J.D. For international students who are willing to understand the common law tradition, the faculty offers a D.E.C.L (Degree in Common Law) as well.[1]

Transsystemic teaching of law, as is also often found in multilingual contexts of legal education, can and have been celebrated as powerful remedies to the dominant paradigm of legal education, rooted in a legal positivistic ("LP") view. This view is generally accepted[2] as the dominant model of teaching, reasoning, and adjudicating legal matters.[3] The limits of such a model are, perhaps incidentally, made more visible in a transsystemic or multilinguistic contexts of teaching, as those are the conditions in which we train legal minds at the *Université de Moncton*. May these short iterations be of use to many who face the challenges of multilingual, or multisystemic, contexts of legal education.

2 A First Dogma of Legal Positivism: The Rule-Paradigm[4]

Multilingual and transsystemic education, be it through the generally available mean of comparative law, unravel the deeply rooted polysemy inherent to even the most casual legal concepts to be encountered. Multiple explanations to this un-fixedness of the meaning of legal concepts are offered by the legal literature; this polysemy is perhaps one the first "terrors" to be faced by legal students. How tragic it is to be facing norms purporting to be just and universal, which are also modeled using that profoundly imprecise medium of language! This finding, in itself, as stemmed a whole field of legal studies gravitating around the now classic *themata* of the hartian "open texture of the (legal) language".

One of the many consequences of this relative imprecision of legal language, as most eloquently revealed to a lawyer endeavoring a transsystemic reflexion, is to reveal the relative unavailability of the rule-paradigm as the only method of resolving legal matters. The "canonic" syllogism, as a means of resolving legal problems was developed, and possibly meant to be applied, to premises that are fixed, and objective.[5] How can the syllogism as a tool retains its centrality when the major

[1] See the interesting presentation offered by the Canada Law Schools resources, available online at http://www.canadalawschools.ca/atlantic-canada/new-brunswick-universities/13-university-of-moncton-faculty-of-law.

[2] Generally, see: Samuel (2003), p. 30.

[3] This is not to be understood as meaning that the notion of Legal Positivism *itself* is non-contentious. Many myths exist *about* what Legal Positivism is or is not, as suggested by a variety of authors such as Norberto Bobbio and John Gardner. For the finality of this short note, we are concentrating on myths conveyed by LP itself and not the myths *about* LP.

[4] For Samuels, the success of Legal positivism is in part due to two fundamental assumptions: "The first is that legal knowledge consists of legal rules; the second is that these legal rules are identifiable in terms of their particular sources and independent of all other social norms arising from other, non-legal sources". Samuel (2003), p. 22.

[5] Huhn (2002), p. 813.

premise, the enunciation of the Rule, be it enshrined in common law judgments or in a piece of legislation, is often times irremediably mobile?

This perennial problem of legal interpretation, rendered highly vibrant through the problems of transystemism, has guided some legal scholar to offer a variety of means to understand what is *really* happening when one speaks of *legal method* or *legal reasoning*. A now well-documented[6] field of legal research covers the means by which legal solutions take place, especially in the context of transystemism. For a good portion of these scholars, it is unavoidable to take into account the profoundly cultural dimension of legal institutions, as to avoid the risk of "faux amis": similarly phrased concepts buttressed by different cultural context accounts for sometimes very different legal solutions or means of enforcing what seemingly may be the same notions. Recourse to multidisciplinary approaches, such as law and economics, law and literature, law and society, all offer a richer understanding of the true nature of the legal reasoning.

As any fiction, the Rule paradigm has roots in reality and reflects the *habitus* and in many cases the actual practices of legal problem solving. May it be only noted that this method is relative to the complexity of the legal problems at hand, which in some case need to be addressed through a richer matrix, especially in the case of transsystemic or multilinguistic questions of law. In such circumstances, law perhaps cease to be a matter of rules, and students, lawyers and judges alike encounter law-as-a-social-fact, a living, and forever context-bound content-matter that it would be of disservice to treat only through the lens of a rule paradigm meant for much simpler matters.... than human ones.

3 A Second Dogma of Legal Positivism: A "Realist" Epistemology

A recent field of legal methodology and legal epistemology covers a ground that remained relatively un-touched up until the recent years: that is, the role of facts in the legal reasoning, as opposed to the role of rules. Likewise to rules, facts themselves have long held a status of undisputable objectivity, but this status has often been put into question through the works of comparative law, and transsystemic contexts.

It may very well, according to prominent legal epistemologists such as Geoffrey Samuel, Christian Atias or Theodor Ivainer, that facts themselves are an object of construction and interpretation and: "the idea that legal science is a discourse that has its objet actual factual situation is to misunderstand, fundamentally, legal thought."[7]

[6] As a seminal source, see: Teubner (1989), p. 727.

[7] Samuel (2004), p. 74.

Legal epistemology's recent findings touches on the mode(s) legal reason uses to constructs the "object-matter"[8] of legal knowledge, and notably how "facts" are received and treated in legal reasoning, Beyond the content of the rules of evidence and of procedure, legal epistemology sheds light on the principles and often unarticulated premises leading to the translation of a "fact" to a "norm" in a judiciary context. For Professor Geoffrey Samuel, the study of the modelization through which norms and fact interact and are construed by legal reasoning is on the first problems of legal science and legal epistemology:

> [Legal science is to be envisaged through a constructive form]. That is to say it has to be envisaged through a structure which mediates between facts and science (law), allowing the legal scientist both to make sense of the facts and to discover solutions from transformation within the structure. Such a structure is what one calls a "model". What, then, is the basis for such a legal model? This, of course, is the fundamental question that should motivate and direct any work on legal epistemology.[9]

Legal epistemology thus underlines that facts are constructs and not "empirical" when seen through the lens of legal reasoning: some facts are chosen (by the trial lawyer, by the judge, etc...) as relevant, others are disqualified. In this operation that could be described as the *naturalization*[10] of the "real" to the needs of legal knowledge, facts and norms coalesce to a great extent.

For the author Astolfi, this may also further reveal that what is habitually referred to as "facts" do not have an *a priori* independent existence: facts take on meaning only in relation to a system of thought or a theoretical framework, or in other words, facts exist only when they are seen and recognized through a pre-existing structure. Identifying this underlying structure by which legal reason "constructs" facts could very well reveal incidentally reveal that there is a legal world-conception,[11] a general conceptual foundation to law that guides its relation both to facts and norms, that could be distinguished from other views, such as the scientific world-conception (*wissenschaftlichen Weltauffassung*).[12]

4 Concluding Remarks

What happens next? Facts lose their standing power as neutral, stable and objective anchors against rules, statutes, and cases ever evolving, ever changing. Facts themselves are objects *inside* and not *outside* of legal reasoning: they are themselves

[8] Berthelot (2008), p. 124.

[9] Samuel (2003), p. 19.

[10] Thomas (1973), p. 103. Teubner (1992), p. 1149.

[11] Astolfi and Develay (1996), p. 25. See also: Hanson (1958).

[12] *Schriften zur wissenschaftlichen Weltauffassung. Monographs on the Scientific World-Conception*, ed. by Schlick und Frank, 1928–1937.

mediated, translated, transformed and interpreted through the (meta)methods governing legal reasoning:

> This epistemological thesis is [...] applicable to law since this is a discourse or "science" (*intellectus*) which does not operate directly on the facts (*res*). What the lawyer do is to construct a model of the social world and it is, arguably, this model which acts as the bridge between the social and the legal worlds. That model is both the *res* (object of knowledge) and the *intellectus* (knowing subject).[13]

It is now clear that the way by which law constructs facts is only superficially encompassed by the formal rules and statutes relating to evidence and procedure[14] of a given jurisdiction. For some authors, to access the deeper structure of the legal reasoning one could set aside the usual sources of positive law. The authentic method of a discipline such as law could also be approached by the study of the paradox and controversies in legal knowledge, as opposed to its apparent unity. For Hammer, legal fictions imagined by law can even go so far as to make facts "disappear",[15] or to substitute themselves to reality.[16] As final remarks, uncovering the underlying assumptions of, and shedding light on, the authentic method of legal reasoning is crucial and urgent. Indeed, when fictions defeat facts in a judicial context it is often times to the peril of vulnerable parties from linguistic, sexual or ethnic minorities.[17] The method by which a judge constructs facts, if it is not satisfyingly encompassed by the legal rules or by what is known as "legal methodology", thus chart the course of legal epistemology towards uncovering a "deeper" level or legal reasoning.

---

[13] Samuel (2003), p. 2.

[14] For Dubouchet, simple factual and legal situations can be solved by the application of the traditional legal syllogism and the special type of reasoning it involves: (1) the formal reasoning. When faced with complexity, when facts are to a lesser extent isomorphic to applicable case law and statute law, a second type of reasoning, the (2) dialectical reasoning, is put forth. For authors such as Dubouchet and Carl Schmitt, some factual situations may arise that are simply not encompassed by relevant positive law, leading the judge to use (3) rhetorical reasoning in the rendering of an equitable solution. Dubouchet (2008), p. 118.

Précité, note 34, à la p. 118 et suiv.

[15] Hammer (2015), p. 119.

[16] Atias (1994), p. 21. "tendance de toute fiction à se substituer purement et simplement à la réalité".

[17] "Competent judges should be able to prioritize facts over legal fictions. Judges should not be so distracted by difference that they fail to recognize facts. "The politics of control and domination are interrupted when we embrace our own fears and anxieties to transcend them." Competent judges should be able to notice, recognize, acknowledge, evaluate, and then set aside their own discomfort and emotional reactions.' Those reactions are a source of information, but just one of the sources of information available to judges. They are not the guiding principles. Even if courts do not love transgender people, they are tasked with working justice and, at a minimum, tolerating difference. In courts' decisions, love, or the lack of it, should not determine whether the result is justice." Hammer (2015), p. 161.

References

Astolfi J-P, Develay M (1996) La didactique des sciences, 4e édn. PUF, Paris
Atias C (1994) Épistémologie juridique. LGDJ, Paris
Berthelot J-M (2008) La construction de la sociologie, 6e édn. PUF, Paris
Dubouchet P (2008) Droit et épistémologie: l'Organon du droit. l'Harmattan, Paris, p 118
Hammer G (2015) Transparent: when legal fictions and judicial imagination make facts disappear, they enforce transphobic discrimination. Columbia J Gender Law 30(1):119
Hanson NR (1958) Patterns of discovery: an inquiry into the conceptual foundations of science. Cambridge University Press
Huhn WR (2002) Use and limits of syllogistic reasoning in briefing cases. Santa Clara Law Rev 42:813
Samuel G (2003) Epistemology and method in law. Ashgate, Chippenham
Samuel G (2004) Epistemology and comparative law. In: dans M Van Hoecke (Dir) Epistemology and methodology of comparative law. Hart, Bruxelles
Schriften zur wissenschaftlichen Weltauffassung. *Monographs on the Scientific World-Conception*, ed. by Schlick und Frank, pp 1928–1937
Teubner G (1989) How the law thinks: toward a constructivist epistemology of law. Law Soc Rev 23(5):727–757
Teubner G (1992) Pour une épistémologie constructiviste du droit. Annales Économies Sociétés Civilisations 47(6):1149
Thomas Y (1973) La langue du droit romain. Archives de Philosophie du Droit, pp 103–125

National Report: Bilingual Legal Education in China

Xiangshun Ding

1 Bilingual Legal Education in China

The so-called "Bilingual Legal Education" refers to cultivating students' basic qualities, legal knowledge and skills of cross-language and cross-disciplinary work so as to enable them to acquire foreign legal knowledge by reading foreign original materials and selecting foreign law courses with a comprehensive understanding of the corresponding foreign laws and cultures as well as the common international legal culture, to make the students practice in law more proficiently in a multi language-speaking and international legal work environment after graduation.

Under the international background of globalization and the "One Belt and One Road" initiative, this "Bilingual Legal Education" teaching model has provided a comprehensive and systematic legal exploration for fostering more new legal professionals who can safeguard China's interests in the international legal arena and build an international order of the rule of law.

Since the late 1990s, bilingual education has been practiced in our country for nearly 20 years. Most of the undergraduate colleges and universities have already set up multiple bilingual courses. Most law schools also set up a number of bilingual legal courses. We will introduce some of the famous and well-known law schools in China.

Bilingual Legal Education can be divided into two kinds from the perspective of subject and object: 1. one is based on Chinese students as the object of acceptance, teachers of this type are mostly domestic teachers who have good foreign languages ability or foreign teachers who was invited from other countries as the subjects of teaching; 2. the other is to recruit foreign students as the object of education, such as the "Chinese Law" program.

X. Ding (✉)
Renmin University of China Law School, Beijing, China

N. Etcheverry Estrázulas (ed.), *Bilingual Study and Research*, Ius Comparatum – Global Studies in Comparative Law 58,
https://doi.org/10.1007/978-3-030-84550-6_4

2 Bilingual Legal Education for Chinese students

The most important point of "Bilingual Legal Education" is "Bilingual", it related to two kinds of languages. In China, Mandarin Chinese is the country's official language. The standard spoken and written Chinese language means Putonghua (a common speech with pronunciation based on the Beijing dialect) and the standardized Chinese characters.[1] So Putonghua and the standardized Chinese characters shall be used as the basic language for teaching in schools and other institutions of education. And the Chinese textbooks used shall be in conformity with the norms of the standard spoken and written Chinese language.[2] All the staff members who need to use Putonghua as their working language shall have the ability to speak Putonghua, like the school teachers and university professors.[3] But China is a multi-ethnic, multi-lingual, multi-dialect, and multi-character country, we have 56 ethnic groups and many of them have their own languages. In the Article 4 and Article 19 of our Constitution, it regulates that "The state promotes the nationwide use of Putonghua" and "The people of all ethnic minorities have the freedom to use and develop their own spoken and written languages".

2.1 Bilingual Legal Education in Ethnic Minority Areas in China

As "Bilingual" generally means two kinds of languages, so in a broad sense, the meaning of "Bilingual" for Chinese students does not only focus on Chinese and one foreign language for most Chinese students, but also could means Chinese and one of ethnic minorities languages for ethnic students. Like Inner Mongolia University Law School, they have more than nearly 30 years bilingual legal education by Chinese and Mongolian for undergraduate students.

2.1.1 Inner Mongolia University Law School

Since 1988, Inner Mongolia University Law School has enrolled some undergraduates majoring in law but taught by Mongolian every year. After nearly 30 years of practice and exploration, the law school improved and formed its own characteristics gradually. The bilingual undergraduate training are by the Mongolian teaching

[1] Law on the Standard Spoken and Written Chinese Language of the People's Republic of China, Article 2.

[2] Law on the Standard Spoken and Written Chinese Language of the People's Republic of China, Article 10.

[3] Law on the Standard Spoken and Written Chinese Language of the People's Republic of China, Article 19.

professors and Chinese teaching professors to complete together, and some courses are with ordinary law school students together, but in the specific curriculum settings, there has a certain particularity in Mongolian Bilingual legal education program.

Inner Mongolia University law School enrolled the undergraduate students who were taught by Mongolian before college study in this bilingual legal education program. As a result, some of the law school undergraduate courses of this program are taught in Mongolian to enable students to acquire the skills to deal with legal matters both in Chinese and Mongolian. For example, the Mongolian Law Introduction, Ancient Mongolian Law Introduction courses are taught in Mongolian and other courses are taught in Chinese.

Now, there are about ten professors engaged in bilingual legal education in Mongolian teaching, and basically formed a contingent of senior legal education teaching group with reasonable age structure and higher academic level, which can meet the needs of teaching and cultivating top legal talents of ethnic minorities both in Mongolian and Chinese. These professors also organized to write three textbooks of Mongolian Criminal Law, Economic Law and Administrative Law, as well as 10 kinds of internal handouts (non-publications), which basically met the needs of undergraduate education in law. These teaching materials received good response from the students during the teaching practice. About the teaching methods, the professors in this program always use cases, discussions, interactions and other methods to teach and pay attention to cultivating students' ability to express legal concepts, systems and related issues accurately in their own native language.

2.2 *Bilingual Legal Education in Non-Ethnic Minority Areas*

Except the above type for ethnic students, the main form of Bilingual legal education for Chinese students is usually focus on Chinese and one foreign language.

2.2.1 Chinese and English

The combination of Chinese and English, which is the most common form of bilingual education in colleges and universities in China. We did some research on a number of the well-known law schools in China, and made some summaries of them.

Renmin University of China Law School

The Law School of Renmin University of China set up the "Program for Comparative Law" in 2009, focusing on strengthening cooperation with foreign law schools and international organizations, and engaging internationally renowned foreign professors, scholars and lawyers to carry out Bilingual Legal Education.

In the selection of students in this program, mainly focus on choosing the students who have foreign language expertise, especially English language proficiency, and who are interested in international legal work.

As for the allocation of teachers resources, on the basis of utilizing the existing teachers at the Law School (especially those who have experience of overseas study), foreign teachers should be vigorously recruited and introduced to carry out teaching in relevant foreign laws in English.

In terms of curricula settings, the Comparative Law Department has not only set up curriculums in jurisprudence but also emphasizes the development and training of English courses that help students improve their skills in legal matters so that students can not only lay a foundation for Chinese law, but also have a basic grasp of the Chinese and foreign laws to form a well-integrated knowledge system and eventually be able to engage in foreign-related legal practice in an international legal environment where Chinese and English are the main working languages.

In addition to this normal systematic curriculum, comparative law faculties often seize every opportunity to actively invite internationally renowned professors, scholars and lawyers visiting us through the "Comparative Law Academic Seminar" to share academic frontier topics in their field of study.

We also offer our students some English courses in different directions aimed at students' ambitions. These courses select and integrate the original textbooks from Common Law countries and the teachers are mainly from other countries and those who have overseas study experience. The course contents also cover foreign lawyers practice, international business, corporate law and other fields.

Many curricula have introduced teaching methods abroad, such as case teaching which as an enlightening interactive teaching method that enables students not only to be able to read English legal documents, make translators and interpreters, but also to use foreign legal databases, like Lexis -Nexis, Westlaw to conduct legal search, research and analysis of problems and the writing of legal instruments.

The English courses that our "Program for Comparative Law" set up are:

Firstly, International Business Course, including international commercial litigation, international commercial arbitration, international commercial contracts, and corporate business law planning. This course is mainly taught by foreign lawyers who have many years of legal business experience in foreign affairs.

Secondly, such as American law courses. Including the introduction of American law, the Contract Law in United States, the Tort Law in United States and the analysis of the classic cases in United States. The course is mainly taught by American professors and the law professors who have studied in the United States. They select the representative legal system and adopt a case-based approach. Through these courses, students' English reading, writing and oral communication skills have been greatly improved, laying a solid foundation for them to engage in foreign affairs.

Thirdly, lawyers practice courses, including legal searching, skill training for adversarial trial, law negotiation courses, etc. The course is mainly taught by

American professors and in the teaching form of simulated cases, like the legal clinic in the United States. Students can help clients solve legal problems as a lawyer.

Fourth, EU law courses, which are taught by foreign teachers from Sweden, the Netherlands and France. The courses are around the EU constitution as the main content, then to develop the teaching with EU trade law, tort law and intellectual property law and other relevant laws.

In the area of international exchange and communication, the Law School has established long-term exchanges and cooperation with many well-known foreign institutions and international institutions. The cooperation project not only covers exchange visits and lectures at the teachers level, but also provides remote education for foreign teachers as well as the exchange and cooperation between students.

At the same time, our Comparative Law Program uses the international resources of the university to hire first-rate scholars from the universities of Geneva, Tokyo University and Waseda University to teach courses such as "Comparative Contract Law", "Comparative Trust Law between China and Japan" "Comparative Contract Law between China and Japan" and other contents.

Peking University School of Transnational Law

Peking University School of Transnational Law ("STL"), part of PKU's Shenzhen Graduate School, is the only law school in the world that combines an American-style Juris Doctor degree (J.D.) with a China law Juris Master degree (J.M.) and enroll students from China and other countries in the world. STL provides an academically rigorous, bilingual four-year program of legal education that prepares students for the mixture of common law, civil law, and Chinese legal traditions increasingly characteristic of the global economy.

STL has assembled an outstanding multinational faculty of scholars from China, the U.S. and the EU. The four-year program of J.D./J.M. dual-degree program at Peking University School of Transnational Law sets the J.D.'s core curriculum in the first year, and supplemented with (1) a cross-border law overview course that introduces to students the world's major jurisdictions to dispute resolutions and their legal norms; (2) legal writing courses, this course is taught by a dedicated linguist to improve the language proficiency of non-native English speakers and help students with their studies in specialized fields. The second year is mainly based on the Chinese Juris Master's courses, supplemented by a small amount of JD and comparative law courses, which are in order to maintain students' English proficiency. The curriculums of the third and fourth years place more emphasis on offering courses on legal issues involving China and the United States, which include those perspectives from the EU and other areas, to ensure that the transnational legal education program become more valuable.

China University of Political Science and Law

China: EU School of Law(ECSL)

The China-EU School of Law (ECSL) at the China University of Political Law and Science (CUPL) was co-sponsored by the Chinese government and the European Union in 2008. It is a unique institution for educating law students; for conducting and facilitating legal research and consultancy; for professional training of judges, prosecutors, lawyers, and other legal professionals; and a platform for China-EU research, teaching, legal academic and professional exchanges and collaboration.

In pursuit of its purpose, ECSL will engage in the legal and scientific education and training of students and of legal professionals in European, Comparative and International law by implementing a qualification program leading to a Chinese post-graduate qualification and/or a European post-graduate qualification (the "Master Program"), an exhaustive program of professional training (the "Professional Training"), and engaging in research and consultancy activities, including joint training for Ph.D. students (the "Research and Consultancy Activities".

The "Double Degree Program" consisting of the "Juris Master of Chinese Law" (JM) and the "European Law Master Program" (LL.M.), is the central program of ECSL. As an integrated part of the Double Degree Program which will last for 3 consecutive academic years/6 consecutive semesters, the duration of "Juris Master of Chinese Law" can be technically identified as for 3 semesters. The "European Law Master Program" will have a duration of 3 consecutive semesters. Upon graduation, these students receive both a graduate diploma and a master's degree certificate from China University of Political Science and Law and a master's degree certificate from the University of Hamburg (the European partner of ECSL).

Courses of the European Law Master program should be taught in English and courses of the Chinese Juris Master program should be taught in Chinese with the exception of courses targeted specifically at international students and courses on International Law and Comparative Law, which should be taught in English. Professional Training Courses will be held in Chinese and/or in the English language depending on the language skills of the audience and the subject of the relevant class. If necessary, ECSL will provide for the translation of lectures and class materials in order to meet the audience's needs.

Many of its English courses are taught by foreign professors. For example, the number of English courses taught by foreign professors account for 23% of the total number of Chinese law courses for the entire academic year. However, ECSL has also developed a Chinese Law Program(LL.M in Chinese Law) in English teaching for foreign students. All the courses of this program are taught by Chinese professors in English, the content mainly focus on China's laws, and allows Chinese students to choose these courses. Chinese and foreign students attend the class together, is conducive to oral practice, and enhance the class more interactive and inclusive.

ECSL does not use the traditional textbook for courses. Instead, the curriculum materials of each course are carefully prepared by the teachers for the students who need to read a large amount of pages, ranging from as little as one hundred pages to as many as hundreds of pages.

As for faculty, ECSL professors have basic background of overseas experience. Taking the first semester of the 2017–2018 academic year as an example, there are 16 Chinese law professors, almost all of whom have overseas experience and 21 are European law professors, all of them are foreign professors.

College of Comparative Law of CUPL

The College of Comparative Law of CUPL was founded on 15 October, 2009 by integrating the Institute of Comparative Law, the School of Sino-German Law and the School of Sino-American Law. It is the only comparative law teaching and research institution in the Chinese higher education and research sector.

The College comprises 42 staff members, including 30 academic staff. Among the academic staff, 29 of them hold doctoral degrees, accounting for 97%. The College boasts high qualifications of its academic staff and distinctive feature of internationalization as 16 academic staff have attained their degrees from world-known overseas universities, making up 53% of the total. The academic staff are proficient in the world's major languages like English, German, Italy, Russian, French and Japanese.

Shanghai Jiao Tong University, Koguan School of Law

Shanghai Jiao Tong University adopts the "three plus three years system" legal education model to break the traditional curriculum system to cultivate undergraduate and master's law school students. It emphasizes the integration of foreign languages and law major during the curriculum. This model mainly enroll students with foreign language college jointly through the college entrance examination admitted to the foreign language college for undergraduate study first. Then as the exemption, students transfer into the law school to finish the three years of English major and law major undergraduate-graduate training together. This means the undergraduate education finish at the end of the third year, and starting from the fourth year to diversion to select a few outstanding undergraduate students to accept three consecutive years of high-level legal education, and received a master's degree eventually. This project calls for mastery of two UN languages and mastering the knowledge of economic, financial, trade, business management and international relations. Introducing foreign teachers to teach courses in comparative law and foreign laws directly in English to mainly emphasis of the students' international perspective.

Southwest University of Political Science and Law, School of International Law

In order to adapt to the multi-polarization of the world, the in-depth development of economic globalization and the need of the country for opening, School of International Law sets up "Foreign Legal Talents Education Program". Its general object is to cultivate a host of foreign legal talents who are well-versed in international rules, competent in dealing with transnational legal affair. The students' election is through the college. From the graduate admission process, the School of International Law will select 10 people to implement the 3 + 2 + 1 year mode: 3 semesters to learn professional knowledge which focus on case study and supplemented by practice. They carried out the activities for legal negotiations, debates and other legal skills competitions that target at cultivating foreign legal capabilities through the course practices in addition to foreign legal expertise knowledge. After finish the courses, there are two semesters practice training, which includes three months foreign law practices or overseas short-term study and one semester graduation thesis writing (WTO cases and foreign laws practice cases) and career choosing and planning.

They set up a multi-mentor system to make full use of the platform for cooperation with the substantive departments, to adopt a system of co-cultivation of tutors and practical experts in schools; Also they make a guidance system which include the teachers in school and teachers overseas' cooperation through various remote and teaching combined with their guidance together. The program is bilingual. Bilingual courses cover one-fourth of the whole courses which focus on the WTO cases and other foreign-related cases. Each semester they will hire at least one foreign professor to engage in teaching professional legal courses. There are also many kinds of legal English activities like Legal English Debate Competition, Legal English Writing Competition or other forms of competition, so as to develop students' professional English ability. And they also promote students' practical training to increase the proportion of practical teaching, and strengthen exchanges and cooperation between domestic law schools and high-level overseas law schools.

Shanghai University of Finance and Economics School of Law

Based on the Collaborative Innovation Center of China Pilot Free Trade Zone, Shanghai University of Finance and Economics sets up a training program for senior legal personnel in the free trade area through the integration of specialization and localization. 75% of the courses (international financial law, international trade law, international investment law) are taught in English, and invite professors in school and experienced practical experts outside the school to teach and strengthen the close cooperation with Free Trade Zone Administrative Committee to strengthen students' practical training. The project is also served as an elective course. After finishing the course, students can obtain a certificate of "Free Trade Zone Senior Legal Person Training Program" from Shanghai University of Finance and Economics.

2.2.2 Chinese and One Foreign Language

However, bilingual legal education in other languages in China is rare. The reason for this phenomenon is that there are very few teachers know other languages. Furthermore, due to China's primary and secondary education system, students who understand other languages are accounted as a relatively small proportion. Although English is the mainstream, but for some local colleges and universities, because of their regional characteristics of the location, they will also add some elements of other languages to legal education. For example, Guangxi University for Nationalities mainly uses Chinese-English Model or Chinese-one of Southeast Asian country's language Model to teach major legal courses so as to cultivate and enhance students' ability to solve legal problems in English or other Southeast Asian languages. We also have other well-known law schools to open Chinese and other languages combined with the bilingual legal education, such as the Chinese bilingual teaching project of Law School of Shandong University, we will describe it in the next section detailly.

Law School of Shandong University

The characteristic of Bilingual Legal Education of Law School of Shandong University is that it uses not only the combination of Chinese and English selected by most of the colleges, but also set the "Chinese-Japanese Economic and Trade Law Class" for undergraduates. It is the first university in China that uses Japanese as a professional foreign language for Legal undergraduate education which aims to cultivate legal professionals with a high level of Japanese proficiency and familiarity with the economic and trade laws in China and Japan. Students in this class should not only need study English and Chinese law like general undergraduate classes in law school, but also have to study most Japanese language courses and the Introduction of Japanese law, Japanese civil law, Japanese criminal law and other courses such as Comparative Law between China and Japan. This class also invited a number of Japanese law experts to participate in the teaching work and endeavored to enhance the internationalization and teaching level of Japanese legal education. The law school also send students to law schools in Japan for exchange study. Most of the graduates of this class will go to Japan for continue legal study or work in foreign-related law firms, public security organs and foreign-funded enterprises.

2.3 Short Analysis and Summary

In terms of curricula, colleges and universities that carry out bilingual education are mainly started with the subjects of private international law, international economic law, international trade law, international commercial law and the system of WTO.

This mainly takes into account the nature of the curriculum in line with international standards.

As for teachers, bilingual teachers in our country are relatively weak and unevenly distributed. However, after more than a decade of development, the faculty of bilingual legal education has been greatly improved. In many national famous law schools, mostly teachers have overseas exchanged experiences and most of them are Doctor returnees. However, the bilingual teaching staffs in most local undergraduate colleges or universities are still weak. In some places, undergraduate colleges are unable to attract Doctor returnees because they are located in remote areas. Moreover, it is difficult for them to send teachers to go abroad for further studies. Some schools do not have a strong faculty in law originally which rarely have the overseas experience. Their own ability of English application is not very good, they can just cope with the normal legal education, but for the bilingual education is powerless. Even there are some law schools in order to realize the bilingual legal education, they arrange for English majors to practice bilingual legal courses, although there is no problem in their English abilities, but they are still not able to realize the goal of bilingual legal education very well because of their poor understanding of professional legal knowledge.

In the use of textbooks, there are relatively few. Taking international economic law as an example, until December 2016, there are a few full-text or bilingual educational materials on the market such as International Economic Law, International Commercial Law, International Trade Law, International Commercial Arbitration, etc. Most law schools teachers will choose to use well-known foreign experts and classic cases to flexibly teach bilingual legal knowledge so as to replace the stereotyped textbooks in the traditional sense. Some teaching materials are introduced on the basis of the original foreign textbooks, plus some necessary Chinese content to make them more suitable for bilingual learning of Chinese students. For example, "Introduction to Law", edited by Jiang Dong, makes some changes that is more suitable for Chinese students on the basis of the original. It chooses the ten chapters in the original twenty-four chapters which are more suitable for Chinese students to learn relatively, and they are divided into two parts—Chinese and English. The English part still uses of the original textbooks, the Chinese part is added by "basic vocabulary definitions" "key words" "key legal knowledge analysis" and so on. The textbook takes into account the integrity of English textbooks and students' English level, from a practical point of view to make it easier to promote.

3 Bilingual Legal Education for Foreign Students-Chinese Law Program

3.1 Introduction of Chinese Law Program

With the improvement of China's economy, the laws of China have also drawn international attention and created a market demand for studying Chinese laws. Traditionally, if the law schools would like to include the foreign students in established undergraduate and graduate students training systems, which require the foreign students to reach a certain level of Chinese, or language barriers will limit the increase in the number of foreign students. At present, some law schools follow the LL.M program of the American Law School, set up a Master's program in Chinese Law for foreign students (LL.M Program in Chinese Law, hereinafter referred to as Master of Chinese Law Project). Teaching all in English has facilitated the study of Chinese law by foreign students and has expanded the student community with great potential for development. The significance of this project lies not only in the implementation of the internationalization strategy for law school, but also in the strategy of "going global" in Chinese law, even having a profound impact on the future direction of Chinese education. Since Tsinghua University first launched the Master's Program on Chinese Law Education in 2005, it has developed to eight universities including Peking University, Renmin University of China, China University of Political Science and Law and Beijing Normal University.

Since the Ministry of Education has no special regulations on the enrollment of Chinese law masters and the teaching methods, it only uses them as one of the education of external qualifications and encourages the qualified colleges and universities to carry out their activities actively. Therefore, the Chinese law Programs of colleges and universities till in the groping stage, there is still a problem or more of its educational orientation, teaching methods, teaching content, etc.

The Chinese Law program in China is generally two years. The first year is mainly for courses teaching. The second year is mainly for research internship and essay writing. The college offers courses in English for these students, including compulsory and elective courses. According to the Courses Setting of Chinese Law Program, it mainly offers the courses in Chinese Civil and Commercial law, Economic law and International law. Specific courses of various schools varies according to the faculty conditions. The reason why the law schools that set up the Chinese Law Program chose these courses spontaneously is determined by the characteristics of these courses. Most of the legal systems involved in these courses are similar to Anglo-American law. Some legal systems are mainly the result of transplanting American laws or are based on international conventions and treaties. They are less affected by the differences in legal cultures and traditions. Generally speaking, Chinese professional terms can be roughly found considerable English vocabulary, can be more accurately translated, facilitate teaching in English, and these legal systems related to translation into English laws and regulations, a large number of cases, teachers and students can use these as the class discussion materials and reading materials. From the view of faculty conditions, it is mainly focus on the professors who both has Chinese legal education background and degrees or further education in foreign law schools. Those who are well versed in Chinese law and have a good foundation in English can handle the task of teaching Chinese law in English, especially who has a law degree or have legal work experience as a prerequisite or priority for the teaching job admission.

3.2 *Career Development After Graduation*

Obtaining the Chinese lawyer qualification requires passing the national bar examination. One of the qualifications for joining the bar examination is that should has the citizenship of the People's Republic of China. This means that foreigners are currently unable to obtain the Chinese lawyer qualification. According to the law of our country, foreign law firms and foreign lawyers are also not allowed to engage in legal affairs in China. This means that a foreign student who has obtained a master's degree in China is also not qualify for the bar examination and cannot engage in legal affairs in China. Foreign enterprises and foreign law firms need to cooperate with Chinese law firms when they involve legal affairs related to China. Foreign students who study the Chinese Law Program can establish a basic understanding of Chinese law and handle the communication with Chinese law firms.

3.3 *Bilingual Legal Education in Chinese Law Program*

In many cases, the Master of Chinese Law program not only needs to teach Chinese language knowledge, but also needs to teach Chinese culture knowledge. Law is more of a "local knowledge," legal education must be combined with China's special national conditions, traditional culture and values to carry out. Many colleges and universities have opened "Chinese traditional law" and "Chinese society and law" courses in Chinese Laws program. These courses must involve special expressions of the legal system in the Chinese language. Therefore, in the setting of the courses, the course of "Legal Chinese" is particularly necessary. This course should focus on Chinese language knowledge related to legal concepts and legal principles, which not only meets the needs of students to learn Chinese and Chinese traditional culture, but also it can effectively replace the Chinese teaching in law courses, draw a clear line between legal courses and language courses, and lay out the position of legal courses. The universities which opened Chinese language courses are Tsinghua University, Shanghai Jiaotong University, China University of Political Science and Law, Xiamen University, University of International Business and Economics and other universities. However, it seems that the establishment of "Legal Chinese" is more appropriate to meet the needs. For example, Peking University Law School set up the Legal Chinese Course.

3.4 *Examples*

3.4.1 Peking University

The Mater of Laws (LL.M.) Program in Chinese Law in Peking University is a Graduate Law program which focusing on Chinese civil and commercial law. Peking University Law School established the LL.M. Program in Chinese Law to address the needs of an international community seeking a comprehensive and systematic understanding of Chinese law from a first-rate legal institution. In this program, leading faculty members will offer Chinese law courses specially designed for international students. Teaching will comprise of both lectures and small-group seminars. There are also optional subjects in non-law areas such as politics, economy and society to facilitate students' understanding of China's culture. Moreover, courses on Mandarin Chinese are available for the improvement of language skill and adaption to local residence.

In their course system for Chinese Law LL.M students, mainly are used English as teaching language for the core courses, like Chinese Civil Law, Chinese Company Law, Chinese Constitutional and Administrative Law and so on, but they also set Legal Chinese and Elementary Chinese(1) for the Fall Semester and Elementary Chinese(2) for the Spring Semester. These language courses will improve students' Chinese language capacity and will be easier for students to understand and study Chinese law.

3.4.2 Tsinghua University

The LL.M Program in Chinese Law offered at Tsinghua was specifically designed for international students and legal professionals who are interested in studying the Chinese legal system. The program offers 15 courses taught entirely in English. This program at Tsinghua is the first formal legal education offered in China for foreign law students and professionals. About the courses, this program consists two types of courses: mandatory and elective. Both of them are about Chinese laws, and will be taught by the Tsinghua Law School faculty in English, as well as adjunct faculty of experienced, practicing lawyers. As other law schools that have Chinese Law LL.M Program, Tsinghua also has Chinese language course each semester for the LL.M Students, but they do not set a Legal Chinese course. Students who demonstrate Chinese language abilities and wish to audit courses taught in Chinese may seek permission from the LL.M Program to do so.

3.4.3 Fudan University

Since the fall of 2010, Fudan Law School has launched an English-instructed program—LL.M. in Chinese Business Law, especially for foreign lawyers, executives, students, and professionals engaging in international trade and/or interested in Chinese business and financial law.

Each LL.M. student will be assigned an academic advisor for study and thesis writing. In addition, Fudan Law School will arrange regular academic and extra-curricular activities for both foreign students and Chinese students so that they may interact with each other.

About the courses, almost all the courses are around with Chinese business and financial law, and the faculty for LL.M program are all in possession of experience and good reputation within their fields. Fudan do not set a Chinese language course, but they set a course called "Legal Mandarin", which likes the legal Chinese in Peking University.

3.4.4 Renmin University of China

The LL.M Program in Chinese Law offered by Renmin Law School is served fully in English, it is a unique opportunity for students from abroad, Hong Kong, Macau and Taiwan. The teaching faculty in the LL.M Program have extraordinary academic credentials. Most professors have experience studying and/or teaching in leading law schools in the most prestigious universities, such as Harvard, Yale, Oxford and Cambridge. They all have deep understandings of both western law and Chinese Law. At the same time, Renmin Law School offers valuable internship opportunities in top law firms and other institutions for students to achieve their career planning.

The LL.M Program in Chinese law provided by Renmin Law School is a two-year English Graduate Program. It is taught in English. The first year is full-time coursework with class attendance. It focuses on Chinese civil and business laws. There are also optional subjects in non-law areas such as Chinese politics, Chinese economy and Chinese society to facilitate the students' understanding of Chinese culture. The second year is set aside for dissertation writing, legal practice and internship. The students can either choose to stay in China or return to their own residence in the second academic year, but they must attend the dissertation defense scheduled in the 4th semester. Compulsory Courses and General Courses will be arranged at the first academic year. Students are required to take all the Compulsory Courses and General Courses. The Chinese language course belongs to the General Courses. There isn't a course like Legal Chinese.

Language Aspects of Legal Education and Research in Czechia: Recent Dominance of English in International Communication and Heritage of Other Languages in a Nominally Monolingual Country

Filip Křepelka

1 Introduction

1.1 Foreword

Interesting contributions of national reporters and lively debate in section *Bilingual Legal Education: the Challenges and the Need* held on 24th July 2018 at the 20th Congress of International Academy of Comparative Law in Fukuoka (Japan) inspired me for the asking to join this section with subsequent reporting on the Czech Republic.

I have repeatedly tackled linguistic issues of both European and Czech laws and legal education also in the comparative perspective in papers[1] and presentations.[2] Being an associate professor at the Law Faculty of the Masaryk University in Brno, I have domestic experiences with evolving language policies.

1.2 Approach

The questionnaire initiating the section focused on bilingual legal education (BLE) without specification. Most presenters understood the adjective "bilingual" as an education in their national language and English as a language of international

[1] Křepelka (2010, 2012, 2019).

[2] This text expand presentation "English as emerging parallel academic language" at the European Legal English Teachers' Association Conference held on 23rd September 2017 in Brno.

F. Křepelka (✉)
Masaryk University, Faculty of Law, Brno, Czechia
e-mail: filip.krepelka@law.muni.cz

N. Etcheverry Estrázulas (ed.), *Bilingual Study and Research*, Ius Comparatum – Global Studies in Comparative Law 58,
https://doi.org/10.1007/978-3-030-84550-6_5

communication. Education in two languages in bilingual countries or cities seems to be a minority experience.

Czechia forms no exception. Education is mainly in the Czech language. However, complementary or additional courses are often in English. There are pressures for further Anglicisation in tertiary education. This trend is challenging for the law as an academic discipline. Moreover, other languages also need to be considered. Language issues in (legal) education and research become a contentious issue in a *nominally monolingual country.*

1.3 Minority Languages in Czechia

The protection of minorities and their languages in national legislation is robust in Czechia. Besides the Constitution,[3] international law guarantees it, among others, the European Charter for Regional or Minority Languages.[4] Czechia pledged to protect the languages of indigenous minorities: German, Polish, Roma, and Slovak.

Bulgarian, Greek, Romanian, Russian, Ukrainian, and Vietnamese are the most populous immigrant minorities. Contrary to other countries, there is a willingness to recognize even their languages as minority languages.[5]

1.4 Czech as National and State Language

Nevertheless, the enumeration of minority languages should not confuse international readers. Czechia is a monolingual country. Minorities are small. The ask primarily for subsidies for their cultural activity. Solely Poles living in a specific border region have their schools. Minority languages are absent in politics, administration, and judiciary.

Insistence on the Czech language is lukewarm. There are few requirements for its use. The absence of any rival language explains this attitude. Additionally, the non-revolutionary establishment of the Czech Republic is worth mentioning.

---

[3] Article 25 of *Listina základních práv a svobod* [Charter of Fundamental Right and Freedom], https://www.usoud.cz/fileadmin/user_upload/ustavni_soud_www/Pravni_uprava/AJ/Listina_English_version.pdf.

[4] Adopted in 1992, effective, CETS no. 148, see Declaration of the Czech Republic contained in the instrument of ratification deposited on 15 November 2006.

[5] *Zákon č. 273/2001 Sb. o právech příslušníků národnostních menšin* [Law on Rights of Members of Ethnic Minorities] does not list language minorities. The Government Council for National Minorities as statutory representative (for English info see https://www.vlada.cz/en/ppov/rnm/historie-a-soucasnost-rady-en-16666/) includes representatives of both traditional and immigrant minorities such as Vietnamese, which in turn English Wikipedia lists as recognized minority language.

This monolingualism is so evident that the Constitution of the Czech Republic (1993) does not proclaim Czech as national or state language. Linguistic legislation bills repeatedly die in the Parliament. Lawmakers specified language aspects in administrative and judicial proceedings only when facing excessive expectations on translation.[6]

1.5 *English in Czechia*

Similarly, as in other countries, English has become the language for communication in international trade, investment, modernization, culture, and tourism. Most pupils and students learn English.[7] Unsurprisingly, younger people master it more than elderly ones. However, even they know English words. Many English words entered the Czech language.[8]

This Anglicisation is spontaneous. Standards for education, employment, or public space barely recognize it explicitly. Nevertheless, several politicians, officials, and journalists regard knowledge of English as an essential precondition for development. Therefore, they demand support and interventions. Among others, they call for prohibition of dubbing of movies, ignoring thus their audience and other languages, if Hollywood movies only existed. Some journalists even call for elevating English to co-official language. Other people are skeptical or reject these policies. *Anglicization* becomes a principal challenge for monolingual Czechia.

[6]There was tendency to interpret § 18 of the Code on Civil Procedure [*Zákon č. 99/1963 Sb., občanský soudní řád*) that anybody has right for interpretation and translation at the expenses of the State. This provision applied by analogy in administrative judiciary proved absurd with increasing number of cases of migrants, asylum seekers and other cases related to foreigners after the accession to the EU. On the contrary, § 16 of the Code of Administrative Procedure [*Zákon č. 500/2004 Sb., správní řád*] stipulates that Czech is the official language of Czech administrative authorities, while documents in Slovak are generally accepted and authorities can dispense from certified translation, which is relevant in supervision of pharmaceuticals, air transport etc.

[7]For recent figures in the member states of the EU, see Eurostat, Foreing Launguage Learning, 2017. https://ec.europa.eu/eurostat/statistics-explained/index.php/Foreign_language_learning_statistics. According to them, 73% Czech pupils learn English in primary education and 99% in upper secondary education, while most have the second foreign language: German, French and Spanish.

[8]Adam (2012).

2 English as Global *Lingua Franca* and Its Impact on Academia

2.1 Remark of Esperanto

Numerous individuals developed planned languages in the nineteenth and twentieth centuries, intending to promote them as a language for universal communication. Esperanto was the most successful. Czechia belongs to countries with the strongest Esperantist movement. Several professional communities have developed their terminology in Esperanto.[9]

Participation at the conference addressing linguistic policies attached to the 2016 World Esperanto Congress in Nitra, Slovakia, revealed for me a community of *verda stelo* aficionados. Extolling of this constructed language resembles religious missionaries. However, concern emerged that they ignore likely results of its hypothetical success. Intense propagation or even imposition of Esperanto would incite disgust and resistance.

2.2 Consequences of the Dominance of English

Nevertheless, we can forget Esperanto because it has never played the role strived by many Esperantists. English has become a global *lingua franca* as the first language in history. According to *de Swaan*, English is the only *hypercentral* language.[10]

As tourists, we expect information on transportation, accommodation, sights, food, and regulations in English. We hope that everybody will answer our simple questions in English. Indeed, people meet our expectations. As professionals, we communicate with our foreign counterparts in English. This dominance as practical. We do not need to try to understand, read, and speak in several major languages.

Some people call for finalizing this trend. There is a tendency to praise English as having features absent in other languages. However, other people feel discomfort and disgust. "Full steam" is becoming controversial.

English eases communication even among the enemies of the West, such as Islamist terrorists. Nevertheless, this dominance generally results in preference of culture, society, economy, and politics of the United Kingdom and the United

[9]We find legal practitioners and scholars among Esperantists. However, physicians or engineers seem to be more active. We can hypothesise about pragmatism, but also about exhaustion resulting from extensive use of any language in legal activities. Esperantists-lawyers focused primarily on international law, see Harry (1978).

[10]*Abram de Swaan* (de Swaan 2013) identifies English as the only hypercentral language, dozen supercentral languages serving international communication in particular regions or fields, approxiately one hundred central languages and many peripheral languages.

States.[11] It puts them to the center of the world. Let us realize the frequent dropping of "Great Britain and "America" in their names.

The dominance of the English language creates an advantage for Great Britain, the United States of America, and other English-speaking countries, including these where it is the language of interethnic communication such as India. Profits generated thanks to this dominance are estimated so high to incite discussion about compensation or taxation.[12]

The Anglicization of touristic, expert, and political communication has an impact on this language. Specific sorts of this language besides its varieties in two dozen English-speaking countries emerge. Linguists coin Globish, International English, and Euro-English for them.[13]

The dominance of English has serious consequences for other languages. Dozen other major languages, i.e. *supercentral* languages, according to *de Swaan* demise as languages of international communication. Moreover, English starts to compete with one hundred *central* languages, i. e. national languages of particular countries or their parts in domestic settings.

2.3 Academia as a Forefront of Anglicisation and Overlap with Internationalisation

Publishing in international journals with the impact-factor required in most fields of science means publishing in English. Scholars and scientists use it in their presentations and lectures at international conferences and workshops.[14] English eases communication in international research teams. Guest lecturers provide their lectures in English. Courses offered for exchange students and programs aimed at international students capable and willing to pay, are mostly in English.

Many politicians, officials, journalists, professors, and students think that international exchange and cooperation are essential for academic excellence. Internationalization has become a mantra and slogan in academia.

Anglicization undoubtedly eases this effort. Scholars and students need not master several languages for their understanding in international settings. Interpretation disappeared from conferences. Translations of scientific literature vanished. Education in English attracts more international students than education in most national languages. It eases the recruitment of professors and lecturers. Therefore,

[11] See publications of *Robert Phillipson* discussing language imperialism, among others his seminal works Phillipson (1992, 2009).

[12] Grin (2005), pp. 82–97.

[13] McCrum (2011).

[14] Among others, Ammon (2001), and Lillis and Curry (2010).

internationalization overlaps with Anglicisation. Unsurprisingly, English pushes of national language even from purely domestic situations.[15]

2.4 Students Exchange and Education of Domestic Students

Few talented individuals enjoyed short-term and post-graduate courses abroad a few decades ago. The European Union's programs *Socrates/Erasmus* launched mass student mobility. Law students in Brno now enjoy more opportunities than they are capable of using. There is little interest in studies in other central European countries. Instead, students long for America and compete fiercely for few scholarships offered by partner *John Marshall Law School* in Chicago.

European exchange programs should promote multilingualism. Nowadays, "English-only" prevailed. Namely, universities in countries in central and Eastern Europe offer courses exclusively in English.[16] Interest in the language of the host country is rare.

Fees paid by international students have become significant revenue for Czech faculties of medicine. English language programs also exist in some fields of science and technology. Despite subsidies and support for the establishment of English language programs, results are modest in social sciences and humanities.

As mentioned, professors and lecturers teach in Czech. However, there are various incentives for education in English. Additional credits—if compared with similarly extensive courses in Czech—stimulate enrolment into courses taught by both local and visiting teachers. However, foreign lecturers arriving in sufficient numbers due to support of academic mobility or requirement for it face disinterest if such stimulation is absent. The state supports delivering diploma theses in English with subsidies turned into wages. Even teachers sceptical towards this option thus encourage their students to write in English under their supervision.

2.5 Shortcomings of Anglicisation

Czechia is a welfare state. Public financing encompasses tertiary education. There are no study fees. Proposals to introduce them failed repeatedly. However, public money is scarce. Czech education is underfinanced if compared with other developed countries.[17]

---

[15] Ljosland (2007).

[16] Kalocsai (2009).

[17] OECD, "Education at a Glance 2018. OECD Indicators", see https://read.oecdilibrary.org/education/education-at-a-glance-2018_eag-2018-en#page8.

Unsurprisingly, efforts to internationalize and Anglicize the Czech academic landscape suffers from shortcomings. Few pay attention to the quality of English. Support for its enhancement is absent. The recruitment of international professors and researchers has mixed results. The principal question is, however, whether students are ready for education in English and interested in it.

2.6 English Advertisement for Academic Jobs and Mandatory English Habilitations

Two controversial measures aimed at the author's Masaryk University deserve mention.

The International Scientific Advisory Board established by the Masaryk University underlined international selection of teachers and researchers. Czech law on tertiary education does not require Czech citizenship. The eventual requirement would be incompatible with the free movement of workers in the European Union in the case of its citizens.[18] We need not fear such an approach. Academia is mentally and institutionally xenophile. Foreign academicians are a proxy for excellence. Therefore, Masaryk University implemented this recommendation with job announcements in English. Interconnected webpages invited numerous academicians from poorer countries.

The Masaryk University has mandated that the theses submitted within *habilitation* shall be in English since 2020, while another language is permitted only if usual in a particular field.[19]

Habilitation is an evaluation of educational and scientific performance expected in Czech law. The procedure is lengthy, demanding, cumbersome, and its results unpredictable. Unsurprisingly, Czech academicians become *docents* at various ages. Success usually enhances individual positions, including indefinite contracts (tenure). *Professors* are the supreme rank, and many academicians do not achieve this rank in their careers.

Supporters justified mandatory English with an extended pool of reviewers. Hectic deliberation resulted in a compromise. Narrowly defined subfields could allow theses in Czech if renowned foreign professors attest unfeasibility of English.

Appraisal of this requirement as an important step towards the genuine internationalization of tertiary education was lesser than we would expect. Literates

[18] Articles 45–48 of the Treaty on the Functioning of the European Union.

[19] See section 1 (3) of the Masaryk University Habilitation Procedure and Professor Appointment Procedure Regulations (English version available at: https://www.muni.cz/en/about-us/official-notice-board/masaryk-university-habilitation-procedure-and-professor-appointment-procedure-regulations): "Habilitation thesis may be submitted in Czech, Slovak or English or other foreign language commonly used in a given field. In the case of habilitation procedures initiated after 31 December 2020, the habilitation thesis must be submitted in English or other foreign language commonly used in a given field (with the exception of Slovak)."

criticized it sarcastically.[20] Other universities declined to follow. Representatives of technical universities confirmed that valuable publications are already written in English, while representatives of universities timidly embraced choice or remained silent. Legal scholars uttered that the Masaryk University undermines its position. Mandatory English is—at least in the field of law—unprecedented in central Europe.[21]

2.7 *Relation Between Law and Language*

Deliberation about mandatory English in theses for habilitation showed isolation of the law faculty. Few professors of arts and pedagogy joined our critique. Sciences, medicine, technologies became Anglicized during the last decades. Valuable publications—i. e. papers in journals with impact factor—are in English. Publications in their respective national language are regarded largely as communication towards professionals or students. Even if taught in a national language, most programs and courses are universal.

Questioning the relevance of international publications in the field of law incites debates on whether the law is science. Indeed, it is specific. Lawyers ascertain the legality of human behavior (required/allowed/prohibited) while interpreting statutes. Attorneys and in-house counsels argue in favor of their clients, enterprises, and institutions. Officials and judges balance arguments in their decisions and judgments. Legal scholars analyze the law in textbooks for the education of students, for information of legal practitioners, and their discourse.

Law is enacted, interpreted, and applied in a particular national language. The meaning of words in that particular language is crucial. Therefore, it has little sense to publish texts about national law primarily in any foreign language. Moreover, potential respectable foreign reviewers would decline its review with unfamiliarity with Czech law.

2.8 *Specifics of Internationalisation of Legal Practice, Education and Publishing*

Attorneys and in-house counsels are pragmatic. Broad resort to English makes their international communication easier than interpretation and translation provided by

[20] Jamek (2017).

[21] I thank for comments to *Jacek Mazurkiewicz*, professor of the Faculty of Law, Administration and Economy of Wroclaw University, Poland, *Janja Hojnik* of the Faculty of Law, the Maribor University, Slovenia and professor *Peter Christian Müller-Graff* of the Faculty of Law, the Heidelberg University, Germany.

professional interpreters and communication in several major languages. We can only speculate how linguistic shortcomings affect this communication.

Language barriers and limited knowledge of foreign law have a profound impact on cross-border legal practice. Attorneys and in-house counsels avoid advice on foreign law, not talking about the representation of their clients and employers at offices and before courts abroad, even if they were allowed to do it. Few lawyers master excellently local law and language. Therefore, they contact local lawyers instead. Many law firms join international networks for this purpose.

As mentioned, English has become the principal language of courses aimed at international students. We shall debate whether international students speaking countries realize sufficiently the pitfalls of international communication in the field of law, which is primarily national phenomenon closely connected with the national language. Legal scholars at international conferences also switched to English.

English also dominated in Fukuoka. Several rapporteurs, mostly from Romance language countries, used French as the second language of the organizer.[22] Still, other French-speaking participants mixed the two languages in their oral and power-point presentations or switched to English because they preferred understanding by all participants.

Journal articles, papers for collections, chapters of books, and monographs in the field of law are lengthy (dozens to hundreds of pages). Complex sentences are frequent. The final version results from repeated reformulations aimed at both precise argumentation and linguistic elegance.

Therefore, rendering scholarly texts in the field of law in English instead of their national language is burdensome and expensive, even for those with sufficient command of English. We shall not expect excellence in complex formulations without *proof-reading*, i. e. the correction of grammatical and stylistic errors by a native speaker.

Other sciences publications are different. Figures, tables, graphs, diagrams, depictions, and photographs deliver principal. Texts summarize research results on the few pages at most. Formulations are terse. Proof-reading is a minor effort. Journals improve these texts.[23]

Moreover, many terms in the field of law require an explanation for an international readership,[24] because they denote concepts of national law. A brief outline of *habilitation* was necessary here because there is no comparable procedure at universities in English-speaking countries.

Comparative studies are explicit in this regard. National rapporteurs write national reports. Their initiators and organizers summarize findings in so-called

[22] One presenter mentioned that French authorities encourage (if not demand) French professors to present at the international conferences where French is expected or allowed, and not in English.

[23] One leading professor of geology highlighted that their research consists of terrain work, deployment of machinery, challenging measurements, and completing tables, diagrams, and schemes. Publications have multiple authors, someone summarizes results in English on few lines. Effort of eventual proof-reading or even translation of entire text is marginal.

[24] On translatability of legal institutes, see Kocbek (2008), p. 60.

general reports.[25] Unsurprisingly, the selection of topics usually reflects the interest of scholars from elite countries.[26] Sets of questions can contort findings of national reports.

Many other papers published "abroad" are *de facto* national reports. Authors write on particular topics because they have studied and practice particular law while understanding the national language. National affiliation plays a small role, and the author is hard to identify if concealed solely in papers addressing the legal theory of international and European law.

Despite huge efforts spent by most authors of national reports or papers based on domestic experience, we read texts summarizing national law and its practice accompanied by the necessary outline of political, social, and economic aspects. Minutely interpretation of particular provisions is downplayed because it requires an explanation of terms in the particular national language.

Moreover, most legal themes are relevant primarily in national settings. Authors of dissertations and theses for habilitation publish them as monographs. Their readership is domestic. English version would find few readers.

At all, pressures for English in legal research and education and discontent with it is not specific for Czechia. Many scholars in Fukuoka highlighted the relation between national language and law and deplored pressure for Anglicisation. It seems that consensus emerged on it. We can note here that all these scholars expressed this criticism in English.

2.9 Complementarity of International and European Laws

The supporters of mentioned trends highlight that international and European laws differ from national law and should thus be subject to similar requirements as other sciences if confronted with outlined arguments.

Indeed, international law is different. Countries select several languages as the authentic languages of international treaties and official languages of international organizations. Diplomats and experts communicate in these languages. For example, English, French, Spanish, Russian, Chinese, and Arabic are official languages of the United Nations Organisation, and authentic languages of international treaties agreed under its auspices. Official multilingualism seems necessary in the European Union law. There is no language of interethnic communication in this

[25] Kischel (2015), p. 5.

[26] I was glad to participate in the section Genetic Testing in Insurance and Employment in Fukuoka. I thank to Professor *Lara Khoury* for excellent coordination. Nevertheless, genetic testing in the field of employment is absent in Czechia, while life insurance is underdeveloped. The topic is not salient in Czechia. At least, it provided an impulse for preparation of the first national treatise of legal aspects of genetic testing.

unique supranational structure. Nevertheless, resort to English, French, and German as its working languages[27] results in a similar situation.

Therefore, academic discourse about international and European law emerges in major languages. Legal scholars specialized in these fields routinely read texts in these languages. Knowledge of foreign languages is indispensable. Nevertheless, we should not ignore the parallel domestic reflection conducted in national languages. International and European laws interact with national laws. National authorities shall apply or consider international law. The European Union relies on its member states for enforcement of its law. Mandatory English could undermine this internal reflection.

2.10 Dominance of a Language of Common Law in International Legal Discourse

English is the language of countries where Anglo-American *common law* exists. However, common law is the second major legal system of the world, which differs from continental *civil law* in most European countries. It is difficult to describe institutes of the latter with English without descriptions or with the troublesome resort to terms rooted in common law settings.[28] We shall not be surprised if linguists identify "continental lawyers" English.

Moreover, this specific linguistic situation seems to incite the preference for common law concepts. Most legal scholars and practitioners know the different perceptions of whether judgments could and shoud be regarded as (case-)law.[29] Different roles of statutes also deserve our attention. Moreover, entire academic reflection diverges.[30]

Patriotism accompanied eventually with disgust towards the Anglo-American model of society, government, and the law could result in hostility towards English. There are Czech and Polish professors with good command of English, which try to suppress it at conferences by them, expecting mutual intelligibility among Slavic languages or preferring other major languages. Mentioning them hints us to pay attention to the role of *other foreign languages*.

[27] Křepelka (2012).

[28] Kocbek (2008), p. 63.

[29] Among others, Kischel (2015), from various perspectives, p. 667 (convergence) and p. 49 (legal imperialism).

[30] Grechenig and Gelter (2008).

3 Other Foreign Languages in Czech Law, Legal Education, and Research

3.1 History Changing Language Landscape

Corona Regni Bohemiae was an important European state composed of autonomous lands Bohemia, Moravia, Silesia, Lower Lusatia, and Upper Lusatia. It lost its independence at the dawn of modern history with the ascension of the Habsburg dynasty. Emerging European superpower encompassed these provinces since 1547 and with a tighter grip since 1620.

The multinational monarchy demised with the First World War (1914–1918). Humanism and modernization marked the interwar Czechoslovak Republic (1918–1939), but its complex ethnic makeup contributed to its collapse and occupation by Nazi Germany at the beginning of the Second World War (1939–1945).

Liberation by the Soviet Union marked the path to communist totalitarianism (since 1948). Nevertheless, distinguishing is desirable. The regime had its revolutionary phase (50ties), moderation (60ties) culminating with "the Prague Spring" (1968) stopped with occupation by Soviets, so-called normalization (70ties) followed by stagnation (80ties) with faint reforms (*perestroika*).

The Velvet Revolution (1989) launched a transition to liberal democracy and market economy. The dissolution of Czechoslovakia (1992) was ephemeral trouble. Czechia joined the Council of Europe (1993), the North Atlantic Treaty Organisation (1999), and the European Union (2004). International trade, investment, and mobility increased significantly during the last decades, thanks to this integration and globalization in general.

Outlined periods resulted in the encounter of Czech society with several major and minor languages. We will mention them together with their importance in law and legal science.

3.2 Turbulent Developments of Czech Law

Law in Czech territory changed profoundly in the twentieth century. Wars had a severe impact on people. Injustice and violence emerged. Hastily adopted law expressed policies of new regimes. Nevertheless, legal thinking remained largely intact.[31]

Socialism had a different impact. Local legal scholars claimed that a distinct socialist legal system emerged, while western authors accepted it.[32] Ignorance for law characterized its first totalitarian phase. The so-called socialist legality marked

[31] For example, regarding the impact of Nazi occupation, see Schelle K, Tauchen J (2009).

[32] See Kischel (2015), p. 218 (citing David, René, Jauffret-Spinosi, Camille, *Les grand systémes de droit contemporains*, 11th edition, 2002) and 219 (citing Eörsi, Gyula, *Comparative civil (private) law*, 1979).

the stabilization of the regime. However, Czechoslovak legal thinking gradually vulgarised. Frequent amendments and recodifications in the period of transition destabilized law, while formalism alternated with revolts against it. For various reasons, authorities applied law selectively. Unsurprisingly, widespread nihilism emerging in the twentieth century continues.[33]

3.3 *Latin: Roots of European Culture*

Latin as a former official language of the Roman Empire and as a liturgical and doctrinal language of the Roman Catholic Church enabled communication of educated people in medieval Europe, while masses were illiterate. Therefore, reformation (fifteenth and sixteenth century) emphasized vernacular languages, i. e. Czech and German languages for Czech lands. Bible translations marked the emergence of modern languages.

Nevertheless, Latin continued to serve the communication of diplomats, clergy, scientists, and scholars, including these opposing triumphant Catholicism, such as exiled educationist John Amos Comenius. It retained its position of primary classical language in secondary education for centuries. It was indispensable until the twentieth century at *gymnasia*. Unsurprisingly, socialism neglected Latin but did not dare to suppress it overtly.

Latin also dominated European academia. Terminology in many fields of science originated from Greek[34] and Latin. This dominance was so strong that it has not disappeared until now. Academic emblems contain Latin, and ceremonies rely on it.

However, the role of Latin in law goes beyond symbols. Latin was the language of Roman law, which contributed to the development of law and legal thinking in many European countries. Latin phrases are shorthand for legal principles. Even laypeople understand many of these phrases. The law of the Roman Catholic Church is also Latin. Unsurprisingly, legal education in socialism downplayed Roman law and suppressed canonic law. The Roman law revived during the transition to democracy as an introduction to private law.

Despite the little interest, law faculties offer facultative courses of Latin. However, nobody expects to communicate in Latin. Academic ceremonies reveal that most academicians hardly understand Latin phrases they pronounce. Nobody writes

[33] Kischel (2015), pp. 571–594. Author explains slow transformation of law, legal practice and legal doctrine in post-socialist countries, impetuous law-making, relics of socialist thinking in the field of law, widespread formalism, crisis of leadership in the field of law, perfunctory enforcement, conservative education, influence of old elites, legal nihilism. However, he distinguishes post-Soviet sphere in general and Russia with revived self-confidence and new member states of the EU to which Czechia belongs.

[34] Classic *gymnasia* taught also (old) Greek and its suppression in favour of living languages was subject of debates one century ago, while (biblical) Hebrew was restricted to seminars for clergy.

now legal treatises in Latin. Even our teachers of Roman law considered eventual writing of their theses in Latin as a joke.

3.4 German: Former Dominance and Recent Impulse

Japan and Korea decided the reception of German law.[35] Czechia's adherence to the Germanic subgroup of continental law (civil law) is a consequence of being part of the Habsburg monarchy in the nineteenth century when foundations of modern civil (*Allgemeines Bürgerliches Gesetzbuch* in 1811), criminal and administrative laws emerged.[36]

The Czech Kingdom was an important member of medieval German *Reich*. German was present in Czech lands since German colonization in the thirteenth and fourteenth centuries. The country was bilingual for centuries. Austrian German (numerous *Austriazisms*) was the primary official language in provinces Bohemia, Moravia, and (Austrian) Silesia in the nineteenth century.

Czech emancipated during the so-called Czech National Revival. However, German remained primary.[37] Judges, officials, attorneys, and in-house counsels knew German. Legal scholars than law faculty in Prague treated law primarily in German. Resort to Czech in politics and law increased gradually. Czech legal journal *Právník* (the Lawyer) published since 1861 belongs to the oldest legal journals worldwide. Czech legal terminology derives from Austrian-German one and remains compatible with it.

The position of the two languages reversed in the interwar period.[38] Czech (or Czechoslovak) became the official language of the Czechoslovak Republic. German-speaking public servants should master it. Nevertheless, minority languages enjoyed protection.[39] Czech schools continued to teach German as a major foreign language. There was an immense trade and cultural exchange between Germany and Austria. Czech (Czechoslovak) legal scholars, including these newly established faculties in Brno, and Bratislava (in Slovakia), resorted routinely to German. Furthermore, the law faculty within the German section of the Charles University (established 1882) lectured and published about Czechoslovak law in German.[40]

Nazi occupation (1939–1945) made German dominant again, while terror endangered Czechs as a nation.[41] The retaliatory expulsion of Germans in 1945 caused an abrupt change in the linguistic landscape of re-established Czechoslovakia.

---

[35] Hertel (2009), p. 167.

[36] Hertel (2009), p. 164.

[37] Velčovský (2014), pp. 78–141.

[38] Velčovský (2014), pp. 144–182.

[39] For detailed analysis in German language, see Epstein (1927).

[40] Skřejpková (2013).

[41] Velčovský (2014), pp. 183–216.

The resurgence of economic and cultural interaction with both socialist East and capitalist West Germany caused a gradual return of German to secondary and tertiary education. Several academicians, including legal scholars, recognized the importance of German.

Germany and Austria became major trade partners and investors in the period of transition. Many German-speaking tourists visit Czechia. Czechs found well-paid jobs in Germany and Austria. Nevertheless, German is strictly facultative. Despite the advantages of its mastering, many parents, pupils, and students perceive German as complicated and unsympathetic.

Post-war (West) German constitutionalism provided an important inspiration for modern Czech constitutionalism. Several talented students and lecturers found their path to Germany and other German-speaking countries. Several legal scholars resort extensively to German and Austrian legal literature. German seems to be the only language besides English in which visiting professors deliver lectures attracting some audience. Several conferences and courses are in German.[42]

Some of these scholars regard literature written in German as a crucial prerequisite for the cultivation of domestic law. However, other scholars claim that English is sufficient. Cleavage emerges between legal scholars oriented on German and Anglo-American laws.[43] We can observe similar differentiation among judges, officials, attorneys, and in-house counsels. Several ones take advantage of their knowledge of German, while others find it unnecessary.

3.5 *French: Remembering Its Importance in International Culture and Politics*

The French language achieved a prominent position during the nineteenth-century in culture, arts, society, diplomacy, administration, management, and law. Artists, business people, politicians, and scholars mastered it. However, the French lost this position in favor of English during the twentieth-century. Its retention as an official language in many international organizations and associations,[44] the International Academy of Comparative Law included,[45] is heritage resulting from its previous dominance.

---

[42] Among others, Austrian-Czech-Slovak summer school of private law, organized by professors of the Faculty of Law in Olomouc and Wirtschaftsuniversität Wien.

[43] For similar impact on legal scholars, elite attorneys and superior court judges in Japan, South Korea and Taiwan, see Kischel (2015), p. 800.

[44] Calvet (2017), pp. 225–230.

[45] See Internet presentation at www.aidc-iacl.org. This bilingualism, however, is not anchored in published statutes and by-laws of the Academy established as association according to law of the Netherlands.

Gymnasia and vocational schools in the Austrian-Hungarian monarchy taught French as a major language. French flourished in the interwar period thanks orientation of Czechoslovakia towards France as then superpower co-orchestrating the Versailles Conference (1919) and disgust towards German as the language of the ancient monarchy. Despite the official preference for Russian and gradual switch towards English, French remained among facultative languages in the period of socialism similarly as German.

Francophone students could enjoy generous support by the French Republic, trying to support retention of its position. Graduates of law, international relations, and public administration realized that French boosts their careers in diplomacy and global and European international organizations.[46] The Faculty of Economics and Administration of the Masaryk University and the Université Rennes II teach *Maitre Franco-tcheque de l'administration publique*. The program suffered from declining interest because recent Czech students lack knowledge of French. Unsurprisingly, France reduced its support.

There are Francophone academicians in Czechia. Nevertheless, the French language disappears from academia. We can hypothesize that the distance makes research in libraries and participation at conferences expensive. We can also perceive the disinterest of French academia for Eastern Europe, resulting in few invitations to conferences and publications.

As regards law, differences between Germanistic and Romanistic (Napoleonic) law and less voluminous literature if compared with German one could explain limited interest. I do not remember any Francophone conference, workshop, summer school, and research project in the field of law in Czechia since 2000.

3.6 *Russian: Surprisingly Weak Impact*

International readers know that Czechoslovakia was part of the communist bloc dominated by the Soviet Union. Perhaps, they expect that the Russian language played an important role.

Indeed, socialist Czechoslovakia promoted the Russian as a language for the future communist planet. Russian was compulsory in primary and secondary education. Many Czechs and Slovaks mastered this Slavic language. However, attitudes towards Russian changed. Widespread sympathies based on the nineteenth-century pan-Slavism and gratitude for liberation in 1945 turned into antipathy after 1968.

Russian language exam was compulsory at universities. However, attempts to promote Russian failed. Soviet scientific literature was relevant in math or physics. However, tightly controlled social sciences could not deliver anything attractive. The economic and social underdevelopment of the Soviet Union has become apparent.

[46] For contemporary reflection of both official multilingualism and retention of French as internal working language at the Court of Justice of the European Union, see McAuliffe (2013).

We need to realize attitudes towards law in socialism to understand little importance of Russian in the field of law. Soviet legal doctrine gradually acknowledged law as an instrument of governance, highlighting specifics of the law in socialist countries.[47] However, obvious primitivism limited central European legal scholars' interest in Soviet literature. References to it usually served to show authors' compliance with Marxism-Leninism.

Unsurprisingly, Russian disappeared with the collapse of socialism. Lists of facultative languages contained it for the surplus of its teachers. The resurgence of trade with Russia and other post-soviet countries, investment in them, and immigration from them spared Russian from disappearance. However, it is a minority option. The recent absence of Russian at Czech law faculties results from its lack in secondary education.

We can explain the recent marginality of Russian in legal academia with its orientation towards the West, the peripheral position of Russia in European organizations, and labile, shaky, and formalist law in post-soviet countries. Even older scholars and practitioners with tested Russian would hardly be capable of discussing legal topics in this language now.

3.7 *Polish: Stronger Role than Expected*

Many inhabitants of Czech Silesia understand Polish thanks to television. Curious intellectuals master reading and understanding quickly when recognizing many false friends.

Despite turbulences in communist Poland, Polish professors were audacious. Western literature was available thanks to translations to the Polish, especially in the field of humanities and social sciences. Poland belonged to few countries allowed to visit. Moreover, Czechoslovaks enjoyed the sympathies of Poles.

Shared experience with both socialism and transition, linguistic and geographic proximity, and mutual interest boost cooperation. Several Czech legal scholars hold Polish legal literature in high esteem and study it for the refinement of Czech law. However, Polish does not rank to major languages. Therefore, nobody expects and demands its knowledge.

3.8 *Slovak: Younger Brother*

Slovak and Czech are mutually intelligible languages. Contrary to emancipating Czech, Slovak faced suppression in the Hungarian part of the Habsburg monarchy.

[47] For recent retrospective reflection of Soviet law, see Berman (2014). However, international readers shall bear in mind that socialist countries differed significantly.

Moreover, Slovakia lacked any tradition of autonomy or statehood. Czechoslovakia thus enabled the resurgence of Slovaks as a nation.

Interwar Czechoslovakia regarded Slovak for political convenience as a variety of Czechoslovak language. The Second World War, when Germany misused Slovak desire for emancipation, resulted in abandoning this approach. The federalization of Czechoslovakia (1968) made its dissolution (1992) easy after brief democratization and liberalization.

This divorce proved as the best solution. Bilateral relations are intense and friendly. There are extensive trade, investment, joint business, job migration, cultural exchange, and many mixed marriages. The Czech and Slovak languages are deemed mutually intelligible also for official purposes. Numerous Slovak students study now at Czech universities, resorting to Slovak.[48]

Czechs assisted Slovaks with the transition from Hungarian administration since 1918. Slovakia retained Hungarian law, while uniform Czechoslovak law emerged after 1945. However, the Czech impact on Slovak legal terminology precedes the establishment of Czechoslovakia, because Slovaks used Czech in writing. Unsurprisingly, emancipatory tendencies encompassed attention for Slovak legal language.[49]

Czech and Slovak laws diverged since the dissolution of Czechoslovakia. We can regret that the comparison of the two close national legal systems is not systematic. Probably, tackling the quickly changing law, and various pressures in underfinanced tertiary education in both countries explains it.

4 Conclusions

4.1 Czechia as Namibia and Pakistan in Tertiary Education?

There is excessive and inappropriate Anglicisation of education in various countries. We can mention Namibia for primary education[50] and Pakistan for the secondary one.[51] Namibian government promoted English for strengthening national identity

[48] Bilateral agreement agreed in 1999 established free access of Czech and Slovak students to universities of other contracting party. However, migration is asymmetric. Slovaks in Czechia largely outnumber Czechs in Slovakia. These studies are at the expense of Czech taxpayers if not re-paid with taxes generated from subsequent job in Czechia. Activist case law of the European Court of Justice cements this asymmetry.

[49] Fundárek (1940).

[50] Sukumane Joyce (1998).

[51] For journalist reflection, see de Lotbiniere, Max, Pakistan facing language crisis in education, the Guardian, 7. 12. 2010, https://www.theguardian.com/education/2010/dec/07/pakistan-schools-language-crisis-lotbiniere, even the report commissioned by the British Council as an organisation promoting English worldwide recognizes problematic outcomes of premature Anglicisation, see Coleman (2010).

in a multilingual country, while Pakistani parents prefer English as a matter of prestige. However, pupils with a poor understanding of English taught by teachers with limited skills learn hardly anything.

Czechia is can unwittingly emulate these countries in tertiary education. Scarce financing is the first ingredient. Problematic governance of universities and their faculties is the second ingredient. Students enjoy significant representation in academic senates.[52] Rectors and deans elected by them seek their support for their policies. Many students embrace Anglicisation. Weak Czech patriotism is the third ingredient. Polish colleagues stressed that English would be regarded—at least in the field of law—inappropriate for habilitation theses.[53]

4.2 Balance of Czech, English and Other Languages in Legal Education and Research

English has become the language of international communication, also among legal practitioners and scholars. Its knowledge is indispensable. Therefore, legal English is an enhancement of this language learned by most students.[54] Exposure of students to lectures provided by visiting professors increases their preparedness for international communication.

Nevertheless, the law is a national phenomenon. International and European laws are complementary. Therefore, Anglicisation resulting in suppression of national language is troublesome in general. It is especially worrisome in underfinanced education and research of national law destabilized after all political, economic, and societal changes.

Additionally, we shall not ignore other languages. Foremost, German deserves attention for its importance in the foundation of Czech law in the former bilingual territory and inspiration in German, Austrian, and Swiss laws. Undue Anglicization reduces the capability to consider national laws closer to the Czech one than Anglo-American laws.

Certainly, English is the language of international students arriving for weeks or months. A systematic comparative approach relying on literature written in English could be suitable for post-graduate courses, doctoral studies, and desirable among legal scholars.

---

[52] International readers can found critical appraisal in Kudrová (2011).

[53] As explained by the professor *Elzbieta Kuzelewska* from Faculty of law and administration of the University in Bialystok for (centralized) habilitation proceedings in Poland.

[54] Traditionally, curriculum at Czech faculties included courses of two languages focusing on professional terminology—Russian and selected major non-Slavic, i.e.Western language.

However, the core law study could not be de-nationalized.[55] Therefore, we shall be skeptical toward efforts to render the entire study program in English. Teaching law in English would be problematic because most graduates will practice law in the national language, even if it were similarly demanding. The opposite is true. Teaching and learning in English are exhaustive.

We shall not overestimate the capability of people to learn foreign languages. English known by the young generation deserves critical appraisal. Nevertheless, we shall demand more from intellectuals. Multilingual professors and students learning some other language besides English and using it for the understanding of foreign laws is an alternative to a law school where impetuous Anglicisation undermines satisfactory reflection and desirable cultivation of national law separating it from practice in Czech.

Besides German, French, and Russian, a surprising number of Czech pupils and students learn Spanish, perceiving it easier than other foreign languages. Individuals study major Asian languages: Arabic, Chinese, or Japanese. Job, hobby, ancestry, or partner motivate individuals to study also minor languages. It is unfortunate if achieved knowledge of these language vanishes in tertiary education.

4.3 Impetuous Anglicisation Averted

Quickly added Czech language requirement rendered mentioned announcements of vacant academic positions nonsense. Foreign "post-docs" do not understand it, continue to apply, and face exclusion on formal grounds. Fortunately, supporters of Anglicisation fail in their effort to compel local teachers and students to switch for English with the recruitment of international lecturers lacking knowledge of Czech.

We shall also appreciate that the Scientific Council dispensed from mandatory English in habilitation theses in fields of domestic law—civil, commercial, labor, constitutional, criminal, administrative, financial laws, as well as in legal theory and legal history. Professors from neighboring countries helped with explicit opinions. Legal scholars in Brno started to consider the relationship between law and language.[56] Unfortunately, such a waiver is hard to achieve for international law, international private law, and the European Union law.

However, the partial failure of the Faculty of Art to convince the same body and timorousness of the Faculty of Education, which prepares teachers for schools teaching almost exclusively in Czech, indicates that struggle for balance between Czech and English continues in Brno. Fortunately, the requirement did not survive

---

[55] Kischel (2015) considers non-existence of genuine in-depth study of foreign law (pp. 5–6). De-nationalisation cannot be perceived in tendency of American school of law towards teaching *eine Art fiktives, einheitlich amerikanisches Recht* (p. 303), because state laws are significantly closer and linguistically homogenous.

[56] Bejček (2017).

before its materialisation scheduled for 2022. New rector and his team recognised its strangeness and—perhaps, thanks to the COVID-19 pandemic distance deliberation—the University Academic Senate abolished it without, while stressing other forms of desirable internationalisation in exchange. Nevertheless, many Czech scholars and politicians continue to regard this form of Anglicisation as desirable.

4.4 *Need for Language Policy and Icelandic Inspiration*

Certainly, we can explain the measures mentioned above with psychology. Masaryk University is the 2nd biggest and strongest university in most rankings in Brno, which is the 2nd most populous city of Czechia. Ironically, Czechoslovakia established it as "the second Czech university" just one century ago in 1919.[57]

Masaryk University shall carefully ascertain the role of Czech as the national language (plus Slovak), English as global lingua franca, and other major and minor foreign languages. An explicit academic language policy is desirable. *Málstefna*, the language policy of *Háskoli Íslands* (the University of Iceland)[58] as a keystone institution of tertiary education established by a small nation defending its linguistic identity, could inspire.

References

Adam R (2012) Anglicizace češtiny a českého komunikačního prostoru [Anglicisation of Czech language and Czech communication space]. In: Hasil J (ed): Přednášky z 55. běhu Letní školy slovanských studií [Lectures of 55 year of Summer school of Slavic studies]. Filosofická fakulta Univerzity Karlovy, Praha pp 21–36

Ammon U (2001) The dominance of English as a language of science: effects on other languages and language communities. de Gruyter, Berlin

Bejček J (2017) Povinně cizojazyčné habilitace: mezi absurditou a "světovostí"? [Mandatory foreign-language theses for habilition proceedings: absurdity and worldwide reputation]. Časopis pro právní vědu a praxi [J Legal Sci Pract] 25(2):339–348

Berman H-J (2014) Justice in the U.S.S.R. An interpretation of soviet law. Harward University Press

Calvet L-J (2017) Les langues: quel avenir? Les effets linguistiques de la mondialisation [The languages: which future ? Language effects of globalisation]. CNRS Éditions, Paris

Coleman H (2010) Teaching and learning in Pakistan: the Role of Languages, the British Council

de Swaan A (2013) Words of the world: the global language system. Wiley

[57] *Zákon č. 50/1919 Sb. z. a n., kterým se zřizuje druhá česká univerzita* (Law on establishment of the second Czech university), adopted by the (provisional) National Assembly in 26th January 1919, see https://www.muni.cz/media/3062591/zakon_o_zrizeni_muni.gif.

[58] University of Iceland Language Policy, as approved by the University Forum on 10 May and by the University Council on 19 May 2016, https://english.hi.is/university/university_of_iceland_language_policy.

Epstein L (1927) Das Sprachenrecht der Tschechoslowakischen Republik: unter Berücksichtigung der Gesetzesmaterialien und der Rechtssprechung, mit Hinweisen und erläuternden Bemerkungen versehen. [Language law of Czechoslovak Republic. Consideration of travaux preparatoires and case-law…]. Verlag von Gebrüder Stiepel, Reichenberg (Liberec)

Fundárek J (1940) Tvorba slovenskej právnej terminologie [Establishing Slovak legal terminology]. Slovenská reč – Mesačník pre záujmy spisovného jazyka [Slovak language – Monthly for interest of codified language] 1:35–38

Grechenig K, Gelter M (2008) Divergente Evolution des Rechtsdenkens – Von Amerikanischen Rechtsökonomie und Deutscher Dogmatik [Diverging development of legal thought – about American law and economics and German dogmatics]. Rabels Zeitschrift für Ausländisches und Internationales Privatrecht 3:513–561

Grin F (2005) L'enseignement des langues comme politique publique (rapport Grin), Haut Conseil de l'evaluation de l'ecole, No 19. Available at http://www.ladocumentationfrancaise.fr/var/storage/rapports-publics/054000678.pdf

Harry RL (1978) Esperanto: an international language for international law. Cape West Reserve J Int Law 10(3):817–826

Hertel C (2009) Rechtskreise in Überblick [Legal circles in overview]. Notarius Int 1–2:157–170

Jamek V (2017) Pyl kapradiny aneb Ďjó, moře [Fern Pollen and Yeah, Sea]. Listy 4:30–32

Kalocsai K (2009) Erasmus exchange students: a behind-the-scenes view into an ELF community of practice. Apple J Appl Lang Stud 1:25–49

Kischel U (2015) Rechtsvergleichung, C. H. Beck, München

Kocbek A (2008) The challenges of intercultural legal communication. Int J Euro-Mediterr Stud 1 (1):53–70

Křepelka F (2010) Probleme mit neuen Sprachversionen des Europarechts [Problems with new versions of European law]. In: Fischer R (ed) Sprache und Recht in großen europäischen Sprachen [Language and law in major European Languages]. Universitätsverlag Regensburg, Regensburg, pp 233–246

Křepelka F (2012) Between legitimacy and efficiency. Recent developments of language regime in the European Union. In: Kuzelewska E, Kloza (eds) The challenges of modern democracy and European integration. Univerzytet w Bialymstoku, Oficyna Wydawnicza ASPRA-JR, Warszawa – Bialystok, pp 101–116

Křepelka F (2019) Soudobé jazykově-právní otázky v evropském Česku se zaostřením na akademické prostředí [Recent language-legal questions in European Czechia with Focus on Academia]. In: Kyselovská T, Sehnálek D, Rozehnalová N (eds) In varietate concordia - soubor vědeckých statí k poctě prof. Vladimíra Týče [In varietate Concordia – Collection of Papers Honouring Professor Vladimír Týč], Masarykova univerzita, Brno

Kudrová V (2011) Student's participation in higher education institution's bodies: czech experience. In: The international higher education congress: new trends and issues. Turkish Council of Higher Education, Istanbul, pp 2022–2028

Lillis T, Curry MJ (2010) Academic writing in a global context: the politics and practices of publishing in English. Routledge, London

Ljosland R (2007) English in Norwegian Academia: a step towards Diglossia? World Engl 26 (4):395–410

McAuliffe K (2013) The limitations of a multilingual legal system. Int J Semiot Law 26:861–882

McCrum R (2011) Globish: how the English Language became the worlds language. W.W. Norton & Company, New York

Phillipson R (1992) Linguistic imperialism. Oxford University Press, Oxford

Phillipson R (2009) Linguistic imperialism continued. Routledge, New York

Schelle K, Tauchen J (2009) Recht und Verwaltung im Protektorat Böhmen und Mähren Verlag Dr. Hut, München

Skřejpková P (2013) Profesor Robert Mayr-Harting a právnická fakulta Německé univerzity v Praze [Professor R. M.-H. and faculty of law of German University in Prague]. In: Tauchen J, Schelle K (eds) Češi a Němci v meziválečném Československu [Czechs and Germans in Interwar Czechoslovakia]. Key Publishing a European Society for History of Law, Ostrava, Brno, pp 250–252

Sukumane Joyce BG (1998) African languages, English, and educational policy in Namibia. Stud Linguist Sci 28(1):207–219

Velčovský V (2014) Nesoužití: česko-německá jazyková politika 18. - 20. Století [Living Apart: Czech-German Language Policy in 18th – 20th century]. Nakladatelství Lidové noviny, Praha

Bilingual Legal Education in Finland

Marcus Norrgård and Alicia Nylund

1 Finland and Bilingualism

1.1 The Notion of Bilingualism

Finland has two constitutionally recognized national languages, Finnish and Swedish, which means that bilingualism is a national cornerstone.

1.2 Finland and Bilingualism in General

Finland's judicial system is a civil law system and the primary source of law is the codified laws and statutes. The court system has two branches: courts with civil and criminal jurisdiction (District Courts—Courts of Appeal—Supreme Court) and courts with jurisdiction in administrative matters (Administrative Courts—Supreme Administrative Court).

The official languages of Finland are Finnish and Swedish, which is stated in the Constitution. However, on the Åland Islands which is an autonomous and demilitarized region, the official language is Swedish only. The Constitution further states that everyone has the right to use either Finnish or Swedish in communication with the national authorities. Finnish is spoken by approximately 90% of the population and Swedish by little over 5%. The Swedish-speaking Finns live mostly in the coastal areas of Finland and on the Åland Islands.

M. Norrgård · A. Nylund (✉)
University of Helsinki, Vaasa, Finland
e-mail: marcus.norrgard@helsinki.fi; alicia.nylund@helsinki.fi

N. Etcheverry Estrázulas (ed.), *Bilingual Study and Research*, Ius Comparatum – Global Studies in Comparative Law 58,
https://doi.org/10.1007/978-3-030-84550-6_6

1.3 Bilingualism in the Education System

Children permanently residing in Finland must attend compulsory schooling, which starts in the year the child turns seven (7 years old). Finland does not have compulsory school attendance since a child can be given instructions at home on the condition that the instructions correspond to the basic education. Basic education is free of charge and encompasses 9 years from the age of 7 to 16 years (7 to 16 years old).

Section 12 of the Basic Education Act (628/1998) states that, in keeping with the instruction language of the school, the pupils shall be taught Finnish, Swedish or Saami as a mother tongue, alternatively the Roma language, Sign language or some other language which is the pupil's native language. The instruction in mother tongue starts in the 1st form.

In schools where the instruction language is Swedish, the instruction in Finnish as the second national language normally starts in the lower forms (1st and 2nd form), while in Finnish schools the instruction in Swedish as the second national language generally starts later in the 6th or 7th form.

In the upper secondary education (optional after the completion of the basic education), there are also compulsory as well as optional (advanced) courses in the second national language. However, in the Matriculation Examination, it is no longer compulsory to take the test in the second national language. Since 2005, the only compulsory test is the one in the mother tongue.

English is normally taught as the first foreign language in the basic education as well as in the upper secondary education.

The higher education in Finland is divided into universities and polytechnics. Most of the universities have Finnish as their administrative language. These universities also do not, generally, have any of the teaching in Swedish. Courses given in English are nowadays, however, prevalent at all Finnish universities. Hanken School of Economics (with campuses in Helsinki and Vaasa) and Åbo Akademi University (with campuses in Turku and Vaasa) are the only two universities that are Swedish-speaking. The University of Helsinki is bilingual (Finnish/Swedish), which makes it a bit peculiar.

2 Bilingual Legal Education at the University of Helsinki

2.1 General Facts About the University of Helsinki and the Faculty of Law

The University of Helsinki was established in 1640 and is the oldest and largest university in Finland. The total number of the students at all levels is little over 32,000.

The University of Helsinki is the only bilingual university in Finland. The language of instruction and examination are Finnish, Swedish or English. The University of Helsinki is the only university in Finland that offers academic education in Swedish in the fields of law, medicine, social work, social psychology, veterinary medicine, agronomy, geography and journalism. According to section 74 of the Universities Act (558/2009), there shall be at least 28 professorships with Swedish being the teaching language at the University of Helsinki. Services and student counseling are provided in Finnish, Swedish and in English. There are also education programmes and courses in English in some fields at the university.

There are eleven faculties at the University of Helsinki. The Faculty of Law is the leading institute of legal education and research in Finland. The Faculty employs about 140 teachers and researchers.

About 2300 students are pursuing degrees in Finnish, Swedish and in English at the Faculty of Law. In addition, the Faculty hosts on a yearly basis about 140 exchange students from all over the world. Doctoral studies can be completed in any of the three languages as well. Studying abroad for a period is also a popular choice among law students. Since 1991, there is a Master of Laws diploma programme fully taught in English at the Faculty. This particular Master's programme is focusing on International Business Law (IBL), including: contract law, company law, intellectual property law, competition law and commercial disputes resolution.

There are separate tests and quotas for Finnish-speaking and Swedish-speaking applicants; therefore the applicants must, when applying, choose which of the two national languages will be the main language of their law degree. About 200 Finnish-speaking and 22 Swedish-speaking applicants are annually admitted to the education programme in Helsinki. The numbers for Vaasa are around 26 and 12 respectively.

2.2 *Structure and Content of the Legal Education*

2.2.1 Structure

The Bachelor of Laws degree comprises 180 ECTS credits, which is equivalent to 3 years of full-time studies. The Bachelor's programme includes a variety of studies and examination in compulsory as well as optional disciplines. It is possible to complete the Bachelor's degree as a bilingual degree, this implies that the student completes at least one third of the Bachelor's programme in the national language (Finnish or Swedish), that is not the student's main language of the degree. The student will then get a specific mention of the bilingualism in the degree diploma. The Bachelor of Laws degree does not qualify for the legal profession, hence law students generally pursue the Master of Laws degree that comprises 300 ECTS credits (180 + 120). The Master's programme comprises 120 ECTS credits, which is equivalent to 2 years of full-time studies. The Master's programme includes some compulsory disciplines and advanced studies in discipline(s) of the student's own choice. The emphasis of the Master's programme lies, however, on the Master's thesis.

2.2.2 Studies, Courses and Examination

The legal studies include courses and examinations, which generally require a lot of individual reading of textbooks. Lectures series are held annually in every compulsory discipline. Normally the lecture series end with a minor exam, an essay or a study diary. The final exams are usually in the form of book exams or take-home exams.

The teaching language depends on the teacher; in some disciplines, there are parallel lectures in Finnish and in Swedish, and in other disciplines the lectures are given in one language only. Sometimes there are also lectures in English if the teacher does not speak either of the two national languages or if the subject is very international such as public international law or energy law. The students are, however, always entitled to write their exams and course work in Finnish or in Swedish regardless of the language of the lectures. In exceptional cases, though, where the teacher is foreign, the students may be asked to do the lecture exam or the written assignment in English, but then the students are allowed to use dictionaries.

The course material is usually in the language of the lectures or the language of the course. However, the literature relating to the specific disciplines, i.e. the exam literature, is mainly in Finnish. There is a shortage of Swedish legal literature dealing with Finnish law, which puts the students who are pursuing a degree in Swedish at a disadvantage.

There are compulsory seminars in specific disciplines, where the students train in academic legal writing and in acting as an opponent of another student's text; hence the seminar courses comprise of both writing and discussions. These seminars are held in Finnish, Swedish and/or English.

2.3 *The Vaasa Unit of Legal Studies*

Since 1991, the Faculty of Law at the University of Helsinki has maintained a unit of legal studies in Vaasa. The population of Vaasa is about 67,000, 70% of whom have Finnish, 23% Swedish and 7% other languages as their mother tongue.

The main reason behind the establishment of a campus in Vaasa was the need for bilingual legal practitioners in the region. The city has a District Court, a Court of Appeal, an Administrative Court with special competence in environmental matters, a prosecutor's office, a Regional State Administrative Agency, a Center for Economic Development, Transport and the Environment, a Tax Office and many solicitor's offices. In addition to this, the Vaasa region is the home of the largest energy technology cluster of the Nordic Countries and many international enterprises. Due to this there is a growing need for multilingual legal expertise in these business fields.

In the late 1980s it was felt that there was a clear shortage of lawyers competent in both national languages in the Vaasa region. Thus, the Faculty of Law at the University of Helsinki established a campus in Vaasa.

The aim at the Vaasa Unit is to ensure that equal instruction proportions are given in Finnish and in Swedish. The study environment in Vaasa is truly bilingual; both students and teachers use Finnish and Swedish interchangeably. The students are not required to become fully fluent in both national languages, but they must be able to understand instruction and study materials in Finnish, Swedish and also in English to some extent.

3 Evaluation of the Bilingual Legal Education System

It is essential for a country with two national languages and where the citizens have the right to communicate in either one of these languages, that the Faculty of Law is able to educate lawyers with sufficient skills in both national languages.

The language policy of the Vaasa Unit is a bit peculiar; it could be characterized as extremely liberal: everybody—teachers, students, and administrative staff—can use either Finnish or Swedish of their own choosing and the recipient must accept that choice and be prepared to understand the speaker.

The discussion on bilingualism is, at least in Finland, **actually more a question of multilingualism**. The University of Helsinki has a great national responsibility regarding the legal education in Finland, since it is the only provider of a full law degree in both national languages.

Over the years, the legal education has been permeated with an international perspective. In addition to the International Master's programme, the Faculty of Law is involved in several international projects. Collaboration with researchers outside Finland is also very common. Furthermore, the main publication language in some of the more international fields is English. Companies, and thus also legal counsel, work increasingly in an English-speaking environment with all communication (including contracts) being drawn up in English. Thus, legal education programmes are today in fact tri- or multilingual, albeit that officially degrees are still only mono- or bilingual.

Bilingual Legal Education: A French Perspective

Anne Brunon-Ernst

1 Background to Bilingual Legal Education

Language has always been key to the building of nation-states in Europe, thus explaining the prevalence of monolingual States. Their promotion was justified on grounds that the territory of a State ought to be defined by common linguistic and cultural boundaries. Conversely, this gave rise to independence movements and greater demands for minority-language recognition, thus paving the way for the first bilingual higher education institutions as early as the 19th c (Arzoz 2012a,

The reporter wishes to extend her warmest thanks for their help in identifying the relevant sources and collecting data: Mr Manuel Miler (Chief Registrar, University Paris 2), Professor Jennifer Merchant (University Paris 2), Dr Georgia Schneider (University Paris 2), Professor Sandrine Clavel (Head of the French Law Faculty Dean Board, University Versailles Saint-Quentin), Professor Pascale Laborier (University Paris 10), Professor Christine Neau-Leduc (University Paris 1), Professor Miguel-Angel Campos-Pardillos (University of Alicante), Professor Charles Videgain (Université de Pau et des Pays de l'Adour), Dr Eneritz Zabaleta, Mrs Emilie Desconet (Université de Pau et des Pays de l'Adour). She is also grateful to her colleagues: Professor Catherine Resche, Dr Marc Eline and Mrs Solène Semichon (University Paris 2) for their comments on the draft.

A. Brunon-Ernst (✉)
Panthéon-Assas University, Paris, France
e-mail: anne.brunon-ernst@u-paris2.fr

N. Etcheverry Estrázulas (ed.), *Bilingual Study and Research*, Ius Comparatum – Global Studies in Comparative Law 58,
https://doi.org/10.1007/978-3-030-84550-6_7

p. 11).[1] Nowadays, the preservation of national[2] and regional languages[3] has been given supra-national legal support by France's membership of the European Union (EU). Bilingual education thus has a long-standing history, which predates the EU integration, and which cannot be isolated from the social, political and institutional contexts of its creation and continued existence (Purser 2002, pp. 20–22).[4] Because of the relative decline of the nation-state models in the Post War era and globalised higher-education and employment markets, it is reasonable to assume that bilingual education is bound to be on the rise.[5]

The case of "bilingual *legal* education" (BLE) is unique in more ways than one. Law cannot exist outside language (Arzoz 2012b, p. 24). Law is drafted, enforced and administered through acts of language. Moreover, legal concepts take meaning within their own legal system, thus they are highly dependent on the frame of reference set by the legal order. To a more limited extent, this can also be true of trans-national legal subjects such as EU law (Taylor 2005, pp. 221–243). Far more than in any bilingual programme involving any other discipline, BLE has always entailed more than simply using a different language as a teaching medium, as the very content of the law is system-bound (Sarcevic 2000, p. 233). Some concepts might not have any equivalent in another legal system (e.g.: there is no translation for the English legal concept of trust in French law), or might describe a particular position in the justice system which has no equivalent in another (e.g.: there is no

[1] In Europe, the first established bilingual university was the University of Freiburg in 1889.

[2] The European Union is committed to protecting the linguistic diversity of the Union, as evidenced by the availability of legal documents in all the official languages of the Union. Article 3 of the Treaty on the European Union, Article 165(1) of the Treaty on the Functioning of the European Union and Article 22 of the Charter of Fundamental Rights of the European Union are the legal basis for the protection of the official languages of the member States.

[3] The European Charter for Regional or Minority Languages protects regional and minority languages. Article 1 (a) of the Charter defines the concept "'regional or minority languages' means languages that are (i) traditionally used within a given territory of a State by nationals of that State who form a group numerically smaller than the rest of the State's population; and (ii) different from the official language(s) of that State. It does not include either dialects of the official language(s) of the State or the languages of migrants". The Charter promotes education in the regional language (Article 7). Article 8 clearly recommends that "the Parties undertake ... to make available university and other higher education in regional or minority languages; or to provide facilities for the study of these languages as university and higher education subjects". France signed the Charter in 1999 but has not yet ratified it. Local governments are encouraged to apply the principles contained in the Charter within their area of competence. Seven regional languages have been identified in France: Basque, Breton, Catalan, Corsican, Dutch (Western Flemish and standard Dutch), German (dialects of German and standard German, regional language of Alsace-Moselle) and Occitan. See http://www.coe.int/en/web/european-charter-regional-or-minority-languages/promoting-ratification-in-france.

[4] The Bologna Declaration also stresses the social, cultural, political and economic importance of education in the EU construction: it states that: "the importance of education and educational co-operation in the development and strengthening of stable, peaceful and democratic societies is universally acknowledged as paramount".

[5] Although not dealt with in the present report, the issue of the rise in immigration to the EU might bolster the need for bilingual education while at the same time radically changing its landscape.

equivalent in the common law of the French *juge d'instruction*). Thus, BLE has to teach also skills which are not legal *per se,* but linguistic, such as, but not restricted to, the ability to translate, switch languages and design information bilingually (Garcia 2009, p. 297).

2 Defining Bilingual Legal Education in the French Context

France has one official language: French. It is a one-language State. If it has indeed promoted the revival of regional dialects (*Basque, Breton, Alsacien*, etc.) through a wide range of initiatives, including primary and secondary education teaching and cultural awareness programmes, the knowledge of these regional languages is neither mandatory in the education system nor required to hold any public office. To the author's knowledge, there are no bilingual legal programmes in France which would include the teaching of law in any one of those regional languages.[6] Although historically bilingual education originated with the rise of minority-language recognition, in the French context, the meaning of BLE is necessarily restricted to the teaching of law(s) in two different national languages (as opposed to a regional and a national language).

The present report therefore considers the use of BLE as referring to the teaching of a law programme in two different languages, one of which would be French, and the other a foreign language (referred to for the purpose of the report as the target language). The most widely taught bilingual law programmes are in French and English,[7] but there are a wide range of possible combinations (Spanish, German, Italian, Russian, Mandarin-Chinese, etc.).

Bilingual legal programmes can be taught exclusively in France, or include one or more university terms in the country whose legal system is taught (referred to for the purpose of the report as the target legal system). The report excludes from its scope any programme which might be taught exclusively in an institution outside France. It thus considers only programmes taught either in France, or part in France and part abroad. The restriction of the scope of the study arises from the fact that any different

[6] Arzoz's paper on "Basque-Medium Legal Education in the Basque Country" (pp. 135–166) describes Basque legal education in the Basque region. I am grateful to Emilie Desconet, Professor Charles Videgain and Dr. Eneritz Zabaleta (Université de Pau et des Pays de l'Adour) for confirming that there was presently no French-Basque legal education programme in the French Basque region (contrary to the Spanish Basque region).

[7] When programmes have a strong international focus, they always include English as one of the languages of instruction (Arzoz 2012b, p. 24). On the issue of English as a *lingua franca*, see: Ammon (2001); Ammon and McConnell (2003); Crystal (2003); Phillipson (2003); Smith (2010); Jenkins (2007); Campos (2010), pp. 175–194; Modiano (1999), pp. 23–25.

In the wake of the Brexit referendum, politicians, journalists and academics are wondering what will be the fate of English as a *lingua franca* in a European Union without the British membership (Campos 2017).

institutional, academic, linguistic and teaching context makes access to relevant data more complex.

The underlying assumption in BLE is that part of a law programme is being taught in another language. The focus is therefore on the language in which law is taught, rather than the legal system which is being taught in a foreign language. Three different cases may arise:

- Firstly, the most common type of bilingual legal programmes is to teach the law of the target legal system fully or partially in the target language; an instance of this would be English common law taught either fully in English, or partly in English and French.
- Secondly, wishing to develop programmes to attract international students or French students seeking a truly BLE training, programmes are designed which teach a certain number of legal subjects in the target language, especially subjects which deal typically with trans-national law, such as international law, human rights law, international criminal law, EU law, etc.
- Thirdly, programmes which offer French law taught exclusively in a foreign language (English mainly) target mainly international students. As the language of law often describes concepts and a system which are unique and specific to a particular legal order, the teaching of the target legal system in a language other than the target language represents a challenge in itself.

There is a wide range of programmes which offer some form of BLE, with varying degrees of legal and linguistic specialisation. Many undergraduate or post-graduate programmes in France offer law as one of the modules students may choose from when they major in economics, history of art, languages, sciences, etc. For the sake of simplicity—and because the report is addressed to jurists of the *Académie internationale de droit comparé*—only law degrees *per se* are considered here. The present report does not consider any law course which is not part of a recognised law degree. The French legal education landscape is made more complex by the com-pulsion to teach at least one foreign language at master's level.[8] The report addresses the preliminary conditions under which a legal programme in France may be considered as bilingual, relating to teaching time allocated to the target language. Does a law programme require a minimum number of hours taught in the target language to qualify as "bilingual"? Is one module (18 to 37.5 h of teaching per year) sufficient to fulfil the "bilingual programme" requirement, or should a more sub-stantial proportion of the teaching be taught in the target language to meet the standard? Moreover, the concept of BLE itself seems to point to something more than just a module or a minimum number of ECTS. Indeed, the underlying assump-tion in the concept of "bilingual education" is that the target language is given equal

[8]The master's degree can only be awarded in France if a foreign language module is offered in first (master 1) or in second (master 2) year of the master's programme, and if the mastery of at least one foreign language is certified. See Article 16 of Title III of Decree of 22 January 2014 on the national framework of programmes allowing the issue of national degrees of bachelor, vocational bachelor and master.

status in terms of contents and teaching time as subjects matters taught in French. However, instances of such programmes are rare in France (double degrees: *bi-licence,* and joint-degrees: *double diplôme*). It would unjustifiably reduce the scope of the study to focus only on these limited initiatives and exclude those which fail to meet the stringent standard of an equal number of hours taught in French and in the target language.

The rationale of the present report is to be as *inclusive* as possible to look into all the different ways in which some form of BLE is provided by the French higher education system. This means that the mere presence of legal teaching in a target language qualifies the programme for inclusion in the discussion. While it might be a little strained to consider language tutorials (18- to 37.5 h per year) as qualifying any French degree for BLE, the reporter, a legal English academic, will explore the input of the teaching methods and approaches used in legal English and discuss whether the model could be adapted to design effective bilingual legal education in Sect. 7.

These preliminary comments aim at circumscribing the scope of the study. However, they also highlight diversity in BLE. The report tries to dis-entangle the complex workings of the system by first offering an analytical table of the types of bilingual programmes (Sect. 3), in the extended meaning given above, before moving on to describing the French institutional setting which underlines the constraints bearing on the system and the reasons for such a diverse landscape (Sect. 4). This explains in part why the system is mainly demand-oriented, responding to the increased calls from students (Sect. 5) and from employers (Sect. 6). The layout and workings of BLE lays the groundwork to consider the challenges facing this type of initiatives and suggestions are made to make BLE an effective tool for graduate employment in a competitive and globalised economy (Sect. 7).

3 Mapping French Bilingual Legal Education

In 2015–2016, there were 209,894 students enrolled in law and political sciences programmes at university.[9] 124,610 were enrolled in an undergraduate course, 78,058 in a postgraduate course and 7226 in a PhD programme. 23,202 bachelor's degrees (*licence*),[10] 19,426 master's degrees (*master 1* and *master 2*),[11] and 887 doctorates were awarded. 26.8% of undergraduate students in law, political sciences and economics passed their undergraduate degree within the statutory 3 years. There

[9]Data in this section are taken from the 2016 "Repères, références et statistiques: Enseignement, formation, recherche", issued by the Direction de l'évaluation, de la prospective et de la performance of the Ministry of Education, Higher Education and Research, p. 154f and p. 246f. Official statistics do not distinguish law from political sciences.

[10]Among which 1829 vocational degrees (*licence professionnelle*).

[11]9787 master's degrees (professional track (*master professionnel*)) and 2575 master's degrees (research track (*master recherche*)), were awarded in 2015–2016.

were 14.1% foreign students in French universities,[12] an increase from 13.5% 30 years ago. Half of the foreign students came from the African continent, a quarter from Europe (4/5th of them came from the EU), a fifth from Asia and the rest from the Americas.

Within the French higher education context, BLE is to be construed as a relatively new and developing area of legal education. It is to be assessed as against the background of a "standard track law degree", which would include foundation subjects in law at the undergraduate level and non-mandatory language classes;[13] and specialised legal subjects in law at the post-graduate level and compulsory language classes and certification. Any programme departing from this traditional track will be termed "specific-track". Table 1 maps cases when BLE is taught in French universities or in programmes set up by French universities. In order to present an exhaustive picture, all cases have been registered, however, entries with asterisks will not be dealt with in the present study as explained above (Sect. 2):

The table contributes to highlight the different audiences targeted by different types of programmes: some aim to target French students exclusively, others a mix of French and foreign students (e.g.: in joint-programmes), others focus exclusively on foreign students (e.g.: LLM programmes in France or abroad, or specific Erasmus tracks). This has an impact on the level of knowledge programme entrants are expected to have in the French and the target legal system, as well as in French and any target language of teaching. The heterogeneous audiences for which standard-track or specific-track programmes are designed might have a direct or indirect impact on which subjects are taught, how, by whom and when. As the purpose of the programmes is to train quality jurists, selection for specific-track and exchange programmes, as well as for optional/advanced certificates, is not based on target language proficiency. Even if some universities require minimum CEFR levels (B2 or C1),[14] the language level of entrants is often deemed insufficient by host institutions.

The table helps identify four categories of BLE:

- **Exchange programmes**: Students who have participated in an Erasmus or other international exchange programme can be considered as having had a BLE; the report focuses on French students sent to institutions abroad and not incoming students;
- **Double and joint-degrees**: Undergraduates in double degrees involving a law degree and a language degree in a French university can be considered as having

[12] This table includes foreign nationals who have studied in the French secondary school system but are not French nationals.

[13] There is no legal obligation to teach a foreign language at undergraduate level. Each university is free to make it a mandatory requirement for the award of a bachelor's degree. In practice, very few programmes do not offer either optional or mandatory language classes at undergraduate level.

[14] *Common European Framework of Reference for Languages: Learning, teaching, assessment* (CEFR). See note 34 and section 7 for further discussion on this point.

Table 1 Table of the different BLE-programme categories in France

Programme type	Target audience	Language of teaching law	Country of teaching
Standard-track law degree			
Law degree	French students mainly	French in the standard track law programme Foreign language if language tutorials	France
Law degree with optional certificate/advanced programme specializing in another legal system	French students mainly	French in the standard track law programme Foreign language if language tutorials Certificate/advanced programme: Fully or partially in the target language	France
Law degree with selection for an exchange programme (e.g. Erasmus)	French students mainly	In France: French in the standard track law programme Foreign language if language tutorials During the exchange: Target language with the standard track law programme or Target language in seminars designed for exchange students and possibly Target language classes designed for exchange students	France and target country
Specific-track law degree			
Double degrees awarded by a French university	French students mainly	In the law degree French and Target language, if one or more modules taught on the target system In the language degree Target language	France
Double degrees awarded by a French university with selection for an exchange programme (e.g. Erasmus)	French students mainly	In France: In the law degree French and Target language, if one or more modules taught on the target system In the language degree Target language	France and target country

(continued)

Table 1 (continued)

Programme type	Target audience	Language of teaching law	Country of teaching
		During the exchange: Target language with the standard track law programme or Target language in seminars designed for exchange students And possibly Target language classes designed for exchange students	
Joint-degree or joint-programme jointly awarded with a foreign institution	French students and students from the foreign joint-university	In France French and Target language, if one or more modules taught on the target system Foreign language (generally target language) if compulsory language tutorials In the target country Target language	France and target country
Programmes designed for foreign law students			
*Exchange programme (e.g.: Erasmus)[a]	Incoming foreign students	French in the standard track law programme Foreign language if compulsory language tutorials French if compulsory or optional academic or legal French language classes or French or English in seminars designed for exchange students	France
*LLM[b]	Foreign students exclusively	English exclusively[c] French if compulsory or optional academic or legal French language classes[d]	France exclusively and/or France and abroad

(continued)

Table 1 (continued)

Programme type	Target audience	Language of teaching law	Country of teaching
*LLM	French and foreign students	English exclusively	Abroad exclusively (Dubai, Singapore, China etc)

[a]Universities at a local level will choose different strategies to deal with exchange students: some will allow students to register in the standard track law programme, some set up special programmes taught in English, others allow a mix of both

[b]French legal provisions relating to the obligation to teach in French do not apply to these programmes. See the French Education Code: "Foreign institutions or institutions set up for students who are foreign nationals, as well as institutions teaching international programmes do not need to comply with the obligations (to be taught in French)" (Article L. 121-3)

[c]French law forbids the exclusive teaching of a programme in a foreign language: "Higher education programmes can only be partially offered in a foreign language" (French Code of Education, Article L. 121-3). However, an overview of the French LLM programmes targeting foreign students shows that either they are exclusively taught in English (students can also attend French as a second language classes) or that students can ask to register for a module taught in French. All these programmes need to be approved by the French Ministry of Higher Education and Research

[d]For foreign students enrolled in these programmes, attending French language classes depends on their entry level in French. See the French Education Code: "Foreign students attending programmes taught in a foreign language are enrolled in classes of French as a foreign language if their mastery of French is not deemed adequate" (Article L. 121-3)

Entries with asterisks list programmes that are not dealt with in the present study

had a BLE; as well as those enrolled in joint-degrees involving a programme of teaching over several years in one or more universities;

- **Degrees partially taught in a foreign language**: Under- or post-graduates who hold standard track law degrees with compulsory legal English language modules coupled with optional certificate/advanced programmes specializing in another legal system are considered as having a BLE;
- **Degrees exclusively taught in a foreign language**: LLM-type programmes are taught generally in English and are fee-paying; whether in France or abroad, they target foreign students mainly and fall outside the scope of the present study.

Of note the fact that all law students are registered for language classes which are compulsory at master level. The contents of the language teaching might qualify the module for inclusion in BLE. If so, all French students reading law are given a BLE in a limited degree.

Notwithstanding this diverse landscape, it is possible to identify common features and challenges in bilingual legal education in France.

4 Institutional Settings

The French public university system is fully or partially State-funded.[15] Certification of programmes for the award of national degrees is granted exclusively by the State. The same procedure applies also to private higher education institutions which are allowed to award standard French undergraduate and post-graduate degrees (*licence* (LLB), *master* (LLM), *doctorat* (doctorate)) if their legal programme complies with the standards set by the French Ministry of Higher Education and Research.[16] Although over the past decade, there has been a drive towards more autonomous management of French universities,[17] which has not always been successful,[18] the certification system has not evolved significantly.[19] Thus the French State has sufficient leverage to create effective incentives for universities to comply with any education policy. However, it stands in a double-bind. On the one hand, it seeks to encourage foreign student enrolments and French student mobility,[20] but on the other hand, it imposes French as the compulsory language of teaching.[21] Only a certain number of exceptions to the "Loi Toubon" make it possible for French universities to teach their programmes in another language than French.[22] In prac-

[15] French Code of Education, Article L. 712-9.

[16] French Code of Education, Article L. 613-1.

[17] French Code of Education, Article L. 712-8.

[18] See for instance the motion moved by the Advisory Body of University Presidents on the National University budget dated 25 October 2013.

[19] Over the last 10 years, the number of undergraduate law and political sciences programmes has increased from 10,085 to 21,373 (and from 704 to 1829 in the vocational track). For the postgraduate law and political sciences programmes, the increase has been from 7218 to 9787 in the professional track and from 2449 to 2572 in the research track (which leads to doctoral thesis). For doctoral studies, programmes have increased from 710 to 952. The overall increase in the number of programmes contributes to the complexity and the diversity of legal education in France. The rise is spread across all disciplines, and the loss of attractiveness in research master tracks is similar. See "Repères, références et statistiques: Enseignement, formation, recherché", issued by the Direction de l'évaluation, de la prospective et de la performance of the Ministry of Education, Higher Education and Research, 2016, p. 154f and p. 246f.

[20] France is a signatory of the Bologna Convention (1999) which sets up mechanisms to encourage student mobility.

[21] Referred to as Loi Toubon, the legal obligation is encapsulated in Law n°94-665 of 4 August 1994 on the use of French language and reads as follows: "Pursuant to the Constitution, French is the official language of the Republic (. . .). It is the language used in education, communication, the work place and public services." (Article 1). This obligation is affirmed in the French Code of Education "French is the language of teaching, assessment and competitive exams, as well as of doctorates and theses in public and private teaching institutions" (Article 2).

[22] Referred to as Loi Fioraso, the exceptions are encapsulated in Article 2 of Law n°2013-660 of 22 July 2013 on higher education and research which amend Article L121-3 of the French Code of Education, and provide that: "French is the language of teaching, assessment and competitive

tice, law faculties have been able to make use of the exceptions provided in the "Loi Fioraso" to develop the wide range of BLE presented in Table 1. Nonetheless the official language requirement might slow down the growth of BLE in the future.

Setting aside the transnational forums, such as the European Research Area and the Ius Commune Research School (Sibony 2016, pp. 47–60), and scientific associations (such as the APLIUT and GERAS in France),[23] discussions about the introduction of a bilingual legal programme are carried out at the level of each faculty, university or university consortium.[24] The development of bilingual legal education relies heavily on the endeavours of some academics, with some form of institutional support either from the university or from the consortium. Recognition of the role played locally by academics is essential to understand the structure of BLE in France. This makes for a very diverse landscape of BLE, as sketched in Table 1. The local nature of the bilingual initiatives also entails that it is difficult to identify a single driving force behind the development of these programmes. Opportunity for designing BLE arises from individual interest and the existence of an international network of academics, as well as a mix of push and pull factors, as individual academic initiatives are supported by increased demands on the part of students for BLE (Sect. 5) and on the part of employers (law firm, in-house legal departments, government positions, etc) for graduates with a command of one or more foreign language(s) (Sect. 6 below).

The description of the institutional settings of BLE did not consider whether there might be a hidden agenda in the pace of its development. Indeed, as aptly stated by research in the field: "behind the educational agenda are political, social, and economic agendas that serve to protect the interests of particular political and social groups" (Tsu and Tollefson 2004, p. 4). The reporter does not challenge this assessment, however on account of the local nature of the development of BLE, she has been unable to identify one single driving force which would help pinpoint a unique interest that is being protected by its promotion or impediment.

There are of course stumbling blocks in the path of BLE: some arise at the level of the French Ministry of Higher Education and Research, and might be prompted by the need to keep university budgets within manageable bounds, and some originate from local opposition to BLE. Indeed, in the latter case, opposition can be grounded on diverging positions as to the foundation subjects which are essential to ensure

---

exams, as well as of doctorates and theses in public and private teaching institutions. Exceptions can be justified

(1) on account of the specific requirements of teaching regional or foreign languages and cultures;
(2) when the teachers are associate or invited professors from foreign institutions;
(3) on account of teaching-related requirements, as when the courses are taught pursuant to an agreement with a foreign or international institution (. . .) or pursuant to a European programme;
(4) on account of the development of trans-national and multi-lingual programmes and degrees."

[23] APLIUT (Association des Professeurs de Langues des Instituts Universitaires de Technologie) and GERAS (Groupe d'Etude et de Recherche en Anglais de Spécialité) are scientific associations which aims at promoting teaching of and research on English for Specific Purposes.

[24] University consortiums group several universities and/or higher education institutions.

effective legal education, or on retaining existing curricula (as introducing BLE would lead to the reduction of teaching hours in existing programmes), or on the insufficient pool of academics with the required legal and linguistic skills to teach those programmes, or then again on failing to identify the need for BLE. These problems will be further discussed in Sects. 6.2 and 7.

This section has sought to identify the horizontal and vertical institutional, professional and interpersonal settings which make the development of BLE possible. As set out in a research paper, linguistic policies are "never simply an accident, but rather results of deliberate decisions involving more than simply the academic community" (Purser 2002, p. 452). Among the other players which have a stake in legal education policies, students and employers have a key role in creating a demand-led market for BLE.

5 Global Drive for Bilingual Legal Programmes

Students are well aware that speaking a foreign language is an asset in the workplace. Although the mastery of at least one foreign language is compulsory to be awarded a master's degree,[25] employers tend to rely on international certification levels, evidence of linguistic stays or traineeship abroad, dual-national status, or any other bilingual/multilingual legal education programme as evidence of the mastery of effective language skills. Studies on graduate employment do not establish a causal link between a stay abroad and increased employment rate in comparison with peers (Calmand et al. 2016). However, when the impact of extended stays (more than 6 months) or certificating exchange programmes is considered singly, the marginal advantage of international experience is clear.

This section looks into three sets of BLE: international exchange programmes, double and joint-degrees and degrees partially taught in a foreign language.

5.1 International Exchange Programmes

Widespread undergraduate and postgraduate interest in bilingual legal programmes certainly springs from the rise in EU student mobility programmes, especially the Erasmus exchange programme.[26] Even if in practice language requirements are not the determining factor of selection for an exchange programme, the opportunities offered by such programmes give more clout to language-teaching and learning in law faculties. Moreover, the availability of English-language programmes tailored

[25] See note 9.

[26] The Erasmus programme was set up following the Bologna Declaration of 19 June 1999 (Joint declaration of the European Ministers of Education).

for foreign exchange students should not be underestimated in the rising demands from French students for access to equivalent programmes in their own under- or postgraduate degrees. Conversely, French students returning from an exchange abroad (especially non-English speaking countries) having experienced adapted law programmes generally taught in English also wish the creation of similar programmes in France.

The driving force behind the Bologna Declaration was the development of a European area of higher education to promote employability.[27] Student mobility was key to achieving the competitiveness and attractiveness of the European system of higher education. However, the effective benefits of the programme are a far cry from the wide-ranging principles of the different declarations. In 2004–2005, only 1% of French students went on an Erasmus exchange (22,000 students/year). 7% of these students were registered in legal programmes abroad (1500 students). Two-thirds of Erasmus students went to Spanish, British, German and Italian universities (Agbossou et al. 2007). Students who participate in the Erasmus exchange programme get a bilingual legal education for one-to-two university terms in a foreign country.

Erasmus programmes are not the only possibility for legal students to study abroad. At the local level, and in accordance with the recommendations of the Bologna Convention, universities have developed exchange programmes with other universities. This creates more opportunities for students to get a BLE for one-to-two terms. As programmes are administered locally and as universities have their individually-negotiated partnership agreements, it is difficult to have a bird's-eye view on these programmes as well as national data on the number of students involved. As in the case of Erasmus, students who are selected for these programmes are the happy few.

The common feature of both types of exchange programmes is that students are generally integrated within programmes in the host university, attending some or all of the law classes either in the target language or in English. This practice raises two separate issues. The first relates to the legal content of the programme. The modules taught to the student might not be geared towards building the students' *legal* skills but chosen or imposed on account of availability of the module in English, or of the relevance of teaching law in a language other than that of the host country (trans-national subjects). Students generally also attend introductory courses to the law of the host country. The second pertains to language skills. As students are required to have minimum language level entry requirements for application to most host universities, language support might be inexistent or insufficient to meet student's academic needs. Moreover, even if the student does acquire bilingual legal skills, it is rarely done by a structured and tutored approach, and whatever bilingual legal skills are learnt, they are not evidenced by any form of specific certification (Blons-Pierre 2016, p. 184).

[27] The Sorbonne Declaration of 25th of May 1998.

The available data shows that only a minority of law students can take advantage of a term in a law faculty abroad. Notwithstanding grants available (Erasmus grants, etc.), there are also effective financial hurdles for students from non-affluent backgrounds. Other options are nonetheless available to offer BLE to a greater number of law students.

5.2 Double Degrees and Joint Law Degrees

Double degrees are to be distinguished from joint-degrees. In this report, a double degree refers exclusively to a programme which includes the completion of both a law degree and a language degree (*bi-licence*), whereas a joint-law degree is awarded by two law faculties in two different institutions, one of which is abroad (*bi-diplôme*). The aim of these degrees is to make students conversant in two or more legal systems and provide them with the required language skills to work in both languages. These programmes can be considered as the only two instances of a truly integrated BLE in France.

The rationale in the conception of joint-degrees is a purpose-built programme providing the necessary skills and foundation knowledge to be proficient to understand and apply the law of two different legal systems. The conception of double degrees follows different rules. At any time, students enrolled in double degrees can switch to take only one degree (either law or language). They need to be taught the minimum foundation subjects that will make the switch possible. The principles underlying the design of double degrees therefore differ significantly from those of joint-degrees.

There are very few programmes in France which give students such a level of integrated BLE.[28] The selection process for access to these programmes is stringent. The programme itself requires a high level of student commitment.

The advantage for under- and post-graduates is their effective knowledge of two legal systems, thus enabling them, theoretically at least, to become certified lawyers in two different countries—provided graduates take 1 year of preparation (or more) to the bar exam (generally in France and in the target country)—, to practice in companies in France or abroad, or in the legal departments of international corporations.

[28] University Paris 10-Nanterre, University of Versailles Saint-Quentin, University of Nantes, University of Tours, University of Amiens, University of Grenoble, University Paris 2-Panthéon-Assas in association with ISIT Translation School, etc.

5.3 Degrees Partially Taught in a Foreign Language

These degrees are standard-track undergraduate or post-graduate law degrees with additional modules built into the programme. Access to these modules is generally selective and leads to the award of a certificate or diploma for successful students after a 1- to 3-year course. They can be managed by language departments, which can award a legal language certificate, or by law faculties. In the latter case, they either grant diplomas, offering an additional track to students (e.g.: diploma in common law, in German law etc) or integrated modules in advanced legal language or law taught in the target language (e.g.: *Magistère* programmes).

- In the case of the certificate taught by language departments, the module is taught in the target language. As the classes are taught by language teachers, the focus is on the legal terminology/phraseology of the target legal system.
- For diplomas administered by law faculties, there are two different approaches:
  - Additional diplomas: The focus is on teaching the target legal system in French or in the target language, but not on developing language communication skills. The perspective is that of comparative law, giving students a bird's-eye view of another legal system, and aims at enhancing their knowledge of law, acquired in other law classes.
  - Integrated advanced module: The focus is on improving both the legal and the language skills in a particular target legal system. Some form if Content and Language Integrated Learning is included in these modules.

The advantage for under- and post-graduates is the additional skills they can add to their resume. Depending on the reputation of the diploma/certificate, the diploma/certificate holder will increase likelihood of admission to a selective post-graduate programme in France or abroad, or employability in sought-for legal positions.

The rationale for BLE is the competitive advantage granted by additional language and legal skills. The focus is very strongly on the employability of graduates and meeting demands for international jurists in the workplace.

6 Need for Bilingual Jurists and How to Meet It

6.1 Bilingual Legal Skills in the Workplace

In France, law graduates are a very diverse body of students and not all of them move on to becoming lawyers. Law is often considered as a wise undergraduate choice, as it gives technical knowledge and allows easy bridges towards other specialties (politics, civil service, journalism, management, economics, academia, etc.).

Notwithstanding the career choices law graduates make, the primary aim of legal education is to train jurists, in the public or private sector, who are specialists in their own legal systems. Except in cases of joint-degrees, graduates do not have the same

Table 2 Legal and language skills taught and matching employment needs

Profession	Legal skills needed in the target system	Language skills needed in the target language
Lawyer/Jurists		
In a French law firm	Knowledge of the legal rules and procedures of the target system in the specialty	Ability to translate and design information bilingually Ability to communicate clearly and effectively (present, discuss, convince and negotiate)
In a law firm in the target country	Extra-qualifications needed (esp. Bar exam)	Extra-skills needed (esp. ability to use language on a par with a native speaker)
In a legal department	Knowledge of the legal rules and procedures of the target system in the specialty	Ability to translate and design information bilingually Ability to communicate clearly and effectively (present, discuss, convince and negotiate)
In an international NGO	Knowledge of the legal rules and procedures in international law and in the target system in the specialty	Ability to translate and design information bilingually Ability to communicate clearly and effectively (present, discuss, convince and negotiate)
Civil servant		
In an international organisation	Knowledge of the legal rules and procedures in international law	Ability to translate and design information bilingually Ability to communicate clearly and effectively (present, discuss, convince and negotiate)
In a government department	Knowledge of the legal rules and procedures of the target system in the field	Ability to translate and design information bilingually Ability to communicate clearly and effectively (present, discuss, convince and negotiate)
In a local government department	Limited knowledge needed unless interactions with foreign partners	Limited knowledge needed unless interactions with foreign partners
In the justice system	Limited knowledge needed unless specialisation in litigation involving cross-border issues	Limited knowledge needed unless specialisation in litigation involving cross-border issues
Academic		
At university or research institutions	In-depth legal knowledge of the target system in the specialty needed if international or comparative element to the research Otherwise knowledge of the legal rules and procedures of the target system in the specialty	Ability to present, discuss and defend complex and innovative concepts in the target language Ability to design information bilingually and present system-bound findings in the target-system frame of reference

legal skills in their own system as in the target system. They can neither practice the law nor plead a case in a court in a target jurisdiction without extensive further education in the target legal system. When litigation involves foreign legal issues or litigation, local lawyers are usually hired to advise or plead abroad. What do students and professionals gain from BLE then? Comparative skills: the ability to identify different institutional settings, legal principles and procedure in the target system, to communicate effectively with lawyers/experts in the target system, and to use the appropriate language to understand, explain and convince foreign partners and clients.

The syllabus in law school is designed to ensure mastery of legal skills that will make graduates efficient in the workplace. The issue therefore is to determine what legal and language skills BLE teaches and how they match employment needs (see Table 2).

The increase in global business makes graduates who have bilingual legal skills extremely attractive. However, as of yet BLE does not train fully competent jurists in two legal systems (except for the notable exception of joint-degrees, which still require additional qualification). BLE skills are nonetheless adequate for most workplace tasks. BLE skills are not expert skills in another legal system but rather comparative legal and language skills which allow jurists to find their way around the institutional setting, legal rules and procedures of another legal system, translate and design information bilingually in their own system for jurists from other systems and to negotiate efficiently with target country lawyers.

If French jurists want to meet employment demands in a global economy, they need to master the legal and linguistic tools of comparative communication. Only BLE trains jurists for these skills.

6.2 *Bilingual Legal Skills in the Academia*

As mentioned in Sect. 4, the development of BLE essentially relies on academics who assess scientific and employment needs, and rely on their existing network of international partners to set up and develop BLE in whatever form presented in Sect. 5. They have obstacles to contend with. The academic community might not share their assessment of BLE needs in the workplace, or might be reluctant to cut down legal teaching hours on subjects they deem essential for a complete legal education to make way for BLE. Generally, these diverging positions can be negotiated locally to allow for BLE to be established. There is not a single law faculty in France which does not offer different degrees of BLE. However, the issue at the present stage of development of BLE in France is not so much its continued existence or its relevance, but rather its growth.

BLE is essential to the development of a globalised economy. More BLE programmes need to be set up, to ensure all students are given bilingual legal tools. But this must be done without slimming down core law programmes, as legal technical skills are the *raison d'être* of legal training. The present hurdles in the wake of BLE growth need to be examined.

- **International exchange programmes** have some room for further expansion as the growing demand for exchange from other foreign universities triggers equivalent space for French students to participate in such programmes. But it is a virtuous circle which the EU Commission, national governments and universities need to contribute to. Brexit creates some uncertainty concerning the conditions under which exchange programmes with the UK will continue.
- **Double and joint-degrees**, on account of the amount of work involved, have always attracted an elite group of undergraduates. Thus, their indefinite extension cannot be the aim of any reasonable BLE policy. However, as there are more outstanding students than available opportunities for them to participate in these BLE programmes, work should be done to continue expanding these programmes.
- **Degrees partially taught in a foreign language** would need to be developed to make up an integral part of the foundation subjects taught in law faculties, as comparative legal and linguistic skills are becoming essential in a globalised world. Law curricula could be rethought to give a greater share to BLE. There is however a main barrier to the expansion of BLE: the lack of a sufficient number of academics to teach BLE. At present, these BLE programmes rely on academics with strong language skills or on invited professors. Any further development of BLE will not be able to rely only on invited professorship but will need to tap into existing academic resources or train academics to teach limited and relevant subjects in a target language.

There are increasing needs for bilingual legal academics, either in their researching capacity to contribute to the growth of international research, or in their teaching capacity to develop BLE programmes.

7 Challenges of Bilingual Education in France

BLE is a major challenge for higher education in the next decade. BLE entails additional costs for the university system but is necessary if legal education wishes to produce jurists which meet the needs of an increasingly globalised workplace.

As the report has shown so far, BLE offers a wide range of programmes. However, they are rarely designed to meet specific legal language skills needed in the workplace. Indeed, the curriculum of exchange students is not built specifically to achieve the required legal and language skills; double degrees tend to run two independent programmes side by side without designing the language track specifically to meet the need of would-be jurists; and degrees partially taught in a foreign language seek primarily to give students a knowledge of the target legal system rather than work on the specific language skills required to ensure effective legal communication. Indeed, in this last category of BLE, the curriculum is devised around lectures on the target system in the target language. From a language acquisition perspective, lectures in degrees partially taught in a foreign language only focus on one skill: listening comprehension. The other four skills necessary to acquire full language proficiency are little practiced (reading comprehension, writing production, oral production and interaction).[29] Content—but not language—is corrected by the academic teaching the seminar. However, in the long run the quality of the target language is bound to impact on the professional credibility of the drafter.

There needs to be regular reassessment of the *language* needs of jurists in the workplace to determine whether under- and post-graduates are trained specifically to acquire these skills.

The present report suggests rethinking existing BLE programmes:

- **International exchange programmes** should seek also to give students strong legal language based skills, fostering the ability to design information bilingually and to assess levels of proficiency in this core BLE skill;
- **Double degrees** should regularly check and update the relevance of modules taught in language degrees so as to build effective linguistic skills geared towards achieving a level of cultural awareness, linguistic proficiency and translation skills that are of use for a jurist;
- **Degrees partially taught in a foreign language** should ensure the students acquire language as well as legal skills.

Law professors focus on the legal skills required to train a good jurist. Language issues are understandably not paramount in designing BLE programmes or teaching them. The report hopes to open new avenues of investigation by presenting a new approach on language curriculum in law faculties. It suggests that law professors work alongside linguists to build BLE programmes which give under- and post-graduates the legal *language* skills in the target system. The approach of language teachers teaching specialised target language classes is to consider that language is embedded in culture, which relates to the target country's legal culture and the culture of the legal professions.

Language classes are compulsory in law faculties, at least at master level. Academics teaching languages in law faculties have been working for almost 60 years on how to teach language skills which would be relevant to graduates in the workplace.[30] Their work falls within the scope of a discipline called Language for Specific Purposes (LSP) (Swales 1990). LSP is defined as: "the teaching and

[29] The Council of Europe designed the CEFR as the framework of reference that would provide a basis for the elaboration of language syllabuses and curriculum guidelines, the conception of teaching and learning materials, and the assessment of foreign language proficiency.

[30] On an assessement of ESP and ASP, see: Swales (1983), pp. 1–19; Resche (2001); M. Petit. 2010. Le discours spécialisé et le spécialisé du discours: repères pour l'analyse du discours en anglais de spécialité. In *E-rea,* Retrieved from <http://erea.revues.org/1400> on 18th July 2017; Sarré and Whyte (2016), pp. 139–164; Van der Yeught (2016), pp. 41–63; Charpy (2011), pp. 25–42.

learning of English as a second or foreign language where the goal of the learners is to use English in a particular domain" (Paltridge and Starfield 2013, p. 2). This goal is further defined in another definition in relation to English (ESP) as: "ESP is an approach to language learning, which is based on learner need. The foundation of all ESP is the simple question: Why does this learner need to learn a foreign language?" (Hutchinson and Waters 1987, p. 19). The very purpose of ESP is to identify student needs in specialised fields. Language ESP teaching relies on robust research in linguistics, cultural studies and ESP to identify ways in which the target language is embedded in the legal and professional culture of a given community. What is the specific terminology in the field? What are the recurrent language structures student will use in the different tasks they will be asked to carry out in the workplace? How does language reflect the professional culture of the target country? Research is carried out in these fields to bring answers to these questions, and help devise programmes that are tailored to the professional needs of students. This expertise is of paramount interest to ensure BLE programmes match the language needs of students, jurists and employers. The report contends that language academics have valuable experience to assist law professors in devising language-teaching strategies in BLE programmes or in the existing compulsory language modules in law schools.

ESP academic approach in France (*Anglais de spécialité*, *ASP*) is based on research and is defined as "the branch of English language studies which concerns the language, discourse and culture of English-language professional communities and specialised social groups, as well as the teaching of this object" (Petit 2002,p. 3). Its object is not only didactics, but stands at the cross-roads of socio-linguistics, applied linguistics, culture studies, literature (Isani 2005), discourse and genre analysis. Its research helps identify relevant features of communication (terminology (Resche 2015),[31] phraseology (Pic and Furmaniak 2014), genres (Wozniak 2015), communicative situations (Domenec 2017), culture (Saber 2006),[32] etc) in a specialized domain, such as law. In France, *ASP* is being studied by members of the GERAS Society.

ASP studies discourses of English-language professional communities. Two approaches are of note here: terminology and genres. First, language lecturers can bring their legal language expertise to help better understand the terminology in a given specialty. Law cannot be set apart from the language used to express legal concepts. In this respect, terminology lies at the very heart of any legal English teaching and research. Terminology is rooted in the culture of a discipline, and how it evolves tells a lot about theoretical changes in the field. It is also of interest to show that a legal concept can only be at best partly equivalent to a given translation in the target language. Additionally, identifying the appropriate terminology of a specialised field can be done thanks to the use of computer-assisted corpus analysis.

[31] See also for example: Raus (2013).

[32] See also for example: M. Charret-Del Bove. 2013. L'évolution paradoxale du droit de garder le silence: analyse de l'argumentation juridique de deux arrêts de la Cour suprême des États-Unis, *Miranda* (1966) et *Berghuis* (2010). In *ASp*, 63: 93–111; Gadbin-George (2013), pp. 75–93.

Second, professional discourses hinge round the identification of features specific to particular genres in a given communicative situation. Three examples to justify this approach: an internal memorandum has different communicative aims than a code of conduct; the length of contracts varies from one country to another; and identifying understatements in negotiation is key to making a successful deal. Thus the internal structure of a message and its language features reflect the intent conveyed. Law students in any BLE programme could be trained to identify the intent of any communicative situation and tailor their language to meet these ends. In the example of an internal memorandum, students could identify its generic features, its communicative settings, its specific linguistic features before being asked to produce their own internal memo. The genre approach can be applied to other professional documents or tasks students have to produce in the workplace (e-mails, written submissions, client interviews, case summaries, negotiation etc.).

These are only some of two of the approaches *ASP* explores in research and applies to teaching with a view to help students be linguistically efficient in a work-related environment.

8 Conclusion

In France, BLE can be found in varying degrees many law programmes offer to under- and post-graduates. These programmes equip students to carry out most of the communicative tasks they are asked to fulfil in a work-related environment. However, BLE is not specifically designed to give students the *linguistic* tools to communicate effectively. BLE could be improved by the input of language academics. By advocating for interdisciplinary cooperation between Law and Language, the report hopes to make the best use of BLE to prepare students to the demands of a globalised workplace.

References

Legal Documents

Bologna Declaration of 19 June 1999 (Joint declaration of the European Ministers of Education)

Common European Framework of Reference for Languages: Learning, teaching, assessment (CEFR)

European Charter for Regional or Minority Languages. http://www.coe.int/en/web/european-charter-regional-or-minority-languages/promoting-ratification-in-france

Loi Fioraso

Loi Toubon

Sorbonne Declaration of 25th of May 1998

Secondary Sources

Agbossou I, Carel-Bergeon S, Caro P (2007) Les échanges européens Erasmus: accroître la mobilité des enseignants pour développer celle des étudiants. *Céreq Bref*, 246. Accessed at http://www.cereq.fr/publications/Cereq-Bref/Les-echanges-europeens-Erasmus-accroitre-la-mobilite-des-enseignants-pour-developper-celle-des-etudiants on 20 July 2017

Ammon U (2001) The dominance of english as a language of sciences: effects on other languages and language communities. Berlin

Ammon U, McConnell G (2003) English as an Academic Language in Europe. Peter Lang, Francfort-am-Main

Arzoz X (2012a) Legal education in bilingual contexts: a conceptual, historical and comparative introduction. In: Arzoz X (ed) Bilingual higher education in the legal context: group rights, state policies and globalisation. Martinus Nijhoff Publishers, Leiden

Arzoz X (2012b) Bilingual higher education in the legal context: group rights, state policies and globalisation. Martinus Nijhoff Publishers, Leiden

Blons-Pierre C (2016) Mobilités et compétences en langues étrangères et dans le domaine interculturel: outils et réflexions pour la description, l'évaluation et la reconnaissance de ces compétences. J Int Mobil 1/4

Calmand J, Rouaud P, Sulzer E (2016) Séjours à l'étranger en cours d'études, une plus-value sur l'insertion en France?. Céreq Bref, 48. Accessed at http://www.cereq.fr/publications/Cereq-Bref/Sejours-a-l-etranger-en-cours-d-etudes-une-plus-value-sur-l-insertion-en-France on 20 July 2017

Campos MA (2010) Going beyond the obvious in English for legal purposes: a few remarks on international legal English as a Lingua Franca in Europe. In: Linde A, Crespo R (eds) Professional English in the European context: the EHEA challenge. Peter Lang, Bern, pp 175–194

Campos MA (2017) Whither legal English Now? Non-native approaches in post-brexit for judicial approaches to training in the EU Today. In: International Conference of the GERAS on Norms, Practices and Transgressions in English for Specific Purposes, Lyon III University

Charpy J-P (2011) Les premiers dictionnaires médicaux en langue anglaise: glissements diachroniques du spécialisé au non-spécialisé. ASp 59:25–42

Charret-Del Bove M (2013) L'évolution paradoxale du droit de garder le silence: analyse de l'argumentation juridique de deux arrêts de la Cour suprême des États-Unis, *Miranda* (1966) et *Berghuis* (2010). ASp 63:93–111

Crystal D (2003) English as a global language, 2nd edn. CUP, Cambridge

Domenec F (2017) Légitimer des technologies controversées: le rôle croissant des spécialistes et des scientifiques dans la communication d'entreprise en ligne. ASp 71:93–121

Gadbin-George G (2013) To quote or not to quote: 'Literature in law' in European court decisions and legal English teaching. ASp 64:75–93

Garcia O (2009) Bilingual education in the 21st century: a global perspective. Willey-Blackwell, London

Hutchinson T, Waters A (1987) English for specific purposes. Cambridge University Press, Cambridge

Isani S (2005) From idealisation to demonisation and in-between: representations of American lawyers in legal FASP. ASp 47(48):67–81

Jenkins J (2007) English as a Lingua Franca: Attitude and Identity. OUP, Oxford

Modiano M (1999) International English in the Global Village. English Today 15(2):23–25

Paltridge B, Starfield S (2013) The handbook of English for specific purposes. Wiley Blackwell, Boston

Petit M (2002) Éditorial. ASp 35/36: 3–5

Phillipson R (2003) English-Only Europe? challenging language policy. Routledge, London

Pic E, Furmaniak G (2014) Impact du lectorat visé sur la grammaire. ASp 65:69–86

Purser L (2002) The Bilingual University-General reflections on its origins, mission and functioning. In: Bergan S (ed) Language policies in higher education: invitation to a debate. Council of Europe Publishing, Strasbourg
Raus R (2013) La terminologie multilingue: la traduction des termes de l'égalité homme/femme dans le discours international. De Boeck, Louvain-la-Neuve
Resche C (2001) Réflexion sur la frontière entre langue générale et langue spécialisée. In: Mémet M, Petit M (eds) L'anglais de spécialité en France: mélanges en l'honneur de Michel Perrin. ASp GERAS Éditeur, Bordeaux, pp 37–46
Resche C (2015) Réflexions sur les termes-valises en anglais de l'économie, de la gestion et de la finance. ASp 68:67–85
Saber A (2006) Tradition, mémoire et préconstruit chez les militaires américains. ASp 49–50:35–48
Sarcevic S (2000) New approach to legal translation. Kluwer Law International, The Hague
Sarré C, Whyte S (2016) Research in ESP teaching and learning in French higher education: developing the construct of ESP didactics. ASp 69:139–164
Sibony A-L (2016) L'internationalisation de la formation juridique: Un point de vue Belge. In: Jamin C, van Caenegem W (eds) The internationalisation of legal education. Springer, New York
Smith U (2010) English as a Lingua Franca in higher education: a longitudinal study of classroom discourse. Mouton de Gruyter, Berlin
Swales (1983) ESP comes of age? – 21 years after. Some measurable characteristics of modern scientific prose. In: Perrin M (ed) Pratiques d'aujourd'hui et besoins de demain, Proceedings of the 4th European symposium on languages for specific purposes, Bordeaux 2 University, 29 August-2 September 1983. ASp GERAS Éditeur, Bordeaux, pp 1–19
Swales JM (1990) Genre analysis: English in academic and research settings. Cambridge University Press, Cambridge
Taylor S (2005) Harmonisation or divergence ? A comparison of French and English product liability rules. In: Fairgrieve D (ed) Product liability in comparative perspective. Cambridge University Press, Cambridge
Tsu A, Tollefson JW (2004) The centrality of medium-of-instruction policy in socio-political processes. In: Tollefson JW, Tsu A (eds) Medium-of-instruction policies: which Agenda? Whose Agenda? Lawrence Erlbaum Associates, Mahwah
Van der Yeught M (2016) A proposal to establish epistemological foundations for the study of specialised languages. ASp 69:41–63
Wozniak S (2015) Étude des domaines spécialisés et de leurs discours en diachronie: le cas des genres spécialisés de la littérature d'alpinisme aux États-Unis. ASp 67:81–99

Language in Law and in German Universities' Legal Education: With a Glance on European Networks

Stefan Grundmann

This contribution is about ***language*** in law and legal education and points to the fact that reduction to one global language carries the risk to impoverish law, namely its pluralism that conveys as well the idea and the essence of pluralism in societal models. The contribution also explains the steps taken in Germany (as well as in Europe) to counter this trend. This is, after all, a country report on plurality of languages in German universities' legal education (but not limited to this). Über die ***Schönheit von Sprache*** kann man streiten. Vielleicht sind die Sonette und Dramen Shakespeares in der Tat noch schöner als diejenigen Goethes, wie mein bester Freund mich seit Jugendtagen zu überzeugen sucht (aber auch als die Balladen und Dramen Schillers?). Jedenfalls jedoch ist Mehrsprachigkeit so wichtig für die Vielfältigkeit von Geist, einen echten Austausch – und auch Streit – von Ideen, damit nicht zuletzt auch Sozialmodellen und ihrer Sinnhaftigkeit, dass der Beitrag in den konzeptionellen Teilen auch in Deutsch vorgetragen wird (Annex 1) und desgleichen in Französisch (Annex 2). Denn diese beiden sind die Gründungssprachen von Rechtsvergleichung. Allein der (ausführlichere) technische Überblick zu fremdsprachlichen Angeboten an/mit deutschen rechtswissenschaftlichen Fakultäten (unten II.) wird aus Platzgründen allein in Englisch abgedruckt. La langue – c'est une arme, et en me référant en ceci librement aussi à Foucault, je soutiens dans cet article que le ***plurilinguisme***, en droit, de nos jours, est considéré surtout comme un obstacle où il devrait en vérité être entendu comme ***un des plus grands pouvoirs***. Les parties conceptuelles sont donc données dans les trois langues, seul le récit plutôt technique de la situation concrète dans les universités allemandes (en bas, section II.) y faisant exception.

S. Grundmann (✉)
European University Institute, Florence, Italy

Humboldt-Universität, Berlin, Germany
e-mail: Stefan.Grundmann@EUI.eu

N. Etcheverry Estrázulas (ed.), *Bilingual Study and Research*, Ius Comparatum – Global Studies in Comparative Law 58,
https://doi.org/10.1007/978-3-030-84550-6_8

1 By Way of Introduction: A Few Foundational Words on the Importance of Language and Its Diversity in Law

Law is language based. Legal education therefore is language oriented—more than many other studies, even if beauty of writing may be a strong impact factor of research more generally (at least) in social sciences, also in 'more sober' and 'more rigorously formal' economics.[1] There are voices that compare the exegetic thrust in law to that in theology or philology.[2] A prominent contemporary legal philosopher has aligned legal writing and practice with Shakespeare's plays—putting original legal interpretation on an equal footing with original interpretation of, say, Hamlet.[3] In knowledge theory, a majority trend coming close to unanimity points into the direction that language informs or influences formation of thought and language—strongly, very strongly, perhaps even as the major factor of all.[4]

These few considerations—reduced to their very essence—already convey one core message: language forms thought, thought about legal and societal models. Hence, *reduction to one language is completely at odds with* a world of multiple legal and societal models and even more at odds with a world in which *pluralism of societal models*—a form of individualism—is seen as being paramount and foundational also from a normative perspective. One may point to the fact that pluralism in legal and societal models and beliefs is even seen as a foundational value enshrined in constitutions (at least in the Western world).[5] One may even go so far to say that the global legal community, if it does not want to betray to some extent the foundational value of pluralism, has a moral duty to foster (much more vigorously and actively) a form of discourse that is based on a variety of languages.

In my own faculty at Humboldt University, the first holder of the chair of comparative law and private international law after the fall of the wall, Axel Flessner, a cosmopolitan man who put enormous energy into the research and education relating to the Europeanization of private law,[6] very strongly and consistently upheld the flag of German language. He did so for legal scholarly writing, for

[1] Vogel (2017) (original: *Das Gespenst des Kapitals*, Zurich: Diaphanes, 2011), passim; Putnam (2002), pp. 135–146 (ch 8 on the role aesthetic values, such as 'elegance,' in scientific conduct); Lee and Lloyd (2005), pp. 65–86.

[2] See, e.g., Gadamer (2006), p. 30; id. *Hermeneutik I. Wahrheit und Methode,* Gesammelte Werke, vol. 1 (Tübingen: Mohr (Siebeck), 1990 [1960]) 334; Betti (1987); Viola and Zaccaria (1999).

[3] Raz (2009), pp. 299–322 (chapter 12 on 'interpretation').

[4] Ground-breaking L. Wittgenstein (1922); even more so id., *Philosophical Investigations* (Chichester et al.: Wiley-Blackwell, 2009 [1953]) see also Goldman (2002), p. 154 et seq.

[5] See, Delmas Marty (2006). From the French constitutional law discourse: Auby (2010). Similarly from a German constitutional law perspective: Häberle (1980); van Ooyen and Möllers (2016).

[6] Among his main accomplishments is the installation at Humboldt University in 1996 of a German Research foundation funded curriculum of structured PhD studies on the 'Europeanisation of Private Law'—for nine consecutive years. For the broad array of PhD theses written in this framework, see, for instance https://www.rewi.hu-berlin.de/de/lf/oe/gkpwr. Among the writings by A. Flessner, see Juristische Methode und Europäisches Privatrecht, *Juristenzeitung* 2002, 14–23.

educational offers, more broadly for the participation in the international discourse in law—at least, as he once specified in a conversation with me, for Humboldt university and at least for a country like Germany. Thereby he equally upheld—and this is still more important and indeed paramount—the flag of the autonomy of German scholarly thinking in law, of practice of law "made in Austria, Germany, Switzerland", and even of the societal models they depict. Indeed, while this may not be of similar importance for small countries or less important universities, it may be paramount for leading universities in jurisdictions that really substantially have shaped and still shape legal thought—other than that in the Anglo-American world. Axel Flessner therefore blamed me for having accepted and indeed proposed the name of 'European Law School' for the network described below and the title of '*Juriste Européen*' for those who have successfully completed its curriculum and the Master exams in three European countries (in three languages).[7] It did not help that I insisted on the fact that this institution and curriculum is, in its essence, about multiplicity of languages ('*plurilinguism*'), of styles and of models—more than any other offer and model existing before. Similarly, he will blame me for writing this account in English and perhaps not even 'forgive' me for the mere fact that, at the end, I add a shorter variant of this text in German (and also in French), containing all major arguments. (by so doing, I am, of course, forced also to play with the paradox of choosing the language which I master less elegantly for the longer version, also accepting the disadvantage that virtually all non-native speakers face when they choose as the intellectual arms the 'mother tongue' spoken by prince Hamlet).

The latter does not even constitute the most important paradox related to language in law and its formative power in the creation of thought, especially legal thought. While Flessner never really formulated this idea in my presence, his consideration is particularly strong if seen as being categorical—and Flessner's *way* of arguing, his insistence on keeping German as a language of discussion, scholarly writing and teaching was categorical indeed. In my view, Flessner's argument is strongest if taken as a plea for pluri-linguist legal education and discourse. Namely so because reduction of the global discussion to one language, a lingua franca, carries the risk that a good number or even most of the ideas developed in the larger part of the world, in their native languages, is de facto excluded from the discourse or strongly reduced in importance. This risk is exacerbated by a dominant attitude in the global discussion of law to see a diversity of languages mainly as an obstacle to a common discourse and much less as a chance for richer, more nuanced, more pluralist discussion of legal and societal models. This implies that *poverty in languages* is seen as constituting the most efficient arrangement of discussion while it could also well be perceived as an *intellectual shortcoming—reducing knowledge and diversity in the global discourse(s)*. History would seem to tell us that the former risk does indeed crystalize all over.

---

[7] See below Sect. 4.

If, for instance, Thomas Piketty with all his originality, puts much of the essence of Karl Marx—or later of Hugo Sinzheimer—into economic models and into modern English[8]—as an educated and globally educated French-born scholar addressing (mainly) an English speaking global audience—this creates an absolute hype in the social sciences.[9] The question how much is Marx, how much Sinzheimer, and where the originality of Piketty is really starting cannot be asked at a global level—because there is not large enough an audience linguistically educated to an extent that allows for such a global conversation and even if Piketty would have liked such a discourse (and actually started out in French and German). State borders become almost a barrier that can be neglected—*une quantité négligeable*—as compared to language borders in the global intellectual discourse, for instance in law, but also more generally in core social sciences.

This first example is, however, still relatively unimportant. Just to 'reinvent' (pervasively) is one risk. Still more important is the risk that core trends are left out and do not influence the global discourse (adequately) and therefore also often do not share in the impact of scholarly thinking on real world developments. One of the most striking developments—separating as well large parts of the U.S. development (not that of the whole Anglo-American world) from that in most other jurisdictions—is often (and convincingly) seen in the impact that law and economics exercises on the evaluation and the development of legal solutions. If this is one of the most important kinds of interplay between disciplines for law and legal thinking nowadays, the choice of which approach should be endorsed would seem to be paramount indeed. In comparison to nowadays' law and economics as shaped mainly in U.S.-American academia and practice as of the 1960s—from Ronald Coase, Guido Calabresi via Oliver Williamson to Richard Posner and others—,[10] another strong academic and legal practice approach on the relationship between law and economics is often almost neglected. This alternative approach—the ordo-liberal school—had a considerable impact on the development mainly of public interest regulation in Europe and most prominently in Germany, much stronger than

[8]See Piketty (2014); original: Piketty (2013) and *Das Kapital im 21. Jahrhundert* (Munich: Beck, 2014) and earlier Piketty (2015); original: Piketty (1997) and *Ökonomie der Ungleichheit – eine Einführung*, (Munich: Beck, 2016). Relating back, among others, to Marx (1867) (vols. 2 + 3 edited by F. Engels 1885 and 1894, also Meissner); Marx (1872); but also Sinzheimer (1921) passim and *Arbeitsrecht und Rechtssoziologie – Gesammelte Aufsätze und Reden* (edited by O. Kahn-Freud and Th. Ramm, Frankfurt/M.: Europäische Verlagsanstalt, 1976); see, for instance, Blanke (2005).

[9]See for instance Kaufmann and Stützle (2015).

[10]See namely Coase (1960), pp. 1–44; id., The Nature of the Firm', 4 *Economica* 386–405 (1937); Calabresi (1961), pp. 499–553; id., *The Cost of Accidents – A Legal and Economic Analysis* (New Haven, Yale University Press, 1970); id. / Melamed (1972), pp. 1089–1128; Williamson (1979), pp. 233–261; id., *The Economic Institutions of Capitalism* (New York/London: MacMillan, 1985), esp. chapter 1: Transaction Cost Economics (distinguishing one 'Antitrust' and one 'Efficiency' branch which have to be assessed against each other); for the broader context of theories preceding (most of) these papers and being based on these papers later on, see, S. Grundmann, in: Grundmann et al. (2018), chapters 3 and 17; seminal as a textbook based on these theories: Posner (1973), now *Economic Analysis of Law* (9th ed., New York, Aspen, 2014).

its relatively modest role in the global academic discussion would suggest.[11] The development of both approaches was different both in substance and in method. They differed in substance—very roughly speaking—insofar as the latter favoured more robust public interest regulation, for instance required more solid proof of advantages to all market participants if (exceptionally) restrictions of competition should be allowed—while the former increasingly favoured a 'more economic approach' in which any future economic advantage was to be set-off against the losses caused by restrictions of competition. This difference in substantive solutions is not really important in our context. Both approaches differ, however, also in method and do so insofar as the law and economics approach shaped in the U.S. soon adopted more stringently economic models as benchmark, a clear orientation towards total welfare and efficiency considerations, and a strong inclination towards calculus on the basis of certain assumptions (the latter only after Coase and some of this not being fully welcome by Calabresi)—while the ordo-liberal approach did not rely on formalizations and tended more to a consideration of potential advantages and disadvantages in real world scenarios and historic contexts, strongly influenced by the existing legal and political institutions, and favoured a more substantive balancing of advantages and disadvantages and plausibility checks.

This is not the place to formulate, let alone to elaborate a profound judgement on both trends, but rather to point to three consequences from such difference (as exemplified in this one example). (1) The difference between both approaches is enormous, the law and economics approach having the main advantage of being so readily 'applicable', but also the main shortcoming of basing its results on assumptions that often abstract (strongly) from real world settings and often fail to have plausibility checks. One could speak in the one case of an approach more rigorously based on a formalisation and calculus, in the other of a value based approach that is more reality oriented but formally less precise. (2) Despite the importance of the difference, the latter is relatively little discussed and therefore we are relatively little aware of the comparative advantages and disadvantages of the two approaches either.[12] We do not really discuss whether dependence on models and calculus

---

[11] See Böhm (1966), pp. 75–151; partial translation into English: Böhm (1989), pp. 46–67; Eucken (2004), p. 278 et seqq. (1st edn., Tübingen, Mohr, 1952, p. 241 *et seqq.*); the most important comments on and further developments of this theoretical approach are: Mestmäcker (1973), pp. 97–111; id., 'Auf dem Weg zu einer Ordnungspolitik für Europa', *Festschrift v. der Groeben* (Baden-Baden: Nomos, 1987), pp. 9–50; id., 'Franz Böhm', in: S. Grundmann/K. Riesenhuber (eds.), *Private Law Development in Context – Private Law Scholars and Development in Germany and Beyond*, (Antwerp / Cambridge: Intersentia, 2017), p. 31-56; see also Grundmann (2008), pp. 553–581; and for the context and the impact the concept had later on: S. Grundmann, in: S. Grundmann/H.-W. Micklitz/M. Renner, *New Private Law Theory* (last footnote), chapter 6. In German literature, the theory has lately aroused increased interest again, see Riesenhuber (2007); Möslein (2015); for a good view on the theory from an international perspective, see Schnyder and Siems (2013), pp. 250–268 (the title, however, rather questionable or even misleading).

[12] See Fikentscher et al. (2013) chapter 1; see also Mestmäcker (2007) (and also his writings named in the last footnote). Also R. Coase was still hostile towards models and calculus, but transaction cost and institutional economics took another path.

does not exclude large parts of lawyers' communities from the discourse to a larger extent than an approach that is more principle and value oriented. (3) This lack of discussion is by no means limited to the Anglo-American world, but would seem to be influenced by the virtual lack of a pluri-linguist global discussion platform. This lack of pluri-linguist global discussion would seem to have different outcomes on both sides of the Atlantic—namely that an alternative approach is more easily neglected in the Anglo-American world, but also that, in jurisdictions such as those of continental Europe, the law and economics approach as shaped in the U.S. is either 'followed' or rather rebutted, not discussed, modified and transformed. It might well be that law and its discussion globally have to pay a high price for the global unwillingness at least to learn and to follow discourses in a few (additional) 'global' languages. If a calculus and model oriented approach to transnational economic transactions was not able to detect the flaws of a process bundling masses of sub-prime loans via securitization and outsourcing into SPVs, manufactured into CDO/CDS under the guidance of global rating agencies and then rated by them, with an investor community relying collectively and in a uniform way on the correctness of such models, might not the existence of alternative approaches in a global discourse have been helpful to cast doubt? Approaches that favour more robustness and plausibility checks instead of 'exact' calculus. After all, we say today that the flaws leading to the crisis have not been obvious only "by hindsight".

These considerations pose the question of who has *responsibilities in maintaining enough linguistic diversity*, and they explain as well why Flessner is right at least in categorical terms when insisting on German as a tool for explaining a whole legal world of thought. It would seem rather obvious that in such an endeavour of maintaining richness of views those have an increased responsibility who convey ideas developed in jurisdictions that still have the chance to be heard in a global discussion. This plea for more diversity—in languages and hence in societal models—can remain realistic only if one admits that the circle of languages consistently participating in a global discourse will (and must) remain relatively restricted even in a global discourse community more adequately shaped than that based on English only.[13] If in such a global discourse Europe may still have an additional voice—besides English—French, German and perhaps Spanish (see last footnote) would appear to be the most obvious candidates. Similarly, in those jurisdictions those universities have a particular responsibility that still attract globally to a large extent—and Axel Flessner's Humboldt university is one of the relatively few in Germany that quite blatantly does so. Therefore, it is difficult not to see Axel

[13] This article is not the place to discuss the possible structure and the prerequisites of such a changed global discourse community. Typical market structures would, however, seem to imply that 5–10 'offers' is still a manageable size and that more is difficult to handle. If then diversity in societal models constitutes one or even *the* core aspect, probably French and/or German (for Europe), Chinese, Arabic, and one or two languages of the global South (among them probably Spanish or perhaps Portuguese) could be 'natural' candidates. The core challenge would then be to create enough 'overlapping knowledge or discourse' among them—and not always only via the one common and thereby dominant channel of English—in a global social sciences community.

Flessner's point when he insists so much on sticking to German as a language to convey ideas about legal and societal thought. The responsibilities are, however, not only with those who bring in jurisdictions of the type described and those who shape discourses from such globally visible universities outside the Anglo-American world. If law is about fairness and social sciences discussion should be shaped such that it can most adequately further the common understanding and welfare, responsibilities for a more diversified discourse environment are probably just as much and perhaps even more with the Anglo-American world itself. This may sound counter-intuitive, but it could well be still more convincing if the impetus for a discourse rich in languages and hence in legal and societal models came as well—and very prominently—from key institutions and key players in the Anglo-American world.[14] The role of the U.S. may even be paramount in this as it is not renowned for taking in ideas and diversity views from other parts of the world very easily (some even speak of 'academic imperialism'). Opting for diversity, formulating a plea of diversity would seem particularly convincing if based on the particular strong position of those who start from the dominant language. We will come back to these questions—more from a perspective of comparative law approaches—after the survey on German universities' pluri-linguist offers in legal education. My suggestion may sound bold, perhaps even naïve. I would hope, however, that while this will not be mainstream, for instance in the US, cutting-edge scholarship might find some interest in such developments and fostering it.

2 Survey on German Universities' Pluri-Linguist Offers in Legal Education

In the following, a survey is given on German Universities' offers related to a teaching of legal content in another language. Three kinds of offers would seem to stand out and are taken up in turn. (1) Courses taught in other languages than German are often required in the German general final law exam, the so-called State's exam ('Staatsexamen'), organized by the Ministry of Justice of each 'Land' (state), such as Bavaria, in a good number of cases by several states jointly, and comprising all the legal core areas.[15] Hence, this type of foreign language courses/

[14]There is some discussion—mainly between German scholars globally trained, but teaching on different sides of the Atlantic—on the perceived 'superiority' of U.S.-American and European approaches to law: see Reimann (2014), pp. 1–36; and Micklitz (2017), pp. 262–309. The question of what role language—and the shaping of a multi-language discourse community—play or would play in all this, is little or not at all considered.

[15]The state exam consists of an exam on all major areas of national law (with its European Law underpinnings), composed of 6–10 cases to be solved in approx. 5 h each, i.e. in 6–10 consecutive days (in writing), supplemented by oral examinations on all these areas (typically 4 × 1 h plus the presentation of a case taken from practice—with the materials—, handed out an hour before the exam itself). The exact content (exam cases/questions) and the examiners are determined by a

requirements applies—wherever it applies—to all lawyers leaving German universities with the regular law degree (close to 100%). (2) Curricula and study courses for foreign students (more accurately: requiring a law degree other than the German State Exam) leading to Master degree at German universities. These courses can be found in German, but as well in other languages, mostly English. (3) Genuine double degree programmes, with integration of genuine university leaving exams both in a German *and* in a foreign university. Issues of funding—so important for the actual impact—will be shortly taken up in this section and Sect. 4. below. The genuine double degree programmes constitute, of course, the most fully integrated one and go well beyond the other two, more modest offers—namely when it comes to foreign language education of students of German law. This segment is made use of by about 10% of the students studying for a German law degree. There is one offer though which still goes well beyond such double degree offers as well. This is the European Law School network (Berlin/London/Paris/Rome/Amsterdam) that will be taken up separately (see below Sect. 4), also because it is based on additional and more sophisticated educational and policy considerations (see below Sect. 3). A few more specialised courses—for instance in law and economics—come closer to this polycentric study arrangement and will be taken up below as well.

2.1 Foreign Language Requirements/Courses in the State Exam (German Final Exam in Law)[16]

2.1.1 Overall Framework

Nowadays, in virtually all catalogues for the State Exam in the different *Länder*, in a number of cases catalogues applying to several of them jointly, there is some type of a requirement to have finished a law course or several law courses in a foreign

sub-section of the Ministry of Justice of that State (or several States jointly). In some (few) universities, part of the exam is as well—and typically in addition—an exam (case) on European Law proper. This is so also in the European Law School scheme (see below Sect. 4). This ‘state part’ of the state exam is credited at 70% to the overall grades. The rest of the credits is decided on by the universities themselves, based on special curricula for specialisation. For one example of a set of specialisation curricula, see https://www.rewi.hu-berlin.de/de/sp/2015/sp. Often, as in this case, there are specialisations offered with respect to subject matters—for instance the law of the enterprise (in the broad sense) or IP law–, with respect to theoretical foundations (legal history and philosophy) or as well with respect to putting law into practice (drafting, dispute resolution, pleading etc.), the latter often in conjunction with teaching practitioners. The credits for these specialisation courses amount to 30% of the overall grades.

[16]This survey has been sent to all law faculties in Germany and their amendments have been integrated. We are particularly grateful for this help.

language. In some cases, this is or these are English language based courses, in the majority of cases, however, the language to be chosen is left open, with some discretion (a catalogue of a few languages) or full discretion (limited, however, to the existing offer). Thus, virtually 100% of graduates acquiring the traditional German law degree, nowadays have to have passed some kind of foreign language requirement.

In a good number of cases, these law courses are also designed to convey knowledge of the jurisdiction(s) in which that language is the official language. For instance English taught courses are then on UK or U.S. Law or also on common law more generally, French taught courses on the Law of France (and potentially others), Portuguese taught courses on the Law of Portugal and/or of Brazil etc. (the so-called *"Fremdsprachiges Rechtsstudium", "FRS"*). While this used to be an extraordinary feature in the 1980s—attracting many students namely to Passau university—, many universities followed later and have now extended programmes. The example of Humboldt university is to the point where one of the most extended programmes—if not *the* most extended one (with Heidelberg and Munich)—is offered today, but has been 'imported' from Passau by a former Passau professor in the 1990s.

These '*FRS*'-programmes are so manifold that only a list of the most extended ones is given in the following (see below b))—followed by a much shorter list of those universities which allow for some part of their studies to be taken abroad (see below c)). While these two possibilities both have a relevance within the State Exam scheme, they differ substantially with respect to importance and role. The requirement of following foreign language taught courses at German universities (below b)) is one of the requirements to be *admitted* to the State Exam and is applicable to all students, while the schemes listed below c) are much more extended in time and substance and *replace the university part* of the State Exam and therefore are credited for 30% of the latter. Conversely, they apply to a much more restricted student body, certainly not more than 10% of the students opting for this scheme even in the universities offering this possibility.

2.1.2 List of Universities with Extended Programmes of Foreign Law Taught in Mother Tongue (*"Fremdsprachiges Rechtsstudium", "FRS"*)

The most important offers of foreign law taught in foreign languages (in their official language) are listed below. In a good number of cases, the foreign language taught courses in foreign law are also part of the (more extended) double degree programmes (if this university has such a scheme), i.e. are used in both contexts. The list—given in alphabetical order of the city—is not exhaustive, as it is very long anyhow. Similar, less extensive offers can be found on the websites of still more universities as well.

(a) *Augsburg* University [http://www.jura.uni-augsburg.de/de/lehre/fra/], offers in US-American, Chinese, French, Japanese, Polish, Russian, Spanish, Turkish Law—all in the official languages of those countries/jurisdictions;
(b) *Berlin* University (*Freie Universität*) [http://www.jura.fu-berlin.de/studium/studiengang_rechtswissenschaft2015/04_Module/modul_fremdspracheAB.pdf], offers in English, French, Italian or Spanish Law—all in the official languages of those countries/jurisdictions or as well language courses in these languages.
(c) *Berlin* University (*Humboldt*) [https://www.rewi.hu-berlin.de/de/ip/cert/frs], requirement as so-called BZQ II, offers in US-American, Brazilian, Chinese, English, French, Italian, Polish, Russian, Spanish, Turkish Law—all in the official languages of those countries/jurisdictions.[17]
(d) *Bielefeld* University [http://www.jura.uni-bielefeld.de/angebote/fremdsprachen/ffa/ and https://ekvv.uni-bielefeld.de/kvv_publ/publ/Studiengang_Vorlesungsverzeichnis.jsp?id=29188817], offers in US-American, English, French, Russian, and Turkish Law—all in the official languages of those countries/jurisdictions.
(e) *Bochum* University (*Ruhr*) [http://www.ruhr-uni-bochum.de/zfi-jura/index.html#], offers courses on common law (US-American, English, South African), French, Spanish and Turkish Law—all in the official languages of those countries/jurisdictions.
(f) *Bonn* University with one more extended programme in English and also a higher degree (with possible extension of the exam period) [https://www.jura.uni-bonn.de/studium/lehrangebote/fremdsprachen/ffa-auf-unicertr-stufe-iii/ and https://www.jura.uni-bonn.de/studium/lehrangebote/fremdsprachen/ffa-lpp-auf-unicertr-stufe-iv/], and one ‚regular' programme for other languages [https://www.jura.uni-bonn.de/studium/lehrangebote/fremdsprachen/internationale-rechtsterminologien/], offers in US-American, English (more extended version, English legal system, English case law and court system), French, Italian, Russian, Spanish, Turkish Law—all in the official languages of those countries/jurisdictions.
(g) *Bremen* University offers a number of foreign / EU law courses in English, particularly within the LL.B. degree course Comparative and European Law and the LL.M. degree course Transnational Law (both Hanse Law School), foreign language certificate (English) required within the State exam course, based on a written exam in an English taught law course or legal English course [https://www.jura.uni-bremen.de/studium/staatsexamen/fremdsprachenschein/], occasionally Turkish law courses taught in Turkish.

[17] Additional offers in Augsburg (Japanese), Bochum, Frankfurt/Main, Würzburg (South African), Heidelberg (Arabic), Munich and Saarland University (Greek), Munich and Trier (Portuguese) and Würzburg (Latin-American, Subsahara-African). The programme in Bonn is particularly nuanced for English law.

(h) *Cologne* University (*Albertus Magnus*) with a specific certificate on US-American Law [http://www.us-recht.jura.uni-koeln.de/1935.html] and additional offers on foreign legal terminology [http://www.zib.jura.uni-koeln.de/14779.html].
(i) *Düsseldorf* University (within the double degree with Cergy-Pontoise, see below Sect. 3.) [https://www.dfh-ufa.org/studium/studienfuehrer/mode/detail/id/rechtswissenschaften/pointer /0/], very extended offer in French Law (Business, Labour and Social Law), in French.
(j) *Frankfurt (Main)* University (*Goethe*) [http://www.jura.uni-frankfurt.de/43078948/4fremdsprachige-Rechtskenntnisse3], offers in US-American, English, French, Italian, South African, Turkish Law—all in the official languages of those jurisdictions/countries.
(k) *Freiburg* University (*Albert-Ludwig*) with one more extended programme in English and French [http://www.jura.uni-freiburg.de/de/institute/ioeffr5/franzoesische-rechtsschule/deutsch-franzoesische-rechtsschule] [French Law School with specific certificate] and in European, International and foreign law [https://www.jura.uni-freiburg.de/de/zusatzprogramme/europaeisches-internationales-und-auslaendisches-recht], offers in English and French as the official languages of those countries/jurisdictions.
(l) *Halle* University (*Martin-Luther*) with one more extended programme in English and French, but also International Law [http://www.jura.uni-halle.de/studium_lehre_pruefung/studium_lehre/lehrveranstaltungen/_fachspez._fremdspr.-ausb.__i_/], can be replaced by moot court participation.
(m) *Hamburg* University [https://www.jura.uni-hamburg.de/studium/lehrveranstaltungen /fremdsprachenangebote.html], offers in English, French, Polish, Spanish, Turkish and Russian Law—all in the official language of those countries/jurisdictions. Also the specialisation (*Schwerpunkt*) can be taken in English (https://www.jura.uni-hamburg.de/en/einrichtungen/institute-seminare/institut-recht-oekonomik/lehre/schwerpunkt.html) and more lectures are given in English for foreign students.
(n) *Heidelberg* University (Ruprecht-Karl) [http://www.jura.uni-heidelberg.de/studium/internationales/fremdsprachige_veranstaltungen.html], offers in US-American, Arabic, Brazilian, English, French, Italian, Polish, Portuguese, Spanish, Turkish Law—all in the official languages of those countries/jurisdictions.
(o) *Jena* University (*Friedrich Schiller*), besides the Law & Language Center [http://www.rewi.uni-jena.de/Studium/Law+_+Language+Center-p-1853.html] with an 'Introduction to the English Legal System', more extended offers [http://www.rewi.uni-jena.de/Studium/Law+_+Language+Center-p-1853.html and for a LL.B. http://www.rewi.uni-jena.de/LLB.html] are on US-American, English, French, Russian, and Spanish Law—all in the official languages of those countries/jurisdictions.
(p) *Kiel* University [http://www.jura.uni-kiel.de/de/StuPrue/ffazertifikat], in English on US-American and English Law (with certificate, running over four terms).

(q) *Konstanz* University [https://www.jura.uni-konstanz.de/studium/staatsexamensstudiengang/vorlesungsverzeichnisse/aktuelles-vorlesungsverzeichnis/] with offers on English, French, Italian, Spanish and Turkish Law—all in the official language of those countries/jurisdictions.
(r) *Leipzig* University [https://www.jura.uni-leipzig.de/studium/studiengang-rechtswissenschaft/fremdsprachennachweis/], offers in US-American, English, French, and Russian Law—all in the official languages of those countries/jurisdictions.
(s) *Mainz* University [http://www.jura.uni-mainz.de/369_DEU_HTML.php], offers in US-American, English, French, Italian, and Spanish Law—all in the official languages of those countries/jurisdictions.
(t) *Marburg* University with offers on US and UK Law (Common Law) and Italian Law—all in the official languages of those countries/jurisdictions, and a course on domestic and international commercial arbitration taught in English.
(u) *Munich* University (*Ludwig-Maximilian*) [http://www.jura.uni-muenchen.de/fakultaet/fachsprachenzentrum/index.html], offers in Chinese, English, French, Greek, Italian, Portuguese, Russian, Spanish, and Turkish Law—all in the official languages of those countries/jurisdictions.
(v) *Münster* University [https://www.jura.uni-muenster.de/de/studium/studienmoeglichkeiten/ffa-fachspezifische-fremdsprachenausbildung/organisatorisches/], offers on the common law, International Law, and in French and Spanish Law—all in the official languages of those countries/jurisdictions. Some of these courses can also be recognized in some branches of the university exam (*Schwerpunktbereich*).
(w) *Osnabrück* University [https://www.jura.uni-osnabrueck.de/studium/fremdsprachliche_fachausbildung/], offers in US-American, Chinese, English, French, Spanish and Polish Law—all in the official languages of those countries/jurisdictions.
(x) *Passau* University with one more extended programme in English , leading to a Certificate of Studies in European, Comparative and International Law (CECIL) [http://www.jura.uni-passau.de/internationales/studienangebote/cecil/lehrveranstaltungen/], and "regular" offers [http://www.sprachenzentrum.uni-passau.de/fremdsprachenausbildung/ffa/ffa-fuer-juristen/] in US-American, English, French, Italian, Russian, and Spanish Law—all in the official languages of those countries/jurisdictions.
(y) *Regensburg* University with two programmes, one on the Anglo-American Legal System [http://www.uni-regensburg.de/zentrum-sprache-kommunikation/sfa/kursangebot/englisch/index.html#EnglischJura] and one on Russian Law [http://www.uni-regensburg.de/rechtswissenschaft/oeffentliches-recht/manssen/ostwissenschaftliches-begleitstudium/index.html], both running over four terms.
(z) *Saarland* University [https://www.uni-saarland.de/fakultaet/r/lehre/terminologie.html], offers in English, French, Greek, Italian, and Spanish Law—all in the official languages of those countries/jurisdictions.

(z1) *Trier* University [https://www.uni-trier.de/index.php?id=63522] (impressively extended, 4-6 terms), offers in US-American, Chinese, English, French, Italian, Japanese, Portuguese, Spanish, and Turkish Law—all in the official languages of those countries/jurisdictions.

(z2) *Tübingen* University [https://www.jura.uni-tuebingen.de/studium/lehrveranstaltungen/] with offers in US-American, English, French, Turkish and Russian Law—all in the official languages of those countries/jurisdictions.

(z3) *Würzburg* University [https://www.jura.uni-wuerzburg.de/studium/fachsprachen-und-auslaendisches-recht/aktuelles/] offers in US-American, English, Australian/New Zealand, French, Italian, Latin-American, Polish, Russian, Spanish, Subsahara-African and Turkish Law—all in the official languages of those countries/jurisdictions.

2.1.3 List of Universities Allowing the Year of Specialisation to be Passed Abroad ("*Schwerpunkt im Ausland*")

In some universities, the year of specialisation that is at the discretion of each university (see above footnote 15) and for which they establish the curricula and the requirements (within certain limits set by the German Lawyers' Act)[18] follows a regime which allows for substitution by a parallel curriculum at a university abroad. This requires a particular clause in the state bylaws on the State Exam and therefore is not completely at the discretion of the universities. In such cases, the year abroad—with all exams—counts 30% to the German State Exam—after recognition and transfer of grades into the German grading system. This possibility is much more exceptional than the one to do courses in a foreign language at the domestic (German) university (above b)).

This more extended scheme is offered at

- the two *Berlin* universities (*Freie Universität*, http://www.jura.fu-berlin.de/international/studierendenaustausch/outgoings/anerkennung/schwerpunkt2sem.html, and *Humboldt Universität*, https://www.rewi.hu-berlin.de/de/ip/out/sp), on the basis of the express authorization of the Berlin bylaws that to my knowledge were path-breaking in this respect (and a condition for developing the European Law School scheme, below Sect. 4), and at
- *Bonn* University (https://www.jura.uni-bonn.de/fileadmin/Fachbereich_Rechtswissenschaft/Einrichtungen/Pruefungsausschuss/Rechtsgrundlagen/Amtl._Bek._1535-3_SPB-PO_2015.pdf).
- *Düsseldorf* University (see http://www.jura.hhu.de/dfs.html, https://www.dfh-ufa.org/studium/studienfuehrer/mode/detail/id/rechtswissenschaften/pointer/0/).
- *Heidelberg* University, in one specialisation area, European and International Capital Market and Financial Services Law (https://jura.urz.uni-heidelberg.de/mat/materialien/uni_hd_jura_material_14895.pdf) and for the written thesis

[18] See § 5d (2) DRiG (*Bundesgesetzblatt* – official Gazette. I p. 1474).

forming part of the requirements (http://www.jura.uni-heidelberg.de/studium/Studienarbeit.html#Ausland).
- *Jena* University (§ 12 of Jena's regulation on the specification curriculum).
- *Kiel* University, in particular cases (see http://www.eastlaw.uni-kiel.de/de/schwerpunkt).
- *Mainz* University, with Glasgow University (see http://www.jura.uni-mainz.de/auslandsbuero/373.php#Schottisches_Recht).
- *Passau* University (see http://www.jura.uni-passau.de/studium/auslandsstudium/schwerpunktbereich-auslaendisches-recht/).
- *Saarland* University (see https://www.uni-saarland.de/fakultaet/r/interessenten/studium/schwerpunktbereiche.html).
- *Würzburg* University (see https://www.jura.uni-wuerzburg.de/studium/rechtswissenschaft/erste-juristische-pruefung/schwerpunktbereichsstudium/stpro-2008-stand-2016/s-14-franzoesisches-recht/ and https://www.jura.uni-wuerzburg.de/fileadmin/02000100/studium/Studienplan/2017-11-20_-__WS_-Studienplan_Beschluss_Fakultaetsrat.pdf)

In some of the double degree programmes, the same possibility is offered, if continued towards a state exam (see below Sect. 3., namely *Berlin, Cologne, Düsseldorf, Erlangen-Nürnberg, Munich, Potsdam, Saarbrücken*), some, such as *Marburg* University, recognise only single subjects taken abroad (https://www.uni-marburg.de/fb01/studium/spbs/schwerpunktbereich_dateien/schwerpunktbereichpruefungsordnung_170713.pdf).

2.2 *Master Programmes (LL.M.) at German Universities (in German and Foreign Language)*

2.2.1 Overall Framework

Many German universities offer LL.M. in their law faculties, a good number in German, namely those on German law and sub-areas of it, the others, targeted on specific areas (almost) exclusively in English. While both types of offers cannot always be neatly distinguished, offers of the first type are designed for and targeted to students having a law degree from foreign universities, not to domestic students from less prestigious universities—as is often the case in the U.S.–, as the main benchmark for quality in Germany is the State exam anyhow. At least this type of offers therefore has to do with cross-border legal education and hence also multi-language skills—albeit mostly for students from other countries than Germany (on these curricula, see list below b). A large number of these curricula are on business law—in Germany and beyond. Conversely, the more topic related curricula are designed for students *and* practicing lawyers from Germany *or* abroad. The more specialised curricula can be related to a legal area—reflecting typically a particular strength, also in research, of the particular university—or to a methodological approach (on these offers, see list below c). These curricula, while not excluding views on German law as well, are more on the inherent structure of these areas or comparative law than on German law content. This is the reason for which these curricula are typically targeted to students and practicing lawyers irrespective of their jurisdiction of origin, and more often are taught in English. The German Academic Exchange Service keeps the list of offers of both types updated and covers the whole range of offers.[19]

2.2.2 Master Programmes (LL.M.) on German Law (or Large Sub-Areas)

Genuine master programmes (LL.M.) ***on German Law***—taught in German—are so numerous that only a few very significant ones are named in the following.[20] They can be found at:

- *Berlin* University (*Humboldt*) with its master programmes on German and European Law and Legal Practice (https://www.rewi.hu-berlin.de/de/ip/master/dteur/index.html).
- *Bochum* University (*Ruhr*) with its general programme on German Law (http://www.ruhr-uni-bochum.de/zfi-jura/llmRUB.html) and its programme on criminology, criminalistics and police science (http://www.makrim.de/).
- *Bonn* University with its general programme on German Law for foreign graduates with a wide range of specialisation possibilities (https://www.jura.uni-bonn.de/auslandskoordination/internationales/master-im-deutschen-recht-llm/)
- *Cologne* University (*Albert Magnus*) with its master on German Law for foreign graduates (http://www.zib.jura.uni-koeln.de/llm.html).

---

[19] See https://www.daad.de/deutschland/studienangebote/international-programmes/en/?p=l&q=&degree[]=2&fos=1&subject[]=250&fee[]=0&sortBy=1&page=1&display=list#.

[20] For a full list see https://www.azur-online.de/bildung/deutsche-ll-m and the following universities: *Bayreuth* (https://www.uni-bayreuth.de/de/studium/masterstudium/LLM_auslaendische_juristen/index.php), *Bielefeld* (http://www.jura.uni-bielefeld.de/angebote/dokumente_ordnungen/ordnung_legum_magister), *Freiburg* (https://www.jura.uni-freiburg.de/de/internationales/incomings/ll-m), *Gießen* (https://www.uni-giessen.de/fbz/fb01/fakultaet-institutionen/dekanat/studiengaenge%20abschluesse/Magister/llm), *Jena* (http://www.rewi.uni-jena.de/Studium/Studieng%C3%A4nge/Rechtswissenschaft+f%C3%BCr+au%C3%9Ferhalb+des+Geltungsbereiches+des+Grundgesetzes+graduierte+Juristen+%28LL_M_%29-p-117.html), *Konstanz* (https://www.jura.uni-konstanz.de/studium/llm-im-deutschem-recht-fuer-auslaendische-juristen/), *Marburg* (https://www.uni-marburg.de/de/studium/studienangebot/master/m-grudtschre), *Osnabrück* (https://www.jura.uni-osnabrueck.de/studium/studiengaenge/llm_deutsches_recht.html), *Passau* (http://www.uni-passau.de/master-deutsches-recht/), *Potsdam* (http://www.jura-potsdam), *Regensburg* (http://www.uni-regensburg.de/rechtswissenschaft/fakultaet/internationales/llm/index.html) and *Tübingen* (https://www.jura.uni-tuebingen.de/studium/llm/).

- *Frankfurt (Main)* University *(Goethe)* with its general programme on German Law for foreign graduates (http://www.jura.uni-frankfurt.de/39838982/LL_M_-fuer-im-Ausland-graduierte-Juristinnen-und-Juristen)
- *Frankfurt (Oder)* University (*Viadrina*) with a general programme (https://www.rewi.europa-uni.de/de/studium/master/Magister.html), but more well-known its German-Polish Law programme (https://www.rewi.europa-uni.de/de/studium/polnisch/master_gplaw/index.html).
- *Heidelberg* University with its general programme on German Law (since 1987) (http://www.unifr.ch/rectorat/reglements/pdf/92421.pdf).
- *München* University *(Ludwigs-Maximillian)* with its general Programme on German Law for foreign graduates (http://www.jura.uni-muenchen.de/studium/studiengaenge/aufbaustudiengaenge/aufb_dr/index.html).
- *Münster* University with its general programme on German Law for foreign graduates (https://www.jura.uni-muenster.de/de/international/master-deutsches-recht-ll-m/).
- *Würzburg* University with its master programme on German Law for foreign graduates (https://www.jura.uni-wuerzburg.de/studium/postgraduales-studium/aufbau-und-masterstudiengaenge/llm-fuer-im-ausland-graduierte-juristen/).
- *Saarbrücken* University with its general programme on German Law ((http://http://martinek.jura.uni-saarland.de/llm_en.html) and specially a programme on German Law, that is taught in French (http://llm.cjfa.eu/).

More typical are, however, master programmes (LL.M.) ***on business law*** in particular, some still rather strongly related to German law, others rather loosely. In the following, we name only those in foreign language—there are, of course, numerous specialised master programs on specific topics in German.[21] The foreign language curricula on business law are offered namely in:

(a) *Berlin* University (*Freie Universität*) with its Master of Business, Competition and Regulatory Law (MBL-FU) (http://www.jura.fu-berlin.de/en/studium/masterstudiengaenge/mbl-fu/index.html), all in English, in particular for practicing lawyers.
(b) *Berlin* (Polytechnic) University (*Hochschule für Wirtschaft und Recht*) with its master programme on Business Law in an International Context (LL.M.) (http://www.hwr-berlin.de/studium/studienangebot/fb-1-kurzform/unternehmensrecht-im-internationalen-kontext/), partly in English, partly in German, but anchored at the economics department.
(c) *Bucerius* Law School, *Hamburg* (the only outstanding private law school), offering the Bucerius Master of Law and Business (LL.M. or MLB) (see https://www.law-school.de/master/?utm_source=daad&utm_medium=listing&utm_campaign=brand-mlb), all in English, with the main purpose of 'exploring a company's lifecycle'.

[21] See https://www.azur-online.de/bildung/deutsche-ll-m.

(d) *Cologne* University (*Albertus Magnus*) with its master programme on German-Turkish business law, (*Deutsches und Türkisches Wirtschaftsrecht*, see http://www.dtm.jura.uni-koeln.de), taught in Cologne (German) and Istanbul (Turkish), mainly for Turkish or double nationality/origin students. The programme can be studied as a double degree programme (for more double degree programmes in Cologne—French and Italian –, see below Sect. 3).
(e) *Mannheim* University with its (strongly interdisciplinary) master of Comparative Business Law (M.C.B.L., Mannheim/Adelaide or only Mannheim) (see https://www.jura.uni-mannheim.de/studium/master-of-comparative-business-law/), all taught in English.

Finally, there are also a few master programs mainly oriented ***towards EU Law***. These are the following ones:

(a) *Hamburg* University with its Master European and European Legal Studies (see https://europa-kolleg-hamburg.de/en/master-programme-european-legal-studies/at-a-glance/), all in English, with strong emphasis also on political and economic aspects of European integration, and its Master of European and International Law (MEIL) (see http://en.cesl.edu.cn / https://www.jura.uni-hamburg.de/internationales/china-eu-school-law.html), all in English, taught (mainly) at China University of Political Science and Law in Bejing. Moreover a Master in Law and Economics in the Arab Region is offered (https://www.jura.uni-hamburg.de/en/einrichtungen/institute-seminare/institut-recht-oekonomik/lehre/masterprogramme/mlea.html).
(b) *Hannover* University with its two years master programme in European Legal Practices (see https://www.elpis-hannover.eu/elpis2.html), taught in German and English and with the possibility to study parts in Rouen, Lisbon and/or Vilnius. This programme comes closest to the European Law School scheme described below—however, without the explicit interplay of diversity and unity.
(c) *Saarland* University with its master programme in European and International Law (LL.M.) (see http://www.europainstitut.de/index.php?id=248), in English and/or German.
(d) *Würzburg* University with its two year master programme in European Law, taught in English and/or German (see https://www.jura.uni-wuerzburg.de/studium/postgraduales-studium/aufbau-und-masterstudiengaenge/aufbaustudiengang/startseite/).

2.2.3 Master Programmes (LL.M.) on Targeted Subject Areas or Regional Contexts

More targeted programmes can, again, mostly be found with respect to areas of business law, a good number in IP law, otherwise with a particular methodological approach. The following should be named.

(a) *Berlin* University (*Humboldt*) offers three masters of specialisation in three areas in which particularly strong research interests (and a number of particular chairs) can be found at the faculty: international criminal law, IP law and ADR/international dispute resolution. These are the master programmes in Transnational Criminal Justice and Crime Prevention—an International and African Perspective (with the University of the Western Cape, see http://www.transcrim.org), on Intellectual Property and Media Law (see https://www.hu-berlin.de/de/studium/beruf/wissenschaftliche-weiterbildung/weiterbildende-masterstudiengaenge/immaterialgueterrecht-und-medienrecht), and on International Dispute Resolution (see https://www.rewi.hu-berlin.de/en/sp/angebote/master/idr/about-the-idr-master-program), the first and the last in English.

(b) *Berlin* University (*Technische Universität*) offers—in a completely different setting—also a master programme in European and International Energy Law (MBL) (https://master-in-energy.com/courses/energy-law/), leading to a master in business law in a highly regulated and also separate specific area.

(c) Bremen University with its Hanse Law School (HLS) network, offers an LL.M. in Transnational Law in German and English (see http://studdb2.dez6.uni-bremen.de/sixcms/detail.php?id=4298&template=fach_lang&js=1), in cooperation with Oldenburg University (*Carl von Ossietzky*) and, optionally, Groningen University (*Rijksuniversiteit*) (see also below Sect. 3). The curriculum provides one optional semester at a foreign university. The programme focusses on transnationalisation, allows specialisation in the legal fields of e. g. labour and social law, information and health law, economic law, private law, public law, criminal and security law.

(d) *Dresden* University offers a master programme in the International Studies in Intellectual Property Law (https://tu-dresden.de/gsw/jura/igewem/ipllm/), taught in English and German, with partner universities abroad (Exeter, Krakow, London, Seattle, Prague, Szeged, Strasbourg).

(e) *Düsseldorf* University with its master on medical law (http://imr.duslaw.de/llm-medizinrecht.html).

(f) *Erlangen-Nürnberg* University offers a master programme on Human Rights (see https://www.humanrights-master.fau.de), taught completely in English.

(g) *Frankfurt (Oder)* University (*Viadrina*) with master programmes on International Human Rights and Humanitarian Law (https://www.rewi.europa-uni.de/de/studium/master/ihl/index.html), European Business Law (https://www.rewi.europa-uni.de/de/studium/master/euwirtrecht/index.html) and Mediation and Conflict Management (https://www.rewi.europa-uni.de/de/studium/master/mediation/index.html).

(h) *Frankfurt (Main)* University (*Goethe*) with master programmes on two focal points of the research agenda of that faculty, namely the one on Legal Theory (see http://www.legaltheory.eu/llm_in_legal_theory) and the one on Finance, also International Finance (see http://www.ilf-frankfurt.de/gain-the-competitive-advantage/). Both programmes are taught in English, the first within an international network of universities, also with a double degree option (Brussels University). See moreover a programme on European Economy Law (http://www.jura.uni-frankfurt.de/39838993/LL_M_-Eur).

(i) *Göttingen* University with its master programme on European and Transnational Intellectual Property and Information Technology Law (see https://www.uni-goettingen.de/en/545891.html), all taught in English.
(j) *Hamburg* University with its master programme in International Taxation (see http://www.m-i-tax.de), taught mostly in German, some English, with interdisciplinary contents and its programme on insurance law (https://www.jura.uni-hamburg.de/studium/postgraduiertenstudiengaenge/versicherungsrecht.html)
(k) *Hannover* University (Leibniz) with its old specialization in and its master programme on European Legal Informatics (LL.M. in IP or IT Law) (see http://www.eulisp.de), in part in English.
(l) *Heidelberg* University with its Investment, Trade and Arbitration programme (with Santiago de Chile University) (http://www.hcla.uni-hd.de/english/kurs_master_jur_2018.html), and also one in corporate restructuring (http://www.igw.uni-heidelberg.de/corp_restruc/) and one in dispute resolution (http://www.ipr.uni-heidelberg.de/internationale-kontakte/pepperdine-llm.html).
(m) *Leipzig* University with its master programmes on European Private Law (https://ipr.jura.uni-leipzig.de/masterstudium/) and on International Public Law and European Integration (https://europarecht.jura.uni-leipzig.de/llm-internationales-recht/).
(n) *Lüneburg* University (*Leuphana*) with its master programme in Competition Law and Regulation (see https://www.leuphana.de/en/professional-school/masters-studies/competition-regulation-llm.html), all taught in English.
(o) *Marburg* University with its master programmes on Pharmaceutical Law (http://www.pharmarecht-master.de/) and Construction Law (http://www.baurecht-master.de/)
(p) *Munich* University (*Ludwig-Maximilian/Max-Planck-Institute*) with its master programme in Intellectual Property and Competition Law (see, https://www.miplc.de), all taught in English, possible with exchange to Washington D.C., and European and International Business Law Master (http://www.jura.uni-muenchen.de/studium/studiengaenge/aufbaustudiengaenge/aufb_eur/index.html).
(q) *Speyer* University with its master programme State and Administration in Europe (http://www.uni-speyer.de/en/studies/the-various-courses/llm-state-and-administration-in-europe.php).

2.3 *Double Degree Programmes (with Participation of German Universities)*

Besides the double degree programmes in specialised areas, often master programmes where the double degree is optional (see above Sect. 2. sub b) and c), namely in Cologne, Hannover, Mannheim, and Frankfurt), there are a good number of double degree programmes on two jurisdictions more generally. They cover in the major part virtually all areas that the domestic law degrees would cover in both countries. There are, however, also a few offers focusing the double degree on business law (*Bochum*, *Lüneburg*). Exceptional are the *Frankfurt* Legal Theory curriculum and the *Hamburg* Law & Economics curriculum that can be studied as a double degree curriculum as well. The offer is particularly broad in Cologne and Berlin (*Humboldt*) with three such jurisdictions/programmes. These (in the large majority of cases) genuine broad double degrees in law comprise the following offers:

(a) *Bayreuth* University (German/Spanish, with Sevilla University—Pablo de Olavide) (http://www.jura-derecho.uni-bayreuth.de/de/index.html), four years' curriculum, leading to a Grado en Derecho and a LL.B. (Bayreuth).
(b) *Berlin* University (*Freie Universität*) (German/US-American, with the University of Connecticut, U.S.A.) (http://www.jura.fu-berlin.de/international/studierendenaustausch/outgoings/partnerunis/uconn_double-degree/index.html), three years' curriculum, leading to a LL.M. at both universities, two more years for a State Exam.
(c) *Berlin* University (*Humboldt*). Three double degree curricula (besides the European Law School, see below Sect.), with English, French and Chinese/English content. Namely:

    (1) German-French three years' study course Berlin, Munich, Paris (so-called BerMüPa, https://www.rewi.hu-berlin.de/de/ip/mfa/dfr), leading to a Licence in Paris which can be credited towards the university part of the State Exam in Berlin, additional two years for the State Exam. For the French students leading to a LL.M. in Berlin.
    (2) German-English five years' study course Berlin, King's College London (https://www.rewi.hu-berlin.de/de/ip/mfa/dd), leading to a LL.B. in London (first two years) and then either an LL.M. in Berlin and Paris (three more years) or a full State Exam curriculum.
    (3) German-European-Chinese two years' study course Berlin, Shanghai (Tongji University) (https://www.rewi.hu-berlin.de/de/ip/master/cn), with a LL.M. degree at each of the universities. In Shanghai courses in English accompanied by language courses in Chinese.

(d) *Bochum* University (German/French, with the University of Tours) (http://www.ruhr-uni-bochum.de/dfbs/), three years' curriculum, concentrating on the business law of both jurisdictions and leading to a LL.B: in Bochum and a Licence in Tours. As of 2018/19 also Maîtrise in Tours and LL.M in Bochum (http://www.ruhr-uni-bochum.de/dfbs/master.html).
(e) *Cologne* University (*Albertus Magnus*) has two (more) curricula (besides the German-Turkish curriculum in business law, named above), one German/French, one German/Italian, namely:

    (1) German-French four years' study course with Paris 1 (*Sorbonne*) (http://www.dfr.jura.uni-koeln.de/14694.html and http://www.dfr.jura.uni-koeln.de/14696.html), leading to a Maîtrise in Paris and a /LL.B. in Cologne. Can be credited towards the State Exam in the university part.

(2) German-Italian four years' study course with Florence University, with three terms abroad (http://www.zib.jura.uni-koeln.de/dib.html), leading to a Laurea Magistrale in Florence and a LL.B. in Cologne. Can be credited towards the State Exam in the university part.

(f) *Düsseldorf* University (German/French, with the University of Cergy-Pontoise) (http://www.jura.hhu.de/dfs.html), three years' curriculum, leading to a 'university certificate' in Düsseldorf and a Licence at Cergy-Pontoise University. Can be continued towards a German State exam (in this case recognition of the French exams as university exam).
(g) *Erlangen-Nürnberg* University (German/French, with the University of Rennes I) (https://www.dfr.rw.fau.de/), five years' curriculum leading to a master degree in Rennes and a State Exam in Erlangen.
(h) *Frankfurt (Main)* University (*Goethe*) (German/French, with Bruxelles University) (http://www.legaltheory.eu/mobility_windows), two years' curriculum, leading to an LL.M. at both universities, focusing on legal theory. For a course organised with Université Lumière Lyon II, leading to two university diplomas see http://iversr.uni-frankfurt.de/studium/studiengang-dudf-duda.
(i) *Freiburg* University (*Albert-Ludwig*) (German/French, with Strasbourg and Basel University) (https://www.jura.uni-freiburg.de/de/internationales/incomings/eucor-master), (typically) two years' curriculum, focusing on comparative and European law, and leading to a LL.M. in Freiburg, a Master Droit et études européennes in Strasbourg and a Master of Law in Basel.
(j) *Göttingen* University (German/Chinese, with Nanjing University) (http://www.uni-goettingen.de/de/studium/423312.html), two years' (comparative law) curriculum leading to a LL.M. in Nanjing and a LL.M. for German and a Magister for Chinese students in Göttingen.
(k) *Hamburg* University (English programme with Aix-Marseille, Ghent, Bologna, Haifa, Mumbai, Rotterdam, Vienna, Warzaw Universities) (http://www.emle.org), three terms' (one year) curriculum on Law & Economics, leading to a LL.M. degree both at Hamburg and the (one) partner university chosen.
(l) *Konstanz* University (German/Chinese, with Tongji University Shanghai, courses taught in English) (https://www.jura.uni-konstanz.de/stadler/kooperationen-mit-china/doppelmaster-tongji-universitaet/), two years' curriculum on comparative law, leading to a LL.M. from both Tongji University and Konstanz.
(m) *Mainz* University, two German/French curricula. The first with Nantes and Paris 12 Universities (http://www.jura.uni-mainz.de/auslandsbuero/126.php), four years' curriculum, leading to a LL.B. in Mainz and a Master at the French universities, possibility to follow on with a State Exam. The second with Dijon University (http://www.jura.uni-mainz.de/auslandsbuero/330.php), same structure, but in the 5th year possibility of a LL.M. in Mainz / Master 2 in Dijon.
(n) *Mannheim* University (German/French with Université Toulouse I—Capitole), adding one year in Toulouse to the three years' LL.B. curriculum with an emphasis on civil and business law in Mannheim, leading to an LL.B. and a

license en droit for Mannheim students respectively adding one year in Mannheim, leading to a license en droit and a "Zertifikat Wirtschaftsrecht Universität Mannheim / Certificate de l'Université de Mannheim – mention droit économique" for Toulouse students.

(o) *Marburg* University (German/Russian with Immanuel-Kant-University Kaliningrad).

(p) *Münster* University (German/Italian with the Università di Torino and German/Spanish with the Universidad Carlos III de Madrid) (https://www.jura.uni-muenster.de/de/international/auslandsstudium-fuer-jurastudierende/doppelabschluss/), six years' curriculum with three semesters abroad in Madrid *or* Turin leading to a State exam in Münster and a Laurea Magistrale in Studi Guiridici Europei in Turin *or* a Grado en derecho in Madrid.

(q) *Munich* University (*Ludwig-Maximilian*) (German/French with Paris 2 University—Panthéon-Assas [see same scheme for *Berlin, Humboldt*]) (http://www.jura.uni-muenchen.de/studium/studiengaenge/auslandsstudium/parisprogramm/studienprogramm/index.html), State Exam with 5th–7th term in Paris, leading to a Licence, after the State Exam converted into a Master.

(r) *Passau* University with two curricula, one German/Russian and one German/French

   (1) German-Russian with the Siberian Federal University Krasnojarsk (http://www.uni-passau.de/deutsches-und-russisches-recht/), two years' curriculum leading to a LL.M. from each university.
   (2) German-French with Université Toulouse I Capitole (http://www.jura.uni-passau.de/studium/studienangebote/internationale-studienangebote/doppelabschluss-toulouse/), the curriculum includes 1 year in Toulouse, leading to a licence and which can be credited towards the university part of the state exam.

(s) *Potsdam* University (German-French, with Paris Ouest University) (http://www.jura-potsdam-paris.de/images/stories/pdf/Infoblatt-Nov.2015-Internet.pdf), three years' curriculum, leading to a LL.B. in Potsdam and a Licence at Paris Ouest University or a Master 1 if one term is added. Can be credited towards the State Exam in the university part.

(t) *Regensburg* University (German/Russian with Lomonosov Moscow State University) (http://www.uni-regensburg.de/studium/pruefungsordnungen/medien/magister-master/magorechtwiss__7_voll.pdf), two years' curriculum leading to a LL.M. from each university.

(u) *Saarland* University with two curricula, one German/French, one German/English/French

   (1) German-French three years' study course with Paris 2, Université de Lorraine, Strasbourg, Toulouse I Capitole, Nice Sophia Antipolis, Grenobles Alpes Universities (see http://www.cjfa.eu/home_de), leading to a Licence in the partner universities which can be credited towards the university part

of the State Exam in Saarbrücken, additional two years for the State Exam. For the French students leading to a LL.B. in Saarbrücken.
(2) German-English-French two years' study course with Lille and Warwick Universities, with three terms abroad (https://www.uni-saarland.de/campus/studium/studienangebot/internationale-studienprogramme/doppelabschluesse/rechtswissenschaft-programm-lille-saarbruecken-warwick.html), leading to a Master 2 in Lille and includes studying at Warwick University. Possible only after successful completion of a three years' law curriculum.

(v) *Tübingen* University (German/French, with the University of Aix-en-Provence) (https://www.jura.uni-tuebingen.de/international/master-in-aix-en-provence), five years' curriculum leading to a master degree (one year in Aix, Master I bevor the State Exam/Master II after the State Exam) in Aix and a State Exam in Tübingen.

A few of the *specialised master programmes* (see above Sect. 2) can be studied as well as a double degree programme. This is the case in

- *Bremen* University, with its Hanse Law School (HLS) network, offers an LL.M. in Transnational Law in German and English (see http://studdb2.dez6.uni-bremen.de/sixcms/detail.php?id=4298&template=fach_lang&js=1), in cooperation with Oldenburg University (*Carl von Ossietzky*), and additionally with the option of a double degree, Groningen University (*Rijksuniversiteit*) (see also above Sect. 2).
- the *Frankfurt (Oder)* programme on German-Polish Law, organised with the *Adam-Mickiewiecz*-University Poznan.
- the *Hamburg* MEIL programme (with China University of Political Science and Law) leading to a LL.M. degree from both universities.
- the *Hannover* IT/IP law programme (with Oslo University) (see http://www.eulisp.de/double-degree-430.html), leading to a LL.M. in both universities.
- the *Heidelberg* Investment, Trade and Arbitration programme (with Santiago de Chile University) (http://www.hcla.uni-hd.de/english/kurs_master_jur_2018.html), leading to a LL.M. in both universities.
- the *Lüneburg* (*Leuphana*) International Economic Law programme (with Glasgow University) (https://www.leuphana.de/graduate-school/master/studienangebot/international-economic-law-llm.html), leading to a LL.M. in both universities.

Double degree programmes typically comprise some basic funding—either via Erasmus funds or as part of the individual scheme–,[22] typically, however not

[22] By way of example, the scheme of the European Law School described below, provides for every student in the Paris-Berlin exchange some 250,- € per month (Erasmus Grant) and 270,- € per month (via the French-German University, Université Franco-Allemande, Deutsch-Französische Hochschule) – in addition to some further scholarships of approx. 5.000- € (for the whole year) granted by participating law firms which can be combined with the sum named above of approx.

covering the costs and not excluding full-cost scholarships for which participants in such schemes apply in addition.

2.4 Funding and Summary

Finally, one should add that scholarships for studying abroad are available also outside such double degree programmes, and this is the majority of cases. They are available in good numbers and from many foundations, the most important being the German Academic Exchange Service (*Deutscher Akademischer Austauschdienst, DAAD*).[23]

The survey given shows considerable importance of an education in law in two (or more) languages, with two main branches: (1) at a minimal level virtually for all graduates with the normal German final law exam and degree ('*Staatsexamen*'), typically with English as an additional language (see above Sect. 1); (2) at a more advanced level with multiple structured offers for those capable and willing to invest more—i.e. approx. 10% of the graduates–, offers, however, which rather provide a framework to go abroad and 'see the original' and are not arranged for at the German universities any longer (no 'internationalization at home') (see above Sect. 3). German universities do offer, however, the counterpart and do so substantially: master studies (almost exclusively in German) for foreign students (see above Sect. 2).

3 Educational and Policy Considerations

The given survey shows considerable importance of an education in law in two (sometimes more) languages—as has been shown both at a minimal level applying virtually to all graduates (mostly in English) and in a more ambitious way for some 10% of the graduates who choose to invest more (in a larger range of languages/ possibilities from which they choose). This result does, however, not imply that the educational and policy considerations behind such shaping of the German university landscape are very elaborate. There is little theoretical discussion about the different purposes of such an international education—international in languages and international in places/jurisdictions. Mostly, it would seem that open-mindedness and a

520,- € per month. See https://www.european-law-school.eu/de/humboldt-european-law-school/finanzierung/. Still, an application to a foundation for a full-cost scholarship remains possible and typically more than half of the students of the European Law School have such full cost scholarships.

[23] For a useful survey from this organisation and also on a long list of other foundations giving such scholarships, see https://www.daad.de/ausland/studieren/stipendium/de/120-foerderungsorganisationen-im-berblick/.

particular kind of initiative and skill of adaptation is seen to be furthered in graduates that have engaged in (some kind of) foreign language studies or even studied abroad. Explicit arguments in writing are very scarce.

No broad discussion can be found about the impact such studies may have on a more pluralist view on law, and even less so on how such a goal—if it is to be furthered—could be advanced by a particular shaping of the offers. While in practice, the decision processes—and clearly the legislative processes—are influenced by the multi-national background of the drafting groups and decision bodies—namely within the EU Commission, but as well within other institutions such as the ECB etc.–, this does not seem to have a counterpart in the design of educational offers (with participation of German universities). The European Law School described below (Sect. 4) forms an exception to this. Therefore, a consistent discussion is lacking on how educational offers should best be shaped with a view to enhance and streamline processes of integration of pluralist approaches within legal practice, academia and rule-setting in Europe (and beyond). This discussion would be about governance models how best exchange views on legal models and the models themselves. While there is, of course, a huge literature on multi-level governance within the EU,[24] this literature focuses on the interplay between different levels, and not the horizontal exchange and good ways to further the understanding of such governance problems already within the curricula in law.

The underlying assumption of this contribution is almost completely absent from the discussion—namely that a diversity of languages and models expressed in those different languages arguably should not be seen primarily as an obstacle, but rather as a powerful discovery tool and tool for pluralistic world views. The lack of such discourse may well be owed to the fact that Europe—which would be a natural proponent and even leader for such a view—remained virtually silent in the theoretical discussion and empowerment of the potential of such diversity.

In law, the *comparative law method* would probably first come to mind when differences of language and of legal styles are at stake. It forms the *natural key discipline* for questions of *diversity*. Looking at this discipline and also comparing it to parallel strands of theoretical approach(es) in social sciences, may not really be conclusive with respect to questions of pluralism, but still be telling to some extent. In a nutshell:

German and French were the languages of comparative law. The founding fathers were writing in French and German—*translated* into English. Until the last decades of the twentieth century, the functional method developed on the basis of René David's and perhaps still more on the basis of Ernst Rabel's writings—formulated in its most developed form by Konrad Zweigert and Hein Kötz—was accepted as the key approach. Legal institutions and instruments, for instance rules, were compared

[24] Ground breaking Rokkan and Urwin (1983); today Chevallier (2003); Marks (1993), pp. 391–411; Marks et al. (1996), pp. 341–378; Hooghe and Marks (2001); Große Hüttmann and Knodt (2012), pp. 186–194; Joerges and Schmid (2011), pp. 277–310; Piattoni (2009), pp. 163–180; broad survey in the contributions to: de Búrca and Scott (2006).

mainly with respect to their function in solving particular problems, pushing their wording—mere terminology—or their place in a legal system—questions of system—to the background.[25] One can speak of a parallel method to that of an interest approach in doctrinal thinking. With respect to pluralism of legal solutions or models, it can be gathered from the literature based on this approach that diversity of ideas and legal approaches is accepted (quite prominently in René David's writings), albeit not really praised as enriching and furthering dynamics of new developments. As the approach has, however, increasingly formed the methodological basis of international unification or also supranational harmonization of the law (already since Rabel for International sales law),[26] there are at least two trends inherent: While the functional approach was typically seen as being rather neutral with respect to evaluating different jurisdictions and the solutions they find, there is nevertheless a claim of superiority for some rules/solutions over others when opting for one solution or another for harmonization/unification purposes—probably still more outspoken in the 1990s and 2000s when it then came to developing principles for European private law. The idea of neutrality is at odds with such endeavours. Moreover, it is noteworthy that the endeavour of developing uniform rules or principles has completely dominated the comparative law world in Europe in the last two or three decades. Would this not imply that diversity was rather seen as an obstacle than as richness in the European main stream discourse?

The functional comparative law approach has come under pressure from two sides in the last two decades, nourished by the social sciences more than by legal scholarship. The most prominent contribution to comparative law in English (American), nourished by economics, at least the one that has been most quoted by far, is much more radical than the European counterpart of the last decades. It now is very outspoken on superiority—no longer only for single solutions, some being picked from this jurisdiction, some others from that one. It claims superiority for whole jurisdictions. In very rough terms, legal origins theory[27] basically reached the conclusion that US-American law would make the world—virtually all countries—better-off, law of Germanic roots still being acceptable, law related to French origin being detrimental outright (it is paradoxical how René David's idea of legal families, first formulated in his native French, was revived here with this outcome). The high impact of this theory has certainly been favoured by the fact that it was termed as being developed statistically (with 'mathematical' precision), and that is was developed by economists. While the basic holding, upon more detailed

[25] For the functional comparative law approach, see for instance: Zweigert and Kötz (1996), p. 33 et seqq.

[26] See for instance: Strömholm (1992), pp. 611–623. For Rabel as the 'mastermind' behind the Hague Uniform Sales Law of 1964 and therefore also behind the Vienna Convention on the International Sale of Goods of 1980, see, among so many Bianca and Bonell (1987), pp. 1–7. The endeavours of unification/harmonization of European private law have consistently referred to this model. See, for instance A. Schwartze in Riesenhuber (2015), p. 64 et seq.

[27] Path breaking La Porta et al. (1997), pp. 1131–1150.

investigation, had to be taken back completely and was indeed taken back,[28] and while this is, of course, not the whole picture of comparative law in English/ American language, one can still not deny the strong prominence of this development (with a strong impact, for instance, on lending by the World Bank and a plethora of literature). This fact further adds to the overall plea made here that the overall picture of an English-centred world resulting in de facto evaluation in favour of legal scholarship and education in only one language mainly urgently requires corrective steps.

The most prominent development on the issue of diversity in political sciences differs to a remarkable extent from legal origins theory—despite sharing the broad, almost statistical approach of fact and pattern finding and gathering. Misfortunately it does not really find a strong counterpart in legal scholarship either. The 'Varieties of Capitalism' research—with the seminal piece by Peter Hall and David Soskice –[29] very prominently asks the questions whether the differences between social models—here those of capitalist kind—do not only constitute a fact, but also are helpful in the pursuit of two goals mainly: respond adequately to the diverging institutional contexts of different countries or regions and even further the arsenal of institutional settings at hand—for learning purposes or for different preferences etc. Superiority claims are weak or inexistent in this approach, it comes closest to seeing variety as a value.

In a comparative law approach, one trend which would perhaps come closest to such a 'varieties' approach could be called '*comparative legal foundations' approach*'. Instead of looking at single solutions for concrete problems, it would focus on the interplay of the main structures and determinants of the legal architecture, for instance which role plays the constitution, namely fundamental rights, in the development of private law (direct/indirect/no application), which court develops these ideas, how do other social sciences influence the development of the legal academic discourse, how practice and which social sciences, etc. etc., and relate this to the institutional structure of this jurisdiction, including the question of who are the main law authorities.[30] Such a comparative legal foundations' approach acknowledges these varieties, it also does not follow an approach of—in principle—the 'superior model'. It could even add foundations to an approach in which a pluralism of models is positively seen, at least in principle. While there is in my view no

[28] See only La Porta et al. (2008), pp. 285–322, responding to a variety of criticism. For critics of the approach, see, for example Klerman et al. (2011), pp. 379–409; Spamann (2010), pp. 149–165; id.: *Contemporary Legal Transplants: Legal Families and the Diffusion of (Coroporate) Law*, 2009 BYU Law Review, 1813–1877 (2010); id.: Large Sample, Quantitative Research Designs for Comparative Law?, 57 *American Journal of Comparative Law*, 797–810 (2009); For an overview on the topic of Legal Origins, see the collection and survey by Deakin and Pistor (2012).

[29] Path breaking Hall and Soskice (2001); and then Amable (2003); Crouch (2005), pp. 439–456; Hancke et al. (2007); Rhodes (2005), pp. 363-370; Sabel and Zeitlin (2008), pp. 271–327; Schröder (2013).

[30] For one first try, see Grundmann and Thiessen (2015); also see the review by Ch. Schmidt, *RabelsZ* 81 (2017) pp. 934–942.

equally seminal piece in legal scholarship to the 'varieties of capitalism' work by Hall and Soskice yet, a prominent and parallel line of thinking could clearly be developed on this basis and this could be the basis of a broad, innovative research agenda.

4 Language in Europe and in the European Law School in Particular

The European Law School has been created in 2007 (with rather extensive and complex negotiations from 2004 to 2007), with a first graduation in 2010 (https://www.european-law-school.eu/de)—with a view to give an answer to the policy considerations formulated above. Its basic principle is that graduates must have studied and sit exams in three languages and in three countries with three major 'styles' of legal thinking and practice—doing a full domestic exam in their home country and passing two LL.M. curricula in two different other countries, all three purposefully aligned. The school still grows and is of such shape and complexity that it can be seen more as an institution already than a curriculum or study course. It has created its own foundation securing the continued running of the school. It has study and research elements. It therefore is distinct from the other programmes named in constitution and in content. It starts being a true law school. The focus in the following is on contents, namely languages.

The scheme is fully integrated. It first comprised *Humboldt* University Berlin, *King's* College London and Paris University (Paris2—*Panthéon-Assas*). As of 2014 it was extended first to Rome and Amsterdam, currently to Athens, Lisbon, Madrid and Warzaw. This would already seem fairly 'representative' of the styles and problems in Europe (and still manageable). For all universities, the scheme is to fully train their students (carefully) chosen in their home university's jurisdiction—starting already at that time with foreign language legal courses in the other jurisdictions and thus building up a spirit of comparison from the beginning, however, with completely solid roots in one (national, but Europeanized) jurisdiction. For all universities, the scheme then foresees that their students switch in two consecutive years (the fourth and fifth) to master studies in two other countries, having passed their home state/university exam after the third year. How solid these roots in the home country are, can be gathered from the fact that the grades in the national law exam—for instance in Germany—not only largely outperform the overall national average (and by far!), but also quite considerably the average reached at universities which do choose their students as well and put the highest emphasis on teaching, such as in Germany Bucerius Law School (average grades still 2 credits higher than Bucerius' average which is the equivalent of almost one level A, B, C, D, E—and the highest level—of the overall German total—reached in the one case by 80%, in the other by 97%).[31] The degree to which the graduates of the European Law School outperform the average of other institutions is puzzling to some extent. While these students have been carefully chosen, there is as well some plausibility to the point that their early networking and their training in 'variety' from the beginning, prepared them particularly well for the more creative parts already in the national exam and that this contributed as well to the outstanding success (surprising also for the initiators). The preparation for variety is indeed the main focus: From the beginning, they become part of a varied group (various nationalities and styles of learning). This is fostered by strong networking activities, especially the joint summer schools and the mutual mentor relationships, the team spirit across borders and in different languages created. Students constantly experience the feeling of sometimes being more fluent in their own mother tongues, in understanding certain legal structures as established in their jurisdiction, but sometimes also being the 'newcomers', the ones who rather listen to learn.

The scheme is fully integrated: in the time line of five consecutive years, in the coherence between all cohorts of students of the same, but as well of different years, but very decidedly also by a continuity in subject matters. While it is possible for students also to vary specialisations in the different countries, all universities have also coordinated curricula. Therefore it is equally possible for students to choose one large area of specialisation and get the full range of varieties over the five years: where main branches—for instance private law with contracts, property and companies—are scrutinized from the perspective of each jurisdiction where they are studying, from a comparative solutions perspective, from a social sciences (for instance economics) perspective and put into context, for instance with market regulation or philosophical foundations. Hence students can choose either to have a portfolio of (different) specialisations—besides the multitude of styles they learn—or a broad understanding in one jurisdiction of the law at large combined with a truly European understanding of one area of specialisation (with social sciences background and a highly varied sample of ideas and solutions).

The yearly summer schools are a key component in the overall scheme. They are key socially and in contents, for students and teachers. They centre on a topic—grand and old, modern and cutting edge, rather targeted or very broad—and do so from many angles. With the participation from several countries and jurisdictions on the panels, in the audience, also with training units in multinational law firms. With a

[31] Between 2012 and 2016, 33% of all First German State Exam's candidates reached academic achievements that surpass the average mark (above 9 points: https://www.bundesjustizamt.de/DE/Themen/Buergerdienste/Justizstatistik/Juristen/Ausbildung_node.html;). At the Bucerius Law School, 80% of the candidates passed the first state examination for law students with this level of distinction (https://www.law-school.de/deutsch/die-hochschule/zahlen-und-fakten/) and the same is true for 97% of the students of the European Law School in Berlin. Thus, virtually all students of the ELS reached the formal qualification for embarking on PhD studies ('*Prädikatsexamen*'). This success and the careful selection process made it possible that no additional admission tests are needed and that therefore students can really switch without halts from one curriculum and jurisdiction to the other – in five fully integrated consecutive years.

topic that lends itself to a consideration of different social sciences, sometimes also art, culture and, for instance, behavioural approaches. In winter times, they meet for the annual graduations—each year (‘*promotion*’) having its name, typically linked to a place (of graduation), an event or a development of that year, populism and ‘hate of diversity’ in 2017: So far, the ‘promotions’ carry the names of Michelangelo, Marie Curie, Aristotle, Henri Heine, Hannah Ahrend, George Frederik Händel, Caterina da Siena, Anne Frank.[32]

The European Law School is designed to give life to a ‘narrative’ of Europe in which diversity of languages and styles is seen as opening up the realm of pluralist thought, and not mainly as an obstacle to one global approach on the basis of English.

5 Concluding Remarks

Language issues in legal education are not a matter of skills only, and not merely a technical matter either. It is highly relevant for contents. German universities offer broadly bilingual, less broadly multilingual training. For Europe—which is multilingual and whose characteristic is a historically and philosophically rooted diversity and appreciation of pluralism–, the language issue is arguably still more important than it may be in other countries or regions of the world. With the aspect of training for understanding diversity, language issues may, however, even be paramount in a world of different beliefs, forms of socialisation and legal models.

Annex 1: Einige grundlegende Überlegungen zur Bedeutung von Sprache (und Vielsprachigkeit) im Recht – sowie zur European Law School (Berlin/London/Paris/Rom/Amsterdam)

1. ***Recht gründet in Sprache***. Daher ist Ausbildung in den Rechtswissenschaften sprachbasiert – mehr als in vielen anderen Studien, selbst wenn sprachliche Eleganz auch noch allgemeiner (jedenfalls) in den Gesellschaftswissenschaften die Wirkmacht der Idee erhöhen mag, selbst etwa in der strengeren, modellorientierten Ökonomik (Fn. 1). Teils wird die Wichtigkeit von Exegese für die Rechtswissenschaften ähnlich hoch angesetzt wie in Theologie oder Philologie (Fn. 2). Und ein großer zeitgenössischer Rechtsphilosoph vergleicht

[32] For a description and explanation, see https://www.european-law-school.eu/en/european-law-school-network/network-events/graduations?set_language=en. For a broader and more detailed description of the school https://www.european-law-school.eu/en. The school plans to offer slots also outside the network, first to students from elsewhere in Europe, perhaps worldwide.

Recht mit Shakespeares Theater – setzt originelle Auslegung im Recht daher auf eine Ebene mit einfühlsamem Verständnis für die hohe Literatur (Fn. 3). In der Wissenstheorie geht ein starker Mehrheitstrend – fast schon die einhellige Meinung – dahin, dass Sprache Denken und Sinnstiftung beeinflusse – stark, sehr stark oder gar ganz entscheidend (Fn. 4).
Diese wenigen Überlegungen können auf folgenden Kern reduziert werden: Sprache formt Gedanken, etwa Gedanken zu rechtlichen und gesellschaftlichen Ordnungsmustern. Daher ***widerspricht eine Reduktion des globalen Diskurses auf nur eine Sprache*** nicht nur der Tatsache, dass es eine Vielzahl solcher Ordnungsmuster gibt, sondern der ***Idee selbst eines Pluralismus von gesellschaftlichen Ordnungsmodellen*** – zugleich einer Form von Individualismus –, namentlich dem Gedanken, dass dieser Pluralismus auch zentral und grundlegend aus normativer Perspektive erscheint. Es kann darauf verwiesen werden, dass Pluralismus in der einen oder anderen Form als Verfassungswert gesehen wird (jedenfalls in den westlichen Demokratien, Fn. 5). Man kann sogar so weit gehen, dass eine globale Diskursgemeinschaft zu Fragen des Rechts, die diese grundlegende Wichtigkeit von Pluralismus ernst nimmt, (sehr viel dezidierter und aktiver) Sprachvielfalt im Diskurs fördern müsste.

An meiner eigenen Fakultät an der Humboldt-Universität hat der erste Inhaber des Lehrstuhls für Internationales Privatrecht und Rechtsvergleichung, *Axel Flessner*, ein Kosmopolit, der viel Energie auf einen Europäisierungsprozess des Privatrechts verwandte (Fn. 6), stets dezidiert die Fahne der deutschen Sprache als Wissenschafts- und Ausbildungssprache hochgehalten – allgemein im internationalen Diskurs, jedenfalls für die Humboldt-Universität und ein Land wie Deutschland. Damit hielt er zugleich auch die Fahne einer Autonomie deutschen Rechtsdenkens hoch, zugleich für ein deutsches, österreichisches und schweizerisches Recht und auch die Gesellschaftsmodelle, die sich in diesen niederschlagen. Zwar mag dieses Insistieren für kleinere Staaten oder weniger im Zentrum stehende Universitäten in der Tat weniger wichtig sein als für die Leitrechtsordnungen und ihre großen Universitäten (außerhalb der angloamerikanischen Welt), die Rechtsdenken substantiell mitprägten *Axel Flessner* tadelte mich deswegen dafür, den Namen einer "European Law School" für das unten beschriebene Netz von Universitäten gewählt oder jedenfalls akzeptiert zu haben, desgleichen den Titel eines "*Juriste Européen*" für alle Absolventen, die das gesamte Curriculum durchlaufen haben mit Master-Abschlüssen (oder vergleichbar) in drei großen Europäischen Rechtsordnungen und drei Sprachen (vgl. unten 2. b)). Da zählte es wenig, dass diese Institution und dieses Curriculum im Kern doch gerade primär auf eine Vermittlung der Vielfalt von Sprachen ("*plurilinguism*"), Vielfalt der Stile und Modelle zugeschnitten sind – mehr als jeder andere Verbund zuvor. Mein Kollege *Flessner* wird es vielleicht auch nicht schätzen, dass dieser Beitrag primär auf Englisch geschrieben ist, selbst wenn ich hier im Anhang noch die deutsche "Übersetzung" nachreiche und mit alldem sogar aufzeige, wie mich die globale Diskurskultur dazu zwingt, primär in der Sprache zu formulieren, die ich natürlich weniger elegant einsetze als ein Muttersprachler, ganz zu schweigen vom Dänenprinz Hamlet in den Sätzen, die wir von ihm kennen.

Das Paradox von Sprache und Recht, insbesondere in ihrer Wirkmacht auf Gedankenbildung und damit auch Recht, geht jedoch weiter. *Flessner* hat diesen Gedanken zwar jedenfalls mir gegenüber nicht explizit geäußert, besonders überzeugend erscheint seine Haltung jedoch vor allem dann, wenn man sie als kategorisch versteht – wie ja auch die Art und Weise seines Insistierens auf deutscher Sprache in Rechtslehre und -forschung durchaus etwas Kategorisches hatte. Besonders überzeugend erscheint mir *Flessners* Grundauffassung, wenn man sie als Ruf nach vielsprachiger Ausbildung und Diskussion im Recht versteht. Denn mit der Reduktion auf eine globale Sprache – eine lingua franca – läuft die globale Diskussion zugleich Gefahr, dass eine erhebliche Zahl von Ansätzen – vielleicht der größte Teil –, die im Großteil der Welt entwickelt werden, jeweils in der Landessprache, vom Diskurs ausgeschlossen bleiben oder jedenfalls ungleich weniger Gehör finden. Dieses Risiko wird noch dadurch erhöht, dass Sprachenvielfalt im globalen Umfeld vor allem als ein Hindernis für einen gemeinsamen Diskurs verstanden wird und viel weniger als Chance für einen reicheren, nuancierter und pluralistischer angelegten Austausch von Ideen zu Recht und Gesellschaftsordnung. Mit anderen Worten, Sprachenarmut wird als das effizienteste Arrangement einer weltweiten Diskussion gesehen, wo sie ebenso gut als intellektuelle Schwäche gesehen werden könnte, als eine Minderung von Wissen und Vielfalt in weltweiten Diskursen. Beispiele hierfür liegen auf der Hand.

Wenn beispielsweise *Thomas Piketty* – bei all seiner Originalität – doch primär schlicht die Essenz von *Karl Marx* – und später *Hugo Sinzheimer* – "übersetzt" in ökonomische Modelle und in modernes Englisch (Fn. 8) – ein global gebildeter französischer Wissenschaftler, der sich primär an ein englischsprachiges globales Publikum wendet –, dann erzeugt er damit einen absoluten Hype (Fn. 9). Die Frage jedoch, wie weit schon *Marx* ging, wie weit *Sinzheimer*, und wo *Piketty* wirklich weiter geht, kann auf globaler Ebene schlicht nicht diskutiert werden – weil der Kreis derjenigen, die an der Diskussion gut informiert teilnehmen könnten, rein sprachlich nicht ausreicht, auch wenn *Piketty* selbst sich dem durchaus stellen wollte (und in der Tat zuerst auf Französisch und Deutsch publizierte). Staatsgrenzen werden als Hindernis im globalen Wissenschaftsdiskurs eine "*quantité négligeable*" verglichen mit Sprachbarrieren, sicherlich in den Rechts-, aber wohl auch allgemeiner in den Gesellschaftswissenschaften.

Dieses erste Beispiel ist freilich noch relativ bescheiden. Wenn vielfach – vielleicht gar überwiegend – das "Rad ein zweites Mal erfunden" wird, ist dies das eine. Etwas anderes ist es, wenn aufgrund von Sprachbarrieren Ideenentwicklungen den globalen Wissenschaftsdiskurs nicht mehr (hinreichend) erreichen und daher auch häufig nicht mehr auf die weltweite Wirklichkeit und Praxis durchschlagen. Eine zentrale Entwicklung des letzten halben Jahrhunderts – zugleich eine Wasserscheide zwischen US-amerikanischem Recht (nicht der gesamten angloamerikanischen Welt) und den meisten anderen

Rechtsordnungen – wird häufig (und durchaus überzeugend) darin gesehen, wie sehr die Ökonomik und namentlich die ökonomische Analyse die Fortentwicklung und Ausbildung rechtlicher Konzepte und Auslegung beeinflussen. Wenn dies heute eine der wichtigsten Formen interdisziplinärer Befruchtung in den Rechtswissenschaften und im Rechtsdenken darstellt, erscheint die Frage danach, welcher (Haupt-)Ansatz gewählt wird, allerdings zentral. Derzeit erscheint ein Law & Economics-Ansatz US-amerikanischer Prägung als der dominante, geprägt seit den 1960er Jahren u.a. von *Ronald Coase*, *Guido Calabresi* über *Oliver Williamson* bis hin zu *Richard Posner* und anderen (Fn. 10) –, worüber dann ein alternativer Strang einer Befruchtung rechtswissenschaftlicher Betrachtung durch Modelle der Ökonomik praktisch gänzlich ausgeblendet erscheint. Dieser alternative Strang – in der ordoliberalen Schule – beeinflusste zwar erheblich die Europäische Entwicklung, namentlich im Bereich der Regulierung im öffentlichen Interesse –, doch blieb der Widerhall in der globalen Diskussion vergleichsweise schwach (Fn. 11). Die Entwicklung beider Ansätze verlief verschieden, sowohl in den inhaltlichen Lösungen als auch in der Methodik. In den inhaltlichen Lösungen liegt der Hauptunterschied – etwas holzschnittartig gesprochen – darin, dass der zweitgenannte Strang eine ungleich robustere Ausrichtung am öffentlichen Interesse favorisierte, beispielsweise Wettbewerbsbeschränkungen nur sehr ausnahmsweise und bei sehr konkretem Nachweis überwiegender Vorteile – und auch nicht erst solcher in weiter Zukunft – als gerechtfertigt ansah. Umgekehrt manifestiert sich der erstgenannte Strang im sog "more economic approach", in dem zukünftige erwartete Gesamtwohlfahrtsgewinne mit den Verlusten aus dem wettbewerbsbeschränkenden Verhalten zu vergleichen sind. Dieser Unterschied in den inhaltlichen Lösungen ist vorliegend marginal. Beide Ansätze unterscheiden sich jedoch auch grundlegend im Methodischen. Der US-amerikanisch geprägte Law & Economics-Ansatz war bald von einer Dominanz ökonomischer Modellbildung im technischen Sinne geprägt, eindeutig auf Gesamtwohlfahrtsrechnung und das Effizienzparadigma ausgerichtet, überhaupt stärker mathematisch gefasst und gekennzeichnet durch eine Dominanz eindeutig formulierter (häufig jedoch als unrealistisch kritisierter) Modellannahmen (alles im Wesentlichen erst *nach Coase*, manches auch etwa von *Calabresi* nicht gutgeheißen). Umgekehrt fußte der ordoliberale Ansatz nicht in dieser Art formalisierter Parameter (bei den Annahmen ebenso wie bei der Modellbildung). Er setzte vielmehr vorrangig auf eine gezielte Herausarbeitung von Vor- und Nachteilen bestimmter Lösungen in möglichst realistischen Szenarien (häufig mit realen, auch historischen und institutionellen Kontexten und meist "in Prosa") und ihre vorsichtige Abwägung gegeneinander – gepaart mit der Herausarbeitung von Leitprinzipien und Plausibilitätskontrollen.

Dies ist nicht der Ort, ein Urteil über beide Ansätze zu formulieren oder gar zu begründen, wohl aber, um auf drei Folgen aus den genannten Unterschieden hinzuweisen (für die auch das genannte Beispiel kennzeichnend ist): (1) Der Unterschied zwischen beiden Ansätzen ist keineswegs vor allem formaler Natur und seine Tragweite ist enorm – wobei der US-amerikanische Ansatz den großen

Vorteil der schlagenden Einfachheit, ja einer stringenten "Anwendbarkeit" (oder Subsumierbarkeit) hat, freilich auch den Nachteil eines (teils als viel zu weitgehend empfundenen) Abstrahierens von der Lebenswirklichkeit und (häufig) auch eines Fehlens von Plausibilitätskontrollen. Der Ansatz fußt stringenter in einer Philosophie der Formalisierung und mathematischer Deduktion, während der Alternativansatz stärker wertebasiert und realitätsverhaftet erscheint, freilich auch weniger präzise. (2) Trotz dieser wirklich erheblichen Unterschiede wird der Alternativansatz eher wenig diskutiert, was dann auch eine Diskussion der komparativen Vorteile und Nachteile beider Ansätze in den Hintergrund treten lässt (Fn. 12). Es wird relativ wenig global diskutiert, ob ein Abstellen auf Modelle und eine mathematische Ableitung von Ergebnissen nicht beispielsweise die größten Teile der Rechtswissenschaften und -praxis von der Diskussion ausschließt und ob dies für die interdisziplinäre Diskussion zwingend notwendig ist, und umgekehrt, ob dieser Effekt etwa im Rahmen des Alternativansatzes nicht oder in geringerem Umfang zu konstatieren wäre. (3) Diese Beschreibung der Diskussionslage bezieht sich m.E. nicht nur auf den US-amerikanischen Diskurs, sondern auch auf den globalen, und wird m.E. auch durch den Umstand begünstigt, dass eine vielsprachige, wirklich weltweite Diskussion heute so weitgehend versiegt ist. Dieser Zustand scheint auf beiden Seiten des Atlantiks unterschiedliche Folgen zu zeitigen – jenseits des Atlantiks dahingehend, dass der Alternativansatz praktisch unbekannt und undiskutiert bleibt, diesseits des Atlantiks, namentlich in kontinentaleuropäischen Rechtsordnungen, dahingehend, dass ein Law & Economics-Ansatz meist entweder ganz übernommen oder pauschal abgelehnt wird und nicht wirklich in seiner Methodik diskutiert, ggf. modifiziert und transformiert wird. Es mag also sein, dass der globale Diskurs zu Fragen von Recht und Rechtswissenschaften einen Preis für die Unfähigkeit zu zahlen hat, einige weitere globale Sprachen zu berücksichtigen. Wenn ein stärker an Algorithmen ausgerichteter, modellorientierter Ansatz unfähig war, die Gefahren einer massenweisen Vergabe von Subprime loans, ihrer Bündelung in Wertpapieren ohne Selbstbehalt beim Risiko (CDSs und CDOs), der Konzeptionierung und zugleich der Beurteilung durch Ratingagenturen etc. etc. zu kennen, desgleichen eine durchweg auf diese Modelle eingeschworene Anlegeröffentlichkeit, wir zugleich heute sagen, dass diese Schwächen doch nicht nur ex post ("by hindsight") relativ offensichtlich erscheinen, mag dieser Preis sogar sehr hoch gewesen sein. Wäre es da nicht sinnvoll gewesen, wenn im globalen Diskurs starke Alternativansätze präsent gewesen und möglicherweise Zweifel begründet hätten – Ansätze, die ein Vorsorgeprinzip stärker betonen und Plausibilitätskontrollen systematisch vorsehen, freilich weniger "exakt rechnen"?

Damit ist die Frage aufgeworfen, wer *für die Erhaltung größerer sprachlicher Diversität Verantwortung* trägt. Zugleich zeigt sich, dass *Flessner* mit seinem Insistieren auf Deutsch als Wissenschafts- und Lehrsprache rechthaben mag, jedenfalls wenn er kategorisch argumentiert und es um ganze rechtswissenschaftliche Ideenwelten geht. Relativ offensichtlich liegt eine Verantwortlichkeit in diesen Fragen bei denjenigen Rechtsordnungen (und

Universitäten), bei denen es plausibel erscheint, dass sie "noch" gehört werden könnten. Natürlich ist dieser Ruf nach mehr Diversität – in den Sprachen und damit auch in den Denkansätzen zu Gesellschaftsordnung – nur dann nicht gänzlich realitätsfremd, wenn man sich eingesteht, dass der Kreis der "global hörbaren" Rechtsordnungen und Diskursgemeinschaften dennoch ziemlich beschränkt bleiben wird. Er ist dann freilich dennoch einem rein auf Englisch beschränkten globalen Diskurs im vorliegend beschriebenen Kern schon deutlich überlegen (Fn. 13). Wenn dann Europa in solch einem vielsprachigen globalen Diskurs noch eine weitere "Stimme" haben mag – neben dem Englischen –, haben wohl das Französische, Deutsche und/oder Spanische vielleicht die größten Chancen (letzte Fn.). Und auch bei den Universitäten stehen die global Sichtbaren aus vergleichbaren Gründen besonders in der Verantwortung – und dann in Deutschland wohl tatsächlich auch *Axel Flessners* Humboldt-Universität. Man kann daher *Flessners* Standpunkt schwerlich rundum ablehnen, wenn er so dezidiert das Deutsche als Wissenschafts- und Lehrsprache einfordert. Die Verantwortung liegt freilich nicht nur bei denen, die Rechtsordnungen der beschriebenen Art zu Gehör bringen können, namentlich von weltweit sichtbaren Foren (außerhalb der angloamerikanischen Welt) aus. Wenn es im Recht auch um "Fairness" – im angloamerikanischen Wortverständnis – geht und wenn gesellschaftswissenschaftliche Diskussion weltweit so strukturiert werden soll, dass sie Wohlfahrt global und ein weltweites Verständnis möglichst gut fördert, ist die Verantwortung der angloamerikanischen Welt selbst in dieser Frage vielleicht vergleichbar groß oder sogar noch größer. Mag dies auch zunächst paradox klingen, so ist es möglicherweise noch überzeugender, wenn der Impetus für einen linguistisch reicheren Diskurs, mit mehr Offenheit für die Vielfalt der Gesellschaftsmodelle, von zentralen Institutionen und Stimmen aus der angloamerikanischen Welt formuliert wird und dies sehr prominent (Fn. 14). Gerade den USA, denen häufig die gegenteilige Haltung vorgeworfen wird (teils ist von "akademischem Imperialismus" die Rede), käme hierbei eine zentrale Rolle zu. Ein Ruf nach Diversität würde besonders überzeugen, wenn er aus einer Position der Stärke heraus formuliert würde, d.h. von Institutionen aus dem dominanten Sprachraum heraus. Das mag freilich ein wenig gewagt, ja vielleicht sogar naiv klingen. Meine Hoffnung ginge freilich dahin, dass diese Überlegung zwar nicht den "mainstream" erreichen wird, wohl aber die Avantgarde, diejenigen, die die Entwicklung vorantreiben.

2. Obwohl das Angebot von mehrsprachigen Ausbildungen im Recht (in verschiedenen Rechten) mit Beteiligung deutscher Universitäten umfangreich ist (vgl. die breite Übersicht oben II.), fehlt praktisch jegliche Diskussion zu der ***Frage, welche Ziele mit solchen ("mehrsprachigen') Angeboten verfolgt*** werden und werden sollten und inwieweit die Angebote dahingehend optimiert werden können. Für die ***European Law School*** wurden solche Überlegungen hingegen durchaus prägend, die abstrakter gefasst werden können (unten a), die dann jedoch auch auf das konkrete Design der European Law School (Berlin/London/Paris/Rom/Amsterdam) bezogen werden können (unten b).

(a) Aus dem Überblick zur juristischen Ausbildung in Deutschland ergibt sich, dass zwei-, teils auch mehrsprachige Angebote durchaus Gewicht haben – dies einerseits auf einem flächendeckenden Mindestniveau, weil praktisch alle Staatsexamensabsolventen eine Zusatzsprachqualifikation (idR in Englisch) erwerben müssen, andererseits deutlich weitergehend – etwa ein volles Jahr in fremder Sprache – für ca. 10% der Absolventen, die mehr investieren (und dabei aus einem breiten Kreis von Sprachen auswählen können). Umgekehrt steht jedoch hinter diesem Angebot kein näher diskutiertes und explizit gemachtes Ausbildungsziel. Es gibt kaum theoretische Diskussionen zu der Frage, welche Ziele im einzelnen eine internationale Ausbildung rechtfertigen – international in Sprachen und/oder Orten bzw. Rechtsordnungen. Primär wird offenbar davon ausgegangen, bei den jeweiligen Absolventen werde damit eine generelle Offenheit für andere Ansätze und eine bessere Anpassungsfähigkeit gefördert, namentlich bei solchen, die dabei auch ins Ausland gegangen sind.

Es fehlt an einer breiten Diskussion namentlich zu der Frage, ob solche Studien vielleicht auch ein stärker pluralistisches Bild von Recht befördern, und erst recht zu der Frage, ob deswegen ein bestimmter Zuschnitt des Curriculums den Vorzug verdient. Obwohl die Entscheidungsprozesse in der Praxis der EU – namentlich auch die Rechtssetzungsprozesse – zweifelsohne dadurch beeinflusst werden, dass die Entscheidungskörper regelmäßig aus verschiedenen Staatsangehörigkeiten zusammengesetzt sind – in der EU Kommission oder in anderen Institutionen, etwa der EZB etc. –, ist keine bewusst hierauf abgestimmte Philosophie hinter den Ausbildungsangeboten erkennbar (jedenfalls soweit deutsche Universitäten beteiligt sind). Die European Law School (vgl. oben Abschnitt IV.) erscheint insoweit als Ausnahme. Daher fehlt auch eine gezielte Diskussion der sinnvollsten Zuschnitte von Curricula, die pluralistische Inhalte in Ausbildung, Wissenschaft und (Gesetzgebungs-)Praxis zum Tragen bringen. Hierher würde auch eine Diskussion zu der Frage zählen, wie eine Governance für intensiven Austausch rechtlicher Ansätze und Modelle zuzuschneiden wäre. Obwohl es eine umfangreiche Literatur zu den Mehrebenensystemen – der sog. multi-level governance – in der EU gibt (Fn. 23), betrifft diese doch primär das Zusammenspiel zwischen unterschiedlichen Ebenen, nicht so sehr den horizontalen Austausch und adäquate Wege, ein gegenseitiges Verständnis zu befördern, etwa durch eine bestimmte Gestaltung der juristischen Curricula.

Die hier vorgestellten Überlegungen finden sich praktisch nicht in dieser Diskussion – namentlich auch nicht dahingehend, dass eine Diversität in den Sprachen, Stilen und Modellen keineswegs primär als ein Hindernis für die Verständigung, sondern vielmehr als ein mächtiges Entdeckungsinstrument und als ein Schlüssel für eine pluralistische Weltsicht verstanden werden könnte und sollte. Dies mag seine Ursache in dem Umstand haben, dass Europa – das für solch eine Diskussion besonders prädestiniert erscheint – eine Diskussion über Theorie und Potentiale von Diversität nur wenig befruchtete oder noch weniger anführte.

Soweit Sprachenvielfalt und Unterschiede in den Stilen zur Debatte stehen, erscheint in den Rechtswissenschaften die *Rechtsgleichung als Methode* besonders direkt aufgerufen. Sie bildet gleichsam die *Schlüsseldisziplin* in Fragen von *Diversität*. Die Entwicklung in dieser Disziplin – auch im Vergleich zu Parallelentwicklungen in anderen Gesellschaftswissenschaften – ist jedenfalls bedeutsam, auch wenn sie nicht den Kreis der Möglichkeiten erschöpft. In der gebotenen Kürze:

Deutsch und Französisch waren die Sprachen der Rechtsvergleichung, ihrer Gründungsväter – dann ins Englische übersetzt. Bis in die letzten Dekaden des 20. Jahrhunderts dominierte der funktionale Rechtsvergleich, basierend auf den Werken von *René David* und wohl noch unmittelbarer von *Ernst Rabel* – auf den Punkt gebracht dann von *Konrad Zweigert* und *Hein Kötz*. Rechtsinstrumente und institutionelle Arrangements, etwa Normen, wurden primär in ihrer Funktion miteinander verglichen, namentlich welche Probleme sie mit welchem Ergebnis lösen, dabei Begrifflichkeiten und Fragen der Systematik in den Hintergrund gerückt (Fn. 24). Die Parallelität zu einer Interessenjurisprudenz im Rahmen der Dogmatik ist nicht von der Hand zu weisen. Fragt man nach Pluralismus rechtlicher Lösungen und Modelle, ist die funktional-rechtsvergleichende Literatur zwar durchaus dahin zu verstehen, dass solch ein Pluralismus akzeptiert wird, in *René Davids* Schriften sogar positiv besetzt erscheint, jedoch umgekehrt auch nicht als bereichernd verstanden wird oder gar als Quelle von Dynamik und Entwicklung. Da die funktionale Rechtsvergleichung freilich zunehmend auch die Grundlage für internationale Rechtsvereinheitlichung oder auch supranationale Rechtsangleichung bildete (bereits seit *Rabels* Initiativen für ein Einheitliches Kaufrecht, vgl. Fn. 25), sind ihr zumindest zwei Tendenzen ebenfalls inhärent: Obwohl der funktionale Ansatz grundsätzlich als neutral verstanden wird im Hinblick auf die Bewertung der verschiedenen, verglichenen Lösungen, liegt doch bereits in der Auswahl der einen oder der anderen Lösung für Rechtsvereinheitlichungszwecke zugleich auch ein Werturteil, jedenfalls für die jeweilige einzelne Lösung – und dies noch expliziter seit den 1990er und 2000er Jahren, als inter- und supranationale Prinzipienkataloge entwickelt wurden, namentlich im Europäischen Privatrecht. Grundsätzliche Neutralität als Anspruch ist mit solch einem Unterfangen schwer zu vereinbaren. Außerdem ist bemerkenswert, dass seit Aufnahme der Arbeiten an der Entwicklung einheitlicher Regeln durch Arbeitsgruppen und Unterkommissionen die Welt der Rechtsvergleichung jedenfalls in Europa sehr weitgehend von dieser "Goldgräberstimmung" dominiert erscheint (und klassische Rechtsvergleichung weitgehend in den Hintergrund trat). Impliziert nicht auch diese Entwicklung jedenfalls im Europäischen Diskursumfeld, dass Diversität letztlich eher als ein Hindernis denn als Quelle der Bereicherung gesehen wurde?

Der Ansatz einer funktionalen Rechtsvergleichung geriet freilich spätestens seit den 1990er Jahren von zwei Seiten unter Druck, dies jeweils eher von gesellschafts- als von rechtwissenschaftlicher Seite. Den prominentesten Beitrag zur Rechtsvergleichung in der US-amerikanischen Literatur formulierten

Ökonomen, jedenfalls den am meisten Zitierten. Er ist ungleich radikaler als der zeitgleiche Europäische Vereinheitlichungsstrom. Überlegenheit der jeweiligen Lösung wird nunmehr explizit gemacht und gar zum vorrangigen Thema – und dies für ganze Rechtsordnungen, nicht mehr nur für einzelne Lösungen, die teils dieser, teils dann jener Rechtsordnung entnommen werden konnten. Sehr stark verkürzt kann der Legal Origin-Ansatz (Fn. 26) dahingehend zusammengefasst werden, dass das US-amerikanische (Finanz- und Gesellschafts-)Recht deutlich höhere Gesamtwohlfahrtseffekte zeitige – und dies in praktisch allen Ländern – als kontinentaleuropäisches Recht, wobei das französische Recht und seine Tochterrechtsordnungen als nochmals problematischer eingestuft wurden als Rechte des germanischen Rechtskreises (in der Tat wurde wieder in Rechtsfamilien gedacht, doch so gar nicht mehr im Sinne ihres "Erfinders", René David). Seine starke Verbreitung wurde durch den Umstand begünstigt, dass der Ansatz als statistisch gegründet formuliert wurde (gleichsam als "mathematisch exakt") und dies von Ökonomen. Obwohl die Kernthese – nach genauerer Untersuchung – unhaltbar erschien (und auch weitestgehend von den Autoren selbst zurückgenommen wurde, vgl. Fn. 27), und obwohl auch die angloamerikanische Rechtsvergleichung sich selbstverständlich nicht in diesem Ansatz erschöpft, ist seine Dominanz doch unverkennbar (mit teils durchschlagender Wirkung in der Politik der Weltbank und in einer Flut an Literatur). Dieser Umstand trägt weiter zum vorliegend formulierten Petitum bei, dass in einem vom Englischen dominierten globalen Diskurs in den Rechtswissenschaften Kurskorrekturen – im Sinne von Vielfalt – angezeigt erscheinen.

In den Politikwissenschaften ist die wohl prominenteste Entwicklung in Sachen Diversität eine bemerkenswert andere als in der Ökonomik – obwohl beide Ansätze etwa den breit-empirischen, auch statistischen Ansatz teilen, die Suche nach Tatsachen und Faktenmustern. Leider findet sich jedoch (auch) hierzu keine starke Parallelströmung in den Rechtswissenschaften. Die sog. "Varieties of Capitalism"-Forschung – mit der bahnbrechenden Formulierung der Agenda durch *Peter Hall* und *David Soskice* (Fn. 28) – stellt sehr prominent und im Kern die Frage nach den Unterschieden zwischen verschiedenen Gesellschafts- und Wirtschaftsmodellen – hier jeweils kapitalistischer Prägung –, und diese werden sichtlich nicht nur als Faktum gesehen, sondern auch als förderlich jedenfalls in der Verfolgung von zwei Zielen: Unterschiedliche Modelle erscheinen als unterschiedlich gut auf die verschiedenen institutionellen Rahmenbedingungen verschiedener Länder und Volkswirtschaften zugeschnitten, zudem und darüber hinaus bereichern sie das Arsenal an Lösungsformen – um daraus zu lernen, unterschiedliche Präferenzen zu bedienen etc. Der Anspruch, überlegende Modelle zu ermitteln, wird praktisch nicht formuliert – vielmehr liegt gerade diesem Ansatz am stärksten das Bild einer Diversität, die bereichert, zugrunde.

Als Ansatz in der Rechtsvergleichung steht ein noch verhaltener Trend aus jüngster Zeit dem "Varieties of Capitalism"-Ansatz am nächsten. Diesen könnte man treffend mit dem Begriff eines *Grundlagenrechtsvergleichs* umschreiben.

Darin werden nicht Lösungen für klar umrissene Probleme verglichen, sondern die Parameter eines Zusammenspiels von Grundstrukturen und zentralen Bausteinen in der Architektur der jeweiligen Rechtsordnungen. Dabei fragt man etwa nach der Rolle, die Verfassungen, namentlich Grundrechte, in der Fortentwicklung von Privatrecht spielen (etwa unmittelbare oder mittelbare Drittwirkung), oder, welches Gericht diese Ideen entwickelt, oder auch, wie andere (Gesellschafts-)Wissenschaften in Rechtswissenschaft und -praxis fruchtbar gemacht werden und auf welche man sich primär bezieht, etc. etc., und setzt all dies in Bezug zum institutionellen Arrangement in dieser Rechtsordnung, einschließlich der Frage, wer und welche Institutionen besonders große Beiträge zur Fortentwicklung der jeweiligen Rechtsordnung erbringen – die sog. "Law Authorities" (Fn. 29). Solch ein Grundlagenrechtsvergleich fußt in einem positiven Verständnis von Diversität, geht grundsätzlich nicht von der Überlegenheit einer Rechtsordnung gegenüber anderen aus. Damit steht er auch einer pluralistischen Sicht der Modelle grundsätzlich positiv gegenüber. Obwohl es m.E. in der Rechtsvergleichung an einem vergleichbar bahnbrechenden Werk fehlt wie in der Variaties of Capitalism-Literatur (mit *Hall* und *Soskice*), erscheint doch eine parallele Entwicklung der Diskussion denkbar und könnte eine breite Forschungsrichtung hiervon ihren Ausgang nehmen – mit großem, weitgehend unbearbeitetem Terrain.

(b) Die European Law School nahm 2007 den Betrieb auf (mit komplexen und in die Tiefe gehenden Verhandlungen 2004-2007), die erste Graduierung fand 2010 statt (https://www.european-law-school.eu/de). Ziel war es, Einheit und Vielfalt Europas, nationaler Verankerung von Recht und Schaffung einer Europäischen Rechtsgemeinschaft jeweils *beiden* – im Zusammenspiel – in der juristischen grundständigen Ausbildung adäquates Gewicht einzuräumen. Das Grundprinzip der Schule besteht darin, dass alle Absolventinnen und Absolventen in drei Ländern und drei Sprachen studiert und ihre Examina abgelegt haben müssen, damit auch drei große "Stile" des Rechts und Rechtsdenkens in Europa vertieft kennen – und zwar mit einem vollen Rechtsstudium im Ausgangsland, etwa einem deutschen Staatsexamen, und zwei vollständigen Masterstudiengängen in zwei anderen Ländern, wobei alle akademischen Jahre genau aufeinander abgestimmt sind und unmittelbar aufeinander folgen. Die Schule wächst weiter, das Arrangement ist so vielschichtig und stabil, dass schon heute eher von einer Institution als einem Studienprogramm gesprochen werden sollte. Eine eigene Stiftung wurde gegründet, um die fortgesetzte Durchführung zu garantieren, die Humboldt European Law School Stiftung. Die European Law School vereinigt in sich Lehr- und Forschungsinhalte. Das unterscheidet sie von allen Doppelabschlussprogrammen, der zweithöchsten Stufe an Verdichtung und Komplexität im internationalen Rechtsunterricht. Am wichtigsten ist jedoch ein Blick auf die Inhalte, namentlich der Umgang mit Sprachen und Stilen.

Es handelt sich um einen dicht integrierten Verbund. Dieser umfasste zunächst die *Humboldt* Universität zu Berlin, das *King's* College in London und die Universität Paris2 – *Panthéon-Assas*, die größte Juristische Fakultät Frankreichs. Ab 2013 wurde er ausgeweitet auf Rom (die altehrwürdige 'La Sapienza') und auf Amsterdam, derzeit zudem auf Athen, Lissabon, Madrid und Warschau. Damit erscheinen die Stile und Problemlagen in Europa schon sehr breit im Verbund vertreten, dieser jedoch noch handhabbar. Alle Universitäten verpflichten sich, ihren (sehr sorgfältig ausgewählten) Studenten das jeweilige Examen dieser Rechtsordnung ungeschmälert abzuverlangen – während dieser Phase freilich bereits auch fremdsprachliche Kurse in den anderen Rechtsordnungen anzubieten und so von Anfang an ein Verständnis für den Vergleich, die Vielfältigkeit möglicher Lösungen zu fördern, dies freilich bei einem Aufbau sehr solider Wurzeln in dem einen nationalen (wenn auch vom EU-Recht beeinflussten) Heimatrecht. Für alle Universitäten sieht die Verbundstruktur sodann vor, dass alle Studenten in den zwei auf das Heimatexamen folgenden Jahren (Jahr vier und fünf) zwei Masterstudiengänge an zwei ausländischen Universitäten (mit den jeweiligen Examina) durchlaufen, dies in zwei weiteren Sprachen. Wie solide dabei die Wurzeln im Ausgangsland gebildet werden, zeigt sich daran, dass die Studierenden im jeweiligen Ausgangsland ihr Examen – in Deutschland ihr Staatsexamen – nicht nur um ein Vielfaches besser ablegen als der nationale Durchschnitt, sondern auch recht deutlich besser als Studierende von Universitäten, die ebenfalls diese intensiv auswählen und besonderes Gewicht auf die Lehre legen – wie in Deutschland namentlich die Bucerius Law School (immer noch ca. 2 Punkte höherer Punktedurchschnitt, also fast eine ganze Note Unterschied im Durchschnitt, Prädikatsexamen bei 80% der Absolventen in dem einen Fall, bei 97% in dem anderen, Fn. 30). In gewisser Hinsicht überraschen diese Ergebnisse durchaus, zumal die Zusatzforderungen doch sehr erheblich sind. Zwar erklärt die Auswahl einiges. Daneben erscheint jedoch die Vermutung plausibel, dass die frühe Schaffung transnationaler Netzwerke und das Training in Vielfalt und Unterschieden von Beginn an eine besonders gute Basis dafür schaffen, im Examen mit den ungewöhnlicheren Fällen besonders kreativ umzugehen und dass ebendies auch zum überragenden (und selbst für die Initiatoren überraschenden) Erfolg beitrug. Auf der Ausbildung in Fragen von Vielfalt liegt in der Tat ein besonderes Augenmerk: Von Beginn an bewegen sich alle in heterogenen Gruppen (mit verschiedenen Nationalitäten und Lernstilen), haben intensive Netzwerkaktivitäten mit jeweils gegenseitiger "Patenschaft", einen Teamgeist über Grenzen und Sprachen hinweg. Die Studierenden erleben ständig einerseits, wie sie in der Muttersprache überlegen formulieren und rechtliche Strukturen erkennen können, aber umgekehrt dann in der fremden Rechtskultur wieder mehr die "Lernenden", die Zuhörer sind.

Die Verknüpfung der einzelnen Dimensionen im Verbund ist dicht: Die akademischen Jahre folgen unmittelbar aufeinander (ohne Lücken für Antragsphasen für die nächste Stufe), die Jahrgänge sind eng verbunden, durch gemeinsames Studieren am gleichen Ort, teils überkreuz in den Jahrgängen, durch die jährlichen Sommerschulen, sehr stark schließlich dadurch, dass gewisse Materien und Fragestellungen immer wieder aufgenommen werden, in den verschiedenen Ländern. Studierende sind zwar frei, auch unterschiedliche Spezialisierungen in den verschiedenen Ländern zu wählen, alle Universitäten haben freilich auch mehrere stark parallelisierte Curricula. Daher ist es auch möglich, einen großen Spezialisierungsbereich zu wählen und dann die ganze Vielfalt an Lösungen und Stilen hierzu über die fünf Jahre vertieft zu studieren. Dann werden etwa Hauptinstitutionen des Privatrechts – Vertrag, Delikt, Eigentum, ein wenig Gesellschaftsrecht – aus der Perspektive jeder einzelnen Rechtsordnung studiert, dann spezifisch rechtsvergleichende Überlegungen angestellt, gesellschaftswissenschaftliche Ansätze hierzu diskutiert (etwa ökonomische Modelle) und alles in größere Kontexte gestellt – etwa mit Marktregulierung oder mit den philosophischen Grundlagen. Studierende entscheiden also, ob sie ein Portfolio verschiedener Spezialisierungen bevorzugen – neben der Verschiedenheit der Stile, die mit den verschiedenen Rechtsordnungen ohnehin einhergeht – oder ein Modell, in dem sie eine (Heimat-)Rechtsordnung breit, über die verschiedenen Großbereiche kennenlernen ("Volljurist"), zusätzlich jedoch *einen* Großbereich dann mit all den oben genannten Perspektiven (einschließlich gesellschaftswissenschaftlicher Ansätze und sehr unterschiedlicher Lösungen, auch im bewussten Vergleich).

Die jährlichen Sommerschulden bilden ein Herzstück des Verbundes – im Sozialen ebenso wie im Inhaltlichen, für Studierende und Lehrende. Ihr Generalthema ist teils altehrwürdig, teils prickelnd modern, teils fokussiert, teils breit – und stets wird es aus vielen Perspektiven beleuchtet. Mit Lehrenden aus vielen Ländern, mit Studierenden verschiedener Stufen, mit Ausbildungseinheiten in den Sponsorenkanzleien, stets mit auch interdisziplinären Zuschnitten, teils Kunst, Kultur oder auch verhaltenswissenschaftlichen Ansätzen. Im Wintersemester treffen sich die Jahre beim Graduierungswochenende – jeder Jahrgang (eine '*promotion*') erhält seinen Namen, idR mit Bezug zum Ort der Graduierung und einer Entwicklung, die dieses Jahr prägte, 2017 dem Populismus und dem aufkommenden "Hass gegen das Fremde". Die bisherigen Jahrgänge trugen die Namen von Michelangelo, Marie Curie, Aristoteles, Heinrich Heine, Hannah Ahrend, Georg Friedrich Händel, Caterina von Siena, Anne Frank.

Die European Law School ist einem Bild von Europa verpflichtet, in dem Vielfalt von Stilen und Sprachen ein plurales und reiches Denken fördert oder fördern kann, und nicht primär Schranken begründet in einer globalen Einheitssprache. Als neben der grundständigen Ausbildung eine Graduiertenschule zur juristischen Promotion aus Exzellenzmitteln eingeführt wurde – verankert an der Humboldt-Universität, jedoch offen für alle ELS-Absolventen –, wurde dies explizit gemacht und als Generalthema die "Einheit und Vielfalt im Europäischen Rechtsraum" gewählt.

3. Sprachfragen in Rechtswissenschaften und -lehre sind keine technischen Fragen, nicht nur eine Frage von "Fähigkeiten". Sie beeinflussen erheblich auch die Inhalte. Universitäten in Deutschland bieten einen breiten Kranz bilingualer

und (deutlich weniger) auch multilingualer Curricula an. Für Europa – das multilingual verfasst ist und zu dessen wichtigsten Charakteristika (heute) eine historisch und philosophisch tief verankerte Verfasstheit in Diversität und pluralistischem Denken zu zählen ist – sind Sprachfragen vielleicht noch wichtiger als in anderen Ländern oder Regionen der Welt. Sieht man freilich den Aspekt als zentral, dass mit Sprachenvielfalt auch eine Befürwortung von Diversität einhergeht, mögen Sprachfragen auch für die Welt ganz allgemein überragende Bedeutung haben, für eine Welt mit vielen Weltauffassungen, Sozialisierungsformen und Rechts- und Gesellschaftsmodellen.

Annexe 2: Quelques considérations élémentaires sur l'importance de la langue (et du plurilinguisme) en droit – et sur la European Law School (Berlin/Londres/Paris/Rome/Amsterdam)

1. Le droit se fonde dans la langue. L'éducation juridique est donc orientée par la langue – bien plus que pour beaucoup d'autres domaines d'études, bien que la beauté de l'écriture soit un facteur fort de recherche plus généralement (au moins) dans les sciences sociales, et aussi dans les 'plus sobres' et 'plus rigoureusement formelles' sciences économiques (Fn. 1). Il y a des voix qui comparent la force exégétique en droit à celle de la théologie ou de la philologie (Fn 2). Un important philosophe contemporain du droit a rapproché l'écriture et la pratique juridique avec les pièces de théâtre de Shakespeare – ramenant une interprétation juridique originelle sur un même pied d'égalité avec une interprétation originelle, disons de Hamlet (Fn. 3). En théorie de la connaissance, une tendance majoritaire voire unanime va dans le sens de la langue en ce qu'elle informe ou influence la formation de la pensée et de la langue– fortement, et peut-être même en tant que facteur principal (Fn. 4).
   Ces quelques considérations – réduites à leur essence même – transmettent déjà un message central : la langue forme la pensée, une pensée sur les modèles juridiques et sociétaux. Par conséquent, la réduction à une seule langue est complètement aux antipodes d'un monde aux multiples modèles juridiques et sociaux et encore plus d'un monde dans lequel le pluralisme des modèles sociétaux – une forme d'individualisme – est perçu comme étant essentiel et fondateur d'un point de vue normatif. On peut pointer au fait que le pluralisme dans les modèles juridiques et sociétaux ainsi que dans les croyances est aussi perçu comme une valeur fondatrice entérinée dans les constitutions (du moins dans le monde Occidental, Fn 5). On pourrait aussi aller jusqu'à dire que la communauté juridique globale, si elle ne veut pas trahir dans une certaine mesure la valeur fondatrice du pluralisme, a un devoir moral d'encourager (bien plus vigoureusement et activement) une forme de discours qui est basé sur une variété de langues.

Au sein de ma propre faculté de l'Université Humboldt, le premier titulaire de la chaire de droit comparé et de droit international privé après la chute du mur, Axel Flessner, un homme cosmopolite ayant dédié une immense énergie dans la recherche et l'étude relatives à l'Européanisation du droit privé (Fn. 6), a fortement et régulièrement défendu le drapeau de la langue allemande. Il l'a fait pour les travaux juridiques universitaires, pour les offres de formation, et plus généralement pour la participation au discours international en droit – du moins, comme il l'a déjà précisé lors d'une de nos conversations, pour l'Université Humboldt et pour un pays comme l'Allemagne. Par-là, il a également défendu – et c'est encore plus important et essentiel – le drapeau de l'autonomie de la pensée universitaire allemande en droit, de la pratique du droit « fabriquée en Autriche, Allemagne, Suisse », et même des modèles sociétaux qu'ils décrivent. En effet, alors que cela peut ne pas être de la même importance pour de petits pays ou de moins importantes universités, il peut être essentiel pour des universités de premier plan dans des juridictions nationales qui ont formé et continuent encore à former la pensée juridique – ailleurs que dans le monde Anglo-Américain. Axel Flessner m'a donc désigné coupable d'avoir accepté et d'ailleurs proposé le nom de 'European Law School' pour le réseau décrit ci-dessous et le titre de '*Juriste Européen*' pour ceux ayant achevé le programme d'études ainsi que les examens de Master dans trois pays européens avec succès et dans trois langues (cf. 2.). Cela n'a pas facilité les choses que j'ai insisté que cette institution et ce programme d'études soit, en essence, à propos de la multiplicité des langues ('plurilinguisme'), des styles et des modèles – bien plus que tout autre offre et modèles préexistants. De même, il reprochera d'avoir écrit cette description en anglais et peut être même qu'il ne me 'pardonnera' pas d'avoir, à la fin, ajouté une version plus courte en allemand (et aussi en français), contenant tous les principaux arguments. (Ce faisant, je suis bien sûr obligé de jouer avec le paradoxe de choisir une langue que je maitrise moins élégamment pour la version plus longue, en acceptant donc aussi les inconvénients que pratiquement toutes les personnes dont l'anglais n'est pas la langue natale rencontrent lorsqu'ils choisissent comme arme intellectuelle la 'langue maternelle' parlée par le prince Hamlet).

Le paradoxe du droit et de la langue, notamment dans sa puissance formatrice de la formation de la pensée et en particulier de la pensée juridique, va cependant plus loin. Bien que Flessner n'ait jamais vraiment formulé cette idée en ma présence, sa position est particulièrement convaincante lorsqu'elle est comprise de manière catégorique – et la *méthode* argumentative de Flessner, son insistance à garder l'allemand comme langue de discussion, d'écriture académique et d'enseignement était en effet catégorique. Il m'apparait particulièrement convaincant lorsque l'argument de Flessner est pris comme un appel à une éducation et un discours juridique pluri-linguiste. Par la réduction du discours global à une seule langue, une lingua franca, celui-ci court le risque qu'un grand nombre des idées développées dans une grande partie du monde, dans leurs langues natales, soient de fait exclues de ce discours ou fortement réduites en importance. Ce risque est exacerbé par une attitude dominante au sein de la discussion globale du droit qui considère la diversité linguistique avant tout comme un obstacle plutôt que comme une chance pour une discussion plus riche, nuancée et pluraliste des modèles légaux et sociétaux. Ceci implique que la pauvreté linguistique est perçue comme constituant l'arrangement le plus efficient d'une discussion alors même qu'elle pourrait tout aussi bien être perçue comme une faiblesse intellectuelle – réduisant la connaissance et la diversité des discours globaux. Les exemples pertinents abondent en la matière.

Lorsque par exemple Thomas Piketty dans toute son originalité traduit l'essence de Karl Marx – et plus loin d'Hugo Sinzheimer – en modèles économiques et en anglais moderne (Fn. 8) – en tant que chercheur français formé de manière cosmopolite s'adressant à un public mondial (principalement) anglophone – cela engendre un engouement total (Fn. 9). Cependant, la question de jusqu'où Marx est allé, puis Sinzheimer et Piketty iront vraiment, ne peut pas être discutée à l'échelle mondiale – le cercle de ceux pouvant participer de manière informée à la discussion ne suffisant pas linguistiquement, alors même que Piketty aurait apprécié un tel discours (il a d'ailleurs d'abord été publié en français et en allemand). Les frontières étatiques deviennent alors un obstacle – en quantité négligeable – en comparaison aux barrières linguistiques, indiscutablement en droit ou plus largement en sciences sociales.

Ce premier exemple est toutefois relativement peu important. Il est une chose de « réinventer la roue », fréquemment voire majoritairement. Il en va d'une autre lorsque des idées, à cause d'une barrière linguistique, ne peuvent plus suffisamment influencer le discours scientifique mondial et la pratique mondiale. Une évolution centrale de la deuxième moitié du siècle dernier – dont il faut séparer les développements des Etats-Unis (et non pas de toute la sphère anglo-américaine) de ceux de la plupart des autres juridictions nationales – est souvent perçue (et de manière convaincante) dans l'influence que l'analyse économique du droit exerce sur l'évaluation et le développement de solutions juridiques. Si celle-ci constitue une des interactions interdisciplinaires les plus importantes aujourd'hui, le choix de quelle approche à adopter est davantage essentiel. Actuellement l'analyse économique du droit dominante telle qu'elle a été principalement formulée par les universitaires et praticiens étatsuniens dans les années 1960 – de Ronald Coase, à Guido Calabresi en passant par Oliver Williamson jusqu'à Richard Posner et d'autres encore (Fn. 10) -, néglige une forte approche alternative sur la relation entre droit et économie. Cette approche alternative – l'école ordo-libérale – a eu un impact considérable sur le développement de la régulation d'intérêt public principalement en Europe et surtout en Allemagne, et qui a eu un écho beaucoup plus important que le suggère la discussion universitaire mondiale (Fn.11). Le développement des deux approches s'est déroulé différemment tant du point de vue du contenu que de celui de la méthode. Elles ont différé du point de vue du contenu – de manière très générale – dans la mesure où la dernière a favorisé une régulation d'intérêt public plus robuste, à titre d'exemple elle a nécessité de plus solides preuves des avantages accordés aux participants du marché si (exceptionnellement) des restrictions de concurrence devaient être autorisées – alors que la première a de plus en plus favorisé une « approche plus économique » dans laquelle n'importe quel avantage économique futur serait à mesurer contre les pertes causées par les restrictions de concurrence. Cette différence du point de vue du contenu n'est pas très importante dans notre contexte. Les deux approches diffèrent aussi toutefois du point de vue de la méthode, et ce dans la mesure où l'approche économique du droit formée aux Etats-Unis a très vite adopté des modèles économiques stricts en tant qu'indicateurs, une orientation claire pour des considérations de bien être total et d'efficience, et une inclination forte pour le calcul sur la base de certaines hypothèses (cette dernière seulement d'après Coase, et quelques développements ne pas tout à fait appréciés par Calabresi non plus) – alors que l'approche ordolibérale n'a pas recouru à des formalisations et a eu davantage tendance à des considérations des avantages et inconvénients potentiels dans des scénarios réels et des contextes historiques, fortement influencé par les institutions juridiques et politiques existantes, et a favorisé un équilibrage plus fondamental des avantages et inconvénients ainsi que des contrôles de vraisemblance.

Ce n'est pas le lieu de formuler, et a fortiori d'élaborer un jugement profond sur ces deux tendances, mais plutôt de souligner trois conséquences émanant de cette différence (tel qu'illustré dans l'exemple). (1) La différence entre les deux approches est énorme, l'analyse économique du droit ayant l'avantage principal de pouvoir être aisément « applicable », mais aussi le défaut principal de baser ses résultats sur des hypothèses qui souvent s'abstraient (fortement) du monde réel et qui souvent n'ont pas de contrôles de vraisemblance. On pourrait parler dans un cas d'une approche plus rigoureusement basée sur la formalisation et le calcul, et dans l'autre d'une approche fondée sur des valeurs qui est davantage inspirée par la réalité, et aussi moins précise. (2) Malgré l'importance de la différence, cette dernière approche est relativement peu discutée et nous sommes donc relativement peu conscients des avantages et inconvénients comparatifs des deux approches (Fn. 12). Nous ne discutons pas vraiment de si la dépendance sur des modèles et le calcul n'exclue pas dans une plus grande mesure une large partie des communautés juridiques du discours qu'une approche qui est davantage fondée sur des principes et des valeurs. (3) Cette absence de discussion n'est nullement limitée au monde anglo-américain, mais semble être influencée par l'absence virtuelle d'une plateforme mondiale de discussion pluri-linguiste. Cette absence de discussion pluri-linguiste mondiale semblerait avoir des conséquences différentes sur les deux rives de l'Atlantique – à savoir qu'une approche alternative est plus facilement délaissée dans le monde anglo-américain, mais aussi que dans des juridictions nationales comme celles en Europe continentale, l'approche de l'analyse économique du droit telle qu'elle a été formulée aux Etats-Unis est soit 'suivie' ou réfutée, et non pas discutée, modifiée ou transformée. Il peut bien s'avérer que le droit et sa discussion mondiale doivent payer le prix de la réticence mondiale à apprendre et suivre des discours dans quelques langues 'mondiales' (additionnelles). Si une approche des transactions économiques transnationales fondée sur le calcul et les modèles n'a pas été en mesure de détecter les failles d'un processus de groupement des emprunts sub-prime par la titrisation et l'externalisation dans des SPV transformés en

CDO/CDS sous la supervision d'agences de notation (elles-mêmes aussi fortement engagées dans la confection de ces produits financiers), avec une communauté d'investisseurs comptant collectivement et uniformément sur l'exactitude de ces modèles, alors l'existence des approches alternatives dans le discours mondial, notamment des approches favorisant plus de robustesse et de contrôles de vraisemblance plutôt que de calculs 'exacts', n'aurait-elle pas été utile pour jeter le doute ?

Ces considérations posent la question de qui détient la responsabilité du maintien suffisant d'une diversité linguistique, et elles expliquent pourquoi Flessner a au moins raison en termes catégoriques lorsqu'il insiste sur l'utilisation de l'allemand comme outil d'explication du monde de la pensée juridique. Il paraît quelque peu évident que la responsabilité face à ces questions devrait reposer sur les ordres juridiques (et universités), dans lesquels il paraît 'encore' plausible qu'ils soient écoutés. Cet appel à plus de diversité – en langues et donc en modèles sociétaux – peut seulement demeurer réaliste si l'on admet que le cercle des langues participant constamment au discours mondial va (et doit) demeurer relativement restreint même dans une communauté de discours mondial qui est plus adéquatement formée qu'une qui ne serait fondée que sur l'anglais (Fn.13). Si dans un tel discours mondial, l'Europe souhaite toujours avoir une voix additionnelle – à côté de l'anglais – le français, l'allemand et peut être même l'espagnol (cf. dernière note de bas de page) en seraient les candidats les plus évidents. De la même façon, les universités de ces juridictions nationales ont une responsabilité particulière – et l'Université Humboldt d'Axel Flessner en est une des quelques en Allemagne qui le fassent si évidemment. Par conséquent, il est difficile de ne pas considérer l'argument d'Axel Flessner lorsqu'il insiste à garder la langue allemande pour transmettre des idées sur la pensée juridique et sociétale. La responsabilité incombe cependant non seulement à ceux qui appartiennent aux ordres juridiques du type décrit précédemment, mais aussi à ceux qui produisent des discours à partir des universités qui ont un rayonnement international en dehors du monde anglo-américain. Lorsqu'il s'agit du droit et de l'équité (dans l'acception anglo-américaine du terme de '*fairness*') et lorsque le discours des sciences sociales doit être structuré mondialement, de telle sorte que le bien être mondial rende possible une compréhension mondiale, alors la responsabilité du monde anglo-américain dans cette question est peut être grandement comparable ou tout aussi bien supérieure. Bien que cela puisse passer pour un paradoxe, il est possiblement encore plus convaincant lorsque l'impératif pour un discours linguistiquement plus riche et produisant plus de publicité pour la majorité des modèles sociaux, est formulé par des institutions et acteurs centraux du monde anglo-américain (Fn. 14). Le rôle des Etats-Unis peut même être essentiel en ceci qu'ils ne sont pas reconnus pour leur capacité à recueillir très facilement la diversité des idées et des points de vue venant d'autres parties du monde (certains parlent même 'd'impérialisme académique'). Optant pour la diversité, un plaidoyer en faveur de la diversité serait convaincant s'il était formulé de la position forte de ceux qui s'expriment dans la langue dominante. On peut naturellement douter de l'audace et même de la candeur du souhait précédemment exprimé. Mon espoir serait cependant que bien qu'il soit probablement impossible de convaincre les majorités aux Etats-Unis, des voix révolutionnaires ayant un intérêt pour la recherche de premier plan démontrent effectivement un intérêt.

2. Bien que l'offre de formation plurilingue en droit (dans les droits différents) avec la participation d'universités allemandes soit riche et variée, une quelconque discussion fait défaut à la question de savoir quels buts ces formations multilingues poursuivent et doivent poursuivre et dans quelle mesure leurs cursus peuvent toutefois être optimisés. Pour la ***European Law School***, ces questions se sont posées de manière abstraites (a) et se sont reflétées dans la construction concrète de la European Law School (Berlin/Londres/Paris/Rome/Amsterdam) (b).

(a) Un aperçu des études en Allemagne démontre une importance considérable de l'éducation en droit dans deux langues (parfois plus) – comme l'a été montré d'abord à un niveau minimal s'appliquant à potentiellement tous les étudiants (le plus souvent en anglais), et ensuite de manière plus ambitieuse pour environ 10% des étudiants qui choisissent de s'investir plus avant dans leurs études, voire une année entière à l'étranger (à partir d'un plus grand éventail d'options linguistiques et thématiques). La conséquence n'en est pas cependant que les considérations de la politique éducative allemande en la matière soient particulièrement élaborées. Il y a peu de discussion théorique sur les différents objectifs d'une telle éducation internationale – internationale linguistiquement et géographiquement. Au mieux, il semblerait que l'on perçoive une plus grande ouverture d'esprit et un sens particulier d'initiative ainsi qu'une capacité d'adaptation parmi les étudiants qui se sont engagés dans l'étude de langues étrangères ou qui aient étudié à l'étranger.

Il manque une discussion plus large à la question particulière de savoir si de telles études conduisent peut être aussi à une représentation plus fortement pluraliste du droit, ou comment même un but s'il doit être poursuivi pourrait être promu par le façonnement particulier des offres. Alors qu'en pratique les processus décisionnels – et particulièrement le processus législatif – sont influencés par le profil multinational des groupes de rédaction et des corps décisionnaires – en particulier au sein de la Commission européenne mais également au sein d'autres institutions telles que la BCE, etc., ceci ne semble pas avoir son pendant dans la conception de l'offre éducative. La European Law School décrite ci-après (cf. section b) constitue une exception à cet égard. Ainsi il manque une discussion construite sur la façon dont l'offre éducative pourrait être améliorée avec l'intention de promouvoir et de raffiner les processus d'une intégration des approches pluralistes au sein des pratiques juridiques, académiques et législatives en Europe (et au-delà). Cette discussion porterait sur comment les modèles de gouvernance comment des participants dans un système pluraliste pourraient au mieux échanger leurs points de vues sur les modèles juridiques. Bien qu'il y ait une quantité non négligeable de littérature sur la gouvernance multi-niveaux au sein de l'UE (Fn. 23), celle-ci se concentre sur l'interaction entre les différents niveaux, et non pas sur les échanges horizontaux et les bons moyens de promouvoir une compréhension de tels problèmes de gouvernance au sein des cursus en droit.

L'hypothèse fondamentale de cette contribution est presque entièrement absente de la discussion – à savoir qu'une diversité de langues et de modèles exprimés dans ces différentes langues ne devait pas être vue en premier lieu comme un obstacle, mais plutôt comme un outil de découverte puissant au service de visions pluralistes du monde. L'absence d'un tel discours est certainement due au fait que l'Europe – qui devrait être un partisan naturel et même le thuriféraire d'une telle vision – demeure potentiellement silencieuse dans la discussion théorique et l'émancipation du potentiel d'une telle diversité.

La méthode comparative vient en premier lieu à l'esprit si on pense à comment affronter conceptuellement la diversité des langues et des styles juridiques. Celle-ci constitue la discipline naturelle majeure pour les questions liées à la diversité. Bien que cela ne suffise pas à emporter le débat en matière de pluralisme, il est particulièrement révélateur d'étudier cette discipline et de la comparer à ces alias issus des sciences sociales. En résumé :

L'allemand et le français furent les langues du droit comparé. Les pères fondateurs écrivaient en français et en allemand et traduisaient vers l'anglais. Jusqu'à la dernière décennie du XXe siècle, la méthode fonctionnaliste développée sur la base des travaux de René David et peut être même plus encore de Ernst Rabel, et formulée dans sa forme la plus avancée par Konrad Zweigert et Hein Kötz, était considérée comme l'approche fondamentale. Les institutions et les instruments juridiques, par exemple les règles, étaient comparés principalement au regard de leurs fonctions dans la résolution de problèmes particuliers renvoyant à l'arrière-plan la question de leur expression – simple terminologie – ou de leur place dans un système juridique à des questions de système (Fn. 24). Il s'agit ici d'une méthodologie similaire à celle des approches doctrinales basées sur la détermination des intérêts. Il découle de la littérature fondée sur cette approche que la diversité des idées et des approches juridiques est acceptée (et ce de manière évidente dans les travaux de René David), cependant non pas au point d'enrichir et de développer une dynamique de nouveaux développements. Dans la mesure où cette approche a cependant de manière de plus en plus prégnante formé le cœur méthodologique de l'unification internationale mais aussi de l'harmonisation supranationale du droit (déjà depuis Rabel en matière de droit de la vente internationale, Fn. 25), il existe pourtant au moins deux courants qui changent un peu l'image: tandis que l'approche fonctionnelle était essentiellement vue comme principalement neutre en ce qui concerne l'évaluation des différentes juridictions nationales et des solutions qu'elles trouvent, elles constituent néanmoins une affirmation de la supériorité de certaines règles/solutions sur d'autres lors du choix d'une solution ou d'une autre à des fins d'harmonisation/d'unification, ce qui est probablement plus explicite depuis les années 1990 et 2000 lorsqu'il s'est agi de développer des principes pour un droit privé européen. De tels projets se trouvent en défaut vis-à-vis de l'idée de neutralité. De plus, il est important de relever que le projet de développement de règles et principes uniformes a dominé intégralement le monde du droit comparé en Europe dans les deux ou trois dernières décennies. Ceci n'impliquerait-il pas que la diversité était davantage perçue comme un obstacle plutôt qu'une richesse dans le discours européen dominant ?

L'approche fonctionnelle du droit comparé s'est trouvée sous le feu croisé ces deux dernières décennies des sciences sociales et de la doctrine juridique, et plus particulièrement des premières. La contribution la plus importante en droit comparé en anglais (américain), nourrie par les sciences économiques, et du moins celle qui a de loin été citée le plus jusqu'à présent, est bien plus radicale que son équivalent européen de ces dernières décennies. La revendication d'une supériorité est particulièrement explicite – elle ne concerne plus simplement des solutions particulières, certaines étant issues de certaines juridictions nationales, et d'autres d'autres. Cette revendication concerne désormais les systèmes juridiques dans leur intégralité. En termes particulièrement simplistes, la théorie des origines légales (Fn. 26) en est arrivée à la conclusion que le droit américain rendrait le monde, c'est-à-dire potentiellement tous les pays, meilleur – le droit ayant des racines germaniques étant encore acceptable, le droit d'origine française d'emblée préjudiciable (René David n'aurait peut-être pas bienvenu cette revitalisation de son idée des familles de droit). Le fort impact de cette théorie est certainement dû au fait qu'elle fut formulée en termes statistiques (avec une précision « mathématique ») et par des économistes. Bien que l'hypothèse fondamentale dût être retirée suite à des analyses plus poussées (Fn. 27), et bien qu'il ne s'agisse naturellement pas d'une représentation exhaustive de la littérature anglo-américaine en matière de droit comparé, l'on ne peut néanmoins dénier une grande force à ce développement (avec des répercussions fortes, par exemple, sur les accords de prêt par la Banque Mondiale et une grande partie de la littérature). Cette situation ne fait qu'ajouter au plaidoyer livré ici selon lequel la représentation d'ensemble livrée par une vision anglo-centrée du monde, résultant dans une évaluation en faveur d'une doctrine et d'études dans une seule langue, requiert urgemment une correction.

Le développement le plus important sur la question de la diversité dans les sciences politiques diffère fondamentalement de la théorie des origines juridiques, bien qu'elle partage l'approche large et presque statistique de la détermination des faits et des comportements. Malheureusement, elle ne trouve pas dans la doctrine juridique un équivalent à sa hauteur. Les recherches sur les « Variétés du Capitalisme », et notamment le travail séminal de Peter Hall et David Soskice (Fn. 28), posent les questions fondamentales de savoir si les différences entre modèles sociaux ici, en l'espèce ceux d'une nature capitaliste, ne constituent pas seulement un fait mais sont également nécessaires à la poursuite de deux buts principaux : répondre de manière adéquate au contexte institutionnel divergent des différents pays et régions, et même de promouvoir l'arsenal des dispositifs institutionnels disponibles, dans un but d'accroitre sa compréhension ou de satisfaire diverses préférences, etc. Les arguments de supériorité sont faibles ou inexistants selon cette approche, qui semble considérer la variété comme une valeur.

Parmi les approches de droit comparé, la tendance qui se rapprocherait le plus de l'approche Variétés du Capitalisme pourrait se dénommer « approche comparative des fondements juridiques ». Au lieu de chercher des solutions uniquement à des problèmes concrets, elle se focaliserait plutôt sur la relation des structures et déterminants principaux de l'architecture juridique, par exemple, quel rôle la constitution, c'est à dire les droits fondamentaux, joue-t-elle dans le développement du droit privé (direct/indirect/pas de rôle), quel cours développe ces idées, comment les autres sciences sociales influencent le développement de la doctrine juridique, comment la pratique et quelles sciences sociales, etc., etc., et lier ceci à la structure institutionnelle de cette juridiction nationale incluant la question de qui sont les autorités juridiques principales (Fn. 29). Une telle approche «comparative des fondements juridiques » reconnaît la diversité et ne permet pas non plus une approche de type « modèle supérieur », en principe du moins. Elle pourrait même contribuer aux fondations d'une approche selon laquelle un pluralisme de modèles est vu positivement, du moins en principe. Tandis qu'il n'existe pas selon moi d'équivalent au travail séminal concernant la « Variété des Capitalismes » de Hall et Soskice pour le moment, une agenda similaire pourrait vraisemblablement être développé sur cette base, au point même d'être le fondement d'un projet de recherche ambitieux et innovant.

(b) La European Law School a été créée en 2007 (à la suite de négociations longues et complexes entre 2004 et 2007), et compte sa première remise de diplôme en 2010 (https://www.european-law-school.eu/) – elle vise à apporter une réponse aux considérations formulées précédemment. Son principe fondamental est que les diplômés doivent avoir étudié et passé les examens dans trois langues et trois pays avec trois styles majeurs de raisonnement et de pratique juridiques différents, sans préjudice de leur préparation au Barreau et en incluant deux cursus de LL.M. dans deux autres pays. La European Law School continue à se développer et a atteint une telle dimension qu'elle peut plus précisément être catégorisée comme institution que comme un cursus. Elle a créé sa propre fondation finançant son développement continu. Elle contient des éléments d'études et de recherche qui lui sont spécifiques. Elle est ainsi distincte des autres programmes mentionnés tant sur la forme que sur le fond. Elle tend à devenir une véritable école de droit. Penchons-nous maintenant sur son contenu, et en particulier ses langues.

Le cursus est parfaitement intégré. Il comporte l'Université Humboldt à Berlin, le King's College à Londres, et l'Université Paris II – Panthéon Assas à Paris. Depuis 2014, il a été étendu à Rome et Amsterdam, et présentement à Athènes, Lisbonne, Madrid et Varsovie. Cette étendue paraitrait déjà comme représentative des différents styles et problèmes en Europe (tout en demeurant réalisable). Il s'agit pour toutes les universités d'intégralement former des élèves (soigneusement) sélectionnés dans leur juridiction nationale d'origine – en commençant déjà aussi par des cours de droit étranger en langue étrangère des deux autres juridictions nationales, et ce faisant, créant un esprit de comparaison dès le début des études, avec néanmoins des racines solidement ancrées dans la juridiction nationale (mais européanisée) d'origine. Pour toutes les universités, le cursus prévoit ensuite que leurs étudiants passent deux années consécutives (leur quatrième et cinquième) de master dans deux autres pays, ayant passé leur examen d'Etat allemand ou de Licence après la troisième année. La solidité de cette formation dans le pays d'origine peut être déduite du fait que les notes aux examens nationaux, par exemple en Allemagne, non seulement dépassent la moyenne nationale (et de loin !) mais aussi considérablement la moyenne atteinte par les universités qui sélectionnent également leurs étudiants et donnent une attention toute particulière à la pédagogie, comme c'est la cas par exemple à l'Ecole de droit Bucerius en Allemagne (Fn. 30). Les résultats des étudiants de la European Law School sont remarquablement supérieurs à la moyenne des autres institutions. Bien que ces étudiants aient été sélectionnés, il est également plausible que leur formation et leur socialisation à la diversité dès l'origine les aient préparés particulièrement bien pour les épreuves requérant le plus de créativité lors des examens nationaux, ce qui aurait contribué également à leur succès exceptionnel (surprenant également pour ses fondateurs). La préparation à la diversité est en effet le cœur du programme : dès l'origine, ils forment un groupe divers par ses nationalités et ses modes d'apprentissage. Ceci est encouragé par des activités sociales, en particulier les universités d'été, les parrainages, et l'esprit d'équipe transnational et multilinguistique créé. Les étudiants font ainsi l'expérience constamment de mieux comprendre leur propre langue et leur propre structures juridiques, mais également celle d'être de véritables novices.

Le cursus est parfaitement intégré : en cinq ans d'études, des étudiants de différentes promotions, de différents âges et de différentes spécialités thématiques étudient dans un cursus intégré. Bien qu'il soit possible pour les étudiants de varier les spécialisations dans les différents pays, toutes les universités ont coordonné leurs offres de formation. Ainsi, il est également possible pour les étudiants de choisir une branche de spécialisation et de saisir une variété d'opportunités au long de ces cinq années : il en va ainsi du droit privé (contrats, propriété, entreprises) qui peut être étudié de la perspective de chaque juridiction nationale dans laquelle ils étudient dans une perspective d'apporter des solutions déduites de l'exercice de la comparaison ou dans la perspective d'une approche de type sciences sociales (par exemple l'économie) et de rendre le tout dans son contexte, par exemple ses fondations philosophiques ou la régulation du marché. Ainsi les étudiants peuvent choisir soit d'avoir accès à un ensemble de spécialisations en sus de la multitude des pédagogies qu'ils expérimentent, soit une compréhension générale du droit dans une juridiction nationale combiné à une compréhension véritablement européenne d'un domaine de spécialisation (incluant des éléments de sciences sociales et un grand nombre d'idées et de solutions).

Les universités d'été qui se tiennent annuellement sont une composante clé de l'ensemble du cursus, aussi bien sur le plan social ou substantiel, et ce pour les étudiants et les professeurs. Elles se concentrent sur un sujet classique et fondamental, ou moderne et innovant, spécialisé ou large, et l'étudient de différentes perspectives, la participation des différents pays et juridictions nationales dans le panel, parmi les auditeurs, ainsi qu'avec le concours de cabinets d'avocats internationaux. Les sujets d'étude se prêtent à l'étude du point de vue de différentes sciences sociales, également des arts et de la culture, et par exemple d'approches comportementales. Tous les hivers les étudiants se réunissent à l'occasion de la cérémonie de remise des diplômes, chaque promotion étant baptisée selon le lieu, l'évènement, ou le contexte politique et juridique de l'année (le populisme et la haine de la diversité en 2017). Les promotions jusqu'ici ont porté les noms suivants : Michelangelo, Marie Curie, Aristote, Heinrich Heine, Hannah Ahrend, Georg Frederik Händel, Caterina da Siena, Anne Frank (Fn. 31).

La European Law School a vocation à nourrir un discours sur l'Europe dans lequel la diversité des langues et des styles est perçue comme ouverture sur une pensée pluraliste, et non pas comme un obstacle à une approche globale basée sur l'anglais. Cette conception est aussi explicitement étendue à une école doctorale. L'école doctorale – basée à l'Université Humboldt mais s'étendant aux participants de toute la European Law School – a été établie autour de la thématique « Unité et Différence dans l'espace juridique européen ».

3. Les questions linguistiques en éducation juridique ne sont pas seulement une affaire de compétence technique des étudiants. Elles sont très pertinentes en ce qui concerne le contenu. Les universités allemandes offrent à la fois des cursus bilingues ainsi que, bien qu'en moins grand nombre, des cursus multilingues. Pour l'Europe – qui est multilingue et dont la caractéristique est une diversité historiquement et philosophiquement ancrée et une appréciation du pluralisme –, la question de la langue est sans doute plus importante qu'elle pourrait l'être dans d'autres pays ou régions du monde. Si le plurilinguisme va de pair avec la diversité, les questions linguistiques peuvent aussi être essentielles dans un monde aux différentes croyances, formes de socialisation, et modèles juridiques et sociétaux.

References

Amable B (2003) The diversity of modern capitalism. Oxford University Press, Oxford

Auby J-B (2010) La globalisation le droit et l'État. LGDJ, Paris

Betti E (1987) In: Mura G (ed) L'ermeneutica come metodica generale delle scienze dello spirito. Roma, Città Nuova

Bianca CM, Bonell MJ (1987) Commentary on the international sales law: the 1980 Vienna sales convention. Giuffrè, Milan, pp 1–7

Blanke S (2005) Soziales Recht oder kollektive Privatautonomie? Hugo Sinzheimer im Kontext nach 1990. Mohr-Siebeck, Tübingen

Böhm F (1966) Privatrechtsgesellschaft und Marktwirtschaft. ORDO 17:75–151

Böhm F (1989) Rule of law in a market economy. In: Peacock A, Willgerodt H (eds) Germany's social market economy: origins and evolution. Macmillan, London, pp 46–67

Calabresi G (1961) Some thoughts on risk distribution and the law of torts. Yale Law J 70:499–553

Chevallier J (2003) L'Etat postmodern. LGDJ, Paris

Coase R (1960) The problem of social cost. J Law Econ 3:1–44

Crouch C (2005) Models of capitalism. New Polit Econ 10:439–456
de Búrca G, Scott J (eds) (2006) Law and governance in the US and the EU. Hart, Oxford
Deakin S, Pistor K (2012) Legal origin theory. Edward Elgar Publishing, Cheltenham
Delmas Marty M (2006) Le pluralisme ordonné. Seuil, Paris
Eucken W (2004) Grundsätze der Wirtschaftspolitik, 7th edn. Mohr-Siebeck, Tübingen, p 278 et seqq
Fikentscher W, Hacker P, Podszun R (2013) Fair economy. Springer, Heidelberg
Gadamer H-G (2006) Classical and philosophical hermeneutics. Theory Cult Soc 23:29–56
Goldman A (2002) The sciences and epistemology. In: Moser P (ed) The Oxford handbook of epistemology. Oxford University Press, Oxford, pp 144–176
Große Hüttmann M, Knodt M (2012) Der Multi-Level Governance-Ansatz. In: Bieling H-J, Lerch M (eds) Theorien der europäischen Integration. Springer VS, Tübingen, pp 186–194
Grundmann S (2008) The concept of the private law society after 50 years of European and European Business Law. Eur Rev Priv Law (ERPL):553–581
Grundmann S, Thiessen J (eds) (2015) Recht und Sozialtheorie im Rechtsvergleich – law in the context of disciplines – Interdisziplinäres Denken in Rechtswissenschaft und –praxis. Mohr – Siebeck, Tübingen
Grundmann S, Micklitz H-W, Renner M (2018) New private law theory – global European, social sciences based. Cambridge University Press, Cambridge
Häberle P (1980) Die Verfassung des Pluralismus: Studien zur Verfassungstheorie der offenen Gesellschaft (Königstein am Taunus: Athenäum)
Hall PA, Soskice D (2001) Varieties of capitalism: the institutional foundations of comparative advantage. Oxford University Press, Oxford
Hancke B, Rhodes M, Thatcher M (eds) (2007) Beyond varieties of capitalism. Conflict, contradictions, and complementarities in the European economy. Oxford University Press, Oxford
Hooghe L, Marks G (2001) Multi-level governance and European integration. Rowman & Littlefield, Lanham
Joerges C, Schmid C (2011) Towards proceduralization of private law in the European multi-level system. In: Hartkamp A, Hesselink M, Hondius E, Mak Ch, du Perron E (eds) Towards a European civil code. Hart, Oxford, pp 277–310
Kaufmann S, Stützle I (2015) Kapitalismus. Die ersten 200 Jahre. Thomas Pikettys "Das Kapital im 21. Jahrhundert"– Einführung, Debatte, Kritik, 4th edn. Bertz + Fischer, Berlin
Klerman DM, Mahoney P, Spamann H, Weinstein M (2011) Legal origins or colonial history? J Legal Anal 3:379–409
La Porta R, Lopez-de-Silanes F, Shleifer A, Vishny RW (1997) Legal determinants of external finance. J Financ 52:1131–1150
La Porta R, Lopez-de-Silanes F, Shleifer A (2008) The economic consequences of legal origins. J Econ Liter 46(2):285–322
Lee C, Lloyd PL (2005) Beauty and the economist: the role of aesthetics in economic theory. Kyklos 58:65–86
Marks G (1993) Structural policy and multi-level governance in the EC. In: Cafruny A, Rosenthal G (eds) The state of the European community: the Maastricht debate and beyond. Lynne Rienner, Boulder, pp 391–411
Marks G, Hooghe L, Blank K (1996) European integration from the 1980s: state-centric v. multi-level governance. J Common Mark Stud 34:341–378
Marx K (1867) Das Kapital – Kritik der politischen Ökonomie, Vol. 1. Meissner, Hamburg
Marx K (1872) Le Capital – Critique de l'économie politique, Vol. 1. M. Lachâtre, Paris
Melamed D (1972) Property rules, liability rules and inalienability – one view of the cathedral. Harv Law Rev 85:1089–1128
Mestmäcker E-J (1973) Macht – Recht – Wirtschaftsverfassung. Zeitschrift für das gesamte Handelsrecht (ZHR) 137:97–111
Mestmäcker E-J (2007) A legal theory without law – Posner v. Hayek on economic analysis of law. Tübingen, Mohr-Siebeck

Micklitz H (2017) A European advantage in legal scholarship? In: van Gestel R, Micklitz H, Rubin EL (eds) Rethinking legal scholarship – a transatlantic dialogue. Cambridge University Press, Cambridge, pp 262–309
Möslein F (ed) (2015) Private Macht und privatrechtliche Gestaltungsfreiheit. Mohr-Siebeck, Tübingen
Piattoni S (2009) Multi-level governance: a historical and conceptual analysis. Eur Integr:163–180
Piketty T (1997) L'économie des inégalités. Découverte, Paris
Piketty T (2013) Le Capital au XXIe Siècle. Le Seuil, Paris
Piketty T (2014) The capital in the twenty-first century. Harvard University Press, Cambridge
Piketty T (2015) The economics of inequality. Harvard University Press, Cambridge
Posner R (1973) Economic analysis of law. Little, Brown, Boston
Putnam H (2002) The collapse of the fact/value dichotomy and other essays. Harvard University Press, Cambridge, pp 135–146
Raz J (2009) Between authority and interpretation: on the theory of law and practical reason. Oxford University Press, Oxford, pp 299–322
Reimann M (2014) The American advantage in global lawyering – Dreizehnte Ernst-Rabel-Vorlesung. RabelsZ 78:1–36
Rhodes M (2005) 'Varieties of capitalism' and the political economy of European welfare states. New Polit Econ 10:363–370
Riesenhuber K (ed) (2007) Privatrechtsgesellschaft: Entwicklung, Stand und Verfassung des Privatrechts. Mohr-Siebeck, Tübingen
Riesenhuber K (ed) (2015) European legal method. Intersentia, Mortsel, p 64 et seq
Rokkan S, Urwin DW (1983) Economy, territory, identity: politics of western peripheries. Sage, London
Sabel C, Zeitlin J (2008) Learning from difference: the new architecture of experimentalist governance in the EU. Eur Law J 14:271–327
Schnyder G, Siems M (2013) Ordoliberal variety of neoliberalism. In: Konzelmann SJ, Fovargue-Davies M (eds) Banking systems in the crisis: the faces of liberal capitalism. Routledge Taylor & Francis Group, London/New York, pp 250–268
Schröder M (2013) Integrating varieties of capitalism and welfare state research: a unified typology of capitalisms. Palgrave Macmillan, New York
Sinzheimer H (1921) Grundzüge des Arbeitsrechts. G. Fischer, Jena
Spamann H (2010) Legal origins, civil procedure and the quality of contract enforcement. J Inst Theor Econ 166:149–165
Strömholm S (1992) Rechtsvergleichung und Rechtsangleichung – Theoretische Möglichkeiten und praktische Grenzen in der Gegenwart. RabelsZ 56:611–623
van Ooyen RC, Möllers M (eds) (2016) Verfassungs-Kultur: Staat, Europa und pluralistische Gesellschaft bei Peter Häberle. (Baden-Baden: Nomos)
Viola F, Zaccaria G (1999) Diritto e interpretazione. Lineamenti di teoria ermeneutica del diritto. Laterza, Roma-Bari
Vogel J (2017) The spectre of capital. Stanford University Press, Stanford
Williamson O (1979) Transaction-cost economics: the governance of contractual relations. J Law Econ 22:233–261
Wittgenstein L (1922) Tractatus Logico-Philosophicus. Kegan Paul, Trench, Trubner & Co., London
Zweigert K, Kötz H (1996) Einführung in die Rechtsvergleichung. J.C.B. Mohr (Paul Siebeck), Tübingen, p 33 et seqq

Bilingual Legal Education in Italy: Translating Languages Into Teaching Methods

Elena Ioriatti

1 Introduction

If this contribution did not deal with the language of Italian legal education, but with the legal language of Italy, considerations should start from a far-away past.

As is well-known, the territory we now call "Italy" was the birthland of one of the greatest legal cultures of the world, Roman law, and consequently of its terminology. The jurist, considered as the expert who has access and control over this refined legal terminology, initially expressed in Latin, has his origin in Rome. A part of this legacy of concepts, categories and norms passes through the centuries thanks to a universally valuable opera called *Corpus Iuris Civilis,* written by emperor Justinian in the VI century and part of it—the *Digest* —recovered in Pisa (Italy) in the XII. The *Digest* (also known as *Littera Pisana* or *Pandectae*) is one of the books of the Corpus Iuris and is the text with which Irnerius and the scholars of the University of Bologna used to teach the law, according to their educational mission.[1]

It is exactly from the experience of Bologna University that the *ius commune* originates, being a legal system shared for centuries by jurists all over the European continent as for its language, method and solutions. The Italian legal culture is therefore at the basis of one of the main legal families of the Western Legal Tradition: the *Civil law*.

This is one of the reasons why in academic education *law* has long been one of the core disciplines of the Italian cultural discourse.

Although the main purpose of legal education all over the world is often practical and professinally oriented, in Italy law has been taught for centuries as a science,

[1] Cairns and du Plessis (2010).

E. Ioriatti (✉)
University of Trento, Faculty of Law, Trento, Italy
e-mail: elena.ioriatti@unitn.it

N. Etcheverry Estrázulas (ed.), *Bilingual Study and Research*, Ius Comparatum – Global Studies in Comparative Law 58,
https://doi.org/10.1007/978-3-030-84550-6_9

and therefore on a theoretical basis; thus, the impact of languages other than Italian has been definitively limited, as the acquisition of the national legal culture and terminology has always been the essential part of the training.

This is also true for the bilingual territories of Italy, since the law, even if translated into other minority languages, is still formulated in Italian, and this version is the reference idiom in the interpretation and application of the legal texts by the courts.

However, recently, for reasons that are independent from regional normative bilingualism, the role of foreign languages—namely English—in legal education is rapidly increasing.

The aim of this Chapter is the description of the current situation of bilingual legal education in Italy and particularly of the recent evolution towards the use of foreign languages, namely English, also as a new teaching method.

Italy is not a monolingual State and its regional dimension offers evidence as to the presence of protected minority languages and cultures. However, even if ethno-linguistic groups have gained not only political and linguistic autonomy, but even independence in the recruitment of the key legal professions (notably lawyers and judges), legal education remains substantially monolingual in those areas too.

Bilingual legal education in Italy is much more linked to a trend of favouring the spread of English as a *lingua franca*, facilitating mobility in Europe, as well as to become a differentiating feature for universities in a competitive context. The core of these changes lies in the academic autonomies of the Italian universities—most of them are state universities—but, as we will see, this trend of a more multilingual academic model as opposed to the one of linguistic homogeneity has experienced some forms of resistance on the governmental level.

Thus, the Italian case is an interesting example of a dynamic and ongoing bilingual legal education underpinning new undergraduate programs. However, at the core of these recent trends lies an urgent desire of linguistic normalization.

In order to understand the Italian context, after a brief survey of the linguistic features of Italy, the first section of this contribution is dedicated to the description of the two Italian bilingual regions, where the use of two—and even three—languages is compulsory, not only in teaching and in the administration, but in legislation too. The focus is on the relation between normative bilingualism (or even trilingualism, as we will see) and the function of those languages in legal education.

The second section will analyze the reception of internationalization and Europeanization in legal education as a factor to enhance the use of foreign languages in University studies; how language is turning into a new methodology in the formation of jurists trained to be comfortable with different jurisdictions will be described too.

Finally, the obstacles that this innovative reorientation of legal education has been facing from the very beginning will also be taken into consideration, as still influencing the development of the Italian bilingual legal education system.

2 Bilingual Regions and Legal Education

2.1 Premise

The development of the modern Italian language, and its relationship with the other idioms spoken in Italy, is particularly interesting as it followed a tortious and tangled path, mostly due to the political disaggregation that characterized the Italian peninsula until the nineteenth century.

Up until the early sixteenth century, the language of educated, written and oral communication was Latin. With the passing of time, an intense debate developed throughout Italy as to whether and which "vernacular" languages (dialects) could be generally employed; at the end of this cultural process *Florentine*, a Tuscan idiom, gradually replaced Latin and, due to its influence and prestige,[2] became accepted as the *Italian language* throughout the Nation.[3]

However, even after the establishment of *Florentine* as the language in Italy, its use was limited to the literates, while the vast majority of the population still used to communicate only through local dialects.[4] The habitual use of Italian by most of the population is indeed a rather recent phenomenon, as people [5] started to communicate in this language in all kinds of situations[6] only over the end of the twentieth century.

As it can be imagined, from this situation a very complex language system developed, in which people often had the tendency to use the Italian language to read, write or speak for the purposes of elevated discourse, and at the same time relied on local dialects when dealing with domestic or day-by-day conversations.[7]

Still nowadays in Italy there is an impressive number of local dialects,[8] as well as a number of languages—other than Italian—that have gained official recognition by the Italian State as "minority languages", and which are specifically protected by the Italian Constitution,[9] as well as by the European Charter for Regional or Minority Languages.[10]

---

[2]Italian had previously been the language of interstate commercial relations: Maiden (2002), p. 34.

[3]Lepschy and Lepschy (1977).

[4]Castellani (1982); see also De Mauro (1963).

[5]According to data from the Italian national statistics institute (Istat), in 2018 English was the most known language in Italy (48.1%, compared to French 29.5% and Spanish 11.1%) and is used mainly for study reasons 45.4% (for 35.51% at work and for everyone else for free time).The use of English among family has increased by 6.9% compared to the past (1987/88 0.6% of cases). In Italy 9 residents out of 10 are Italian mother tongue (52 million. Foreign residents amount to 5.2 million).

[6]This was mostly as to the Fascist policy of linguistic unification, Ben-Ghiat (1997), pp. 438–444 as well as to the spread of the media. See hereinafter §2.2.

[7]Sacco (2000), p. 244.

[8]See Maiden and Perry (1997).

[9]Article 6 "The Republic shall safeguard language minorities by means of appropriate measures".

[10]Posner (1996).

At present (2021), twelve minority languages are officially recognized in Italy, among which we can count German, French and Ladin.[11]

2.2 Bilingual Regions and Normative Bilingualism

Even if all the protected minority languages have been regulated by specific legislations, the regime for bilingualism in Italy, which refers to the obligation to draft legislation in more than one language, concerns only two regions: Valle d'Aosta—*Vallée d'Aoste*—for French and *Trentino Alto Adige-Süd Tyrol* (hereinafter, Valle d'Aosta and South Tyrol[12]) for German and Ladin.[13]

In Valle d'Aosta, an autonomous Region of the North West of Italy, the French language had explicitly been recognized a parity status with Italian, also with regard to legislation and a part of the administrative production.

Historically, a form of French bilingualism started to develop under the annexation of Valle d'Aosta to the kingdom of France, becoming the official language in 1961, along with French-Provençal. After the unification of Italy (1861), Italian was made official language of Valle d'Aosta too. On 29th February 1948, the Province of Aosta became an autonomous Region with a special status and Italian-French bilingualism was introduced as the new linguistic regime.

However, even though the whole community is officially bilingual, only few people still rely on French today, and particularly not in "educated" discourse. Italian is the language of current speech, but at the same time is taking the place of French as the medium of "high-register" activities. As to the legal environment, although almost all administrative documents and legislation are equally drafted and enacted in the two languages, the right to use French for instance in court is rather limited if compared to what occurs in other biligual areas of Italy like South Tyrol (see below), where such right is foreseen by art. 100 of the Regulation (Statuto) of Autonomy of the Trentino-South Tyrol: in fact, not only does it guarantee for the application of the constitutional principles of equality and defence, but it also protects linguistic minorities.[14]

---

[11] The 12 minority languages recognised and protected by a statute (Legge 482/1999) are: French, Provençal, Franco-Provençal, German, Ladin, Friulian, Slovene, Sardinian, Catalan, Albanian, Greek and Croatia. Ladin, in particular, is an officially recognized Romance language, spoken only in a few valleys of the provinces of Trentino, South Tyrol and in a small part of the Veneto region. Furthermore Mocheno and Cimbro are protected minority languages at the regional level (see footnote n. 13).

[12] It should be noted that the use of the term "South Tyrol" to indicate the part of the region where German language is mostly used is conventional among the speakers. Technically, the term "Province of Bolzano, of the *Trentino Alto Adige-Süd Tyrol* Region" should be used.

[13] Together with Italian, German and Ladin, two other minority Germanic languages are recognized in *Trentino Alto Adige-Süd Tyrol*: Mocheno and Cimbro.

[14] Art. 6 of the Italian Constitution (Costituzione della Repubblica Italiana).

Nevertheless, in Valle d'Aosta[15] a principle that modern scholars define as *perfect*, *complete* or *total bilingualism*—and which the Italian Constitutional Court qualifies as *"full bilingualism"*[16]—is well established in primary and secondary school;[17] however, this principle is not reflected in advanced education, especially in the field of law. As we will see, the main University in the region[18] does not offer a full curriculum in law, and the few lectures dealing with law are held exclusively in Italian. Furthermore, the situation is even more evident concerning other forms of post-graduate legal education, like lawyers' training, since held outside the Region by Italian entities (*scuole forensi*—schools for the legal professions).

Another interesting and characteristic area in which normative bilingualism in Italy can be analysed is the Province of Bolzano (Bozen).

The Province of Bolzano is an autonomous Province that, along with the autonomous Province of Trento, is part of the autonomous Region Trentino-Alto Adige/Südtirol (South Tyrol), located in the North East of Italy.

Until 1918, this almost entirely German-speaking territory was part of the Austro-Hungarian princely County of Tyrol, and was annexed to the Kingdom of Italy only in 1919, after the end of World War I. This is particularly relevant as, even now, the most spoken language in the province is German: according to the census in 2011, South Tyrol's population consists of 69.15% German speakers, 26.06% Italian speakers and 4.53% Ladin speakers.[19]

After the annexation of South Tyrol to Italy, and with the rise of Fascism, the new regime tried to bring forward the Italianization of South Tyrol, banishing the German language from public services and prohibiting German teaching.

The situation was completely overturned after World War II with the new constitutional asset, which provided for the German-speaking population of South Tyrol the same rights as the Italian speaking inhabitants, offering a broad protection of the development of the German-speaking population.

Today South Tyrol enjoys a broad administrative and legislative autonomy and is known as one the territories in Europe in which the linguistic minorities have been recognized the greatest degree of protection and widest range of rights.

The institutional setting of this Province is specifically designed to permit the cooperation of the two main linguistics groups—German and Italian speakers—where every person has the right to use either language when relating to both the judiciary and the offices of the public administration. As a consequence, public documents are also usually bilingual and the civil servants who work in the judicial and

---

[15] See art. 39 Statute of the Autonomous Region of Valle d'Aosta.

[16] Constitutional Court (Corte Costituzionale), Judgment no.156/1969.

[17] In this regard, the Regulation for the Autonomous Region of Valle d'Aosta (Statuto per la Regione Autonoma della Valle d'Aosta) expressly establishes that "in all types and grades of schools the same number of hours per week as are dedicated to the teaching of the Italian language shall be dedicated to the teaching of French". See also Coonan (2000).

[18] Aosta University.

[19] https://astat.provincia.bz.it/downloads/Siz_2018-eng(1).pdf.

administrative fields are required to be fluent in both languages. Furthermore, legislation and all normative sources and documents must be drafted in bilingual version, and, when involving interests of the Ladin community, in this third language too.

Thus, the development of the legal language is particularly important in both Valle d'Aosta and South Tyrol, especially when dealing with legal terminology.

Consequently, in both territories bilingual legal drafting concerns institutions—and therefore concepts—of Italian law, which are applied within one single legal system, namely the Italian one, and are merely expressed both in Italian and in a second legal language (German in South Tyrol and French in Valle d'Aosta). Thus, legal concepts in Italian translated into French and German often differ from the equivalent terms that are used in France, Austria or Germany.

Thus, in order to facilitate legal translation a special institution has been founded: in South Tyrol the *Joint Terminology Commission*, composed by both Italian and German speaking experts, has the scope of creating, developing and expressing the terminology of the Italian legal system in German. In Valle d'Aosta the legislation is drafted predominantly in Italian and subsequently translated by translators working within the *Service de promotion de la langue française*.[20] Therefore, particularly in South Tyrol, the legal professions—lawyers, judges, notaries—as well as the civil servants, even having a predominant language skill, are required to understand the translation and the correspondence of legal terminology adopted in both languages.[21]

[20]Both in South Tyrol and Valle d'Aosta the drafting process regarding bilingual legislation involves institutions and experts from both linguistic groups, who can guarantee the quality of the drafting, the translation and the correspondence of legal terminology. Until now, legislation in Valle d'Aosta has been drafted predominantly in Italian and subsequently translated into French. On the contrary, in South Tyrol the legal texts are often drafted in both languages, and so also in German, to be then translated into Italian.

As in both South Tyrol and in Valle d'Aosta bilingual drafting concerns institutions—and therefore concepts—of Italian law, which are applied within one single legal system—the Italian one—it is foreseeable that problems regarding the issue of divergent interpretation between the two language versions may arise. In South Tyrol it has been expressly established that the Italian text prevails over the German one and therefore, in case of doubt over interpretation, the Italian text is always to be considered the authentic one. Conversely, in Valle d'Aosta the original authentic text is the one in which the law was drafted (either Italian or French) and this is the language version to which the court must refer to for the purposes of interpretation. It can therefore be concluded that in both regions there is no duty for the courts to take into account both linguistic versions: in Valle d'Aosta the court will consider the first version the original text and the other one as a simple translation, while in South Tyrol a hierarchy between the two versions has already been provided by the law, as being Italian the only authentic text for interpretation. Finally, notwithstanding the formal provisions on interpretation, in case of doubt or contradictions, the court will define a reasonable solution in its juridical background, as well as in the general principles and values of the Italian legal system.

[21]In this regard, the recruitment of lawyers and judges is carried out locally and so not through a national public selection as in the rest of Italy. The access to the legal professions, as well as to the public administration, is subject to the possession of a specific language certificate enacted by the South Tyrol province, demonstrating a certain language knowledge both in Italian and German.

2.3 University Legal Education in Bilingual Regions

In this peculiar environment, it is easy to understand how bilingualism poses very important goals and challenges. To be able to enforce legislation and to administrate justice in the two languages, the system should be able firstly to count on a sufficient number of legally educated bilingual legal professionals and law graduates.

In South Tyrol, as well as in the rest of Italy, responsibility for legal training is shared between law faculties and other schools for the legal professions, that can be established by universities or local bar associations. However, despite the fact that the presence of two languages is a cardinal tenet of legal life in these areas, one may not say that both these institutions respond to the challenges of public policies on bilingualism.

In university education multilingualism has been complied with, leading to the introduction of the extensive use of English, in addition to German and Italian. The trilingual Free University of Bolzano/Bozen—established in 1997—does not currently offer a full curriculum in law, but several classes in law disciplines (mostly in the Economics curriculums) which may be theoretically taught in the three languages.[22] Anyhow, the system is not designed to provide legal education in both Italian and German; according to the teaching regulation[23] of the Faculty of Economics in Bolzano, lectures—in law disciplines too—are offered in Italian, English and German, possibly respecting a proportion among the three languages in the number of courses.[24]

This higher educational system splitting teaching into at least two languages is linguistically conditioned too, as students are required to be fluent in at least two of the three languages. Nevertheless, the educational commitment—as well as this linguistic university policy—is not meant to incentivize the knowledge and the language of the two linguistic communities, neither is this model of education is supposed to prepare lawyers of the two groups for their professional life.

The same applies to the co-official status of French in the special-status autonomous Region of Valle d'Aosta/*Vallée d'Aoste*.[25]

---

[22] Art. 4, art. 5 and art. 6 Law 482/1999, for the protection of linguistic minorities in Italian regions involved in the matter.

[23] Libera Università di Bolzano—Freie Universität Bozen. Regolamento didattico del corso di Laurea Economia e Management—Studiengandsregelung des Bachelor Wirtschaftswiessenschaften und Betriebsfürung. Art. 3: "The study program is offered in three languages: Italian, German and English".

[24] However, operatively, courses in the fields of law are activated in Italian. The two other teaching languages are residual, depending on the subject or the availability of German or English-speaking professors: on the one hand, teachers who are fluent in the two languages may voluntarily accept to teach in English or German. On the other hand, the university might create specific teaching positions in which the knowledge of both these languages is a prerequisite. In this regard, special chairs called "Double belonging" (*Cattedra con doppia appartenenza*) have been recently created within the framework of an agreement among the universities of Trento, Bolzano and Innsbruck ("Euregio" agreement, related to the European Region Tyrol-South Tyrol-Trentino).

[25] The protection of other historical minorities is instead laid down in a statutory instrument: Framework Law no. 482/1999. See Woelk et al. (2007); Woelk (2007), p. 157.

With reference to the Italian-French bilingual area of Valle d'Aosta, higher education in law is entirely held in Italian. As already mentioned, at the university of Aosta, with the exception of the "double degree" projects that are held with foreign universities (as an example, the University of Savoie Mont Blanc and the University of Nice), all classes dealing with law are taught in Italian.

2.4 Post Graduate Legal Education in Bilingual Regions

Post graduate education is a further unsolved problem that legal education in bilingual territories is facing, particularly concerning the training of law graduates who would like to enter the "traditional" legal professions (namely: lawyer, judge, notary).

Again, in both bilingual regions, the system is not designed to provide post university training in law in the two languages (Italian/French or Italian/German). The responsibility for this specific need is more up to the bar associations than to the Universities and the same control over professional appointments is decentralized to those local associations.

The Bolzano school for the legal professions (*Scuola forense—Anwaltsschule*) established by Bolzano Bar Association Council (*Consiglio dell'Ordine degli avvocati di Bolzano—Rechtsanwaltskammer Bozen*) ensures that post-graduate legal education complies with the requirements for accessing the Bar exams, also with regard to bilingualism.

According to the School regulation[26] students may attend classes either in Italian or German, but not all the programs in all disciplines are available in both languages. The data on language offer indicates that only 20–30% of the lectures are offered in German, even though German speaking young jurists attending the school are not a minority. This depends mostly on the availability of German speaking professors more than on the content of the lecture, even if experimental double language classes have been recently introduced.[27] This model is based on a co-teaching method of the same subject by two teachers, each being bilingual, but prevalent in one of the two languages. However, these bilingual classes are part of the general program of the school, the aim of which is not to train young jurists in bilingual legal terminology or legal translation. As a consequence, most case readings and pedagogical material are not available in the two languages.

The French speaking area of Valle d'Aosta is not equipped with a school for the legal professions (*scuola per le professioni legali* or *scuola forense*) and, as noted already, training in law is demanded to the competent associations located in the Italian territory.

---

[26] Art 10, Regulation of the "Scuola forense" of Bolzano.

[27] Information given by the Director of the Scuola forense di Bolzano Alvise Dalla Francesca Cappello (avvocato/ Rechtsanwalt/lawyer).

This is understandable as students residing in Valle d'Aosta are not motivated to study law in a language other than Italian, since the ability to assimilate and understand administrative documents and particularly to learn norms and case law as well as to solve cases is to be carried out in this language only. That is also due to the fact that the regulation of the legal language in Valle d'Aosta is a lot less incisive compared to South Tyrol, where all citizens have the right to use their language when dealing with legal offices and in court: consequently, all legislation, public documents and case law must be translated in the chosen language, where in Valle d'Aosta, translation is foreseen only for specific legal deeds.[28]

In conclusion, bilingualism is one of the main characteristics of the legal environment in Valle d'Aosta, and in South Tyrol in particular, the importance of which is enhanced also by the development and increment of the legislation produced by the institutions of the autonomous Province of Bolzano, with the subsequent rising demand for bilingual jurists. Despite a full curriculum in law is still lacking at the University of Bolzano, it is clear that the bilingual legal education in South Tyrol has considerably developed and will probably increase over the next few years, in order not only to properly train future lawyers and civil servants, but also to offer a legal education that is complete, up with the times and transferable abroad.

Despite these efforts, in Sud-Tyrol the final result of this organization is that each language community has, *de facto*, developed legal education models in its language, without being necessarily concerned with the language of the other community. This is particularly true in the case of the German speaking community, since the crucial importance of German in a territoy adjacent to Austria and the situation of the market of the legal profession where the capability of handling legal German is necessary to successfully access the legal career.

For the time being, outside South Tyrol the nearest universities which offer a full curriculum in law are the University of Trento (Italy) and the University of Innsbruck (Austria); it is interesting to notice how the latter, that is located in the Austrian region of Tyrol, offers an integrated curriculum in law which covers both the Austrian and Italian legal systems and in which classes are taught in German as well as in Italian. Recently, both Universities signed an agreement for the exchange of students within the law courses.[29] This model could represent the starting point for a bilingual curriculum in Italian and Austrian Law, after an initial experimentation period.

Finally, and strangely enough, the Italian Universities offering a bilingual German-Italian training course for lawyers *(avvocato/Rechtsanwalt)* are the University of Florence, offering a programme in which Italian students interested in the legal profession in Germany attend part of the courses in Cologne (Germany)[30] and the University of Turin[31] in cooperation with the University of Münster.

[28] The so called "ordinanza", according to the Decree (Decreto luogotenenziale) no. 545/1945 on the administrative system of Valle d'Aosta.

[29] This is one of the joint projects activated in the framework to the European Region *Tyrol-South Tyrol-Trentino*.

[30] See https://www.giurisprudenzaitalotedesca.unifi.it/changelang-eng.html2.

[31] Double degree University of Turin and Westfälische Wilhelms Universität (WWU) Münster.

3 Bilingual Legal Education on the National Level

3.1 Internationalization

In Italy, the State has the exclusive authority to regulate the matter of high education in law. A university degree (*Laurea Magistrale in Giurisprudenza*[32]) recognized after a five years study programme at the Faculty of Law is the required title to access the legal professions (lawyer, judge, notary).

For a student interested in studying law, but not in the legal traditional legal professions, a different curriculum of three years (bachelor) is the only possible alternative; although this curriculum does not allow the law graduate to continue the required training to become judge, lawyer or notary a consistent number of Italian universities have activated a bachelor degree in law (Degree in Legal Services—*Laurea in Servizi Giuridici*)[33] and this number is destined to increase.[34] This is tangible particularly with regard to aspects concerning the language of teaching, as the three years bachelor is currently the only framework enabling Italian universities to enforce a law degree in a language other than Italian.[35]

Strangely enough, the fact that in Italy a five-year law degree (*Laurea in Giurisprudenza*) can't be offered in two languages, as well as in a language other than Italian, is not due to any reluctance of the State to implement a bachelor model, as in other European States: the real obstacle is of a technical-linguistic nature, as being the five-year degree the only education programme for the traditional legal professions which are still the essence of legal education in Italy and strongly based on the national legal culture and terminology. Outside the "gold circle" of these legal professions, Italian language is getting less and less dominant in legal education.

In Italy the language of teaching and of University programmes is regulated on the national level. The general framework on language discipline in university studies is a statute dated 1933[36] providing that "Italian is the official language of teaching and of examinations in all universities".

---

[32] The so called 1+4 system, requiring five years of training in law was introduced by the Law Decree no. 270/2004.

[33] 33 Universities according to http://www.universitaly.it/index.php/offerta/cercaUniv.

[34] There are currently (2018) 77 law schools providing a five-year degree (Laurea in Giurisprudenza) and 44 three-year bachelors (Laurea in Servizi Giuridici/Degree in Legal Services).

[35] If education in law is considered in a broader sense, outside the Law Faculties, this discipline is taught in the departments (former "faculties") of political and social science, as well as in that of economics and business, PhD schools and masters. Afterwards, the responsibility for legal training is shared among schools for the legal professions, private schools for notaries or courses for training judges.

[36] Art. 271 Regio Decreto no.1593/1933.

However, a more recent statute[37] calls for the "strengthening of internationalization also through courses and forms of selection carried out in a foreign language".[38]

Currently, the foreign language of teaching—any language other than Italian—is the only requirement which is necessary to qualify a University programme as "international".

It is well known that the internationalization process of legal education is a complex phenomenon that has gradually involved all the European education systems, responding to the need of the State to be competitive in a global market, as well as with the neo-liberal idea that universities "produce" services with economic values, that have to be competitive and attractive, as all the other economic activities.[39] Within this complexity, aspects such as competition among law schools, convergence of academic curriculums, attracting students, mobility of researchers and students are the ingredients of a successful education system in the field of law too.[40]

Thus, like in many other European education systems, internationalization has been the "engine" of the recent development of bilingual education in Italy. It is therefore not surprising that the language of teaching in bilingual programmes is English, and legal education makes no exception.

3.2 *Europeanization*

The use of a language other than Italian in legal education could, however, depend on other reasons besides the process of internationalization.

Here, the pressure of adapting the method of teaching to uniform to European criteria has played a role too.

As a matter of principle, in Italy academic and teacher autonomy is very broad. Law Faculties responsible for the organization of teaching in the different areas of the legal training enjoy a significant level of freedom, with the only limit regarding the balance of the number of credits assigned to each course. The adoption of specific teaching and learning methods largely depends on the decisions of the single teachers; as to the field of law, teaching has always been in the form of theoretical lectures, in which the pedagogical approach is mostly to address notions and juridical cultural competencies to students.

In this framework, students are required to demonstrate a certain level of knowledge of the subject which has been presented by the teacher, as well as of reasoning skills. Those abilities are usually verified through oral or written exams, which are particularly demanding from the students' point of view. In general, undergraduate

[37] Art. 2 Law n. 240/2010 on university reorganization.

[38] Ministery Decree no. 98/2016.

[39] Arzoz (2012), p. 30.

[40] Ibid.

legal education is carried out with the aim of providing a general education, with no particular emphasis on professional skills, like those required in the legal professions.

More recently, undergraduate legal education in law has been influenced also by the tension between offering only an academic preparation or training students towards a professional qualification as well.[41]

A decisive role was played by the political decision of the Italian Government to implement the protocol signed in Bologna in 1988 by the Minister of Education of the European Community, which had the declared goal to harmonize the university systems in their respective countries.[42] Italy was one of the very first European nations enforcing this reform—the so called "Bologna process"—[43] by introducing a "3+2 system", a training programme composed of a three-year bachelor followed by the possibility for the students to continue their education for two additional years (*Laurea specialistica*). As noted by Febbrajo, the reform offered the Italian law Schools the chance and the justification for enforcing an honourable compromise between two different models of graduate legal training: on the one hand, the traditional one, that is prevalently cultural.[44] On the other hand, a mostly operational and variegated training, so as to meet the various demands for new professional figures required by the business world and the labour market.[45] Although the "Bologna Process" in Italy was soon modified,[46] a new model of legal education was finally put forward, with more branches of specialization for the judiciary and incorporating some law practical training.

According to this new pedagogical and scientific trend, education in law Schools should assume not only the task of disseminating knowledge, but also that of providing students with more concrete and practical abilities, that are important too for constructing their professional future. The law curriculum must be designed so that, in addition to theoretical legal education, students are trained to learn also what is expected by society and by the labour market. Thus, along with the traditional lectures, teachers are invited to stimulate students through seminars, case analyses, interactive sessions, continuous assessment and other innovative educational methodologies.[47] University legal education has thus been able to establish a

[41] Pascuzzi (2017).

[42] Febbrajo (2007), p. 105.

[43] Law Decree no. 4/2000.

[44] In Italy, the indications of the "Bologna process" were adopted under Ministerial Decree no. 509/1999 which deeply changed the organization of Italian universities. In particular, it introduced a distinction between undergraduate and graduate degrees and gave stronger impulse to Phd studies as a third level of higher education. Furthermore, the system of credits was adopted and universities were given major autonomy as regards the definition of their educational activities.

[45] Febbrajo (2007), p. 105.

[46] The reform was soon changed under Ministerial Decree 270/2004 which introduced a master degree in law, lasting 5 years.

[47] Law Decree no. 28/2000 and Law Decree no. 4/2000 (annex n. 31).

connection with these underlying necessities, which are often left to the personal resourcefulness of the individual law graduate.[48]

Actually, such a pedagogical approach hasn't modified the features of the traditional legal education—systematic teaching, theoretically dominant and culturally guiding—but rather integrated it; on the one hand, universities have introduced elective courses—often in the form of "workshops" (*laboratorio*) having a more activity-based approach in which students do not only "listen and learn", but are required to "do things", so as to develop more creative and practical skills.

It is in this context that law Faculties are placing more emphasis on the proportion of language, legal language and courses offered in a language other than Italian. Thus, more space to languages, like the introduction of English as the language of teaching or the possibility for students to attend specific training programs on some of the legal languages (mainly English, German, French and Spanish) indirectly opens up the professional environment for future jurists. Although students are not trained to be bilingual *per se*, at the end of their studies they should be able to approach a wider market; this is tangible particularly in private practices and business, where linguistic skills are appreciated. Furthermore, with regard to international law firms and companies operating beyond the national market, only a young jurist who indisputably fulfils language qualification requirements may be the ideal candidate for a post.

For this reason, bilingual legal education in Italy is now moving beyond a model that emphasizes national knowledge and is becoming a cross-border form of higher training. Once more, as well as in the case of the internationalization process, a legal education which shifts away from the national State and moves towards the labour and professional market.[49]

This has been particularly relevant over the last ten years, as one of the reasons for which students choose to leave their home country is certainly the world crisis; however, the decision of a university's administration to conduct its "business" bilingually or even in English also has the aim of qualifying students with a wider and more global vision, as well as a sense of concreteness, as the result of the Bologna process.

3.3 A Relevant Example: Trento University Faculty of Law

Besides all traditional opportunities such as the double degree, the Erasmus programme, as well as the involvement of foreign professors in elective courses, the Italian academic environment also offers few bilingual legal education models.

In 2017 a new course was established at the Faculty of Law of Trento, located in Trentino-Alto Adige, not far from South Tyrol, but in an Italian, monolingual

[48] Pascuzzi (2013), p. 16.

[49] Arzoz (2012), p. 30.

environment. In the case of the Trento Faculty, the decision was made to activate the first law bachelor degree entirely offered in English, anticipated by a two years experimental period of assessing students' interests, as well as their performances and results.

Here, the motivation for bilingual legal education is not specifically connected to the social environment, and particularly to the location of Trento Faculty of Law at the border of the bilingual area of the Trentino Region,[50] but to the cultural mission of this top law School, the main goal of which is to train students in comparative and transnational law.[51] Since its establishment, Trento Faculty of Law has indeed always paid special attention to comparative law not only as an important part of the young scholars legal education, but also as a teaching method.[52]

Students' language training has constantly been central, also thanks to the favourable conditions established at a higher level through a generous University language policy, which has always been interpreted and applied according to the cultural model and necessities of each Faculty or department. Thus, some scientific departments (e.g. the Centre for Integrative Biology CIBIO) since the very beginning have been offering courses entirely taught in English, but it is particularly with the Faculty of Law that the university's autonomy and the flexibility of the general teaching language policy of this well known Italian University has proved to be innovative and to have a vision.

Similarly to other law Schools in Italy, Trento Faculty of Law has always cultivated the language skills of its students through International mobility programmes, double degree projects (as for example the *Transnational Law Project*—TLP—, activated in 2008[53]), as well as by offering a good number of elective

---

[50] See previous paragraphs.

[51] Trento Faculty of Law on line Students' Guide: "*The mission has always involved treating "legal phenomena" as distinct from domestic positive law of which it is part, being national laws and regulations worthy of study for obvious, practical reasons but clearly distinguishable from the legal phenomena per se. Indeed, law is a complex reality, which includes domestic positive law, international law, supranational law and, of course, their reciprocal interactions. Thus, it is no surprise that the content of university law programs throughout Europe (and elsewhere) is tending towards uniformity and national differences now often only account for a small part of them. In this light, the method of comparative law is one of the best tools for learning one's own domestic legal system in a broader context, which takes law into account as a social phenomenon. By "denationalizing" the law, one's knowledge of it can only being improved, and its consistency tested with reference to its explicit and implicit justifications. This is the essence of the Theses of Trento, a Manifesto on comparative law which was developed in 1987 by a number of distinguished scholars partly based at the Faculty of Law of the University of Trento, and which has had a lasting influence on the cultural history of the Institution. For these reasons, the choice to study law in Trento offers students a challenging initiation into the realm of law in both its comparative and transnational aspects*".

[52] Grande (2012) (Originally published 2006), Chapter III.

[53] The objective of the Transnational Law Program (TLP), created and directed by the author of this Chapter, is to provide an opportunity for students to obtain a transnational legal education and to be trained as transnational lawyers. The Trento Faculty of Law offers this programme in close cooperation with the Washington University School of Law (WUSTL) in Saint Louis, Missouri

courses in other languages besides Italian. With the passing of time, these choices in legal education have been reinforced with the introduction in the students' curricula of legal language courses in the framework of the Law and Language Program (programma Lingua e Diritto).[54]

Thus, it is no surprise that the very first bilingual Faculty of law in Italy was established in this environment: *Comparative European and International Legal Studies* (CEILS) programme was the only bachelor degree in law in Italy to be entirely offered in English, as well as one of the very few established in Europe.[55]

Very soon, this model was continued in Italy by Turin University (Università degli Studi di Torino) where the English law bachelor "Global Law and Transnational Legal Studies" was launched in 2018. The program offers several courses on comparative law giving students the possibility to deepen the research of different legal models, practices and cultures, according to the aim of global and transnational law. These three-year bachelors[56] are included within an overview in which courses offered in English are developing progressively. Although less considerable in terms of quantity compared to other areas, such development has also involved the legal sphere over the past years. Courses are offered in English, in particular with regard to post-graduate one-year or two-year masters, but also to double degree programmes. All Italian law Schools provide elective courses in various languages besides Italian, mainly by inviting visiting professors or professionals who are experts on a particular subjects.

A different decision has recently been made by some of the most prestigious Italian universities (University of Bologna and Florence) and is related to the activation, within the School of Law, of some compulsory law courses in English Courses like "Comparative Legal Systems", "International law", "European Union Law", are therefore open to students enrolled in the five-year law programme, willing to experiment learning in English, after passing an entry test.

This is the teaching model that the Faculty of Law of Trento decided to experiment in order to assess students' interest, as well as the effectiveness of teaching in a

(USA), where the students enrolled in the project spend one year, during which they obtain an LL.M Degree, as well as the possibility to register for the BAR exam. On the model of the TLP, since 2018 a number of similar double title programs have been proposed at Trento Faculty of Law and recently by other Departments of Trento University).

[54]Legal English, legal French, legal Spanish and legal German. This programme, coordinated by the author of this Chapter, offers a vast range of activities: basic to advanced foreign-language courses, courses to learn foreign legal languages, law courses and workshops held by professors in a language other than Italian, seminars and courses on legal translation within the Doctoral Program in Comparative and European Legal Studies, Italian courses for foreign students, research activity on legal translation, congress organization and seminars.

[55]English law bachelors are offered by Maastricht and Tilburg Universities (The Netherlands), by the European Law and Governance School of Athens (Greece) and since 2018 by Turin University (Italy).

[56]CEILS program, which was launched in 2017, counts 50 enrolled students per year, for a total of 150 students in the 3 years, plus 10 non-UE students per year.

language other than Italian, before actually activating CEILS English bachelor.[57] Thus, the Faculty's professors were involved in the difficult challenge of teaching their subjects in a different language. Regarding some experimental teachings—as in the case of the author of this Chapter with a course "Comparative legal systems", the direct experience of the tight relation between language and teaching methodology proved that language is not simply a means to communicate comparative knowledge. This choice for bilingualism derives from the need to take steps in the direction of the Europeanisation of the law curriculum: in these terms, language is method, as "the law practitioners need to be capable of crossing national borders, not only physically but also intellectually"[58] and English, according to the Eurobarometer,[59] is currently the most spoken foreign language in Europe.

Thus, the responsibility upon teachers is very high and has no comparison with the situation of those involved in the elective law English courses. The formers are *de facto* responsible for programme planning of an essential part of the curriculum leading to a traditional law degree (*Laurea in Giurisprudenza*). Furthermore, they have to fulfil the task of elaborating new teaching materials. At present, this is in all probability the weakness of the process of introducing law courses in English, as the scarcity of English comparative law literature in all fields of law is a specific barrier to the development of innovative teaching methods.

Developing high-quality learning material in the form of specific legal literature remains a challenge for each law professor initiating this teaching adventure,[60] together with the knowledge of the foreign language: teaching in English in general offers serious dares in Italy, posed by the intellectual culture which is strictly identified with the use of Italian.

3.4 Obstacles and Challenges

This change in the culture of academic law is so profound that in Italy it has inevitably led to discussions and obstacles.

Language used at a university level is tightly linked to two characteristics that belong to the Italian legal system: the first refers specifically to legal education and depends on the linguistic regime of the legal professions. The second, which is more general, refers to the protection policy enforced by national institutions to preserve Italian language.

[57] Trento Faculty of law has recently deliberated to continue the teaching in English, and to include the fundamental courses in English in the regular teaching offer of the Faculty.

[58] Kornet (2012), p. 319.

[59] Eurobarometer 2012, European and their languages: http://ec.europa.eu/commfrontoffice/public/opinion/archives/ebs/ebs_386_en.pdf.

[60] Van Erp (2015), p. 1.

As regards the first issue, it is important to remember that University education is mandatory for a student who seeks access to the legal professions, as it is subordinate to the possession of a five-years degree *Laurea in Giurisprudenza* (Five years degree in Law).

In the past, the choice of the national official language as the only teaching language was also influenced by the peculiar environment in which post war legal culture developed in Italy. At that time, academic training in law was deeply influenced by positivism[61] and consequently exclusively based on national law. Transferring knowledge in this rigorous normative context meant the adoption of a dogmatic and national uniform approach[62] in university courses all over the nation.

Even internationalization and Europeanization are progressively influencing the Italian university system, an important element guiding legal education is that still nowadays the legal professions are strongly rooted into the national Italian environment. As noted above, practicing law is a professional activity that is controlled by law bar associations settled at the national or regional level. This is true particularly with regard to access to the Bar: the "on the job" practice remains the primary training method chosen by the law graduate aiming to enter the legal professions, after having obtained a university law degree. Thus, from the very first year of their five-year university studies, students initiate to become familiar with Italian taxonomy, legal language and categories, so as to gradually learn how to handle and understand the Italian legal reasoning. Even if academic legal education is far from being exhaustive in the training of a lawyer, a judge or even a notary,[63] it has great importance from a linguistic point of view. This is the primary reason for which the main Italian university curriculum (*Laurea Magistrale in Giurisprudenza*), obtained after a five-year study programme at the Faculty of law, cannot be provided in a language other than Italian.

The second reason of the ongoing strong connection between university education and national language is the general policy of the Italian institutions with reference to the Italian language.[64] This is particularly clear after the Italian Constitutional Court (*Corte Costituzionale*) and the Supreme Administrative Court of Italy

[61] Febbrajo (2007), p. 94.

[62] Febbrajo (2007), p. 95.

[63] According to a study concerning "the legal graduate education in Italy" one of the structural and institutional specificities of the Italian model is the separation between law faculties and the legal professions, due to the weakness of the impact of academic legal education on the reality of the legal practice: Ballarino (2007), p. 221.

[64] With the decision published on the 29th January 2018 the *Consiglio di Stato*, Italy's high administrative court, ruled that Italian universities cannot offer a degree exclusively in English. The contested provision is art. 2(2)(l) Law 240/2010 on the organization of universities, insofar as it enables the general and exclusive activation (i.e. to the exclusion of the Italian language) of [university education] courses in foreign languages, based on which the Polytechnic Institute of Milan decided to offer all graduate programmes in English in 2012. Against the university's decision, a group of lecturers appealed to the regional administrative court, which ruled in their favour. The ruling was appealed to the *Consiglio di Stato*, which then referred the question to the Constitutional Court.

(*Consiglio di Stato*) ruled on the legitimacy and compatibility with the Italian Constitution of university courses offered entirely in English.

In November 2017 the *Consiglio di Stato*[65] confirmed a principle that had already been laid down by the Constitutional Court in judgement no. 42/2017 and ruled that universities, considering the *special nature and specificity of the individual courses [...] may also choose to offer them exclusively in a foreign language "but" in accordance with the principles of reasonableness, proportionality and adequacy, in order to continue to guarantee that the overall teaching on offer respects the primacy of the Italian language along with the principle of equality, the right to education and academic freedom.*[66]

The decision underlined that the goal of internationalization cannot jeopardize the principles of the primacy of the Italian language, of equal access to university education and of academic freedom, and it cannot relegate the Italian language to a marginal position in academia.

The *Consiglio di Stato* reaffirmed that the Italian language is a fundamental element of cultural identity and primary vehicle for conveying the culture and traditions of the national community. Teaching courses held solely in a foreign language would have the effect of *"entirely and indiscriminately exclud[ing] the official language of the (Italian) Republic from university teaching in entire branches of learning"*.[67] Moreover, it would deny students with no knowledge of any language other than Italian the freedom to choose their own university study programme and prevent them from reaching "the highest level of education". Finally, it would violate academic freedom because it would affect how teachers communicate with students and discriminate against them with regard to the allocation of courses based on an expertise—knowing the foreign language—which has nothing to do with the skills that were examined during recruitment and with the specific knowledge which must be imparted to students.[68]

The holding of the decision then reaches its conclusion by precising that "the aforementioned principles would not be violated by a training offer that gives the possibility to run programmes in both languages in parallel and offer individual English-taught modules, depending on the specific features of the discipline taught".

For the *Accademia della Crusca*, the most important centre of scientific research dedicated to the study and promotion of the Italian language,[69] this was a "*wonderful victory*" and this decision is a "*powerful weapon*" to protect the Italian language, as stated by its President, Claudio Marazzini. According to Marazzini, offering programs only in English is a form of "*pseudo-internationalization*" that contributes to

[65] Consiglio di Stato, (decision) 23 November 2017, published on January 29, 2018.

[66] Ibid.

[67] Ibid.

[68] Ibid.

[69] http://www.accademiadellacrusca.it/en/accademia/history/accademia-today (last visited September 17, 2018).

the marginalization of the Italian language and through which universities only try to climb the international rankings.

The question now is to what extent the Court decisions will affect internationalization at Italian universities where many undergraduate courses, master's and doctoral programmes are already held in English and whether it will have an effect in general on the ongoing linguistic debate regarding the internationalization of higher education in Italy and in Europe.

At present, discussions have not come to an end. Although almost everybody has agreed that the introduction of the English language in legal education is of growing importance, the ongoing diversification of opinions is focusing on whether entire courses offered in a language other than Italian could still grant and maintain the high level of education of Italian universities.

Thus, according to the question as regards "how much English" the system of academic education in general could stand is particularly relevant in the field of law, as on the one hand legal Italian is an essential instrument of the jurist who intends to enter the legal professions in Italy; on the other hand, because of the well-known peculiarities of legal translation, the language in which the legal education is expressed strongly conditions the substance of the educational message too.[70]

4 Conclusions

As we have seen, language rights in Italy are constitutionally recognized and regional governments perform the obligation to promote bilingualism, even in legal drafting. At least in South Tyrol, trilingualism, with German, Italian and Ladin, plays an important role and has definitely become a genuine value. However, universities and schools for the legal professions do not significantly contribute to foster this cultural and legal characteristic of the country. Even in bilingual regions, universities train monolingual law students.

As noted by Arzoz, bilingual or multilingual legal education has different meanings, depending on the way in which a State structures its higher education system: through separate monolingual institutions, through bilingual (or multilingual) institutions or, finally through a combination of both.[71]

The situation of Italy is definitely peculiar and does not precisely fit into any of these models. Even when carried on in a multilingual State, higher legal education in Italy remains principally monolingual; bilingual or multilingual academic institutions are definitely rare, even though this scenario is constantly and rapidly evolving.

At the same time, even with regard to a specific institution, bilingualism means definitely English and can have different applications and levels of deepening, with the use of a second language limited to a certain course or being a compulsory

[70] Blanch-Jouvan et al. (1993).

[71] Arzoz (2012), p. 7.

element of the curriculum even in the legal studies. Furthermore, entire institutions offering bachelor legal education in a language different from the official national one of the country are destined to become a model. This last frontier of non-Italian language legal education seems to be destined to increase, as it very much attracts students[72] and the use of English has proved to be a formidable vehicle for the transfer of comparative and transnational legal knowledge.[73]

Arguably, bilingual legal education in Italy is a methodology, and this methodology is in transition: it is moving away from the techniques used when ties to the key legal professions were predominant, and the development of the "science of law" was a priority,[74] and is turning into a series of gradual and continuing developments and transformations,[75] following current students' agendas. In this context, the use of English as a teaching language is not devoid of consequences on the content of teaching, resulting less connected to a specific legal system aimed at the training of a jurist destined to operating in a global context. A prominent example is the use of the term "giurisprudenza" (case law) in a class of Italian-speaking students, which implies transferring the concept of "interpretation" (interpretazione) and "no source of the law" (non fonte del diritto). On the contrary, the same concept expressed in English "case law" in a class of students also from other countries is recognized as "rule (norm), even if not enacted".

However, obstacles do still exist, due to the difficulties of accepting the fact that a part of the well-rooted national legal education could be not replaced, but integrated, in order to equip students with new means of education.

References

Arzoz X (2012) Legal education in bilingual contexts: a conceptual, historical and comparative introduction. In: Arzoz X (ed) Bilingual higher education in the legal context: Group rights, State policies and globalization. Studies in international minority and group right vol 2. Brill, Leiden, pp 1–34

Ballarino G (2007) Graduate legal education in Italy: an empirical overview. In: Olgiati V (ed) Higher legal culture and postgraduate legal education in Europe. Edizioni Scientifiche Italiane, Naples, pp 205–225

Ben-Ghiat R (1997) Language and the construction of national identity in fascist Italy. Eur Legacy 2 (3):438–443

Blanch-Jouvan X et al (eds) (1993) L'enseignement du droit national aux étudiants étrangers. Société de législation comparée, Paris

Cairns J, du Plessi PJ (ed) (2010) The creation of the Ius Commune: from Casus to Regula (Edinburgh Studies in Law EUP), Edinburgh Studies in Law EUP (Book 7)

[72] Trento English law bachelor CEILS, in its first year of activation (2017), has attracted more than 200 students, applying for 50 positions offered.

[73] Graziadei (2015).

[74] Cownie (2007), p. 120.

[75] Cassese (2017), pp. 143–149.

Cassese S (2017) Legal education under fire. Eur Rev Priv Law 25(1):143–149
Castellani A (1982) Quanti erano gl'italofoni nel 1861? Studi linguistici italiani 8(1):3–26
Coonan CM (2000) Language teacher training and bilingual education. At: http://www.celelc.org/projects/Past_Projects/TNP_Languages/TNP1_resources/SP6NatRepIT.pdf (last visited September 13, 2018)
Cownie F (2007) Transforming a discipline: the changing world of academic lawyers in United Kingdom. In: Olgiati V (ed) Higher legal culture and postgraduate legal education in Europe. Edizioni Scientifiche Italiane, Naples
De Mauro T (1963) Storia linguistica dell'Italia unita. Laterza, Bari
Febbrajo A (2007) Higher legal education and models of legal culture in Italy. In: Olgiati V (ed) Higher legal culture and postgraduate legal education in Europe. Edizioni Scientifiche Italiane, Naples
Grande E (2012) (originally published 2006) Development of comparative law in Italy. In: Reimann M, Zimmerman R (eds) The Oxford handbook of comparative law
Graziadei M (2015) Law, language and multilingualism in Europe: the call for a new legal culture. In: Sarcevic S (ed) Language and culture in EU law: multidisciplinary perspectives. Ashgate, Farnham
Kornet N (2012) English-medium legal education in continental Europe: Maastricht University's European law school: experiences and challenges. In: Arzoz (ed) Bilingual legal education in the legal context: group rights, State policies and globalisation. Studies in international minority and group right vol 2. Brill, Leiden, pp 313–339
Lepschy G, Lepschy AL (1977) The Italian language today. Hutchinson, London
Maiden M (2002) The definition of multilingualism in historical perspective. In: Lepschy AL, Tosi A (eds) Multilingualism in Italy past and present. Studies in linguistics, vol 1. Routledge, Cambridge, pp 32–46
Maiden M, Perry M (1997) The dialects of Italy. Routledge, London
Pascuzzi G (2013) Giuristi si diventa. Il Mulino, Bologna
Pascuzzi G (2017) Il problem solving nelle professioni legali. Il Mulino, Bologna
Posner R (1996) The romances languages. Cambridge University Press, Cambridge
Sacco R (2000) Langue et droit. In: Jayme E (ed) Langue et droit. Bruylant, Bruxelles
Van Erp S (2015) Should English be the shared academic property law languages? Eur Prop Law J 4 (1):1–2
Woelk J (2007) From compromise to process: the implementation of the South Tyrolean autonomy. In: Boltjes M (ed) Implementing negotiated agreements: the real challenge to intrastate peace. T.M.C. Asser Press, The Hague
Woelk J, Palermo F, Marko J (eds) (2007) Tolerance through law: Self-governance and group rights in South Tyrol: The autonomy of South Tyrol. Brill, Leiden

Bilingual Legal Education in Japan

Mark Fenwick

Japan's situation regarding Bilingual Legal Education (BLE) is, at least in the National Reporter's point of view, quite original because of its complexities and somehow contradictions.

To begin with, two different stages must be taken into account: before and after 2004. That year was a key one to introduce and develop a new educational system more alike the US-style of law schools. In reality, Japan has experienced two different and competing institutional pressures in the context of legal education. (A) One pushing to a more diverse form of legal education but aiming to reinforce and enhance better Japanese lawyers inside the country, (B) the other one, with the commitment of the Ministry of Education, to internationalize Japanese universities and undergraduate law faculties in view of globalization and commerce.

The results of the new plan have not been—until now—the ones expected. The reformers and builders of the first current or pressure, hoped for a significant rise in the pass rates for the bar examination in Japan and this did not occur: it still remains low, currently between 20 and 25%. Consequently, law schools and law school students actually have focused their limited study time on "core" examination subjects, leaving little time or reason to pursue more diverse and creative course offerings, including courses taught in languages other than Japanese or courses making extensive use of foreign language materials.

On the other hand, the interest of the Ministry of Education to internationalize its education has obtained some new developments, although it is still uncertain which of these two tendencies shall prevail in the near future.

A little bit of history: "*Prior to 2004, the only pre-condition to take the national bar examination was high school graduation. A university law degree of any kind was not necessary. The bar examination was, however, notoriously difficult, with a*

M. Fenwick (✉)
Kyushu University, Fukuoka, Japan
e-mail: mark@law.kyushu-u.ac.jp

N. Etcheverry Estrázulas (ed.), *Bilingual Study and Research*, Ius Comparatum – Global Studies in Comparative Law 58,
https://doi.org/10.1007/978-3-030-84550-6_10

pass rate fluctuating between 2-3%. This meant that by the year 2000, Japan had less than 30,000 lawyers for a country with a population of over 120 million." (...) In order to assist candidates taking the bar examination, a network of private, specialized "cram" schools emerged independent of the universities. For those talented enough to pass, the bar examination was a gateway to, rather than the end-point of, professional legal training. A special institution run by the Supreme Court, the Legal Research and Training Institute would enroll those who had passed the bar examination and train them for a two-year period. In this way, future prosecutors, judges, and practicing lawyers would be trained together, before entering into the work force..."

The National Reporter adds a clarifying aspect: *"This does mean that Japan had no university-level legal education. Quite the contrary. Rather, the vast majority of students who enrolled on an undergraduate law degree at one of the many (90+) law faculties (hougakubu)* ***had no intention or prospect of pursuing a career in legal practice****. Rather,* ***there was a clear separation – at least, in comparison with other jurisdictions – between university legal education and the legal profession.*** *Instead, an undergraduate law degree* ***was seen as providing a general education, ideally suited to a career in the public sector - as a national or local government official - or in a private company.*** *As such, a law degree from a good university was seen as a ticket to a stable career in the life-long employment system that functioned so effectively in the post-war development of Japan.* (The underlying is the General Reporter's responsibility).

As a consequence, this way of understanding legal education, so separated from the finalities pursued in the legal profession, the "encyclopedian" or generalist culture provided by Universities such as the undergraduate law faculty of Tokyo had one main objective: to produce and form the elite of the national—level bureaucrats as well as the leaders in the fields of finance and commerce. In this process, academic performance at university was accorded much less weight than the particular university one attended. High school students were placed under enormous pressure to get into the best university possible (such as the mentioned above), in order to secure their future employment prospects. (...) *"As such, pre-2004 undergraduate university legal education in Japan was a high status, generalist training, rather than a specialized, graduate, or professional style of legal education. Undergraduate legal education was certainly not designed with a view to produce practicing lawyers or other legal professionals..."*

Complementary, previous to 2004 the main Universities both public or private, had graduate schools of law that offered Master's and Doctoral level courses mainly oriented on comparative law, but again, with one main and specific target: to prepare its students for a career as university teachers and researchers (not as legal practitioners) with a certain mastery of a foreign language and the law of that country in a special field. The two main preferences in terms of language, due to historical reasons, were German or French.

Hence, *"pre-2004 "legal education" in Japan could be divided into several different components: (i) university legal education, comprising a generalist undergraduate program; (ii) research-oriented graduate schools with a strong focus on comparative law; (iii) a series of specialized "cram" schools which would prepare candidates to pass the bar; and, (iv) a professionalized legal education, which came* ***after*** *passing the Bar examination and served as the only real practical legal training one would receive before entry into the three main legal professions of lawyer, prosecutor or judge..."*

In 2004 the Educational Japanese Authorities enhanced what was meant to be a sort of radical change in terms of Legal Education: the introduction of Law Schools with a US JD style education in a 2 or 3 years—program, depending on whether students had studied law as undergraduates. Completing law school became a pre-condition for taking the new national bar examination. Significantly, the new law school system was added **"on top"** of the undergraduate and graduate level legal education described before. This means that—contrary to what other countries such as Korea did a few years later—Japan did not close down the undergraduate law faculties or the research-oriented graduate schools of law. The origin of this reform was the general dissatisfaction with the state of the legal profession by the mid 90ties: *"(...) it was often difficult to obtain legal services and much of the supposed "non-litigiousness" of the Japanese could be better explained by the difficulties and costs of finding a reliable lawyer. Most lawyers tended to be concentrated in the big cities of Tokyo and Osaka, creating an uneven geographical distribution. Many people also criticized the quality of legal professionals, as the lack of genuine competition created little incentive for legal professionals to offer a better standard of service (...) after the Japanese economy fell into recession, pressure emerged to reform the system. The pressure came from several sources. The Ministry of Justice and Supreme Court in Japan wanted to increase the number of prosecutors and judges. Big business began to complain about the lack of quality in the legal profession. And, as the economy declined, more disputes emerged. The trend towards de-regulation meant that government control over the economy was decreasing. The capacity of government to manage conflict was diminishing..."*

As one can observe, this is just another example of how economic issues may impose legal, social and cultural reforms; on the other hand, many legal, social and cultural changes have played a significant role and had tremendous impact in the economy of certain countries and regions.

In any case, "*the key event in the reform of legal education was the creation of a Justice System Reform Council in June 1999. After two years of deliberations, the Council's recommendations were released in June 2001. These recommendations were to the have a profound impact on legal education of Japan and provided the template for the new post-2004 system.*

The primary aim of the Council's recommendations was to reform the justice system and increase reliance on the law as a means of social ordering. A key element of the transition towards a "law-governed society" was the call for an expansion in the number of lawyers, judges and prosecutors...".

There was great optimism and confidence in the creation of these new law schools. The market would determine the number of the new and well prepared lawyers, which in an average of 70 to 80% would be admitted to the legal profession after passing the bar examination. To support the newly created law schools, it was proposed that (at least, until 2011) only those who graduated from a law school could be eligible to sit the new examination, which would still have to be passed to qualify as a lawyer, public prosecutor or judge. Two programs would be offered: a two-year program for those who had studied law as an undergraduate and a three-year program for those who hadn't. The expectations were to have around 3000 lawyers graduating every year. The bet was to increase the quantity but also the quality and diversity of the new lawyers. The new law schools would move away from the narrow focus of private cram schools that had emerged to support students competing to pass the old-style bar examination. In order to accomplish this the Council recommended recruiting law school applicants from a wide range of academic and professional backgrounds: *"A lawyer with a degree in medicine, for instance, would be better placed to assist a client in the context of medical malpractice suite. Or, a lawyer with experience of the creative industries would be more effective in handling a copyright dispute..."*

Another aim was to enlarge and cover the gaps of geographic diversity in order diminish the centered influence of urban cities such as Tokyo and Osaka. And finally, to frame "internationalized lawyers" experts in business and international exchange.

Curiously enough, and maybe because of the pressure and resistance of the stakeholders of the traditional legal education system, the undergraduate law departments or faculties were maintained as a source of employees for government and internal business. As already mentioned, Korea did not follow the same path and many undergraduate law programs and departments were closed down when they opened the new law schools, as it happened in Seoul National University.

Therefore, as from 2004 the majority of law faculties in Japan offered: (i) the traditional general undergraduate legal education; (ii) a research-focused graduate school; and (iii) a new professional Law School, responsible for preparing students for the bar examination.

Sixty-six new law schools opened in that year and the competition to attract the best students was fierce. But the first results of launching and recruiting the new model of lawyers in the new era were not the ones expected. The number of students allowed to pass the bar examination increased much more slowly than originally envisaged. The government had to accept that instead of 3000 graduations per year, only half was reaching that goal. Not only this, but also the percentage pass rates began to drop to disappointing figures: from 48% in 2007 to around 25% in the period 2009–2015. The government's officials tried a feeble excuse: all in all, Japan should not become a litigious society, so 1500 new lawyers per year was enough, especially to avoid unnecessary competition and also to promote quality instead of quantity.

The introduction of an alternative way to pass the bar exam in 2011—a preliminary qualifying bar examination centered in six basic subjects—didn't obtain satisfactory results and simply supposed a return to the basic and traditional roots: the new kind of lawyers was not meant to be so necessary and the new generation of students would focus again in becoming well trained administrative officers, bureaucrats or researchers. The five more distinguished Universities in producing the best pass rates have been Keio, Tokyo, Chuo, Kyoto and Waseda in that order.

Another issue that has to be taken in consideration is the economic cost of attending to private law schools in relation to public ones. In average, it implies a 50% higher and not many students can afford that difference, especially if the light at the end of the academic tunnel seems so distant, dim, and ineffective. A logical consequence of all this is that applications to Law Schools are down from a decade ago, and some schools have been forced to merge or even close down. The persistent declining pass rate for the bar examination—25% on average—forced law school students again to focus on core examination subjects, leaving little time or incentive to pursue courses offered in other languages.

A different path to reimplement the new type of internationalized lawyers in some universities has been the introduction of programs mainly or exclusively taught in English. This can be a way of considering and accepting the term *"Bilingual Education"* in Japan in the last ten years. It was the path, as the National Reporter explains, to "re-invent" the graduate education by offering in some universities Master's and Doctoral programs taught mainly or exclusively in that language.

In order to better understand the trends that have been followed in Japan's BLE the reporter separates three different kinds of programs: (a) the ones offered by professional law schools (b) undergraduate programs with general legal education (c) graduate-level programs. Finally, the reporter signals the personal experience of Kyushu University where he is based, which offers all the three programs mentioned above.

Law Schools As said before, these new institutions experienced an optimistic start that collapsed a few years later. An article written by Dan Rosen—from Chuo University Law School in Tokyo—reflects both stages. From his point of view, many of the subjects taught at the beginning of the new Law Schools never appeared in the future bar exams. At first, they were accepted and chosen by the students as a way to expand their general culture and obtain some level of legal diversity. But things changed radically when the bar exams began to prove that only some core and traditional topics were frequently and persistently asked. What was required to pass the exams was memory and repetition; no need to intertwine knowledge or compare systems. The result? The students learned the lesson: forget the idea and hopes of diversity and internationalization; disregard all subjects and courses that are complementary such as law & economics or law & sociology, legal ethics, Roman or German law. Stick to the only courses and subjects required to approve the bar examination and if that is achieved, afterwards say goodbye to the law schools altogether. Dan Rosen, like many other professors are wondering how many students per year shall be attending courses that are considered a luxury and a waste of time for the new generation of students. As stated by the National reporter, (...) *"No matter how much the government may have emphasized the need for broadly trained lawyers, by maintaining a strict bottleneck on entrance to the profession, students are pushed into focusing on the bar-exam related subjects and away from other* *courses that can quickly come to be seen as a distraction from the core task. This includes courses with a strong foreign language component...*"

In view of this situation two alternatives may rise. Adopt the Korean model that limited the number of law schools but also required some universities with accredited law faculties to stop their undergraduate legal education, or increase the bet on internationalization, such as Luke Nottage's proposition that shows the case of the University of Sydney as a good example of cooperation between Australia and China, by promoting a 3 plus 2 double degree program (see page 19 of the report). Whether any of these alternatives shall be adopted remains doubtful in the National reporter's point of view.

Undergraduate Law Faculties These institutions have been "pushed" towards a different direction, especially by several governmental Ministries: internationalization of undergraduate teaching, learning and research. A example of this tendency was the 2009 Global 30 project that offered English only undergraduate courses and programs, or the Top Global University Initiative which began in 2014 and finishes in 2023. Funded by the Japanese government that approved U$S 77 million to attract more foreign faculty and students in the main Japanese Universities classifying them in two categories, A and B and accordingly giving more or less funds per year to each of them. Kyushu University, rated A, receives U$S 4.2 million annually because of its potential to be ranked among the top 100 in world university rankings. Type B universities receive U$S 1.7 per year. Two main "pushers" of this initiative were former Prime Minister Shinzo Abe and several Japanese companies that need to re-shape and re-invent the new professionals in order to compete in the global race where Japan has been losing presence and markets.

In 2013 the government launched Japan's Revitalization Strategy that aims to doublé the number of Japanese students studying abroad by 2020 (from 60,000 to 120,000). This was complemented with *"the "Tobitate (Leap for Tomorrow) Study Abroad Initiative". This scheme which hopes to make Japan a nation in which "ambitious young people are given the opportunity to go global" offers various chances for students to study abroad. A standout among these opportunities is the so-called "Young Ambassador Program". This program provides scholarships and other aid with the help of private-sector contributions aiming to collect 20 billion yen. The goal is to help 10,000 of these young "ambassadors" by 2020...*"

It is still very soon to predict and evaluate the results of all these strategies and initiatives. At least ten more years will be needed to reap what has been sown.

As already mentioned, Japanese legal education has not followed the usual standards of launching skilled and specialized professionals in such and such area of expertise. On the contrary, it has developed the encyclopedian, general approach helpful to work afterwards in different levels of the government or local companies. Hence, one can find two different and parallel trends or paths in Japanese education: (i) the scientific-research (ii) the practice—oriented. Until recently, the comparative legal education was mainly or exclusively taught in Japanese, although German or French law was the target of the comparative investigation. The finality of such education was to have a better knowledge and understanding of the Western World, but mainly as a mere intellectual curiosity or search for diversity. And there were no urges from up-ward companies or administrations to receive new well practiced and skilled professionals.

But something began to change since the last end of the twentieth century and beginning of the twenty-first: (a) the realization that English would still be necessary to move in commerce, business and politics, and (b) the realization that the Asian region (and particularly China) was beginning to acquire more and more economic and political influence in the Western world. Kyushu University, for example, recognized these changes and began to do something about it by hiring more and more foreign academic professors. Consequently, as the National reporter explains, *"there has been the creation of new four-year undergraduate programs that can be described as genuinely bilingual in the narrow sense that it involves a combination of law courses that are taught in both Japanese and English with the stated aim of producing "global lawyers" or, at least, those with the necessary language and legal skills to become global lawyers. An example of this type of bilingual law program is the so-called "Global Vantage" program (GV) launched in Kyushu University in 2015. This program is only open to 10 students per year and involves a separate English-language entrance examination from the traditional undergraduate program, but students are offered a genuinely bilingual program that aims to build language skills in English, as well as legal knowledge in both Japanese and English…"*

To put this in Samuel Huntington words, in China the slogan was "Ti-Yong" (Chinese knowledge for basic principles, Western knowledge for practical skills) and in Japan the slogan was "Wakon Osey" (Japanese spirit for Western techniques). (**) Samuel Huntington – The clash of civilizations and the remaking of world order.- Ed.Paidós SAICF – 1997 – pag.86 – Spanish edition.

Some of the aims of the GV program are to foster expertise in the fields of law and political science, to develop creative and flexible problem solving, proactive leadership roles both nationally and internationally. Again it is too soon to evaluate the results of this program, especially because of the low number of students that are involved each year.

Graduate Schools The establishment of the new law school system in 2004 reduced the number of students wishing to enter the research-oriented post-graduate law programs offered at a Master's or Doctoral level. The reasons for this decline of interest in a more research oriented graduate level legal education may vary, but one logical one to extract is that the new students have a more practical and very "consumer" way of understanding education. If it is useful and provide skills in the short term, they will take it; if it is a long term and therefore uncertain way to obtain a future employment, they will not. This may explain why several law faculties have broadened their recruitment to bring in former lawyers, prosecutors and judges (i.e. those with practical experience) to teach as professors in the new law schools. The national reporter finds also another reason for this change of orientation: *"…Of course, this "opening up" legal academia to those with more* *experience of the realities of legal practice makes a lot of sense given the demands of the law school system. One of the design issues with the new law school system was that* ***the overwhelming majority of the faculty members responsible for preparing students for the new bar examination had not passed the bar examination themselves, nor did they have any experience of legal practice. They were researchers and not practitioners. "Opening up" of faculty recruitment has been a logical response to the law school system...***"

Consequently, the role of graduate schools after the reform in 2004 remains with a big question mark. The Japan example is another of many which reflects what usually happens when reforms and new programs are designed by persons who may have great theoretical ideas that confront and clash with the practical realities that appear in the short or long term.

The intermediate key that may open new doors in BLE is again internationalization. This is the big focus of Universities such as Kyushu that is more and more providing graduate programs taught either entirely, or substantially, in English at both a Master's and Doctoral level: *"The such first program, the LL.M. in International Economic and Business Law (IEBL) was established in 1994. At the time, it was the only Master's course taught entirely in English within Japan and was designed to overcome the main obstacle to studying law in Japan, namely the Japanese language. Kyushu University's IEBL program focuses on international and comparative trade and business law. An LL.D. program allowing students to complete a doctoral dissertation in English was added in 2000..."*

Other universities such as Keio, Kobe, Nagoya and Waseda followed the path opened by Kyushu. The bilingualism of the programs is quite peculiar, because in strict sense one cannot say they are taught both in English and Japanese; in reality Japanese is offered as an option, but in general, legal education is proposed and taken in English. The advantage of the "*relatively*" low cost of graduate school tuition fees in Japan compared to the US or UK, makes it attractive for Asian students to choose a Master's law degree in English geographically situated in the Eastern region.

Another initiative from Kyushu was to host a new program, the **Young Leaders Program (*YLP in Law*)**. The Ministry of Education designated Kyushu to host and develop (...) "this *Master's level graduate program* (that) *targets young legal professionals and government officials from designated emerging economy countries. Initially the geographical focus of the program was North East and South East Asian countries but recently a number of other countries have been added including India, South Africa and Turkey. Students on the YLP are integrated into the IEBL program where they study legal issues with a particular focus on international and comparative trade and business law. Again, these programs are taught entirely in English...*"

Kyushu University's Bilingual Master's (*LL.M.)* degree program in Law (*BiP*) is another attempt and innovation to offer bilingual legal education. It offers overseas graduates of Japanese language undergraduate programs or those with a legal background and a strong background in the Japanese language, the opportunity to take a Master's degree in law in a bilingual environment: *"The program is designed for students who already have a solid foundation in the Japanese language. (...) As such, the program is principally intended for Japanologists or lawyers with strong Japanese interested in (i) Obtaining a deeper understanding of Japanese culture and society through the study of historical or contemporary issues in Japanese law & politics; or (ii) Preparing for a legal career in Japan or connected to Japan by studying Japanese and international business law...*"

As a part of the Program students have to do a Master's thesis under the supervision of two faculty members. It be on any legal topic and must be written in either English or Japanese. They are also expected to complete a 20 page's summary of the thesis in the other language. Finally, students are offered the opportunity to participate in an internship of 2–4 weeks at either a Tokyo-based international law firm, company or government agency. The *BiP* program is still very small, with only 2–3 international students per year enrolling.

The conclusion that arises after this panorama of Japanese education is somehow enigmatic: Is Japan striving for still a traditional and "core subjects" education, towards new and original forms of internationalization, or thirdly, to somehow a middle-road kind of legal education that remains modern and open to the Western world while keeping faithful to its own culture? The three kinds or types of students found in Japan nowadays do not give us yet a conclusive answer. As it usually happens in the Eastern World, much more time is required to see the result of these tendencies...

Bilingual Legal Education in Mexico: Studying the Native Languages and Looking at Global Law

Efrén Chávez-Hernández

1 Introduction. Some Data About Mexico

In this research, we analyze the situation of bilingual legal education in Mexico: a path formed between two branches, on the one hand, to study and understand the law with a multi-cultural approach that includes the vision of Mexican ethnic groups, and on the other, to look at global law, especially the law of the United States of America, the main commercial partner of Mexico. This involves teaching law in the indigenous languages of Mexico on the one hand, and studying law in the English language, on the other.

First, we present some data about Mexico, regarding its population, territory and languages spoken. Subsequently, data of law students in Mexico and schools are shown, with the purpose of analyzing the situation of legal education in Mexico. Then, we describe the *Master in American Law*, an example of bilingual legal education in Mexico, taught at the National University, indicating the characteristics and challenges of it. Finally, we will present some conclusions about how to advance in this bilingual legal education to train better legal professionals in Mexico.[1]

Mexico is a Federal Republic composed of 31 territorial entities called States and Mexico City, seat of federal powers. It has a territorial extension of 1,964,375 km^2.

It has a population of 112,336,538 inhabitants according to the last population census of 2010, (119,530,753 people estimated in 2015). The composition of the population of Mexico includes:

[1] I thank Professor Juan Javier del Granado, coordinator of the "Masters in American Law" of the UNAM, who provided me with information about the course, which has been captured in this writing.

E. Chávez-Hernández (✉)
National Autonomous University of Mexico (UNAM), Mexico City, Mexico
e-mail: efren.chavez@unam.mx

N. Etcheverry Estrázulas (ed.), *Bilingual Study and Research*, Ius Comparatum – Global Studies in Comparative Law 58,
https://doi.org/10.1007/978-3-030-84550-6_11

- mestizo race person 60%,
- indigenous 30%,
- white 9%,
- another 1%

The official languages are Spanish (Castilian) and 68 indigenous languages, called "linguistic groupings", and are the following: Akateko, Amuzgo, Awakateko, Ayapaneco, Cora, Cucapá, Cuicateco, Chatino, Chichimeco Jonaz, Chinanteco, Chocholteco, Chontal de Oaxaca, Chontal de Tabasco, Chuj, Ch'ol, Guarijío, Huasteco, Huave, Huichol, Ixcateco, Ixil, Jakalteko, Kaqchikel, Kickapoo, Kiliwa, Kumiai, Ku'ahl, K'iche ', Lacandón, Mam, Matlatzinca, Maya, May, Mazahua, Mazateco, Mixe, Mixteco, Nahuatl, Utcoco, Otomí, Paipai, Pame, Pápago, Pima, Popoloca, Popoluca de la Sierra, Qato'k, Q'anjob'al, Q'eqchí, Sayulteco, Seri, Tarahumara, Tarasco, Teko, Tepehua, Tepehuano del Norte, Tepehuano del Sur, Textepequeño, Tlahuica, Tlapaneco, Tojolabal, Totonaco, Triqui, Tseltal, Tsotsil, Yaqui, Zapotec and Zoque.[2]

It is estimated that in 2015 there were 7,382,785 people aged 3 years and over who speak an indigenous language. The languages with the highest number of speakers are: Nahuatl, Maya and Tseltal. At the national level, it is estimated that 7 out of every 100 inhabitants of 3 years and older speak an indigenous language.[3] This is 7% of the population.

Regarding the number of people who speak English in Mexico, according to estimates from the National Institute of Statistics and Geography (INEGI), the population over 18 who speak English is approximately 9.4% of the population.[4]

2 The Teaching of Law

2.1 Universities and Law Students

In Mexico there are 1770 Higher Education institutions (universities) that offer a degree in Law. Of these, 146 are public (federal and state universities) and 1624 are private universities.[5]

---

[2]Instituto Nacional de Lenguas Indígenas (INALI) [National Institute of Indigenous Languages], http://www.inali.gob.mx/clin-inali/#agrupaciones.

[3]Instituto Nacional de Estadística y Geografía (INEGI) [National Institute of Statistics and Geography], "Hablantes de lengua indígena en México", http://cuentame.inegi.org.mx/poblacion/lindigena.aspx?tema=P#uno.

[4]Instituto Mexicano para la Competitividad, A.C. [Mexican Institute for Competitiveness] *Inglés es posible; Propuesta de una Agenda Nacional*, undated, p. 17. Available at: http://imco.org.mx/wp-content/uploads/2015/04/2015_Documento_completo_Ingles_es_posible.pdf.

[5]Nava Arroyo, Ana Cecilia and others, "Infografía Las Escuelas de Derecho en México 2016", Centro de Estudios sobre la Enseñanza y el Aprendizaje del Derecho, A.C., [Center for Studies on Teaching and Law Learning], [Online]. http://www.ceead.org.mx/infografia_ies.html.

Table 1 Universities in Mexico that teach Law

Public	Private	Total
146	1624	1770

Source: Center for Studies on the Teaching and Learning of Law (2017)

Table 2 Students in Mexico who study Law

Men	Women	Total
176,232	178,521	354,753

Source: National Association of Universities and Institutions of Higher Education (ANUIES)

Table 3 Students at the UNAM who study Law (2016)

Men	Women	Total
5498	6105	11,603

Source: National Association of Universities and Institutions of Higher Education (ANUIES)

Table 4 Students at the UNAM Law School

Undergraduate	Postgraduate	Total
11,856	1002	12,858

Source: UNAM 2016 statistical agenda

Table 5 Foreign and national students at the UNAM Law School

	Nationals	Foreign
Bachelor's degree (undergraduate)	98.86%	1.14%
Master's (postgraduate)	99.6%	0.4%
Doctorate (postgraduate)	95.7%	4.3%

Source: Own elaboration with data obtained

The number of students of the law degree in 2016 was 354,753, of which 176,232 are males and 178,521 women (Tables 1, 2, 3, 4, and 5).[6]

[6]"Anuario Educación Superior Licenciatura 2015–2016", *Anuarios Estadísticos de Educación Superior*, Asociación Nacional de Universidades e Instituciones de Educación Superior (ANUIES) [National Association of Universities and Institutions of Higher Education], [Online].http://www.anuies.mx/informacion-y-servicios/informacion-estadistica-de-educacion-superior/anuario-estadistico-de-educacion-superior.

In 2003 it was 203,149 students. Fix-Fierro, Héctor Felipe, "¿Muchos abogados, pero poca profesión? Derecho y profesión jurídica en el México contemporáneo", en *Del gobierno de los abogados al imperio de las leyes: estudios sociojurídicos sobre educación y profesión jurídicas en el México contemporáneo* / Héctor Fix-Fierro, editor -- México: UNAM, Instituto de Investigaciones Jurídicas, 2006, p. 5. [Available online: https://biblio.juridicas.unam.mx/bjv/detalle-libro/2261-del-gobierno-de-los-abogados-al-imperio-de-las-leyes-estudios-sociojuridicos-sobre-educacion-y-profesion-juridicas-en-el-mexico-contemporaneo].

The main educational institution in Mexico is the National Autonomous University of Mexico (UNAM), whose enrollment of law students in 2016 was: 11,603 students (5498 males and 6105 females).[7]

In 2017, the Law School of the UNAM (*Facultad de Derecho de la UNAM*) had a population of 11,856 undergraduate students (undergraduate) and 1002 postgraduate students (Masters and PhD).[8]

2.2 Foreign Students and Visiting Professors

In the Faculty of Law (*Facultad de Derecho*) of the UNAM, the most important law school in the country, the number of foreign students is even lower. In 2016, 101 foreign exchange students were received, who studied a semester at the UNAM.[9]

This indicates that the proportion of foreign students is just 1.14%.

In the Postgraduate Studies, the proportion is 99.6% of national students and 0.4% of foreign students in the Master of Law; and of 95.7% of national students and 4.3% of foreign students, in the Doctorate in Law.[10]

There are 40,184 academics throughout the UNAM, and in 2015, 300 foreign visiting professors were received.[11] Which means that approximately 0.74% are foreign teachers.

Regarding the Faculty of Law of the UNAM, the proportion is similar, that is, less than 1% are foreign professors.

---

[7] "Anuario Educación Superior Licenciatura 2015–2016", *Anuarios Estadísticos de Educación Superior*, Asociación Nacional de Universidades e Instituciones de Educación Superior (ANUIES), [Online].http://www.anuies.mx/informacion-y-servicios/informacion-estadistica-de-educacion-superior/anuario-estadistico-de-educacion-superior.

[8] *Agenda estadística UNAM 2016*, [Online]. http://www.planeacion.unam.mx/Agenda/2016/pdf/Agenda2016.pdf, p. 16 y 18.

[9] According to the annual report of the dean of the Faculty of Law of the UNAM, the Faculty received a total of 443 students, of which 23% were foreigners [that is 101 students]; 39% of national origin from other institutions of higher education; and 38% were students from other Faculties of the UNAM itself. *Primer Informe de actividades del Dr. Raúl Contreras Bustamante Director de la Facultad de Derecho UNIVERSIDAD NACIONAL AUTÓNOMA DE MÉXICO*, Miércoles 29 de marzo de 2017 Aula Magna "Jacinto Pallares", [Online] http://www.derecho.unam.mx/img/pdf/informe.pdf, pp. 26–27.

[10] *El Posgrado en la UNAM en cifras: reporte de avances y perspectivas 2015*, México, D.F.: Coordinación de Estudios de Posgrado, 2015, [Online] http://www.posgrado.unam.mx/sites/default/files/2015/10/el_posgrado_en_cifras.pdf, p 89.

[11] Universidad Nacional Autónoma de México. *Portal de estadística universitaria*, [Online] http://www.estadistica.unam.mx/numeralia.

At the UNAM Law School, the main foreign nationalities represented in the students are Colombians, being the largest group, as well as Spaniards, Peruvians, Canadians, Americans, to name a few.[12]

In 2016, there were 1293 visiting professors from abroad at the UNAM; of a total of 40,184 academics,[13] what amounts to a 3.22%.

Regarding the UNAM Law School, there is no precise information about visiting professors, but in the opinion of the dean, their presence is very important and must be encouraged.[14]

Because the number of foreign students and professors is still limited, in the School of Law of the UNAM there is no bilingual legal education program.

However, in the field of Postgraduate Studies in Law, the Institute of Legal Research (*Instituto de Investigaciones Jurídicas*) of the UNAM has a "*Master's Degree in American Law*" which is taught in four semesters, whose content is equivalent to the *Juris Doctor* taught in the United States, but offered in Mexico. This program is aimed at Mexican students who want to be more than bilingual lawyers: "bi-legal" lawyers.[15]

In the case of the Master of American Law, all professors are residents of Mexico, although there is a professor of American origin.

3 Towards a Bilingual Legal Education

3.1 Intercultural Universities

In the area of undergraduate education, the Bilingual Legal Education in English language no attempt was made to initiate perhaps because the number of foreign students, or nationals who are fluent in English or another foreign language, is even lower.

---

[12]There is no accurate information. Although, in 2016 UNAM in general received students from 32 countries (Australia, Germany, Argentina, Brazil, Belgium, Bolivia, Canada, South Korea, Costa Rica, Colombia, Chile, China, Denmark, Ecuador, United States), Spain, France, Finland, Greece, Honduras, Italy, Japan, Norway, the United Kingdom, the Czech Republic, Russia, the Dominican Republic, Puerto Rico, Serbia, Sweden, Switzerland and Peru) but they do not have the data with precision about which they attended to the Faculty of Law. Bulletin UNAM-DGCS-053. University City. 3:00 p.m. January 24, 2017. Available: http://www.dgcs.unam.mx/boletin/bdboletin/2017_053.html.

[13]"LA UNAM EN NÚMEROS 2016–2017", *Portal de Estadística universitaria [University Statistics Portal],* [Online] http://www.estadistica.unam.mx/numeralia.

[14]Contreras Bustamante, Raúl, *Facultad De Derecho U N A M; Proyecto de Trabajo. Período 2016–2020,* [Online] https://www.derecho.unam.mx/director/ContrerasBustamantePlanTrabajo.pdf, p. 31.

[15]The call for entry to the Master was published in January 2017, available at: https://www.juridicas.unam.mx/actividades-academicas/1117-maestria-en-derecho-estadounidense.

However, in populations where there is an indigenous majority, so-called "intercultural universities" have been implemented, which teach classes in Spanish (Castilian), but incorporate some indigenous languages into the substantive functions, becoming bilingual schools.

As indicated, in Mexico there are 68 indigenous languages; so, the 7% of the population of Mexico speak an indigenous language.

According to information from the Ministry of Public Education (federal ministry of education), there are 11 intercultural universities located in 11 states of the Republic, with 14,008 students enrolled in 2015–2016.[16] Among them, the Intercultural University of Chiapas, Intercultural University of the State of Tabasco, Intercultural University of the State of Puebla and the Veracruzana Intercultural University have a degree program in Law with an intercultural approach.[17]

3.2 The Master in American Law

And as previously noted, there is the "Master's Degree in American Law" taught by the Institute of Legal Research of the National Autonomous University of Mexico (*Instituto de Investigaciones Jurídicas de la UNAM*), the Illustrious and National Bar Association of Mexico (*Ilustre y Nacional Colegio de Abogados de México*), and the School of Law of Sinaloa (*Escuela Libre de Derecho de Sinaloa*). The Master's Degree in American Law is a postgraduate program that is an example of bilingual legal education in Mexico.

They constitute a postgraduate course, therefore, different from the undergraduate.

All the teachers are local and they teach the classes in both languages, but in English the own and specific institutions of the American common law are taught. The professors are Mexicans, except for the coordinator of the Master's Degree, who is American resident in Mexico, researcher at the National Autonomous University of Mexico.

This bilingual legal education program began in 2011 as an initiative of the law professors Hector Fix-Fierro, at that time director of the Institute of Legal Research of the National Autonomous University of Mexico (national public university), and Oscar Cruz Barney, at that time president of the Illustrious and National Bar Association of Mexico (national association of Mexican lawyers); with the idea of studying the legal system of the United States of America. The objective of the Master's Program is to train Mexican jurists to advise companies, offices and

[16] "Universidades Interculturales", Secretaría de Educación Pública [Ministry of Public Education] [Online]] http://eib.sep.gob.mx/diversidad/universidades-interculturales/.

[17] For example, at the Intercultural University of Chiapas, the degree course in law has six semester courses of "Native Language". Universidad Intercultural de Chiapas, "Plan de Estudios de la Licenciatura en Derecho Intercultural" [Online] http://www.unich.edu.mx/wp-content/uploads/2017/06/DERECHO_VUELTA.jpg.

organizations in the United States, which carry out activities in Mexico or Latin America.

Similarly, this program allows a comparative law study to understand and improve local legal institutions, based on the experience of the compared country, in this case: United States.

This Master has had many applications for admission to the Program. However, it is clarified to the students that this Master's degree does not accredit them to practice law in the United States, nor to present the Exam before the Bar of that country.

Nor is it aimed at people who want to live in the United States, because for that, they are recommended to take a Juris Doctor in a university in that country.

The areas of law that are taught in a foreign language are: Private Law, Commercial Law, History of Law, Constitutional Law, Administrative Law, Procedural Law, Legal Methodology, Legal Deontology, International Commercial Law are studied.

The curriculum of the Master in American Law is composed by the following subjects:

First semester.

1.1. History of the Anglo-American Legal System.
1.2. United States Contracts Law I.
1.3. United States Torts Law.
1.4. United States Property Law I.

Second semester.

2.1 Methodology and Legal Writing in the Anglo-American Legal System.
2.2 United States Contract Law II.
2.3 United States Corporate Law.
2.4 United States Property Law II.

Third semester.

3.1 American Civil Procedure.
3.2 United States Constitutional Law.
3.3 American Administrative Law.
3.4 Uniform Commercial Code.

Fourth semester.

4.1 United States Evidence Law.
4.2 Professional Responsibility in the Anglo-American Legal System.
4.3 American Criminal Law.
4.4 Federal Immigration Law and NAFTA.

In the teaching and evaluation of American law the professors use the same methods that are used in the United States, that is, the case method for teaching, and the evaluation through written exams, under the system of "blind grading", that is, the teacher at the time of qualifying the exam, you do not know who the exam is, to guarantee impartiality and objectivity in the qualification.

The selection of professors has been carried out among researchers from the Institute of Legal Research of the UNAM.

The textbooks (casebooks) of the subjects have been purchased directly from the publishers of the United States; as well as specific texts have been developed for the course.[18] The same texts are used, as if they were studied in the United States.

All students are Mexican, who speak fluently the English language.

3.3 Advantages of Bilingual Legal Education in Mexico

We find that students are more competitive in the work force as a result of having received bilingual legal education; the students are more competitive, because they can be hired by companies, associations or other foreign institutions that carry out activities in Mexico and Latin America, since the students are experts in Mexican Law (Civil Law) and United States Law (Common Law) in a globalized world.

Otherwise, such training could only be acquired if the student studied law in Mexico and the United States, and then returned to practice law in Mexico. Something complicated for Mexican lawyers.

The bilingual legal education in Mexico has been an improvement, as interest in teaching American law has increased. Now it is proposed to teach the Master in other States of the Mexican Republic.

This Master began with the idea of being only a Diploma, however, due to the interest of students and academic institutions, it became a Master's course.

In addition, the School of Law of Sinaloa (*Escuela Libre de Derecho de Sinaloa*), a private university, was associated as an organizing institution.

Also, there has been a desire to be taught in the border of the country, since this Master's had been taught only in Mexico City, but from August 2018 will also be taught in the city of Tijuana, Baja California.

The Master in American Law is oriented to solve the needs of law firms in Mexico, especially those that deal with foreign and international entities.

I believe that the interest in bilingual legal education will grow in the country due to the fact that more offers of education will arise, either through the creation of schools or through the delivery of the Master's Degree in agreement with other universities.

[18]Example of them are the following: *Responsabilidad civil extracontractual en Estados Unidos,* by Juan Carlos Marín G., & Juan Javier del Granado -- México: Universidad Nacional Autónoma de México, Instituto de Investigaciones Jurídicas: Ilustre y Nacional Colegio de Abogados de México, 2013. x, 743 pages (Series: Derecho de Estados Unidos de América del Norte; 1). http://bibliohistorico.juridicas.unam.mx/libros/libro.htm?l=3229 / *Obligaciones contractuales en Estados Unidos* by Oscar Cruz Barney & Juan Javier del Granado -- México, D.F.: UNAM, Instituto de Investigaciones Jurídicas: Ilustre y Nacional Colegio de Abogados de México, 2014, (Derecho de Estados Unidos de América del Norte; 2), https://biblio.juridicas.unam.mx/bjv/detalle-libro/3675-obligaciones-contractuales-en-estados-unidos.

The law firms will have more interest in hiring "bi-legal" lawyers, that is, they know the law and legal culture of Mexico and the United States.

I think that in the Law School of the UNAM will grow the number of subjects in which they are taught in English, or another language. That is, bilingual legal education will grow.

Now, the main language as an option for a bilingual legal education is English, because it is the language of the United States, and the most common on the world. Intercultural universities use the most common indigenous languages of the region.

Probably, later bilingual legal education can be carried out in other languages, such as French, if we want to study the law of France and Quebec, Canada; or, the German language, if we wanted to study the German legal system.

The bilingual legal education is conceived in Mexico as an opportunity to compete better in the international order, specifically, in the international commercial sphere; and on the other hand, in the opportunity to promote the development of native indigenous peoples, by promoting the teaching of law in indigenous languages.

4 Conclusions

In Mexico bilingual legal education is still in beginning, it has yet to be developed. There are two initial cases: the intercultural universities where the law is studied with references to indigenous languages; and the Master in American Law, where the United States legal system is studied in English and Spanish. Both cases have had an important degree of acceptance.

To increase the number of bilingual legal education courses, I consider it necessary to promote academic exchange, both for students and foreign professors.

Bilingual legal education contributes significantly to train more qualified lawyers to face the challenges of globalization.

References

Asociación Nacional de Universidades e Instituciones de Educación Superior (ANUIES). "Anuario Educación Superior Licenciatura 2015–2016", *Anuarios Estadísticos de Educación Superior*, [National Association of Universities and Institutions of Higher Education], [Online].http://www.anuies.mx/informacion-y-servicios/informacion-estadistica-de-educacion-superior/anuario-estadistico-de-educacion-superior

Contreras Bustamante R. *Facultad De Derecho U N A M; Proyecto de Trabajo. Período 2016–2020*, [Online] https://www.derecho.unam.mx/director/ContrerasBustamantePlanTrabajo.pdf, p. 31

Cruz Barney O (2014) *Obligaciones contractuales en Estados Unidos* by Oscar Cruz Barney & Juan Javier del Granado -- México, D.F.: UNAM, Instituto de Investigaciones Jurídicas: Ilustre y Nacional Colegio de Abogados de México, (Derecho de Estados Unidos de América del

Norte; 2), https://biblio.juridicas.unam.mx/bjv/detalle-libro/3675-obligaciones-contractuales-en-estados-unidos

Fix-Fierro HF (2006) "¿Muchos abogados, pero poca profesión? Derecho y profesión jurídica en el México contemporáneo", en *Del gobierno de los abogados al imperio de las leyes: estudios sociojurídicos sobre educación y profesión jurídicas en el México contemporáneo*/Héctor Fix-Fierro, editor -- México: UNAM, Instituto de Investigaciones Jurídicas, 2006, p. 5. [Available online: https://biblio.juridicas.unam.mx/bjv/detalle-libro/2261-del-gobierno-de-los-abogados-al-imperio-de-las-leyes-estudios-sociojuridicos-sobre-educacion-y-profesion-juridicas-en-el-mexico-contemporaneo]

Instituto Mexicano para la Competitividad, A.C. [Mexican Institute for Competitiveness] *Inglés es posible; Propuesta de una Agenda Nacional*, undated, p. 17. Available at: http://imco.org.mx/wp-content/uploads/2015/04/2015_Documento_completo_Ingles_es_posible.pdf

Instituto Nacional de Estadística y Geografía (INEGI). [National Institute of Statistics and Geography], "Hablantes de lengua indígena en México", http://cuentame.inegi.org.mx/poblacion/lindigena.aspx?tema=P#uno

Instituto Nacional de Lenguas Indígenas (INALI). [National Institute of Indigenous Languages], http://www.inali.gob.mx/clin-inali/#agrupaciones

Marín GJC (2013) *Responsabilidad civil extracontractual en Estados Unidos,* by Juan Carlos Marín G., & Juan Javier del Granado -- México: Universidad Nacional Autónoma de México, Instituto de Investigaciones Jurídicas: Ilustre y Nacional Colegio de Abogados de México, 2013. x, 743 pages (Series: Derecho de Estados Unidos de América del Norte; 1). http://bibliohistorico.juridicas.unam.mx/libros/libro.htm?l=3229 /

Nava Arroyo, Ana Cecilia and others, "Infografía Las Escuelas de Derecho en México 2016", Centro de Estudios sobre la Enseñanza y el Aprendizaje del Derecho, A.C., [Center for Studies on Teaching and Law Learning], [Online]. http://www.ceead.org.mx/infografia_ies.html

SEP. "Universidades Interculturales", Secretaría de Educación Pública (SEP) [Ministry of Public Education] [Online]] http://eib.sep.gob.mx/diversidad/universidades-interculturales/

UNAM. "LA UNAM EN NÚMEROS 2016–2017", *Portal de Estadística universitaria [University Statistics Portal],* [Online] http://www.estadistica.unam.mx/numeralia

UNAM. Agenda estadística UNAM 2016, [Online]. Mexico. Universidad Nacional Autónoma de México. http://www.planeacion.unam.mx/Agenda/2016/pdf/Agenda2016.pdf p. 16 y 18

UNAM. Bulletin UNAM-DGCS-053. University City. 3:00 p.m. January 24, 2017. Available: http://www.dgcs.unam.mx/boletin/bdboletin/2017_053.html

UNAM. *El Posgrado en la UNAM en cifras: reporte de avances y perspectivas 2015,* México, D.F.: Coordinación de Estudios de Posgrado, 2015, [Online] http://www.posgrado.unam.mx/sites/default/files/2015/10/el_posgrado_en_cifras.pdf, p 89

UNAM. Portal de estadística universitaria, [Online] Universidad Nacional Autónoma de México. http://www.estadistica.unam.mx/numeralia

UNAM. *Primer Informe de actividades del Dr. Raúl Contreras Bustamante Director de la Facultad de Derecho UNIVERSIDAD NACIONAL AUTÓNOMA DE MÉXICO,* Miércoles 29 de marzo de 2017 Aula Magna "Jacinto Pallares", [Online] http://www.derecho.unam.mx/img/pdf/informe.pdf, pp. 26–27

Universidad Intercultural de Chiapas, "Plan de Estudios de la Licenciatura en Derecho Intercultural" [Online] http://www.unich.edu.mx/wp-content/uploads/2017/06/DERECHO_VUELTA.jpg

Efrén Chávez-Hernández Doctor in Law (PhD.) by the National Autonomous University of Mexico (UNAM).

Specialist in Constitutional Law and Political Science by the Center for Political and Constitutional Studies in Madrid, Spain; Diploma in Comparative Law from the International Faculty of Comparative Law in Strasbourg, France. Diploma in Continental Law, at the University of Paris II, Pantheon-Asas, Paris France.

Full-time academic at the Institute of Legal Research since 2000 and Professor at the Law Faculty of the UNAM since 2002. Professor of several courses in master's degrees and graduates in universities in the states of the Mexican Republic. National Researcher Level 1 of the National System of Investigators of the National Council of Science and Technology of Mexico.

Speaker in international and national congresses, seminars, diplomas and interviews, among which are: VIII World Congress of the International Association of Constitutional Law (Mexico, 2010); International Seminar on Probity and Transparency in the National Congress and in the Political Parties System (Santiago, Chile, January 2012); Symposium "Religion and Human Rights" (Utah, United States 2013); International Congress of Human Rights and International Humanitarian Law (Bogotá, Colombia, 2014); World Library and Information Congress: 83rd IFLA General Conference and Assembly (Wrocław, Poland, 2017).

proposent aussi des cours en langues étrangères cyclées sur les différents systèmes de droit. Elles peuvent également proposer des programmes de master en langues étrangères, généralement dans le domaine du droit international et/ou européen, gérés exclusivement par la faculté roumaine ou en partenariat avec des universités étrangères.

Les universites situées dans des zones géographiques ayant une forte dimension multiculturelle et multiethnique (e.g. Université Babes-Bolyai de Cluj-Napoca) proposent également des cours et des programmes de master en langue hongroise, langue maternelle de la principale minorité ethnique de Roumanie.

2.5 Le nombre des professeurs invités par année

Le nombre de professeurs invités connait certaines fluctuations, selon les années. Il y a une présence constante des professeurs français provenant des universités partenaires du consortium du Collège juridique franco-roumain (environ 30/an), auxquels s'ajoutent environ 5 professeurs/an qui visitent notre faculté dans d'autres cadres de coopération (Erasmus, accords bilatéraux, *fellowship* etc). Dans ce total d'environ 35 professeurs invités ne sont pas inclus les professeurs étrangers invités pour des interventions ponctuelles dans le cadre des conférences internationales organisées par notre faculté, dont le nombre est difficile à estimer.

3 L`organisation des programmes d`enseignement juridique en langues étrangères

3.1 L'importance de l'éducation juridique bilingue

L'importance de l'éducation juridique bilingue est reconnue par la constitution, les conditions concrètes de mise en œuvre étant détaillées dans la législation subséquente, notamment la loi de l'éducation nationale. En même temps, il faut rappeler que la mise en œuvre des cours en langues étrangères dépend des conditions matérielles et financières des universités, qui disposent d'une grande autonomie décisionnelle en ce qui concerne l'utilisation de leurs propres ressources.

Dans la Faculté de Droit de l'Université de Bucarest :

Pour les premières 4 années d'études - le parcours facultatif franco-roumain[7], suivi chaque année par environ 200 étudiants, comprend 4-5 cours en français par année universitaire, qui s'ajoutent aux disciplines de droit roumain, environ 10-12

mentionner la Faculté de Droit de l'Université Roumaine-Américaine, qui, *a priori*, propose des études juridiques bilingues.

[7] http://www.collegejuridique.ro/upload/2017_2018Organisation%20des%20enseignements.pdf.

par année universitaire (un total d'environ 15-17 cours en roumain et français par année universitaire).

Au niveau des programmes de Master, actuellement 2 programmes sur 12 sont en langue étrangères (Français, respectivement en Anglais), étant suivis par environ 80 étudiants.

Au niveau du doctorat, 10 thèses sur 179 sont rédigées en langues étrangères (8 en Français, 2 en Anglais), dont 6 sont des cotutelles internationales. Il faut également préciser que les doctorants peuvent, à tout moment pendent les études doctorales, décider de rédiger et soutenir leur thèse dans une langue de circulation internationale.

3.2 La situation des professeurs employés

Les cours en langues étrangères peuvent être enseignés tant par des professeurs étrangers que par des professeurs roumains.

Au niveau du Masters 2 d'Arbitrage international, géré exclusivement par notre faculté, les intervenants sont principalement des professeurs et des professionnels roumains qui enseignent en Anglais. Au niveau du Masters 2 de Droit européen, géré par le Collège juridique, les cours magistraux sont partagés entre les intervenants roumains et français (5 professeurs français et 4 professeurs roumains).

Au niveau du Collège juridique franco-roumain d'études européennes (la seule ligne d'études bilingue de notre faculté), les professeurs français qui enseignent les cours magistraux sont globalement plus nombreux que les professeurs roumains (environ 5 professeurs roumains et environ 30 français, pour tous les niveaux d'études). Par contre, les travaux dirigés (TDs) sont dispensés principalement par les enseignants et doctorants/ post-doctorants roumains (environ 10 chargés de TDs roumains et 1-2 chargés de TDs français).

Les professeurs français assurent chaque année des cours modulaires d'environ 5 jours (20-25 heures de cours pour chaque discipline).

Les chargées de TDs étrangers ont des contrats doctoraux ou postdoctoraux avec une des Universités partenaires et viennent enseigner à Bucarest pendant un semestre (environ 80 heures) ou une année universitaire (environ 160 heures), avec la possibilité de prolonger le contrat. Les chargées de TDs roumains sont des anciens étudiants du Collège qui font des études doctorales ou postdoctorales en français et/ou qui ont déjà intégré des professions juridique prestigieuses.

Les autres professeurs invités viennent à Bucarest pour donner des cours ou des conférences plus ciblées, ayant généralement une durée de une à deux semaines (entre 8h et 15h).

Dans les années précédentes, il y a eu également des professeurs participants aux programmes de type *fellowship*. Ces enseignants des universités des Etats-Unis, Italie, Suisse etc. qui sont restés à Bucarest pour un semestre ou une année universitaire complète et qui ont donnée des cours/conférences hebdomadaires, en langues étrangères, dans leurs domaines de compétence.

3.3 *Le besoin d`organiser des cours bilingues*

Au fil du temps, le besoin d'améliorer la qualité de l'enseignement juridique universitaire a déterminé les universités roumaines à réviser leurs plaquettes des enseignements, afin d'assurer une plus grande ouverture internationale. Cette démarche d'internationalisation des curricula avait pour but, d'un côté, de permettre aux étudiants roumains un accès plus aisé aux études approfondis à l'étranger et au marché international du travail et, d'un autre, d'attirer des étudiants étrangers vers notre faculté.

L'organisation d'un cursus complètement bilingue aurait mobilisé des ressources techniques et humaines extrêmement importantes que la finalité de la démarche ne justifiait pas. Ainsi, notre faculté a choisi de privilégier certains programmes de coopération universitaire internationale et de mettre en œuvre certains programmes bilingues adaptés aux besoins stratégiques.

3.3.1 La nécessite d'organiser un programme universitaire complémentaire en langue française est issue, dans le cas du *Collège Juridique Franco-roumain d'études européens,* des influences culturelles que le droit français a exercé sur le droit roumain a partir du XIXème siècle, du fait que les deux pays aient un patrimoine juridique commun hérité du droit romain, mais aussi du contexte historique dans lequel ce Collège est apparu.

Créé dans les années 1990, quelques années après la chute du régime communiste de Roumanie, ce Collège spécialisé aux études européens répondait aussi, à l'époque, à une nécessite d'ouverture de la Roumanie vers l'Europe occidentale. La formation des juristes aptes à maîtriser les instruments juridiques internationaux et européens n'était possible qu'avec le soutien des enseignants expérimentés dans ce domaine. La Roumanie étant également un pays francophone, l'éducation juridique en Français était la solution la plus logique qui contribuait, parmi autres, au maintien et à la consolidation de la francophonie.

3.3.2 Le besoin d'organiser des cours de droit en langues étrangères est devenu de plus en plus évident avec la multiplication des mobilités internationales, surtout dans le cadre du programme Erasmus.

Vu que notre faculté ne proposait qu'un nombre très limité de cours en langues étrangères (excepté les cours en Français au sein du Collège juridique franco-roumain), nous avons essayé d'offrir du tutorat individuel pour les étudiants étrangers en mobilité (Erasmus ou autre). L'activité de tutorat visait une meilleure ouverture vers l'international et était censé se dérouler en Anglais, pour toute la plaquette des enseignements de notre faculté. Ce projet a durée environ 5 ans, mais depuis 2016 nous avons complètement renoncé à cette pratique pour plusieurs raisons dont les trois principales sont les suivantes: manque de matériel pédagogique en langue étrangère pour les disciplines de droit roumain, activité extrêmement chronophage, difficultés bureaucratique dans la rémunération des enseignants impliqués.

3.4 Les difficultés de coté des étudiants/de la faculté/des autorités

Les autorités sont en principe favorables à l'ouverture internationale via les programmes d'études bi ou multilingues.

Les principales difficultés dans la mise en œuvre de tels programmes concernent l'enseignement en langue étrangère des disciplines de droit roumain; il s'agit notamment de l'identification des professeurs roumains bilingues et de l'élaboration des matériaux pédagogique en langue étrangère. Néanmoins, ayant une applicabilité territoriale limitée, l'enseignement des disciplines de droit roumain en langue étrangère n'est pas une priorité (les étudiants étrangers qui veulent étudier le droit roumain dans une langue étrangère sont peu nombreux). Par contre, l'enseignement des disciplines de droit international/européen se fait de plus en plus dans des langues de large circulation.

Les étudiants roumains qui souhaitent des carrières de juriste international sont très favorables à la mise en œuvre de programmes d'études bilingues ou multilingues. Ceux-ci restent néanmoins minoritaires (environ 10-15%) et souhaites souvent approfondir leurs études et/ou travailler dans des pays où siègent des organisations et institutions internationales/européennes.

3.5 Les domaines du droit enseignant en langues étrangères

Plusieurs disciplines du droit sont enseignées en français ou en anglaise dans tous les niveaux d`études. La situation des cours en langues étrangères est suivante :

Les cours en Français

- Premières 4 années universitaires (Licența en système roumain, Licence + Master 1 en système français): Introduction au droit, Méthodologie et terminologie juridique française, Droit constitutionnel comparé, Introduction au Droit européen, Droit administratif comparé, Droit institutionnel de l'Union européenne, Théorie générale des obligations et de la responsabilité, Droit des affaires, Ordre juridique et contentieux de l'Union européenne, Droit européen des droits de l'homme, Droit du travail, Droit des sociétés, Droit européen des affaires I et II (Les libertés de circulation et la concurrence), Droit international économique, Droit social international et européen, Système juridique et contentieux de l'UE.
- Cinquième année universitaire (Master en système roumain, Master 2 en système français): Droit de la concurrence approfondi, Droit des organisations internationales économiques, Contentieux européen des droits de l'homme, Contentieux international, Droit des sociétés approfondi, Droit international et européen de la distribution, Droit financier international et européen, Arbitrage et investissements internationaux, Droit économique international et européen

approfondi, Droits des affaires et droits de l'homme, Droit des contrats internationaux et européens approfondi, Droit international et européen de la propriété intellectuelle et industrielle, Droit international et européen de la consommation.

- Doctorat: L'institut juridique francophone doctoral et post-doctoral peut, avec l'École doctorale de la Faculté de Droit de l'Université de Bucarest, organiser des activités d'enseignement en langue française, destinées aux doctorants.

Les cours en Anglais

- Premières 4 années universitaires*:* La faculté peut organiser des cours en langues étrangères, a caractère non-permanent, en fonction de la disponibilité des professeurs invitées (e.g. Introduction au droit américain, espagnol, autrichien ou des cours plus spécialisés, tels Le droit américain des contrats, Le droit responsabilité pénale en droit suisse, etc).
- Master
- a. Arbitrage international : International, European and national legal order; European Union law and arbitration; Comparative arbitration law; Romanian law on arbitration; Arbitration in constructions; International commercial contracts; Conflict of law in the matters of contracts; Arbitration before the Court of International Commercial Arbitration attached to the Chamber of Commerce and Industry of Romania; Dispute resolution between states and foreign investors; Intellectual property law arbitration; Comparative arbitration law; Sports law arbitration.
- b. Master Diplomatie culturelle (projet - date estimée pour ouverture 2018/2019): Fundamental Elements of Public International Law; Diplomatic law and practical aspects of cultural diplomacy; The protection of cultural identity of national minorities at international level; EU Law - from a global perspective; International Protection of Human Rights - the European model.

4 La valeur des langues étrangères en activité professionnelle

Maitrisant une langue étrangère de circulation internationale, les étudiants qui font des études bilingues ou dans une langue étrangère peuvent, pendant leur cursus universitaire, participer aux compétitions internationales, ainsi qu'aux programmes de mobilités et stages internationales. A la fin des études, la plupart poursuivent leurs études à l'étranger ou sont recrutés dans des institutions, entreprises et cabinets prestigieux. La maitrise du vocabulaire juridique et la bonne compréhension des situations juridiques avec des éléments d'extranéité sont un avantage incontestable dans le secteur public, ainsi que dans le secteur privé.

Concernant les étudiants qui ont suivi le cursus bilingue au Collège juridique franco-roumain, on peut observer qu'ils bénéficient de conditions particulièrement favorables lorsqu'ils souhaitent poursuivre leurs études en France et que les débouchés à la sortie des études sont particulièrement vastes.

– L'entrée vers les études en France

Ils peuvent ainsi partir en tant qu'étudiants ERASMUS pour un ou deux semestres pendant toute la durée de leurs études, sans avoir des difficultés linguistiques pendant la mobilité.

Les étudiants peuvent également, dès l'obtention de la Licence en Droit, poursuivre leurs études en France et s'inscrire en Master I. Beaucoup d'étudiants attendent cependant la fin de la quatrième année et partent effectuer leur Master II en France. Cette démarche est grandement facilitée pour les étudiants inscrits au Collège: justifiant d'une inscription dans une université française (Paris I Panthéon Sorbonne) et du statut d'étudiant au Collège juridique, leur dossier ne rencontre aucun problème d'équivalence, ce qui peut parfois être la cause du refus d'inscription des étudiants étrangers. La procédure pour postuler est également plus simple pour les titulaires d'un diplôme français de Master I. Enfin, les établissements membres du consortium s'engagent à faciliter l'accès des étudiants du Collège à leur formation de Master et, après, au Doctorat.

– La réussite professionnelle

Si un peu plus de la moitié des diplômés exercent aujourd'hui la profession d'avocat (généralement dans le cadre de grands cabinets roumains ou internationaux), de magistrat, ou de juriste d'entreprise, un quart d'entre eux ont intégré les plus hautes fonctions de l'administration publique roumaine (en particulier dans la diplomatie), internationale ou européenne. D'autres encore sont devenus enseignants-chercheurs d'universités de renom, en Roumanie, en France et ailleurs.En générale, le Collège juridique franco-roumain est une excellente préparation pour intégrer :

– les professions juridiques du secteur privé: avocat - notamment dans les plus grands cabinets d'affaires de la ville - ou conseillers juridiques au sein d'une grande entreprise;
– la fonction publique nationale roumaine, notamment au sein du Ministère des Affaires Etrangères ou de la Justice;
– la fonction publique européenne et internationale, au sein des institutions européennes (comme la Commission Européenne) ou internationales (ONU, organisations internationales économiques de type FMI, Banque Mondiale).

5 Les méthodes d` évaluation les étudiants

Dans le cadre du cursus bilingue franco-roumain, le nombre relativement restreint d'étudiants qui y participent nous permet de faire une véritable évaluation selon des méthodes participatives. Le contrôle continu est beaucoup plus important que dans le cadre du cursus classique, ayant un poids de 50 pourcent de la moyenne finale. Quoique l'examen final se fasse principalement à l'écrit, le contrôle continu est souvent axé sur la participation orale des étudiants aux débats proposés par le chargé de TD et sur les exposés oraux.

6 Les sources de documentation les cours bilingues

La documentation pour les cours de droit en langue étrangère se fait à l'aide de la bibliographie spécifique, obtenue par acquisition directe ou par prêt à la bibliothèque, mais également à l'aide des ressources électroniques. Dans notre faculté il y a également une bibliothèque juridique francophone au sein du Collège juridique.

Le fonctionnement du Collège juridique est soutenu principalement par les autorités françaises. Depuis sa création, le Collège est néanmoins passé par plusieurs étapes de réorganisation, suite auxquelles le soutient financier de la part des autorités publiques s'est diminuée et les universités membres du consortium ont été appelées à mobiliser plus de ressources propres. La Faculté de droit de Bucarest, par exemple, participe avec les locaux, une partie du personnel administratif et enseignant, la prise en charge partielle de l'accueil des enseignants étrangers. Les Universités françaises participent surtout à la prise en charge des missions pédagogiques de leurs enseignants qui se déplacent à Bucarest. Le Collège dispose aussi de certaines ressources propres, provenant des frais d'inscription (environ 200 euros par étudiant).

Il n'y a pas de matériaux pédagogiques spéciaux, chaque enseignant ayant la liberté de choix entre les ressources bibliographiques disponibles. Pour ce qui est de l'enseignement des disciplines de droit roumain, chaque professeur a du faire l'effort d'obtenir des traductions de la législation pertinente, ainsi que de concevoir et de structurer les cours d'une manière accessible tant pour les étudiants roumains que pour les étudiants internationaux.

7 Les défis de l`enseignement en langues étrangères

7.1 Le niveau différent du langue

La plaquette des enseignements de notre faculté inclut des cours obligatoires de langues étrangères. Pour suivre ces cours, les étudiants sont distribués dans des groupes distincts, en fonction de leur niveau initial. Dans le cadre du Collège juridique franco-roumain, les étudiants passent un examen d'entré afin de prouver une connaissance suffisante de la langue française et, après l'admission, ils suivent aussi des cours supplémentaires de langue française (enseignés par des spécialistes de l'Institut français de Bucarest).

7.2 Les changement dans les derniers 5 ans

Au niveau de notre université il y a une tendance claire d'encouragement de la mise en œuvre de programmes d'études en langues de circulation internationale. Pour notre faculté, on constate que les programmes démarrés antérieurement continuent à avoir du succès et que deux autres nouveaux programmes internationaux de Master sont envisagés dans le futur proche.

Les arguments de soutenir ce changement sont:

- Depuis 2007, la qualité d'Etat membre de l'Union Européenne de la Roumanie a déterminé un plus grand intérêt pour les diplômes universitaires roumains;
- Notre Faculté fait des efforts permanents pour adapter la plaquette des enseignements aux exigences d'un marché du travail internationalisé;
- Par conséquent, le prestige de notre faculté a augmenté, ainsi que son attractivité pour des partenaires institutionnels et pour les étudiants étrangers;
- Les étudiants roumains manifestent un grand intérêt pour l'étude du droit en langues étrangères, afin de mieux connaitre les systèmes juridiques d'autres pays et d'approfondir l'étude du droit international/européen.

7.3 Cohésion entre la théorie et la pratique

Certains cours en langues étrangères de notre faculté (surtout au niveau de master) sont organisés avec le soutien et la participation des professionnels (avocats, mais également juges ou fonctionnaires publics). De cette manière, on essaye d'obtenir une plus grande cohésion entre la théorie et la pratique.

7.4 Les perspectives

Dans notre pays, il y a une tendance claire à accorder de plus en plus d'importance au rayonnement international des universités, les partenariat et mobilités internationales étant de plus en plus nombreuses. Il est vrai que les facultés de droit, vu le spécifique des études juridiques, sont moins susceptibles d'attirer des étudiants étrangers, à la différence d'autres facultés ayant un profile plus technique. Les principaux bénéficiaires des programmes en langues étrangères restent donc les étudiants roumains. En même temps, les autorités, les étudiants ainsi que les employeurs sont d'accord qu'un bon juriste doit maitriser au moins une langue de circulation et d'être capable à gérer des situations ayant des éléments d'extranéité.

8 L`option pour la langue

Les principales langues étrangères utilisées dans les études juridiques (dans toutes les facultés de droit qui proposent des cours en langues étrangères) sont l'Anglais et le Français.

L'option pour l'Anglais se justifie tout simplement par le fait que celui-ci est a présent la principale langue de circulation internationale. L'option pour le Français s'explique par le fait que la Roumanie fait partie de la francophonie (même si jeunes générations étudient de moins en moins la langue Française) et que les deux Etats ont une tradition juridique commune.

Les autres langues qui peuvent être utilisés sont : L'Espagnol, l'Allemand et l'Italien.

L'éducation juridique dans une langue étrangère de circulation n'a jamais été considérée une menace à l'adresse de l'identité nationale. Au contraire, les autorités, les étudiants et le secteur privé comprennent l'importance de l'ouverture internationale dans le contexte de la globalisation, de l'intégration européenne, du fluxe migratoire de plus en plus important, etc.

Legal Monolingualism in a Multilingual State: Whither Bilingual Legal Education in Singapore?

Alan K. Koh

1 Introduction

The short, simple, and surprising answer to the question "does Singapore offer bilingual legal education?" is this: "for practical intents and purposes, no". How can a highly-developed and wealthy jurisdiction where four languages are constitutionally recognised as 'official languages'[1] and whose population has always been ethnically, linguistically, and culturally diverse *not* have legal bilingualism—or indeed, multilingualism? The legal monolingualism that has long been—and continues to be—a feature of law in Singapore is startling in contrast with jurisdictions in Europe, where multilingual legal education seems to have thrived together with (or in spite of?) multiethnicity and multilingualism (c.f. Chapter "Language in Law and in German Universities' Legal Education" by Grundmann). Indeed, when it comes to the field of law, Singapore linguistically resembles the Anglophone former

I am grateful to Samantha Tang for our discussions and her comments on earlier drafts, and to my late father Jackson Koh for sharing his experiences as a former member of the Singapore teaching service. I also thank the Centre for Asian Legal Studies, Faculty of Law, National University of Singapore for financial support towards my participation at the International Academy of Comparative Law's XXth General Congress held in Fukuoka in 2018.

[1]Constitution of the Republic of Singapore (Constitution), art 153A(1): "Malay, Mandarin, Tamil and English shall be the 4 official languages in Singapore." Note that the 'national language' is, however, Malay: Constitution, art 153A(2): "The national language shall be the Malay language and shall be in the Roman script . . ." The Constitution (art. 53) further provides that "[u]ntil the Legislature otherwise provides, all debates and discussions in Parliament shall be conducted in Malay, English, Mandarin or Tamil."

A. K. Koh (✉)
Division of Business Law, Nanyang Business School, Nanyang Technological University, Singapore, Singapore
e-mail: alan.koh@ntu.edu.sg

N. Etcheverry Estrázulas (ed.), *Bilingual Study and Research*, Ius Comparatum – Global Studies in Comparative Law 58,
https://doi.org/10.1007/978-3-030-84550-6_13

Dominions (and England itself) more than other ex-British colonies with comparably diverse ethnic, linguistic, and cultural compositions.

The questions are thus: why did Singapore never develop bilingual legal education, and what does this mean for Singapore legal education going forward? The goal of this Chapter is neither to idly speculate, nor to present mountains of hard evidence to support an elegant theory. Written from the perspective of an insider, this Chapter offers a set of hypotheses that are not inconsistent with the facts and the limited extant evidence. The overarching hypothesis may be simply stated: bilingual legal education is difficult, if not impossible, to achieve due to the combined effects of state language policy and economic realities.

The rest of Chapter is as follows. Section 2 offers a brief primer to the past and present of multilingualism in Singapore, with special attention given to the role of state language policy in education post-independence. Section 3 describes the treatment of languages other than English in the judicial process. Section 4 provides a general overview of the legal education landscape in Singapore, with particular focus on one law school, the National University of Singapore Faculty of Law ("NUS Law"). Section 5 introduces the limited opportunities available to students at or through NUS Law to receive legal education in a language other than English. The prospects for bilingual legal education in Singapore are discussed in Sect. 6, and Sect. 7 is a brief conclusion.

As much of the information relevant to this subject is contained in ephemera that are not necessarily archived or kept publicly accessible, much of this Chapter is based on the (possibly flawed) personal recollections of the reporter; caveats are made expressly where an assertion is based on memory, and apologies are offered for any inadvertent errors. Every reasonable effort has been made to state the facts as known to the reporter as of 20 May 2018, although some sources are updated through 30 May 2019.

2 Multilingualism in Singapore

2.1 *History*

A trading port for centuries, Singapore has been ethnically and linguistically diverse since long before its 'founding' as a trading post of the British East India Company (Chew 2013; Bolton and Ng 2014). Shortly before independence, English and Mandarin Chinese were spoken respectively by only 1.8 and 0.1% of the population; the most widely spoken languages were a southern Chinese dialect/language (Hokkien) (understood by 80% of the Chinese community) and Malay (spoken by just under half of the total population). Even within what we would now perceive as more or less a single Chinese ethnic community—that have formed a plurality of the local population since 1891 and a majority since at least 1931—there was considerable linguistic diversity; at independence the plurality first language of the Chinese ethnic community was Hokkien (39%). The Indian community was also linguistically fragmented, albeit less so, with speakers of predominantly Tamil making up 59% of that community. The Malay community was by far the most homogenous with 85% speaking Malay (Bolton and Ng 2014, p. 308). Even well after independence, it is estimated that the average adult Singaporean were conversant in six to eight languages or dialects, but seldom English (Bolton and Ng 2014, p. 309).

For most of its history, different languages served different functions in Singapore. Whereas the local population used a form of Malay or Hokkien for cross-community communication until well after independence, English was the language of administration continuously through British colonial rule and later self- and independent government (Bolton and Ng 2014, p. 309). The differentiated roles of English and other languages—apart from a brief period during which Malay proficiency was a mandatory requirement for would-be public servants[2]—would also be reflected in the official language policies of modern Singapore.

2.2 *State Language Policy*

Language policy has been a key government concern since the attainment of limited and then full self-government in the 1950s, and especially since gaining full independence upon separation from the Federation of Malaysia in 1965. The extent to which language was a politically sensitive issue in Singapore, as it was with other states and nations in the region, was fully appreciated by the (self-governing) state government (Lee 1960). Right from independence, the state took the official position, subsequently constitutionally entrenched, that the four official languages—Mandarin Chinese, English, Malay, and Tamil—would have official and co-equal status (Constitution, art 153A(1)). The national language is Malay (Constitution, art. 153A(2)); in practical terms today, it is the language of the national anthem and for ceremonial purposes.

Singapore citizens are classified for official purposes into four racial categories: 'Chinese', 'Malay', 'Indian', and 'Others' (Au-Yong 2016). A person classified into a particular racial category is required to be taught the language corresponding to that racial category as 'mother tongue'.[3] The government's goal was to encourage

---

[2]The reporter's father was a graduate of Mandarin Chinese-medium high school and served as a public school teacher (and therefore a public servant) from early 1965 (shortly before Singapore gained full independence by separating from Malaysia) to 1971. He recounted that his teachers' training was, with the exception of a single course in Mandarin Chinese, conducted entirely in English. He also recounted that in order to be 'confirmed' (earn tenure), it was necessary to pass a Malay language examination—a requirement that would eventually be abolished some years later.

[3]i.e. Mandarin Chinese for 'Chinese', Malay for 'Malay', Tamil, Hindi, or another Indian language for 'Indian'. For 'Others' the situation is more complicated, but generally speaking the language spoken at home (if one of the recognised Indian languages other than Tamil), an official language other than English, or a another foreign language (French, German, or Japanese) may be acceptable.

students to be bilingual in English and a mother tongue (National Library Board 2016). It is important to note that despite ethnic Chinese making up a supermajority of the post-independence population, the government did not at any time elevate a Chinese language or dialect above Malay or Tamil as a matter of official policy. As Singapore's long-serving Prime Minister Lee Kuan Yew shared in a memoir, making Chinese Singapore's (sole) official language would not have been palatable to the non-Chinese population; English had to be chosen as the 'working language' for 'political and economic reasons', but each member of an ethnic community would also be instructed in its own 'mother tongue' for 'self-confidence and self-respect' (Lee 2012, pp. 59–60). The 'mother tongues' were not necessarily the specific language variety spoken at home by a citizen; rather, Mandarin Chinese was assigned to the Chinese community, Malay to the Malay community, and Tamil to the Indian community as these were considered 'most relevant and applicable' (Bolton and Ng 2014, p. 310). Nevertheless, Mandarin Chinese became a matter of special interest to Prime Minister Lee; he perceived the use of dialects by members of the Chinese community as an 'obstacle to learning Mandarin and English in school' and a threat that would 'displace Mandarin and strengthen the position of English' (Lee 2012, p. 150).[4]

In its early form, government language policy recognised all four official languages as media of instruction in schools, but all vernacular medium schools teaching in Mandarin, Malay, and Tamil were phased out by 1987 due to declining enrolment (Bolton and Ng 2014, p. 309). English thus gained ascendance as the medium of instruction in primary and secondary education (Tan 2014, p. 338), with the vernacular languages reduced to 'second languages' over the course of the twentieth century.[5] Although students are assigned to study 'mother tongues' generally by ethnicity rather than the language that is actually spoken at home (especially if it is not one of the four official languages), individual students may request to be allowed to study as mother tongue an official language (that is not English) that does not match their ethnicity (Silver and Bokhorst-Heng 2016, pp. 10–11).[6] There are also programmes run by the government for secondary school students to study a third language on top of English and mother tongue (Ministry of Education 2017).[7]

[4]To Prime Minister Lee, Mandarin 'unites the different dialect groups' and 'reminds the Singapore Chinese that they are part of an ancient civilisation with an unbroken history of over 5000 years' (Lee 2012, p. 150). There remains, however, resistance from the local ethnic Chinese community against the government's stance on Chinese dialects up to the present (Tan 2012).

[5]There are partial exceptions where subjects such as mathematics are taught on an experimental basis in Chinese in some schools, but these comprise only a very small minority.

[6]The reporter is personally aware of one case where an acquaintance of the same grade level, who is ethnically Chinese, spent most of his pre-secondary education overseas in international schools, and was permitted to substitute French for his mother tongue (which would have been Mandarin Chinese had the general principle been followed) requirement.

[7]As of 2018, the options include Malay, Chinese, Bahasa Indonesia, Arabic, French, Japanese, German, and Spanish.

The clear demarcation between the primarily cultural role played by the 'mother tongues' (in contrast to the technological and economic role of English) in the government's original language policy became blurred around the turn of the century, when the government began attempting to emphasise the economic value of the 'mother tongues' in a shift towards what has been coined 'linguistic instrumentalism' (Wee 2003). In particular, in light of developments in the People's Republic of China, Mandarin Chinese came to be singled out for special treatment for perceived economic advantages (Wee 2003, pp. 216–217; see also Wee 2006, p. 353). The overall trend seems to be towards greater use of English as the primary language at home, so much so that it may be appropriate to consider English not just as an official language, but also a mother tongue in its own right (Tan 2014).[8]

Local university admissions[9]—and especially for law faculties, which are perceived to be (and in reality generally are, at least in recent times) the most selective faculties next to medicine—generally require a passing grade on mother tongue as well as English in school-leaving examinations, it is not unreasonable to assume that most local law students in Singapore have or retain some working knowledge of at least their mother tongue. However, students and graduates of local universities are not necessarily the multilingual elites that they might have been expected to be. Although census data suggests that a substantial minority (12.6%) of university graduates are literate in three or more languages (Siemund et al. 2014, p. 345 tbl 5), research has found that university students are more likely to be only bilingual (usually in English and Mandarin Chinese only), whereas polytechnic[10] students are more likely to be multilingual in English, Mandarin Chinese, and either Hokkien or Cantonese (Siemund et al. 2014, p. 353 fig 5, 358). For the narrow subset of university students and graduates that are from NUS Law, hard statistics do not exist, but in the reporter's experience[11] there is little to suggest that (at best) more than perhaps a bare majority of local students at NUS Law are truly functionally bilingual.

---

[8] The reporter self-identifies as a native speaker of English, despite having Mandarin Chinese as the 'mother tongue' assigned by the Singapore government.

[9] Admission to university faculties in Singapore is competitive; there is no right to a place at a local university just because an applicant has completed the required course of pre-university studies.

[10] Polytechnics are vocational training institutions typically offering three-year courses that enroll the plurality of Singapore secondary school graduates. They correspond to level 5 on UNESCO's International Standard Classification of Education (ISCED) 2011 (or ISCED 1997 level 5B) framework.

[11] Over 3 years in residence as a law undergraduate, 2 years as law faculty teaching staff, 1 year in professional training and practice, and 2 years as law faculty research staff, plus an additional two years' experience teaching law in a Singapore business school.

3 Legal Monolingualism

Whatever the reality of language policy and language use is in the schools, markets, workplaces, or homes of Singapore, the practice of law—and especially court-related work—is its own bubble. Here, only one language matters: English. Order 92 Rule 1 of the Rules of Court (Cap 322, R5, 2014 Rev Ed), which is the main instrument governing civil procedure in Singapore, states unequivocally that

> Every document if not in the English language must be accompanied by a translation thereof certified by a court interpreter or a translation verified by the affidavit of a person qualified to translate it before it may be received, filed or used in the Court.

In similar vein, section 286(2) of the Criminal Procedure Code (Cap 68, 2012 Rev Ed) provides:

> Evidence recorded in writing or, if it is not recorded in writing, the transcript of the evidence recorded, must be in English and signed by the judge hearing the case; and shall form part of the record.

In practice, all legal proceedings except the giving of oral evidence by a witness (which will be interpreted into English, if applicable) are conducted entirely in English. There is no right, whether at civil or criminal law, to conduct legal proceedings even in any of the three official languages other than English. The existing case law further makes it clear that even a judge who is conversant in the language of a non-English document is not permitted to substitute their own understanding for a version translated by a qualified translator or the opinion of expert witnesses.[12] All legislation, whether by Parliament or delegated authorities, are only made in English, with no official versions even in the other three official languages.

Outside the courtroom, however, the three other official languages have a more significant role to play. Constitutionally, legislative deliberations may be conducted in any of the four official languages (Constitution, art 53), and as a matter of practice,[13] government services (in-person only[14]) are provided and government communications are made in all four official languages. Nevertheless, it would not be inaccurate to characterise law and its practice in Singapore as the exclusive domain of the English language.

[12] See the judgment of the Singapore High Court in *Shi Wen Yue v Shi Minjiu and another* [2016] SGHC 137; [2016] 4 SLR 911 at paras. 7–8. However, as any legal practitioner with court experience in Singapore would observe, it is not uncommon for counsel or a judge familiar with the language in which oral evidence is given by a witness to alert the interpreter to possible errors in interpretation.

[13] There are specific statutes and regulations providing for the mandatory use of official languages other than English, but there is no general provision to the best of the reporter's knowledge mandating all government services to be accessible in all official languages.

[14] Online services are generally only available in English.

4 The Legal Education Landscape: General Background

4.1 National University of Singapore Faculty of Law

Founded in 1957 as the Department of Law of the University of Malaya (which was renamed the University of Singapore and later merged with Nanyang University), the National University of Singapore (NUS) Faculty of Law (NUS Law) is the largest law degree-granting institution department in Singapore.[15] It is also generally perceived as the most prestigious, and benefits, as part of a comprehensive university, from the relatively high positions achieved by NUS as a whole in global rankings. NUS Law is for practical intents and purposes the face of Singapore legal academia for international purposes. The rest of the Chapter will focus on the situation within NUS Law as this is the context with which the reporter has the greatest familiarity and personal experience on which to draw on.

4.1.1 Student Body Profile

NUS Law admits approximately 220–240 students every year for its 4-year LL.B. programme.[16] Over 100 students are admitted to its LL.M. programme per year,[17] and 3–5 candidates are admitted to the Ph.D. programme each year.[18]

The vast majority of students (90–95%, by impression) enrolled in the NUS Law LL.B. programme are local (i.e. Singapore citizen[19]) students.[20] The bulk of foreign students enrolled as undergraduates typically have received a substantial part of their

[15] For a general, concise history, see Tan (2017b).

[16] For academic year 2017–2018, 221 (120 men, 101 women) were enrolled as first year undergraduates; 228 (122 men, 106 women) as second year students; 239 (147 men, 92 women) as third years; and 240 (141 men, 99 women) as fourth- (and final-) year students in the LLB programme (http://www.nus.edu.sg/registrar/info/statistics/ug-enrol-20172018.pdf). Note that Singapore does not generally keep statistics on genders other than male and female.

[17] AY 2017–2018: 120 students (36 men and 84 women) over 7 LLM programmes (http://www.nus.edu.sg/registrar/info/statistics/gd-enrol-20172018.pdf);

AY 2016–2017: 105 (36 men, 69 women) over 7 LLM programmes (http://www.nus.edu.sg/registrar/info/statistics/gd-enrol-20162017.pdf);

AY 2015–2016: 122 (37 men, 85 women) (http://www.nus.edu.sg/registrar/info/statistics/gd-enrol-20152016.pdf).

[18] There were 17 PhD candidates enrolled in AY2015–2016; 15 in AY 2016–2017; and 16 in AY 2017–2018 (sources in footnote 3). The PhD is designed to be a 3–4 year full-time programme, although historically part-time candidates were enrolled as well. Anecdotally, there are virtually no cases of candidates dropping out (i.e. not finishing), which makes 3–5 new candidates per year a fairly safe estimate.

[19] For this Chapter, I use 'local' to mean exclusively 'Singapore citizens'. As Singapore does not officially permit dual citizenship for adults (Constitution, Part X on Citizenship), it is safe to assume that a Singapore citizen is, for present intents and purposes and by legal definition solely and exclusively 'local'.

[20] There are no official statistics on this point.

pre-university education, ranging from 2 (high school) to 6 years (middle and high school), in Singapore, and usually under an established government scholarship scheme.[21] However, the proportion is reversed for the graduate programmes. LL. M. programmes are dominated by foreign students, with only a handful of local students enrolled each year,[22] and there have, to the best of the reporter's knowledge, only been a few local students who have graduated from the Ph.D. programme in the last 10 years or so.[23]

As a matter of impression, NUS Law has a relatively diverse student population by national origin at the graduate level and in terms of incoming undergraduate exchange students, but official data on the composition of the student body is not available. Students from (not in any particular order) Malaysia (primarily undergraduate), P.R. China, and India seem to be the most numerous.

4.1.2 Faculty Profile

As of 23 March 2017, counting full-time (excluding emerita), tenured, tenure-track, and untenured positions at the rank of lecturer or above, foreigners make up an estimated 47.6% of the faculty (30 out of 63).[24] This does not include a number of special contract, full-time positions created primarily for locals (for which an estimated 10 out of 11 are locals).[25] I do not include in this count a number of locals who have professorial titles but who neither teach nor conduct research nor contribute materially in any direct, visible way to the faculty,[26] and I do not include a large body of part-time (some of whom are foreigners holding 'fractional appointments'),

---

[21] For an example, see the Singapore Ministry of Education's 'ASEAN Scholarship' scheme: https://www.moe.gov.sg/admissions/scholarships/asean.

[22] Precise figures are not available, but anecdotally, there are no more than five local students in the LLM programmes each year, of which at least one or two are on scholarship.

[23] One was for many years an associate professor of law at the business school of another local university and now a consultant at a local law firm, and the other was an assistant professor before earning tenure and promotion to associate professor at NUS Law in 2021.

[24] Based on the list at https://law.nus.edu.sg/about_us/faculty/staff/staffdiv.asp as of 12 Mar 2018. One local faculty member was then recently deceased but remained on the list. The estimations are based on the reporter's personal knowledge and guesswork. As a rule of thumb, where there is no specific information either publicly- or personally-known to the reporter, the faculty member is assumed to be a citizen of the country in which they received their first degree. Despite this heuristic, the citizenship status of some faculty, especially those holding Malaysian citizenship at some point, is not necessarily clear. For historical reasons, many Malaysian faculty members were educated in Singapore (including at NUS Law itself) and are for general intents and purposes virtually indistinguishable from full naturalised or born locals. Naturalised citizens are counted only as locals as Singapore does not recognize dual citizenship (c.f. note 12 above).

[25] Under the category 'Sheridan Fellow' at https://law.nus.edu.sg/about_us/faculty/staff/staffdiv.asp. One faculty member in this category is known to be foreign-born but their current citizenship status is unknown to the reporter. Disclosure: the reporter worked at NUS Law in this capacity from 2014 to 2016.

[26] This category includes several politicians and diplomats, all in service to Singapore, but whose presence or activity on campus itself is *de minimis* or non-existent.

adjuncts, or legal skills instructors, all of whom are predominantly local. The count also does not include a considerable body of research staff based at the research centres or postdoctoral fellows. To the best of my knowledge, there is no local research staff who also teaches at NUS Law.[27]

Despite the large number of foreign faculty, most hail from other common law jurisdictions and relatively few are legally-trained in a language other than English.[28] As we will see later in 5.1, only two past full-time faculty members appear to have played a long-term role in teaching law courses at NUS Law in another language.

4.1.3 Courses by Visiting Professors

NUS Law receives a substantial number of visiting foreign academics each year who teach usually intensive three-week-long courses. For the academic year 2017–2018, NUS Law welcomed a total of 25 visiting professors based in Canada (1), Japan (1), England (9), Australia (8), United States (7);[29] this figure only includes visitors who taught at least one intensive course over 3 weeks.[30] The reporter can confirm from personal knowledge that the visiting professor from Japan teaches in Japanese in his home institution, but it is unclear whether any other visitor in the above academic year has ever or is able to teach in a language other than English.[31]

In light of the overwhelmingly US/Anglo-Commonwealth origin or dominant affiliation of NUS visiting professors—at least for AY2017/18—combined with the past practice of NUS Law generally not to offer law courses taught in languages other than English (but for one notable exception discussed later), NUS Law's visiting professor programme is yet to be harnessed as a vehicle for bilingual legal education.

4.2 Singapore Management University School of Law

Singapore Management University's (SMU) School of Law (SMU Law) admitted its first degree candidates in 2007 (Wee 2007). Bilingual education opportunities at

[27] Indeed, as of May 2018, there was (to the reporter's knowledge) no local postdoctoral fellow at all.

[28] A precise count is difficult, but a fair estimate would be ten or fewer. On the educational background of NUS Law faculty members, see also Bell (2019), pp. S35–S36.

[29] One is based in both England and Australia and thus double-counted.

[30] https://law.nus.edu.sg/about_us/visitors/visitors_s11718.html; https://law.nus.edu.sg/about_us/visitors/visitors_s21718.html.

[31] A previous (Anglophone) visiting professor from McGill University shared informally with a group of persons (which included the reporter) that he was able to take questions from students in French and to understand and evaluate written work in French, but that he preferred to communicate in English wherever possible.

SMU Law began with the move from NUS Law to SMU Law of a professor hailing from the People's Republic of China. After arriving at SMU Law, she was responsible for the first "Introduction to Chinese History, Culture, Economy and Law" course, which appears to have been taught entirely in Mandarin Chinese (Yang 2009; Singapore Management University n.d.-a). She was also listed as a faculty member responsible for a course featuring a study mission to the People's Republic of China, that featured a course component in the Chinese language (Singapore Management University n.d.-b). The Introduction to Chinese History, Culture, Economy and Law course appears to be currently under the charge of another faculty member, who appears to have also received his first degree from and have roots in the People's Republic of China (Singapore Management University n.d.-c). In this regard, the bilingual legal education situation in SMU is not dissimilar to NUS (discussed in more detail at Sect. 5.1 below).

4.3 Singapore University of Social Sciences School of Law

The Singapore University of Social Sciences ("SUSS") (formerly UniSIM until 11 July 2017) School of Law is the newest of the local law schools, admitting its first students in January 2017 (Tan 2017b, p. 197). This law school was established as a response to the observation of policy makers in 2013 that young lawyers were not entering the practice of criminal and family law in sufficient numbers. A key reason for the dearth of young entrants in these fields was their lack of appeal to both graduates of the existing two law schools (who were mainly top local students) and those who had earned their degrees abroad usually at great expense. The new law school was aimed at remedying this (actual or prospective) shortage by giving preference to candidates 'who demonstrate a genuine interest in the practice of community [i.e. family and criminal] law' (Fourth Committee on the Supply of Lawyers 2013, p. 12).

The official curriculum does not appear to include any course not taught in English (Singapore University of Social Sciences 2019). This is surprising when one takes into consideration this law school's professed orientation towards the practice of criminal and family law, which are precisely the areas in which a good proportion of clients are likely not to be fluent or even conversant in English. Given that there does not seem at the time of writing any component for student exchanges with foreign non-Anglophone universities, SUSS cannot be said to offer any bilingual legal education as of 2018.

4.4 Foreign Universities

Singapore,[32] like several other Commonwealth jurisdictions,[33] recognises some (but not all) law degrees conferred by certain institutions in other jurisdictions (Commonwealth and USA) for the purposes of admission to practise law. In general, a law degree, even if awarded by a recognised foreign university, will not be recognised if the course leading to that law degree is an accelerated or double degree course.[34] As law degrees offering substantial foreign language and foreign law training in the UK are likely to fall outside the scope of recognised degrees, it is improbable that persons admitted to the practice of law in Singapore on the basis of foreign degrees would have received substantial bilingual legal education.

5 Opportunities for Bilingual Legal Education at the National University of Singapore Faculty of Law

5.1 The 'Chinese Legal Tradition and Legal Chinese' Course

As foreshadowed above, no institution in Singapore has—or ever had—'bilingual legal education' in any meaningful sense. As of May 2018, NUS Law offered only one course—'Chinese Legal Tradition and Legal Chinese' (NUS IVLE n.d.)—is taught in a language other than English.[35] This is an elective course taught for many years, until his departure from NUS Law in 2020, by a professor born in and educated in the People's Republic of China.[36,37] The course is read mostly by third- and

[32] See the list published by the Ministry of Law at https://www.mlaw.gov.sg/content/minlaw/en/practising-as-a-lawyer/approved-universities.html.

[33] Another prominent example is Malaysia, which recognizes law degrees from 14 Australian and 5 New Zealand universities, as well as both Barrister and Solicitor qualifications of England and Wales: (http://www.lpqb.org.my/index.php?option=com_content&view=article&id=47&Itemid=61. Most states and territories in Australia apply a set of uniform principles when determining if an overseas-educated or -qualified applicant should be admitted to the practice of law: Law Admissions Consultative Committee, *Uniform Principles for Assessing Qualifications of Overseas Applicants for Admission to the Australian Legal Profession* (August 2015, rev June 2017). Mutual recognition of qualifications for legal practice in Australia and New Zealand is governed by their respective (national-level) legislation (each titled Trans-Tasman Mutual Recognition Act 1997) and state equivalents in Australia.

[34] Legal Profession (Qualified Persons) Rules (R 15, Cap 161), rr 11–12.

[35] Disclosure: the reporter has read this course before (in Academic Year 2012–2013).

[36] The professor received bachelor's and master's from institutions in the People's Republic of China, and also earned degrees from institutions in England (taught master's) and the United States (LL.M. and S.J.D.).

[37] https://scholars.cityu.edu.hk/en/persons/jiangyu-wang(2215380f-8082-4dbd-a3ed-f8e2c7dd0a86).html.

fourth-year undergraduates.[38] The course description is worth quoting at length (NUS IVLE n.d.):

> This course provides an introduction to the contemporary Chinese legal system, covering its historical evolution, legal culture, sources of law, key legal institutions, the legal profession, and selected areas of law, as well as, practical legal Chinese in terms of reading and drafting legal documents in Chinese. **It is conducted entirely in Mandarin and is intended for students who possess a basic level of legal Chinese**. Unfamiliarity with Chinese legal materials and inability to comprehend legal Chinese are common disadvantages faced by Singapore lawyers advising clients who do business in China. This course aims to deal with this by offering practical skills in the context of an understanding of the broader legal system and legal culture of China. Students are given selected Chinese legal articles, statutes, court decisions and other legal documents and instruments to read and are required to undertake practice assignments in Chinese. After the study, students will be expected to be able to interpret Chinese legal concepts in Chinese. After the study, students will be expected to be able to interpret Chinese legal concepts in Chinese. Particularly, we will
>
> - examine the history, structure, and basic principles and methods of the legal system in China;
> - consider the historical, social and cultural contexts in which Chinese law has evolved and operated, and understand the role of law in China's political, social, and economic developments;
> - study original Chinese legal documents including statutes, court rulings, government publications, journal articles, and news and commentaries.
> - learn the skills and methods essential to the understanding and practice of Chinese law, such as statutory interpretation, case analysis, legal research, legal writing and dispute resolution.
>
> (minor typographical errors fixed; bold emphasis in original)

The key features of this course may thus be summarised as follows:

- Taught entirely in Mandarin Chinese by a relatively senior, tenured faculty member
- The law that is taught is the law of the People's Republic of China, not Singapore
- Teaching materials include primary and secondary sources from the source jurisdiction in the original source language
- Assessment involves (at least in part) a practical component and using Mandarin Chinese

Apart from its value as an elective, this course is also compulsory for students who are planning to go on student exchange at law faculties in the People's Republic of China (NUS Law 2017b).[39] The number of enrolling students fluctuates but

[38] Recall that in the regular LL.B. programmes (both 4- and 3-year versions) the first 2 years comprise only compulsory courses.

[39] "**Chinese Language Requirement:**

Students who wish to opt for an exchange programme at a Chinese partner university would need to fulfill one of the following prerequisites:

- minimum Grade B4 in Higher Chinese (HCL or CL1) at GCE 'O' level; or
- minimum Grade B4 in Chinese (CL2) at GCE 'AO' level (old curriculum); or
- minimum Grade C in H1 Chinese at GCE 'A' level; or
- minimum Grade 4 in SL Chinese for the International Baccalaureate (IB) Diploma

seldom exceeds ten or so. From the reporter's personal recollection, less than ten students were enrolled in his year (Academic Year 2012–2013), and in Academic Year 2013–2014 only one student who completed this course went on student exchange to an institution in the People's Republic of China (Koh 2013, p. 46).

The precise origins of this course are unknown, but surviving records indicate that it was offered as least as early as 2004 (NUS Law 2004b).[40] The course was then taught by another faculty member who (has since left NUS Law[41]) also hailed from the People's Republic of China. As it was during 2002–2003 that NUS Law forged links with four leading institutions in the People's Republic of China (Tan 2017b, p. 182), that a course on Chinese law taught in Mandarin Chinese was established around that period was no coincidence. The development of a legal Chinese course in what was then Singapore's only law school also nicely mirrors the contemporaneous move towards linguistic instrumentalism by the Singapore government with respect to Mandarin Chinese in the realm of pre-tertiary education (c.f. Wee 2003).

5.2 *Student Exchange Programmes*

NUS Law's exchange opportunities for undergraduates are too numerous to list in full, but for our purposes, only a few exchange partner institutions offer or require any course of instruction to be in a language other than English. NUS' exchange partners in the People's Republic of China naturally offer courses in Mandarin Chinese.[42] It is not clear whether it is mandatory for a NUS student to take any course taught in Chinese, but it may be worth their while to do so as there appears to be preferential treatment by NUS Law of credits earned by reading Chinese-language medium courses on exchange, based on a report by a law student who went on exchange at Tsinghua University (International Relations Office n.d., p. 2).

As of AY2018/19, students going for exchange at Kyushu University (Japan) are required to read a Japanese language course (NUS Law 2017a). There appears to be

Students may also need to undergo an interview and if selected for exchange at a Chinese partner university, will be required to read LL4009V Chinese Legal Tradition & Legal Chinese module in Semester 1. (Note: the exchange period for Chinese partner universities is in Semester 2)."

[40]This professor was instrumental, amongst other things, for setting up student exchange programmes and fostering other links with law schools in the People's Republic of China (Tan 2017a, p. 232 n 54).

[41]This faculty member joined NUS Law in 1992 (Tan 2017b, p. 207) but has since left (possibly around 2008) to join the (then-) other local law school, SMU Law, although she appears to have also left SMU. See Sect. 4.2.

[42]As of AY 2017/18, they were China University of Political Science and Law; East China University of Political Science and Law; Fudan University; Peking University; Tsinghua University; and Renmin University. Most, if not all these institutions also offer law courses taught in English.

no requirement for a student on exchange at Kyushu to read any law course taught or assessed in Japanese, although it may be an option.[43]

As a matter of historical interest, to the reporter's recollection, the University of Heidelberg was an exchange partner institution at which proficiency in a non-English language (German in this case) was a mandatory requirement; however, Heidelberg was, according to the reporter's recollection, taken off the list of partner institutions around or shortly after AY 2012/13.

5.3 *Miscellaneous*

Apart from the Chinese Legal Tradition and Legal Chinese course, there appears to have been the option to write an undergraduate research dissertation in Chinese.[44] This option was exercised at least once and under the supervision of the professor who taught the legal Chinese course (Chan 2005).[45] This is perhaps the most impressive example of an exercise in bilingual legal education by an NUS Law undergraduate, but this bold experiment does not appear to have been repeated since.

It should also be mentioned for completeness that NUS Law also ran an LL.M. programme in Chinese law from 2004 to 2006, but it played no role in broadening bilingual legal education as the programme was designed to be taught entirely in English (NUS Law 2004a, p. 12).[46]

6 Prospects for Bilingual Legal Education in Singapore

6.1 *Degree Programmes: Promise or Pipe Dream?*

Around early 2012, NUS Law announced that it had entered into a Memorandum of Understanding with Tsinghua University to offer new degree programmes that would have students of each institution spend the final year of their first degree (LL.B.) programme at the other institution, where they would earn a master's degree (LL.M.) (National University of Singapore 2012). Although the Tsinghua portion of the programme leading up to the LL.M. could have been completed by a NUS LL.B. degree student entirely in English as the Tsinghua LL.M. in Chinese law programme

[43] Albeit one that the reporter is unaware that any student has ever exercised.

[44] It is not (and has never been) necessary to write a research dissertation to graduate (with an honours degree) from NUS Law; the students who take up the option of writing one are always in the minority, numbering no more than twenty in a typical year.

[45] I am grateful to Lim Siu Chen of the CJ Koh Law Library of the National University of Singapore for sharing this information with me.

[46] This short-lived programme saw 14 graduates over its 2 years of operation: Tan (2017b), p. 216.

has always been entirely in English (Tsinghua University n.d.), there has since been no mention of any progress on this collaboration between the two institutions. As of May 2018, none of the six bachelor's-master's programmes (Exchange Plus) listed on the official NUS Bulletin involve Tsinghua University (National University of Singapore n.d.).[47]

While it may be premature to write off the NUS-Tsinghua collaboration at this juncture—or indeed any institution from a jurisdiction where the legal language is not English—there remain considerable challenges to bilingual legal education in general that are detailed below.

6.2 *Challenges and Obstacles*

Despite efforts at NUS (and SMU), it is in the reporter's assessment that the following five challenges (or obstacles, if one is to be realistic) would make any substantial progress towards bilingual legal education difficult to achieve.

Student Monolingualism Despite the claimed achievements of state-promoted bilingualism, notional bilingualism for social and cultural purposes does not translate into a basis for effective bilingualism in law, except perhaps where Mandarin Chinese is concerned given that two of the three Singapore law schools offer a course in legal Chinese and offer (until the pandemic that began in 2020) exchange programmes with institutions in the People's Republic of China. As to other languages, the pool of students suitably prepared for serious legal work in a non-official language is vanishingly thin. Anecdotally and from the reporter's personal recollection, students demonstrating proficiency in a language other than English and mother tongue[48] simply do not attend NUS Law in substantial numbers.[49]

[47] The six programmes are with New York University, Boston University, Erasmus University Rotterdam, King's College London, University of Melbourne, and University of Toronto. To the best of the reporter's knowledge, none of the six offer a significant bilingual legal education programme either. Erasmus University Rotterdam's LL.M. programmes are notably all taught in English (Erasmus University Rotterdam n.d.).

[48] For example, of the over thirty students in the reporter's high school graduating class who sat for school leaving examinations in Japanese language, only two went on to study law in Singapore (one in NUS and the other in SMU); of these, only the reporter continued to use Japanese in the course of his professional legal work.

[49] The reporter is aware of two other students in his graduating class who had substantial German language proficiency. One went for student exchange at the University of Helsinki (where she read law courses in English but also Finnish language classes, amongst others), and a few years after graduating from NUS Law proceeded to earn master's (Mag. iur.) (in German) and doctoral degrees (Dr. iur.) (in English) in Austria. The reporter himself later earned a doctorate in law (Dr. jur.) at a German university with a dissertation written in English but which drew on the laws of two non-Anglophone jurisdictions, Germany and Japan. See Koh (forthcoming). The reporter is also aware of a student from an earlier graduating class who went on exchange at the University of Heidelberg.

Degree Programme Structure As there is virtually no flexibility for undergraduate law students in NUS Law to receive intensive instruction in a language other than English or mother tongue in the first two years of study,[50] the only students who are equipped, by the third year of their studies, to read law courses in a third language (whether offered as an elective or during exchange), the existence of any students ready for bilingual legal education each year (other than in Mandarin Chinese) will have been by accident, not design. Any student who proceeds to embark on a serious course of bilingual legal education—other than the one course in Legal Chinese and a one-semester exchange in a law school in the People's Republic of China—would be in the minority of minorities.

Lack of Economic Incentives As Singapore has always adopted and has no reason to deviate in future from legal monolingualism, bilingual legal education offers minimal return on investment for a recipient who practises law in a Singapore-centric setting. Fields such as family and criminal law are notorious among the public imagination for their perceived or real lack of financial reward (Ng 2016), yet it is these fields that require the frequent use of languages other than English due to the nature of the clientele.[51] Even with proficiency in a language other than a Singapore official language even at a level adequate for professional legal work, one's prospects may vary in the job market,[52] perhaps in part due to the substantial presence of English-speaking, foreign-trained and foreign-qualified legal practitioners in Singapore who are better equipped than local graduates to offer legal services in another language.[53]

[50]For students on the standard 4-year LL.B. or 3-year graduate-entry LL.B., as of 2017/18 the first four semesters (two years) of the LL.B. programme are completely taken up by compulsory courses, leaving no room at all for elective courses.

[51]From the reporter's personal experiences as a legal practitioner, as well as anecdotal accounts, clients who are unable or prefer not to communicate in English are often those seeking criminal defence or family law services, and even commercial matters involving client interaction not in English involve invariably small and medium enterprises, with typically (though not always) lower-value work. Having said that, there are a number of small firms in Singapore that specialize in the niche and highly lucrative market for Indonesian business clients.

[52]The reporter's conversations with two different senior lawyers in the same big four Singapore firm separately and on different occasions in 2016 and 2018 yielded a mixed picture for Japanese language proficiency. The first lawyer (the managing partner of the firm) said in 2016 that there is no added value for a Singapore-trained and -qualified practitioner to know Japanese and that the firm would not hire on this basis; the second (a partner) mentioned in 2018 a case in which a Japanese-speaking local law student was offered a training contract (practical legal training apprenticeship in Singapore) at a leading Singapore firm in part due to that student's Japanese language proficiency. There was also at least one case of a Japanese-speaking, locally-trained lawyer working with the Singapore practice of a Japanese law firm, but the reporter was informed in 2020 that this individual had ceased to be with the firm. Anecdotally, however, Indonesian language proficiency is attractive to (predominantly small) firms oriented towards Indonesia-related business.

[53]In addition to foreign-qualified lawyers (who number over a thousand), a number of foreign-qualified lawyers have also passed the Foreign Practitioner Examinations and registered to practice both Singapore and foreign law. For the key statutory provision, see Legal Profession Act (Cap 161, 2009 Rev Ed), s 36B. As of 22 May 2018 there were 23 registered foreign lawyers under this

Continued Focus Exclusively on 'Common Law' and Common Law Jurisdictions Despite strong messaging from leaders of the legal community (see e.g. Menon 2015, pp. 18–19) and somewhat increased awareness amongst members of the practical importance of the law of civil law jurisdictions in our interconnected world,[54] it is difficult to say that locally-educated jurists have, as a whole, outgrown the entrenched affinity towards (and in some cases, outright veneration of) the common law tradition and common law jurisdictions, particularly England and Wales.[55] The language of the common law is English, and no other language is necessary—or even helpful—in understanding common law cases, doctrine, literature, or legislation. Legal education in a language other than English is, for practical intents and purposes, education about law that is *not* common law.[56] Hence, non-English legal education has limited appeal to an Anglophone student or jurist in a common law jurisdiction who is usually free from factors encouraging or compelling such learning to which others in the rest of the world are subject.[57] So long as real demand for non-common law training remains anaemic, bilingual legal education's prospects of achieving mass appeal in Singapore are correspondingly dim. The only bright spot is may be the law (and thus language) of the People's Republic of China, where pragmatic, economic incentives may yet keep the flame alive.

Lack of a Clear Candidate Language for Bilingual Legal Education Even if Singapore were hypothetically to do whatever it takes to implement a substantive bilingual legal education programme, the big question remains: which language should it be in? The influence—and indeed, dominance—of the English language in the international legal education scene presents Singapore, an ethnically and linguistically diverse state, a dilemma. No matter which language it chooses, it will exclude at least a substantial ethnic and linguistic minority. In the interests of fairness and equity between ethnic communities, unless Singapore were ready to bite

---

provision based on a search for lawyers with registration type of "36B LEGAL PROFESSION ACT" on the Legal Services Regulatory Authority E-Services portal at https://www.mlaw.gov.sg/eservices/lsra/search-lawyer-or-law-firm/.

[54] "We also hope to increase their exposure to other Asian legal jurisdictions, in particular civil law as it is practised in Asia." (Chesterman 2015, p. 1). For an analysis of the challenges of civil law instruction in Asia arising from language, see Bell (2019).

[55] This is based on the reporter's experience as a student, junior faculty member, legal practitioner, and researcher in Singapore.

[56] While non-common law can be taught in English (easy examples include international and European law), common law (in the narrow sense and excluding mixed jurisdictions such as Israel and South Africa) cannot be taught on a large scale to would-be practitioners of a common law jurisdiction without great difficulty (with limited exceptions such as Francophone Canada) other than in English.

[57] These factors include commercial pressure (to which much of the entire non-common law world doing business with stubbornly Anglophone common law trading partners is subject), political circumstances (such as those in Europe), or centuries-long or newly-constructed scholarly tradition (Europe and East Asia).

the bullet and implement at least three bilingual legal education programmes featuring Mandarin Chinese, Malay, and Tamil respectively—which would be a tremendously costly, if not impossible endeavour—perhaps the best choice is to stick with what it knows best: legal monolingualism (in English).

7 Conclusion

A multilingual country with only one language for legal purposes—a seeming paradox that is, in a nutshell, Singapore. But as this Chapter demonstrates, the reality and demands of law and legal education are distinct from broader national language policy in government and education more generally. Despite the attractions of bilingualism in legal education, Singapore's circumstances point to a perhaps unsatisfying, but ultimately the most realistic and workable solution: maintaining the status quo of colonial-origin legal monolingualism in a multilingual post-colonial state.

References

Au-Yong R (2016). Debate on whether race classification model is still relevant. Straits Times, 19 January 2016, https://www.straitstimes.com/singapore/debate-on-whether-race-classification-model-is-still-relevant

Bell GF (2019) The civil law, the common law, and the english language—challenges and opportunities in Asia. Asian J Comp Law 14(S1):S29–S49. https://doi.org/10.1017/asjcl.2019.22

Bolton K, Ng BC (2014) The dynamics of multilingualism in contemporary Singapore. World Engl 33:307–318

Chan LH (2005) 中国<合同法>与英美合法的比较: 南辕北辙还是异曲同工? [Zhong guo <he tong fa> yu ying mei he fa de bi jiao: nan yuan bei che huan shi yi qu tong gong?]. National University of Singapore Faculty of Law LL.B. dissertation, 2005

Chesterman S (2015) Letter from the Dean. Faculty of Law, Dean's Office, National University of Singapore, February 2015, https://law.nus.edu.sg/about_us/pdfs/Letter%20from%20the%20Dean%20NUS%20Law%202015.pdf

Chew PG-L (2013) A sociolinguistic history of early identities in Singapore: from colonialism to nationalism. Palgrave MacMillan, Basingstoke. ISBN 978-1-137-01233-3

Erasmus University Rotterdam (n.d.) Erasmus School of Law – Masters. Erasmus University Rotterdam, https://www.eur.nl/en/esl/education/master/overview

Fourth Committee on the Supply of Lawyers (2013) Report of the Fourth Committee on the Supply of Lawyers, May 2013. https://www.mlaw.gov.sg/content/dam/minlaw/corp/News/4th%20Committee%20Report.pdf

International Relations Office (n.d.) SEP Report. International Relations Office (IRO). http://www.nus.edu.sg/gro/assets/doc/prog/sep/reports/cn/sep_report_china_tsinghua.pdf

Koh AK (2013) The educational deficiencies of the Singapore practitioner. Singapore Law Rev 31:45–49

Koh AK (forthcoming) Shareholder protection in close corporations. Cambridge University Press, Cambridge. ISBN 978-110-8496-667

Lee KY (1960) Talk by the Prime Minister, Mr. Lee Kuan Yew to the Nanyang University Political Science Society on March 29, 1960. Singapore Government Press Statement JK/MC.MA 93/60, http://www.nas.gov.sg/archivesonline/data/pdfdoc/lky19600329.pdf

Lee KY (2012) My lifelong challenge: Singapore's bilingual journey. Straits Times Press, Singapore. ISBN 978-981-4342-032

Menon S (2015) International Commercial Courts: Towards a Transnational System of Dispute Resolution, Opening Lecture for the DIFC Courts Lecture Series 2015. https://www.supremecourt.gov.sg/docs/default-source/default-document-library/media-room/opening-lecture%2D%2D-difc-lecture-series-2015.pdf

Ministry of Education (2017) Language Programmes in Secondary School. Ministry of Education Singapore, archived 4 July 2017 at https://web.archive.org/web/20170704120341/https://www.moe.gov.sg/education/secondary/language-programmes/

National Library Board (2016) Bilingual policy. Singapore infopedia, updated 31 August 2016, http://eresources.nlb.gov.sg/infopedia/articles/SIP_2016-09-01_093402.html

National University of Singapore (2012) NUS Law School partners Tsinghua University to offer new degree programmes. Newshub – NUS' News Portal, 3 January 2012, archived 7 March 2017 at https://web.archive.org/web/20170307183621/http://newshub.nus.edu.sg/headlines/0112/tsinghua_03Jan12.php

National University of Singapore (n.d.) 3.3.3 Exchange Plus Programmes. Faculty of Law, NUS Bulletin 2018/19, archived 1 Jun 2019 at https://web.archive.org/save/http://www.nus.edu.sg/nusbulletin/faculty-of-law/undergraduate-education/special-programmes/exchange-plus-programmes/

Ng JY (2016) Criminal, family law need more practitioners to meet demand: Indranee. Today (online), 16 February 2016, https://www.todayonline.com/singapore/criminal-family-law-need-more-practitioners-indranee

NUS IVLE (n.d.) Module Overview: LL4009V/LL5009V/LL6009V – Chinese Legal Tradition and Legal Chinese – 2017/2018, Semester 1. IVLE NUS Learning Management System, archived 1 Jun 2019 at https://web.archive.org/web/20190601084650/https://ivle.nus.edu.sg/V1/lms/public/view_moduleoutline.aspx?CourseID=5B5DE004-6616-4447-8600-458DDF7D2235&ClickFrom=StuViewBtn

NUS Law (2004a) LawLink: The Alumni Magazine of the National University of Singapore Faculty of Law 3(1) (Jan–Jun 2004), https://law.nus.edu.sg/alumni/pdfs/LAWLINK_v3n1.pdf

NUS Law (2004b) Chinese Legal Tradition & Legal Chinese. NUS: Faculty of Law – Course Description, archived 15 August 2004 at https://web.archive.org/web/20040815122241/http://law.nus.edu.sg:80/current/course/courses_desc.asp?MC=LL4009

NUS Law (2017a) AY2018-2019 Credit Requirements for NUS Law Students (Single Degree Programme) at Partner Universities, updated 30 September 2017. https://law.nus.edu.sg/student_matters/student_ex/docs/cre_req1819.xlsx

NUS Law (2017b) Eligibility and Application. NUS – Faculty of Law, updated 30 September 2017. https://law.nus.edu.sg/student_matters/student_ex/application.html

Siemund P, Schulz ME, Schweinberger M (2014) Studying the linguistic ecology of Singapore: a comparison of college and university students. World Englishes 33:340–362

Silver RE, Bokhorst-Heng WD (2016) Overarching themes, bilingual dreams and multilingual landscapes: quadrilingual education in Singapore. In: Silver RE, Bokhorst-Heng WD (eds) Quadrilingual Education in Singapore: Pedagogical Innovation in Language Education. Springer, Singapore. pp 3–19, ISBN 978-981-287-965-3

Singapore Management University (n.d.-a) School of Law Year 2008/09 Term 2 LGST 226 Introduction to Chinese History, Culture, Economy and Law (Mandarin). Singapore Management University. https://inet.smu.edu.sg/sites/courses/Documents/Outlines/UGRD/0820/LGST226_Li_Mei_Qin.pdf

Singapore Management University (n.d.-b) School of Law Year 2010/11 Term 2 Law 002 Law Study Mission (Beijing & Tianjin). Singapore Management University. https://inet.smu.edu.sg/sites/courses/Documents/Outlines/UGRD/1020/LAW002_LiMeiQin.pdf

Singapore Management University (n.d.-c). https://inet.smu.edu.sg/sites/courses/Documents/Outlines/UGRD/1420/LGST226_Henry%20Gao.pdf

Singapore University of Social Sciences (2019) Bachelor of Laws – LAWLLB – Curriculum Plan, updated on 22 February 2019, archived 1 Jun 2019 at https://web.archive.org/web/20190601085506/https://www.suss.edu.sg/Eservice/Public/ViewCP/ViewCP.aspx?progcd=LAWLLB&viewtype=mhtml

Tan C-H (2017a) NUS law in the noughties: becoming Asia's global law school. Singapore J Legal Stud 215–238

Tan KYL (2017b) The lamp of the law: 60 years of legal education at NUS Law. National University of Singapore, Singapore

Tan S (2012) Language ideology in discourses of resistance to dominant hierarchies of linguistic worth: Mandarin Chinese and Chinese 'dialects' in Singapore. Aust J Anthropol 23:340–356

Tan Y-Y (2014) English as a 'mother tongue' in Singapore. World Engl 33:319–339

Tsinghua University (n.d.) FAQs. School of Law, Tsinghua University, archived 1 Feb 2018 at https://web.archive.org/web/20180201200702/http://www.tsinghua.edu.cn/publish/lawen/3547/index.html

Wee L (2003) Linguistic instrumentalism in Singapore. J Multilingual Multicult Dev 24:211–224

Wee L (2006) The semiotics of language ideologies in Singapore. J Socioling 10:344–361

Wee L (2007) SMU law school to welcome inaugural intake in August. Business Times, 6 January 2007, at 8, archived 1 June 2019 at https://web.archive.org/web/20190601085715/https://www.smu.edu.sg/sites/default/files/smu/news_room/smu_in_the_news/2007/sources/BT_20070106_1.pdf

Yang M (杨萌) (2009) 新大法律系首办《走进中国》课程 华语教课·反应热烈 [SMU Law School launches course to understand China]. Lianhe Wanbao *(联合晚报)*, Singapore, 11 April 2009, at p 9, translation available and archived 1 Jun 2019 at https://web.archive.org/web/20190601085752/https://www.smu.edu.sg/sites/default/files/smu/news_room/smu_in_the_news/2009/sources/LHWB_20090411_2.pdf

Bilingual Legal Education in Taiwan

Andrew Jen-Guang Lin

1 The National Taiwan University College of Law

In 2016, the total number of law students at National Taiwan University College of Law was 1526 (including students in the undergraduate, master and Ph.D. programs).

For the purpose of comparison, in 2016, there are 35 universities having the department, college or school of law or having a bachelor or advanced legal studies program. There were 119 legal studies programs, including 40 undergraduate programs, 66 master programs, and 13 Ph.D. programs.

In 2016, the total number of law students in Taiwan was 19,662, including 13,503 students in undergraduate programs (bachelor of laws), 5845 students in master of laws programs and 314 Ph.D. students.

There are two types of foreign students at NTU College of Law. The first type is "degree students" pursuing a degree, such as a bachelor of law degree (LL.B.), master of law degree (LL.M.) or doctoral degree (Ph.D.), who must comply with the same requirements in order to obtain the respective degree. The other type of foreign students is coming as exchange students who usually stay for one or two semesters and enroll in courses they select.

As for the degree students, the number of foreign students at NTU College of Law has maintained at the range of 77 to 82 during 2007 and 2016. The proportion of foreign students to local students at NTU College of Law was 5.6 to 100 in 2016 and 6.6 to 100 in 2007. In other words, foreign students constitute 5.3% if the student body at NTU College of Law in 2016 and 6.19% in 2007.

A. J.-G. Lin (✉)
National Taiwan University, Taipei, Taiwan
e-mail: andrewlin@ntu.edu.tw

N. Etcheverry Estrázulas (ed.), *Bilingual Study and Research*, Ius Comparatum – Global Studies in Comparative Law 58,
https://doi.org/10.1007/978-3-030-84550-6_14

With regard to the Exchange students (foreign students not seeking for degrees) coming to NTU College of Law, there has been an upward trend in the number of exchange students over the last 18 years. The number was in the single digit by 2008, crossed 10 in 2009, and exceeded 100 in 2016.

At the College of Law, National Taiwan University, 100% of full-time faculties are the nationals of Taiwan. However, there are visiting professors who are paid to teach a course (in a regular semester or complete teaching intensively in less than a month) and visiting scholars who are unpaid and come to conduct short-term research.

Many different nationalities are represented in the student's body, there were many international students enrolled in undergraduate, master and doctoral programs at NTU College of Law during the period from Academic Year 2000 to 2017. The top 5 foreign countries in terms of number of degree students at NTU College of Law during that period are China, Japan, Korea, Mongolia and Thailand.

The majority of courses are conducted in Mandarin at NTU College of Law. However, they do provide English courses and some conducted in German and Japanese for local and international students to enroll. In the last 10 years, there were 12 English courses offered in Academic Year 2009 (the fewest offered year), while there were 39 English courses offered in Academic Year 2015 (the most offered year).

The number of visiting professors in 2016 was 344 constituting 8.2% of the faculty at NTU.

2 Bilingual Legal Education Program in Taiwan

What courses can be considered as bilingual legal education courses is, as mentioned by the national reporter, an issue itself. By the definition of bilingual education, we usually refer to courses that are conducted in the native language and another language. In Taiwan, a bilingual legal education course is a legal course that is taught in Mandarin (or Taiwanese), the native language of Taiwan, and English (or other foreign language). From personal observation, there may be very few courses that are considered to be bilingual legal education courses according the strictest definition.

As the national reporter points out, the importance of bilingual legal education courses is that it provides students many benefits in learning the legal regimes. Firstly, students learn how to read foreign legal material in foreign languages, particularly in English. Secondly, they learn how a legal concept is expressed in other foreign jurisdictions. Furthermore, local students may interact with international student in the courses. Finally, students may learn the comparative approach in learning law.

In the National Taiwan University College of Law there are professors that teach courses in both languages. English courses are offered in line with the policy of NTU to accommodate more and more international students who have not yet been able to attend the courses conducted in Taiwan's language. Another type of English courses is designed to train the local students to learn in English environment. These courses are usually related to foreign law, Anglo-American laws and international law. Occasionally, local professors co-teach a course with foreign professors who come for the full semester or for only a few weeks. For example, during 2008 to 2012, Professor Ming-cheng Tsai, former Dean of NTU College of Law, initiated a Comparative Law Course held in several semesters, inviting guest speakers from universities of different countries.

In order to provide local students opportunities to learn directly from foreign scholars, to access to foreign legal regime, to get familiar with foreign legal materials, and partly to accommodate more and more international students, particularly exchange students, professors are encouraged to start a bilingual legal education course.

The first reason to start a bilingual legal education course from the reporter's perspective is to correctly introduce foreign law and legal terminologies to local students. The second reason is to benefit local students to access to different sources of foreign legal materials so that they learn where to find foreign law and legal materials. The third reason is to accommodate the increasing international students who have not been able to attend courses conducted in local language. For this purpose, English courses have become the policy of several top universities to encourage professors to run English taught courses. Most English taught legal courses are in the master program and mainly in comparative legal studies in nature.

From several universities 'point of view, to offer more English taught courses is in response to the trend of globalization and internationalization and to allow students to get used to the English learning environment.

In practice and in reality, from the national reporter perspective, there are, and I quote "several obstacles in carrying out the bilingual legal education program or in running English legal courses in Taiwan".

First, it takes more time to prepare an English taught legal course and there are not many incentives for local professors to conduct legal education courses in English. It is crucial to mention though, as the reporter later expressed, that he has not seen many objections or resistance against bilingual legal education directly, "these objections are mainly against university's policy requiring faculties to offer English taught courses". Professors offering BLE courses do not receive any additional financial concessions comparing with offering regular courses conducted in local language. The criticisms are mainly against the compulsory policy itself.

Another obstacle is that English taught courses are not popular among local students. A course not conducted in local language is not popular if it is not a required course to be taken.

The areas that they have decided to teach in a foreign language are the mentioned below.

Firstly, a popular option is Comparative law or for the purpose of comparative studies. Secondly, it is also commonplace to find courses related to International Law. Thirdly, they may also offer courses to study Anglo American Laws. Furthermore, other topics of law that have caught attention of international society such as

Arbitration and Intellectual Property Law, International Human Rights Law, International Disability Rights Law.

The majority of students who have received bilingual legal education or attended English taught courses have been able to outperform in terms of having better chances to getting into the top law firms and more internationalized listed companies as in-house counsels. Many top law firms look for lawyers with proficiencies in foreign languages, particularly in English.

Different professors evaluate students differently. In most bilingual or foreign language taught courses, students are evaluated by their performance in the class and the final exam or term paper.

Professors teaching bilingual legal education courses usually choose the area of law they specialize. Therefore, they usually are familiar with and able to obtain the necessary resources. Textbooks in some courses are used, such as Anglo-American Contract Law. Legislative materials, statutes, case law, scholarly writing, etc. are easily accessed from online legal research services, such as Westlaw and Lexis.

Different professors design their reaching and materials differently.

Students enrolled in bilingual legal education courses are usually having different levels of proficiencies in the foreign language used in the courses. In order to encourage students with lower proficiency in English, it is a policy for many professors to explain, in the course description, that English is not the major element for evaluating the students.

For BLE courses or English taught courses, the reporter states that the number has increased gradually or at least maintained the same level in the past 5 years.

The number of BLE courses is related with the number of visiting professors.

m. Most professors offer BLE courses mainly from the academic point of view. However, professors have noticed and encouraged students pointing out the advantage that BLE students have when applying for a job in comparison with the rest of students who have not enroll in a BLE course.

Law firms, particularly those with international businesses, will recruit students having received bilingual legal education.

The main language chosen as an option for bilingual legal education is English.

The reason the national reporter refers to English is because most of the literatures in the areas of law are in English.

If another language had to be chosen, due to the fact that Taiwan is a civil law country, they will chose German and Japanese laws, since many areas of law are patterned after those laws.

Bilingual Legal Education is not perceived by students, faculty members, State authorities or Law Firms as a threat to national roots and culture.

Bilingual Legal Education in the United States: The Deficient Status Quo and a Call for More Action

Mathias Reimann

> *"The limits of my language are the limits of my world."—*
> *Ludwig Wittgenstein, Tractatus Logico-Philosophicus*
> *(Proposition 5.6 (1922))*

1 Introduction: The American Problem with English as a Global Legal Language

It is a truism that law is inextricably tied to language since it operates largely through (written or spoken) words. To understand law, one must understand its language. As a result, it is crucial in which language law is expressed.

On a global level, today this language is predominantly English. Its predominance is mainly the result of three consecutive historical developments. Through the vast expansion of the British Empire, a large segment of the world's jurisdictions adopted English as their primary official language.[1] Since the middle of the twentieth century, US-American capital and business came to dominate the world economy. And since the late twentieth century, US-American and British law firms have shaped global legal practice.[2]

This Report focuses on the United States proper and thus excludes Puerto Rico. There, the main language of instruction is of course Spanish. Most lawyers, however, speak English as well and can thus be considered bilingual, albeit to varying degrees.

Thanks to the staff of the University of Michigan Law Library, especially Seth Quidachy-Swan and Virginia Neisler, for their excellent research support. I also thank Vivian Curran and Stacie Strong for their valuable criticisms, hints, and suggestions.

---

[1] This is true for nearly 90 countries, i.e., almost half of the world's jurisdictions, Strong et al. (2016) 5 (fn. 8).

[2] See Reimann (2014).

M. Reimann (✉)
University of Michigan Law School, Ann Arbor, MI, USA

N. Etcheverry Estrázulas (ed.), *Bilingual Study and Research*, Ius Comparatum – Global Studies in Comparative Law 58,
https://doi.org/10.1007/978-3-030-84550-6_15

For US-American lawyers, this creates a peculiar situation. On the one hand, the global predominance of legal English gives them a significant professional advantage: their native language is the lingua franca of the world today.[3] On the other hand, it dramatically diminishes their need to master any other tongue since they can get away with English much, if not most, of the time. Thus, as Judge Posner noted (in a case turning on potentially different meanings in French and English), "most Americans, even when otherwise educated, make little investment in acquiring even a reading knowledge of a foreign language."[4]

Posner's statement also describes, by and large, the status quo in US-American legal education. As we will see, efforts to train students in foreign legal languages play a decidedly marginal role (infra. Sect. 2).[5] This is true despite the fact that acquisition of foreign language capabilities does actually have significant professional and educational benefits (Sect. 3). If US law schools wanted to make greater efforts in foreign language training, they could draw on a significant talent pool, both among their faculty and their student population (Sect. 4). As the Conclusion (Sect. 5) postulates, US law schools actually *should* make greater efforts, albeit within reasonable limits - not only to let more students reap the benefits of exposure to foreign languages, but also to counter the current political trend towards nationalism and isolationism.

At the outset, a clarification is in order. "Bilingual legal education" can be understood in various ways. Strictly speaking, it means teaching full fluency in two legal languages. Yet, this is so difficult to accomplish that it remains beyond the reach of the vast majority of students. This Report construes the term more broadly. It also includes the teaching of modest foreign language skills which most of students can acquire with reasonable effort.

2 The Status Quo: The Marginal Role of Foreign Language Training

Assessing the status quo of foreign language teaching in US-American legal education is difficult because comprehensive data are hard to come by. There are over 200 accredited law schools in the United States. They are not part of the federal system of government. Some are chartered under the laws of the various states and thus public, many are operated as private organizations. Thus, they function in a largely decentralized fashion. They are, however, connected through two nationwide organizations. First, the American Bar Association (ABA) supervises their

[3] Of course, there are many varieties of English, particularly in the law; even in English, legal terms often have somewhat different meaning.

[4] Bodum v. La Cafetière, Inc., 621 F.3d 623, 633 (7th Cir. 2010) (Posner, J., concurring).

[5] For a collection of essays on bilingual legal education in countries where the population speaks more than one language, see Arzoz (2012), reviewed by Strong (2014), pp. 358–360.

compliance with its accreditation standards; yet, since foreign language teaching is not a requirement, the ABA does not collect information about it. Second, the majority of schools are members of the Association of American Law Schools (AALS); that organization, however, does not systematically gather data about foreign language teaching either. As a result, the following descriptions are based on information obtained primarily from the individual law schools' websites by the research staff of the University of Michigan Law Library; these data were gathered in July of 2017. While this information is thus not necessarily fully comprehensive, it does provide a fairly reliable picture of the situation.[6]

This picture shows that foreign language teaching in US law schools is currently quite rare. To be sure, it is no longer true that, as Gloria Sanchez wrote over 20 years ago, there are no foreign language courses.[7] Today, there are a variety of curricular offerings introducing US law students to law in a foreign language, and a few law schools have made serious efforts in that direction.[8] Still, on the whole, exposure to law in a language other than English plays a distinctly marginal role.

The existing offerings can be divided into three groups: dual degree programs (1), individual foreign language courses at US law schools (2), and opportunities to study or work abroad (3).

2.1 *Dual Degree Programs: True Bilingualism?*

More than 30 law schools claim to offer joint degree programs with foreign institutions, sometimes in several countries. In most of these programs, US law students obtain the basic law degree in the respective foreign jurisdiction in addition to their home institution's JD; in some, they spent a year abroad and receive the more limited LLM degree. The total number of these law schools - about one in seven of those accredited by the ABA—looks more impressive than it really is in the context of foreign language teaching. While almost all these joint programs are with institutions in non-English speaking countries, many do not require full fluency in, and some not even significant command of, the partner country's vernacular. In addition, while enrolment numbers are hard to come by, indications are that only a very small number of students actually pursue a joint degree with a foreign university.[9] As a result, these programs immerse only a tiny fraction of US law students in a foreign language.

[6] A list of schools offering courses in foreign languages is also provided by Strong (2014), p. 355 (fn. 6) though it is not, and does not claim to be, complete.

[7] Sanchez (1997), p. 639.

[8] See Rathod (2013), p. 866 (fn. 2).

[9] Again, concrete data are difficult to find. The only information that Columbia Law School, which has dual degree programs both with the University of Paris I (Sorbonne) and the Paris Institute of Political Studies (Sciences Po), could provide was that "at least a few students are going to the Sorbonne every year" (telephone conversation between Virginia Neisler, University of Michigan

Still, where they do require fluency, these programs provide significant exposure to the law of another country in the vernacular. This does not necessarily lead to full-fledged bilingualism in the sense that students become as capable in the foreign tongue as they are in English, especially in the legal and business context. But they can be expected to reach a level of proficiency that enables them to perform professional work in at least one foreign language.

2.2 *Courses at US Law Schools: Degrees of Immersion*

Foreign language courses in US law schools have a surprisingly long history. The Louisiana Law Center offered a course in Legal French as early as in 1930s and 1940s[10] (and does so again today); at the University of Michigan, Konrad Zweigert taught an introductory course in German in 1956/57 on an ad hoc basis;[11] Vanderbilt University Law School began a course in Legal (and Business) Spanish in 1976[12] which, however, seems to have been discontinued; and Herbert Bernstein taught a course in legal German at Duke in the 1990s. Still, for the time being such courses were extremely rare exceptions. They became somewhat more frequent only around the turn of the century in the wake of globalization.

Today, of the accredited law schools in the United States, more than 40 claim on their websites to offer courses in one or more foreign languages—about one in five institutions. This is a significant number, although one must be careful not to overrate it. First, it is still a distinct (ca. 20%) minority. Second, it is unclear how many of the courses advertised are actually taught on a regular basis. Third, as with dual degree programs, the number of participating students seems to be quite small.[13] On the whole, it is fair to assume that, at the very most, a few hundred out of more than 100,000 US law students in the United States ever take a course in a foreign legal language.

The design and coverage of the courses varies. Most of them focus directly on foreign (legal) *language* training for American lawyers; these courses may or may not require preexisting language competence. Where they introduce students also to aspects of the respective foreign legal systems, they do so more or less incidentally

Law School Library, and Columbia representative of the dual degree programs, December 14, 2017). As director of the University of Pittsburgh Law School's dual degree program with the University of Paris I, Vivian Grosswald Curran reported that is not easy to find students able and willing to participate; e-mail from Vivian Grosswald Curran, October 9, 2017.

[10]Ward (1996), p. 1314.

[11]Conard and Stein (1957).

[12]Lacey and Garcia Reyes (1981).

[13]The number of students enrolled in the various foreign language courses at the University of Pittsburgh, for example, has ranged from 3 to 13; statistics provided by Vivian Curran to the author per e-mail, October 9, 2017; see also Crank and Loughrin-Sacco (2001), p. 203 (Boise State University; never more than 12 students).

and in order to provide a cultural context.[14] A few courses, however, are designed as introductions to the basic features of foreign *legal systems* in a foreign language.[15] Here, students can acquire a deeper understanding of the context and culture from which the (legal) language derives its meaning. In addition, there are a few specialized subjects taught in foreign languages.[16] Occasionally, instructors have also combined courses about domestic subjects with a foreign language component. Examples include teaching a regular course in immigration law or criminal justice in English with the option of taking an additional credit in Spanish; this allows students to prepare for working with clients who cannot effectively communicate in English.[17]

2.3 Going Overseas: Studying and Working Abroad

Many US law schools run summer programs abroad, usually in attractive locations and often in non-English speaking environments, sometimes providing more touristic than educational value. The majority of these programs are taught exclusively to US law students and entirely in English. A notable exception is the Inter-American Summer Program offered by the University of the Pacific McGeorge School of Law since 2009 (jointly with the Denver Sturm School of Law since 2011) in Guatemala: students come from both the United States and the host country, and instruction is in both English and Spanish.

A large number of American law schools also offer semester abroad programs in partnership with foreign universities, often in multiple venues (Columbia Law School lists 20).[18] This provides US students with plenty of opportunity to study in a non-English speaking country. Yet, it does not necessarily involve foreign legal language training either. In many of these semester abroad programs, the local coursework is all in English. In others, however, students are required to take classes, in whole or in part, in the local language. They must therefore be generally fluent

[14] See, e.g., Curran (1993).

[15] E.g., the Introduction to the Continental Legal Systems taught in Spanish at the Washington College of Law at American University, see Rathod (2013), p. 899 (fn. 137).

[16] An example is Vivian Grosswald Curran's course *L'arbitrage international* which is taught in French at the University of Pittsburgh Law School; e-mail from Vivian Grosswald Curran, October 9, 2017.

[17] Rathod (2014) (course at American University Washington College of Law); Crank. Loughrin (2001). See also Dutton et al. (2013), p. 43. Law clinics also sometimes conduct meetings in the clients' language, especially in Spanish, see Rathod (2013).

[18] According to the various websites of US law schools, students can spend a semester abroad in a very broad of range of countries, including Argentina, Belgium, Brazil, China, France, Guatemala, Germany, Israel, Italy, Japan, Mexico, the Netherlands, Norway, Sweden, Spain, Taiwan as well as (at least linguistically foreign) Puerto Rico.

when they arrive and can then acquire knowledge of the respective *legal* terminology.

Finally, there are many opportunities for externships in foreign countries. But again, in many cases they do not require fluency in the local language, either because the placement is an English-speaking jurisdiction or because the host institution works in English, as is true for most international governmental or non-governmental organizations. Yet, where US students do work in a foreign language, externships provide valuable opportunities to acquire legal language fluency and, at the same time, to gain an understanding of the respective foreign legal culture.

Of course, if a student has mastered a foreign language, and especially the legal terminology, his or her options for study or externships in other countries are much increased. An ideal combination is thus to study a foreign legal language at home and then to perfect it by immersing oneself in it abroad.

2.4 Languages Covered: Towards a More Global Range

The scope of languages covered by courses in US law schools remains somewhat Euro-centric but there is a trend towards a more global range.

By far the most frequently taught foreign (legal) language in US law schools and programs is Spanish, a global language in its own right. This is unsurprising. By now, Hispanics comprise nearly one fifth of the US population; the United States borders on a country with nearly 130 million Spanish speakers; and business ties with Latin America are extremely important.

Language instruction is also offered in the other two most prominent Western European languages, i.e., French and German, and sometimes in Italian, In addition, today some law schools have classes in languages from other regions of the world, including Arabic, Chinese (Mandarin), and Hebrew.

2.5 Teaching Materials: The Predominance of Spanish

The published teaching materials both reflect and fortify the primacy of Spanish in the language programs of US law schools. In recent years, three books were published for use by teachers of Spanish as a foreign legal language. They vary in objective and character. Victoria Ortiz, Espanol para Abogados (2013), is written in Spanish and aims primarily at the acquisition of Spanish legal terminology. Katia Fach Gómez, El Derecho en Espanol, Terminologia y Habilidades Juridicas para un Ejercicio Legal Exitoso (2014), is also written exclusively in Spanish but proffers more of an introduction to the study and practice of law in Spanish speaking countries as well as to several substantive areas of law. Finally, S.I. Strong, Katia Fach Gómez and Laura Carballo Piñeiro, Comparative Law for Spanish-English

Speaking Lawyers, Derecho Comparado para abogados anglo- e hispanoparlantes (2016), provides a bi-lingual and comparative perspective on key aspects of the Anglo-American and civil law systems in the Hispanic tradition, such as the legal, business, and social cultures, sources of law, select topics of substantive and procedural law, and various "practical issues."

There is also a textbook for teaching legal French: Vivian Curran, Learning French through the Law, A Comparative Treatment of Terms in a Legal Context (1996). Its goal is to make students rapidly reach considerable fluency but also to convey cultural information and to introduce students to aspects of French society.

Beyond these four books covering Spanish and French there are no pertinent publications. The market for teaching materials involving other languages, it seems, is just too small. Thus instructors of legal Arabic, Chinese, German, Italian or Hebrew are on their own. This is in stark contrast to the abundance of teaching materials in English designed for instruction in non-English speaking countries; the market for such materials is essentially global and thus huge.

3 The Benefits: Three Reasons to Teach Law in a Foreign Language

In the last 25 years, the benefits of studying law in a foreign language have been explored quite extensively in US-American legal scholarship.[19] They can be grouped in three categories. The advantage that most immediately comes to mind is directly professional: a lawyer who can work in a foreign language can better attract and communicate with non-English speaking clients—of which there are many not only abroad but also in the United States themselves (1). Beyond that, learning law in a foreign language is an opportunity to acquire sensitivity to foreign cultures—an important professional asset in its own right, particularly in a global environment (2). Finally, there is reason to believe that studying foreign languages is generally good brain training—especially for lawyers (3).[20]

[19] The most thorough discussion is Rathod (2013). This section draws heavily on that article.

[20] To these benefits for US-American law students as individuals, Rathod adds a systemic dimension: bilingual lawyers "will transform and invigorate interactions between attorneys and limited English proficiency (LEP) clients and, more broadly, among attorneys, the parties to a proceeding, and the legal decision makers," Rathod (2013), p. 863. He then explores this systemic dimension in greater detail, id. 890–898.

3.1 Working in a Foreign Language: Clients with Insufficient English

Being able to work in a foreign language generates career advantages (Sect. 3.1.1), avoids misunderstandings (Sect. 3.1.2), and helps to provide access to justice, to protect client dignity, and arguably even to fulfill ethical obligations (Sect. 3.1.3).

3.1.1 Career Advantages

For an American lawyer, the ability to work in a foreign language is, to put it bluntly, good for his or her career and business. It is easy to see why: today, a growing number of attorneys have to represent clients whose native language is not English. This is most obvious in the international context: many US lawyers now work across international boundaries and thus with clients or colleagues from non-English speaking jurisdictions.[21] But it is also true on the purely domestic level: American society has long been, and remains, multilingual, and almost 10% of the US population does not "speak English well."[22]

It is true, of course, that many of these clients, both abroad and at home, will have some command of English. Where that command extends to the legal and business context, as in the case of many Western European lawyers and business people, the American lawyer will be able to work in English without much trouble. Even in that case, however, an understanding of the respective foreign language will help to avoid misunderstandings (see infra. Sect. 3.1.2). Where the foreign party's command is poor, the American lawyer will have to communicate at least in part in the respective foreign tongue. Of course, he or she can, and may even have to, employ a translator, but that is merely a second best, especially if he or she is not versed in the respective legal and business terminology. In either case, command of the foreign parties' language is a distinct professional advantage, even if only because "[c]lients *like* it when their lawyer speaks [their] language."[23]

It is therefore not surprising that in the United States, lawyers with foreign language skills appear to be in growing demand.[24] To be sure, the strength of their market advantage depends on their field of work. It is especially great in international

[21] Note that here, they compete with foreign lawyers whose command of English is usually very good—and often better than the American lawyers' command of the respective foreign language.

[22] According to a 2011 census, that is estimated to be true for 8.7% of the US population, see Language Spoke at Home, U.S. Census Bureau (2011), quoted by Rathod (2013), p. 869. That amounts to about 30 million people—almost equivalent to the population of all of Canada.

[23] Acello (2013).

[24] Anon (2009); Volkert (2013); see Crank and Loughrin-Sacco (2001) (for the special context of criminal justice work); Curran (1993), p. 605.

practice,[25] particularly with Asia and Latin America, as well as in immigration and other public interest work[26] but much smaller, e.g., in the purely domestic commercial context. On the whole, attorneys with foreign language capabilities help firms to attract clients who are not native English speakers, and these clients constitute a very sizeable pool.

For academics, command of a foreign language and its legal terminology opens up avenues of comparative research. It is true that a lot of foreign legal material is now available in English, but serious, in-depth, comparative study still requires access to foreign law in the vernacular.

3.1.2 Avoiding Misunderstandings

As every international lawyer (and every comparative law scholar) knows, legal terms often have very specific meanings which may differ from one language to another.[27] Thus working across linguistic boundaries is rife with opportunities for misunderstanding which are mildly embarrassing at best and catastrophic for client interests at worst. Avoiding them requires understanding the languages involved. How deep that understanding must be depends on the problem.

Sometimes the problem is simply that literal translations are badly misleading, even among Western languages: *jurisprudence* means case law in France but (something like) legal theory in England; a *notario* is a highly qualified legal professional with a quasi-public office in Mexico (similar to a *notaire* in France, a *Notar* in Germany, etc.) but a legally untrained person performing essentially clerical functions in the United States; and a *regulation* under EU law denotes legislation directly applicable in the member states while it is an administrative rule in many domestic legal systems.[28] To avoid such—rather obvious—pitfalls, it is normally sufficient to master the respective legal *terminologies* which can be accomplished in a foreign legal language course.

Other terms translate more directly but their meaning is still highly context specific—they sound alike but still do not mean exactly the same. An Italian *contratto* does not require consideration while an English *contract* normally does;

---

[25] Various international governmental organizations have expressed their interest in a greater number of bilingual lawyers, see Strong (2014), p. 354 (with further references).

[26] See Volkert (2013); Anon (2008).

[27] Of course, this is often true with non-legal terms as well, as illustrated by the well-known contract case of Frigaliment Importing Co. v. B.N.S. International Sales Corp., 190 F.Supp. 116 (S.D.N.Y. 1960); see the discussion by Sanchez (1997), pp. 663–664.

[28] For another striking example (English *investment* v. Spanish *inversion*), see Sanchez (1997), pp. 662–663. Terms can have different meanings even where legal systems share a common language: "judicial review" in the United States usually means constitutional scrutiny of legislation, in England, it commonly means review of administrative action. In Germany, *Verfügung* means a legal act affecting private property rights; in Switzerland, it can also mean an administrative decision (for which the term in German is *Verwaltungsakt*).

the office of the Argentine *Presidente (de la Nacion)* is very different from that of the German *(Bundes)Präsident*; and in France, labor law (*droit du travail*) encompasses individual employment relationships while in the United States, it does not. In fact, some terms are so particular to certain legal environments that they cannot be effectively translated at all, as is the case for *amparo*, *Obligation* or *Conseil d'Etat*. Handling these kinds of difficulties presupposes more than just knowledge of legal terminology. It requires an understanding of the respective foreign *legal system* and can thus only be acquired in an introduction to that system, preferably in the vernacular.

Finally, some terms are so deeply rooted in culture—think of *due process* in Anglo-American English, *Rechtsstaat* in German or *li* in Chinese—that they can be grasped only by someone with a thorough understanding of the respective tradition. Such an understanding requires deep immersion in the foreign legal and social environment. This, in turn, almost invariably requires studying, working or even living in the respective foreign country for a substantial period of time.

3.1.3 Access to Justice, Client Dignity, and Professional Obligations

The ability to communicate with clients who do not have a full command of English is not only a career advantage and a tool to avoid misunderstandings, it also promotes access to justice. It is a widely recognized problem that the nearly 10% of the American population with little or no command of English face particularly great difficulties in a legal system operating overwhelmingly in that language.[29] As a result, they are in dire need of legal assistance and thus of American lawyers with whom they can effectively communicate. This is especially true because limited English capability is strongly related to recent immigrant status and low socioeconomic position as well as to race. The majority of people in this category are poor and poorly educated; thus they already have extremely limited access to justice. As a result, the need for American lawyers with foreign language skills is particularly great in areas like immigration, employment, poverty, and criminal law.[30]

American scholars have also justly pointed out that communicating with a client in his or her own (native) language creates a human connection and avoids degradation. It is a sign of "respect for the individuality of the interlocutor and an acknowledgment of her basic human dignity."[31] A person's language is an important part of his or her identity. Ignoring it "threatens a client's autonomy."[32] In particular,

[29] See Standing Committee on Legal Aid (2012); Dutton et al. (2013), pp. 22–23 (also noting that there is a considerable body of constitutional, statutory and regulatory law on access to courts in the United States); Uyehara (2003), pp. 544–557.

[30] For a fuller discussion of these issues, see Ahmed (2007).

[31] Rathod (2013), p. 885.

[32] Ahmed (2007), p. 1024.

it can severely diminish the client's power to make decisions, to enforce rights or invoke defenses.

There is even an argument that lawyers have a legal duty effectively to address language difficulties of clients without a full command of English. Such a duty can arguably be found in the Rules of Professional Conduct that govern lawyer-client relationships in the United States.[33] While these rules do not specifically address language issues, they do require lawyers to represent their clients competently, i.e., with the requisite skill and diligence, as well as to ensure reasonable communication with their clients.[34] From these duties, several scholars have convincingly derived an obligation for lawyers to bridge the gap between English and their client's language.[35] To be sure, this does not require that the lawyer command the client's (foreign) language, though it will greatly help if he or she does. But it does require that the lawyer be aware of translation and communication pitfalls so that he or she can take the necessary steps to avoid them. That, in turn, is much easier for someone who has experience with a foreign language.

3.2 *Acquiring Cultural Awareness: Foreign Mindsets*

The intimate connection between language, law, and culture has been well-known at least since Friedrich Carl von Savigny propagated it as a foundational idea for his Historical School of Law two centuries ago.[36] It is not only a standard topic in comparative law[37] but has also been much discussed by advocates of multilingual legal education in the United States.[38] The cultural awareness students can acquire by experiencing law in a foreign language has three main dimensions: access to a particular foreign (legal) culture (infra. Sect. 3.2.1), sensitivity regarding cultural differences generally (Sect. 3.2.2), and, as a beneficial side-effect, better understanding of one's own legal culture (Sect. 3.2.3.)[39]

---

[33] While each state has its own set of rules, they are largely based on the American Bar Association's Model Rules of Professional Conduct (1983). In the United States, such rules are known as "professional ethics." The term is somewhat misleading because the rules are actually legal in character; they are enforced by the respective bar associations through a variety of sanctions including disbarment.

[34] See American Bar Association (1983), Rules 1.1., 1.3., and 1.4.

[35] Ahmed (2007), pp. 1019–1024; Rathod (2013), pp. 886–889; Sanchez (1997), p. 641.

[36] von Savigny (1814), pp. 8–16; von Savigny (1831), pp. 24–31. Of course, the intimate connection between law and culture had already been discussed by Montesqieu (1748); and the intimate connection between language, thought, and culture had been pointed out by Herder (1784–1790).

[37] See Curran (2019), pp. 681–709.

[38] See, e.g., Curran (2019); Sanchez (1997), pp. 658–660.

[39] The concept of a "legal culture" is complex and contested. This Report is not the place to delve into the debate. For an overview, see Cotterrell (2019), pp. 710–733.

3.2.1 Access to a Particular Foreign Legal Culture

"[K]nowing a second language allows entry into another world."[40] This is true in a dual sense. First, understanding a foreign (legal) language not only opens up the meaning of its terms and texts, it can also provide access to the way lawyers in the respective legal culture *think*—how they structure legal material, analyze problems, and argue positions—in short: it provides access to their legal mentality and style. Note that this does not require full fluency.[41] Much can be learned about foreign legal mentalities by way of carefully picked illustrations.[42] Second, mastering a foreign (legal) language also allows "entry into another world" in a more literal sense, i.e., by enabling students to go abroad and expose themselves to another legal culture. There, they can experience the foreign mentality from close-up. Such on-the-ground exposure, however, does require fluency because without it, the student cannot to immerse him- or herself in the foreign environment.

In addition, understanding one particular legal culture facilitates access to closely related ones, e.g., those shaped by the strong Spanish influence in Latin America. Understanding Mexican law from a Spanish perspective is much easier than from an US-American point of view. Still, one must resist the assumption that since two legal cultures share a language, they are also otherwise the same. A US-American lawyer need only look to England to recognize how wrong that assumption can be.[43]

Understanding a foreign legal culture is not a mere educational luxury but a significant professional asset. It enables a US-American lawyer to work effectively with colleagues and clients from the respective legal system. He or she will be able not only to avoid linguistic misunderstandings but also to bridge the gap between his or her own and the foreign parties' styles and habits of negotiation, drafting, interpretation, and dispute resolution.[44]

3.2.2 General Cultural Sensitivity

Experiencing the differences between their own and a particular foreign legal environment also makes students more sensitive to cultural differences in general. At minimum they will be aware that lawyers and clients in other countries often make assumptions, have predilections, and cultivate habits that differ significantly, if

---

[40] Curran (2019), p. 680.

[41] This is pointed out by Curran (2005), pp. 779–780, 782.

[42] It is interesting to note, for example, that many (especially civil law) systems define legal concepts much more clearly, precisely, and uniformly than is common in the United States. This shows a much greater preference for clear demarcations of legal concepts and categories and a concomitantly greater discomfort with ambiguous terminology. In the mind of a French, German, or Mexican jurist, law is a precise "science"—at least as a theoretical ideal, even if that ideal cannot always be reached in practice.

[43] 5 See Atiyah and Summers (1987).

[44] For an illustration in the US-Mexican context, see Sanchez (1997), pp. 672–673.

not radically, from the students' own mentality. Even if a lawyer, confronted with an alien culture, does not understand exactly *how* its members' minds operate, he or she will be more attentive to differences, observe more carefully, and hold back with his or her own assumptions. This not only helps to avoid embarrassing blunders, it also increases the speed and efficiency of learning about the other culture.

Such general cultural awareness is an important professional benefit as well. This is especially true in international legal practice where US-American lawyers often have to deal with colleagues and clients from many different systems. Having acquired at least *some* understanding of at least *one* foreign legal culture helps them to navigate even between unknown ones. For these reasons, intercultural skills are high on many employers' lists of job qualifications for lawyers they seek to hire.[45]

3.2.3 Understanding One's Own Culture

About two centuries ago, Goethe famously wrote that "[h]e who does not know foreign languages knows nothing of his own."[46] The same can be said (with equal exaggeration) about law and legal culture. As comparative lawyers have touted for many decades in advertising their discipline, experiencing a foreign legal system and culture almost inevitably entails a much better understanding of our own. It opens our eyes to features of the domestic environment that we did not notice before because we took them for granted. Once we recognize these features, however, it is but a small step to wonder about their underlying reasons, and only a slightly bigger step to reflect upon their advantages and disadvantages. When Americans taking a law course in a foreign language learn that the French and Italians address their lawyers by academic titles ("maitre", "dottore"), they suddenly realize that this is not done in the United States, may think about what explains the difference, and consider the consequences. When they learn that the Spanish term "codigo" has different implications than the Anglo-American word "code", they will realize that in Mexico, more law than in the United States is written down in systematically organized blackletter rules; then they may, again, begin to wonder why Americans tolerate that much of their law remains a more disorganized state.[47] And if they experience that in many other cultures, constitutional law does not play an overwhelming role at all, they will see more clearly how pervasive that role is at home;

---

[45] See Slaughter, The International Dimension of the Law School Curriculum (2004), pp. 417–418.

[46] "Wer fremde Sprachen nicht kennt, weiß nichts von seiner eigenen." Goethe (1907, orig. 1838), p. 18 As was quite common for the educated upper middle class in 18th century Germany, Goethe had studied the classical languages, i.e., Greek, Latin and Hebrew, as well as the most important modern ones, i.e., French and English.

[47] In a similar vein, Sanchez (1997), p. 665, points out the different significance of categorization of legal material in the civil and common law traditions. Modes of categorization, in turn, determine conceptions of reason and reasoning processes, see Lakoff (1987).

then, they can ask why Americans seek so much judicial control of political processes and decisions.

It must be admitted that the immediate professional utility of these reflections upon one's own legal culture is very limited. But they do broaden the students' views, improve their acumen, and stimulate their imagination.

3.3 Enhancing Cognitive Abilities: Brain-Training for Lawyers

Studies suggest that individuals with advanced skills in more than one language acquire mental abilities that go way beyond understanding the languages themselves. Such individuals are not inherently more intelligent than their monolingual colleagues, but there is a strong argument that they better develop particular cognitive functions. This argument is based on vast and complex research in cognitive psychology and psycholinguistics the results of which can be presented here only in very rough outline.[48] Legal scholars have added the—highly plausible—argument that there is a "striking consonance between these advantages and the core skills needed for effective law practice."[49]

To begin with, bilingual persons are particularly apt at "divergent thinking." Operating in just one language "imprisons thought and understanding" but operating in "many languages liberate[s] them."[50] Bilingualism opens the lawyer's mind to multiple options and solutions; it also makes him or her comfortable with a multitude of competing or complementary meanings. For lawyers, this is directly helpful in working through client problems and in interpreting texts. Furthermore, bilingual individuals are often better at "executive control" of information. Switching back and forth between languages, their brains have learned to sort and rank information according to its current relevance. This arguably helps lawyers to distinguish facts or arguments pertinent to their case from less relevant or unimportant matter; is also aids them in focusing on the former without being distracted by the latter. In addition, experience with multiple languages teaches individuals better analytical and critical skills in dealing with verbal information. They are more open to varying grammatical structures and more attentive to nuances of meaning. Finally, using multiple languages entails generally greater sensitivity in communication; this is especially true when it is combined with the experience of living in multiple cultural environments. The results are better ability to detect verbal and non-verbal cues and greater attention to the (often unexpressed) intents and needs of others.

[48] For a much fuller discussion, see Rathod (2013), pp. 871–883.

[49] Rathod (2013), p. 878; see also Curran (2019), pp. 686–687.

[50] Curran (2019), p. 687. As Umberto Eco put it: "A language always is a prison. . .because it imposes a certain vision of the world." quoted after id., fn. 19.

To be sure, the picture is complicated. The degree to which bilinguals really develop these skills is contested in the scientific literature, and it has been shown to depend on a multitude of variables.[51] Some studies also suggest that bilingualism has its downsides, like lower semantic and verbal fluency.[52] On the whole, however, there are strong reasons to believe that studying law in a foreign language enhances a lawyer's "social intelligence"[53] and "communicative sensitivity"[54] Both are highly useful mental assets - even when dealing with domestic clients in English.

3.4 The Varying Scope of Benefits: Language Skills and Beyond

In order properly to gauge the educational value of studying law in a foreign language one must recognize that the benefits we have discussed vary in scope and character.

The direct practical benefit of being able to work with clients and colleagues without a full command of English is largely limited to the language studied: having taken a law class in Spanish does not enable a lawyer to work with a speaker of Russian or Japanese. Yet, even on this purely operational level, *to some extent* the understanding gained by studying in one foreign language is useful with regard to others as well: an American student who has experienced the translation pitfalls, varying meanings, and cultural contingency of terms with regard to Spanish, will also be aware of these difficulties with regard to Russian or Chinese. As a lawyer, he or she will no longer easily trust literal translations from or into any language but rather seek a contextual and culturally informed understanding of terms or texts, if need be with the help of a foreign colleague.

The benefit of understanding foreign cultures is broader than that of mere linguistic skills. Of course, it is also strongest with regard to the particular language and culture studied: a course on Spanish law taught in Spanish and with the requisite attention to the cultural context provides access particularly to the way Spanish jurists think about their law, and perhaps more broadly, to how Spanish people think about their legal system, state, and society. It helps a student less with regard to the (legal) culture of other countries. Yet, as we have seen, it helps even there. It facilitates access to related legal cultures. And it alerts students generally to law's cultural contingency. It thus makes them aware that even if the foreign rules or institutions look similar to their home-grown counterparts, they may function very differently and generate very different outcomes. This will protect even a student

[51] Rathod (2013), pp. 880–882.

[52] Id., 882–883.

[53] Id., 880.

[54] Id., 879.

who took an introduction to Spanish law against the facile assumption that the law in Japan works pretty much like the law at home.

Finally, the benefits of the brain training derived from dealing with law in a foreign language have the broadest scope. It is true that they are not entirely independent of the particular language studied: the more it differs from the student's baseline language, the harder the mental workout and, presumably, the greater the benefits. On the whole, however, the cognitive abilities that can be acquired by studying law in a foreign language are essentially generic: enhanced mental creativity, productive imagination, and social intelligence are generally useful in the practice of law.

As a result of these variations, the choice exactly which foreign language to study is also of varying importance. It is crucial when the student's primary goal is to work with particular foreign countries or segments of the domestic population. In this regard, Spanish must be the top contender in a US law school. The choice of language is somewhat less important when the primary goal is to acquire general cultural sensitivity. In that case, a student may want to pick a language and culture that is not easily experienced close by, but that is still accessible to a Western mind, such as French or German. If the primary goal is brain training, i.e., the acquisition of general cognitive skills, the choice of language is least important. For a maximum workout, the brave can tackle a non-Western language that forces them to think in radically different ways.

4 The Possibilities: Talent Pools and Teaching Options

We have found that when it comes to teaching in a foreign language, US law schools currently do fairly little, but we have also recognized that there are good reasons to do more. It is now time to look at the possibilities. What do American law schools have to work with in terms of student and faculty talent pools, and what are the realistic teaching options?

4.1 Foreign Language Skills Among Students

An important consideration is the existing language talent pool among law students. Of course, law schools can teach a course in a foreign language without requiring any previous knowledge of it. Yet, a course can introduce students to the foreign legal terminology much more quickly and easily if they already have at least a basic knowledge of the respective language. Moreover, an introduction to a foreign legal system in the vernacular requires (at least conversational) fluency.

Americans students (and Americans in general) have the reputation, especially abroad, of being hopelessly monolingual.[55] This reputation is not entirely undeserved when they are compared to students in many other countries where foreign languages are taught and thus spoken much more commonly. Still, there is reason to believe that the problem of American monolingualism is exaggerated. After all, the United States continues to be a country of immigrants with about a million new arrivals per year. By far most immigrants come from non-English speaking jurisdictions (especially Mexico and other Latin American countries as well as China and other Asian nations), bringing foreign languages with them. As a result, about 20% of people living in the United States today speak a language other than English at home.[56] Thus, a substantial percentage of students should know a foreign language at least on the conversational level.[57]

Exactly what percentage of US-American J.D. students[58] have a sufficient command to take a course in a foreign language is almost impossible to determine because nobody seems to keep any statistics.[59] I thus conducted a survey of the J.D. students at my own law school (the University of Michigan) in the fall term of 2017. I asked all students (per e-mail) whether they had the language skills to take an introductory course to a foreign legal system in the vernacular.[60] Of the 196 respondents, 100 said they did. They listed a total of 26 languages, most prominently Spanish (42), Chinese (Mandarin) (16), French (16), and German (14).[61] Of course, these data have to be taken with a huge grain of salt. With a response rate of ca. 20% (196 out of 929), the answers are not necessarily representative for the Law School's whole J.D. population; this is especially true since students with language skills were

[55] See supra note 4 and text.

[56] Dutton et al. (2013), p. 9.

[57] Also, most graduate students in the United States have almost surely been exposed to some foreign language teaching. They all have college degrees, and most colleges still impose a language requirement for graduation. Unfortunately, however, college study of foreign languages rarely results in fluency.

[58] We leave students in the various masters (LLM) programs aside here. It is true that most of them come from foreign, and indeed from non-English speaking, jurisdictions and thus have a native knowledge of a foreign language. Yet, they are obviously not the audience for foreign language courses at a US law school. The domestic students in LLM programs have a obtained a J.D. degree and are thus part of the J.D. language talent pool.

[59] We know the number of J.D. students coming from foreign countries, but it remains small (the ca. 3500 foreign J.D. students amount to less than 3% of the ca. 124,000 students enrolled in US law schools in 2016), and at least some of them come from English-speaking countries like the United Kingdom or Australia. The percentage of Hispanic or Asian students could provide some indication of existing language skills but their overall number is difficult to assess because existing statistics lump all minority students together and because not all of the students from these regions count as minorities. Also, not all of them still speak the language of their family origin.

[60] Note that this is a higher threshold than may be required for a course merely on foreign legal terminology.

[61] Other languages listed by multiple students were Arabic, Japanese, Russian, Hindi, and Korean, Cantonese, and Italian.

probably much more likely to respond than those without, much as I tried to work against that.[62] Assuming that they were twice as likely to do so, the survey would still indicate that almost a quarter of all J.D. students are capable of taking a law course in a foreign language, including about 10% in Spanish.[63] Of course, there is also the question of how representative the student population at the University of Michigan is with regard to all J.D. students in the United States. On the one hand, perhaps students at an elite ("top ten") law school have more language skills than the average; on the other hand, perhaps a law school with very high admission standards does not enroll as many recent immigrants from Latin America and Asia or other regions.

At minimum, the data support the claim that even in US law schools, there is a significant potential audience for classes taught in foreign languages. Unsurprisingly, this is mainly true for Spanish—which also happens to be the language with the greatest practical utility at least in the domestic context. As immigration from Asia continues apace, it will be increasingly true for Chinese as well.

4.2 Foreign Language Skills Among Faculty

Even if a significant number of students have the skills to take classes in a foreign language, law schools still need faculty to teach them. Is there a sufficient number of instructors to perform that task?

Again, there are no statistics about the foreign language capabilities of American law faculty members. Extrapolation from existing data (e.g., about minority membership, non-resident alien instructors or visiting professors) is impossible because these data do not show the respective individuals' countries of origin, and they do not tell us anything at all about the language skills of anyone not in these groups.

In order to get at least one impression, I, again, conducted a survey at my law school, this time among my colleagues. In particular, I asked them whether they feel linguistically competent to teach a law course in a foreign language. Of 81 respondents 18 said yes. They listed mostly French (6) and German (4) but also Spanish (2) and Hebrew (2) as well Chinese (Mandarin), Hindi, Japanese, Lithuanian, and Portuguese (1 each).[64] This time, the response rate was 80% (81 out or 101) so that the data are roughly representative for the faculty. Even assuming that none of the 20 non-respondents could be added to this group, the result still means that almost one in five members of the Michigan law faculty considers him- or herself highly

[62] The instructions specifically encouraged the students without such language skills to check the box for "none," and the questionnaire put that box at the very top of the list of options.

[63] For what it is worth, my experience with our law students suggests that this is entirely plausible.

[64] This count does not include the foreign instructors who come and teach on a regular basis (Cook Global Law Professors). Including them adds one Korean and two German native speakers.

fluent in at least one language other than English.[65] Again, it is difficult to tell to what extent this picture is typical for US law faculties generally. On the one hand, the Michigan Law School is much more internationally oriented than the majority of American law schools; on the other hand, it has very few Hispanic or Asian minority members, nor is it located in area with a strong presence of Hispanics or Asians, unlike law schools in Florida, the Southwest and on the West Coast.

The data is in line with the impressions one gets from interacting with law school teachers in the United States more generally, e.g., at conference or workshops. Like their students, US law faculties are not as multilingual as their counterparts in many other countries, especially in Europe, but, also like their students, they are by no means entirely monolingual either.

4.3 A Dose of Realism

If it is true that a substantial percentage of US law students are linguistically prepared to take, and of law faculty to teach, a course in a foreign language, it is tempting to conclude that most American law schools could easily staff and fill such courses, at least for the languages most important in legal practice. Yet, the possibilities must be assessed with a dose of realism. Four particular caveats are in order.

First, student capability is not the same as student interest, not to mention student enrolment. To be sure, most American law schools will enroll students "who have studied foreign languages in the past and want to continue language acquisition," as well as students "whose goal is to enhance their practical skills for a life abroad or for international practice."[66] But that does not necessarily mean that "[f]oreign language courses in a legal context will find an enthusiastic reception from both [these] kinds of law students."[67] The enrolment numbers we have for such courses suggest that student interest is modest.[68] This is not surprising: law students are often so focused on other subjects, extracurricular activities, and their job search that they are loath to invest time and energy in courses that not only look exotic but are also entirely irrelevant for the bar exam. Yet, one must also consider that the level of student interest is not cast in stone. It is determined in part by a school's educational message and by the courses actually offered. If law schools explain, or even emphasize, the benefits of language training, and if they regularly offer classes in foreign languages, more students will become motivated to take them. This is especially likely if law schools advertise such courses in their promotional materials and thus attract

[65] I also asked who feels sufficiently competent to *take* a law course in a foreign language. 33 of the respondents said yes, i.e., about one third of the faculty. Beyond the languages mentioned in the text, they listed Guarati, Italian, and Russian.

[66] Curran (1993), p. 607.

[67] Id.

[68] Supra notes 9, 13.

applicants with the requisite skills and interests.[69] In addition, organizations of Hispanic, Asian-American or other ethnic student groups can promote the study of foreign languages. Even then, however, courses in a foreign language will engage only a minority of students, although perhaps a much larger one than at present.

Second, the fact that a respectable percentage of faculty members *could* teach in a foreign language does not mean that they *want to*, not to mention actually *will*. Most professors are busy enough with their existing course load and not looking for more time in the classroom, especially since professional rewards tend to result more from publication than from teaching. In addition, fluency in a foreign language is merely a necessary, but not a sufficient, qualification for teaching a law class in it. The instructor must also have sufficient knowledge of the underlying foreign legal system and culture. Ideally, he or she should hold a law degree from the respective jurisdiction. That, however, would narrow the pool of qualified faculty members in the United States to the vanishing point. But even if one requires a merely basic knowledge of the foreign legal system, few current faculty members would qualify. Thus in most law schools, staffing courses in a foreign language would require hiring adjuncts or foreign visitors; in addition to being pedagogically risky, that costs money deans will not spend happily in times of fiscal constraint. In the literature, it has been suggested that courses could be taught by a language instructor without any law degree.[70] This is a dubious proposition because it entails a serious risk that such an instructor lacks a sufficient understanding of (not mention feel for) legal terms and texts so that he or she may do more harm than good. The suggestion to use foreign graduate students enrolled in LLM programs[71] seem to be a safer option, assuming that they have the requisite teaching skills.

Third, there is the issue of teaching materials. As we have seen, there are now a respectable number of quality publications for law courses taught in Spanish and one option for French.[72] Beyond that, however, instructors have to create their own material. As everyone teaching a class from his or her own course pack knows, this is enormously time- and energy-consuming—and not rewarded beyond one's own classroom (or, at best, law school). Chances ever to publish teaching materials in languages other than Spanish are slim; publishers are often reluctant to accept bi- or multilingual texts for fear of an insufficiently large market. The only way to keep the burden of creating foreign language teaching material within reasonable limits is to share the work with several others.

Finally, there is the overarching consideration that, like all other aspects of the curriculum, teaching law in a foreign language must be evaluated from a cost-benefit

---

[69]Former ABA President Roberta Cooper Ramo suggested that in the admissions process, law schools "give some preference" to applicants with foreign language skills; Cooper (1996), pp. 313–314. However, that really makes sense only if law schools then provide students with an opportunity to use their language skills; as we have seen, that is currently much the exception.

[70]Curran (1993), p. 604; Lacey and Garcia Reyes (1981), p. 659.

[71]Curran (1993), p. 604; Lacey and Garcia Reyes (1981), id.

[72]Supra Sect. 2.4.

perspective.[73] In one's enthusiasm for a particular topic, it is easy to forget that law school time, faculty resources, and student energy are limited. Teaching or taking a course in a foreign language means foregoing other options. Whether these opportunity costs are justified depends on the circumstances—such as whether a law school seeks to train students particularly for international practice or for work with domestic minority language clients; whether a significant percentage of its graduates will serve non-English speaking communities; whether it enrolls a particularly substantial number of students with foreign language capabilities and interests; and whether faculty members have both the necessary qualifications and interests to teach law classes in a foreign tongue.

5 Conclusion: A Question of Commitment

American law schools currently proffer very limited training in foreign (legal) languages (supra Sect. 2). This is true even though such training generates multiple professional and educational benefits which are generally recognized in the literature (Sect. 3). The potential for expanding such foreign language training, in particular the talent pool among students and faculty, is stronger than the American reputation for monolingualism intimates; yet, a realistic assessment of the possibilities and a sober cost-benefit analysis suggest that courses in foreign languages neither will nor should be offered by all law schools or taken by a majority of students (Sect. 4).

Still, the current situation is deficient. The vast majority of American law schools, including my own, offer virtually no opportunities to experience law in a language other than English. As a result, the vast majority of American law students do not even have a chance to take a course in a foreign language—no matter how strong their skills and how serious their interests. At least where law schools have a substantial language talent pool among their students as well as the requisite resources, they should provide *some* foreign language options. Not offering a class even in Spanish is difficult to justify for any major US law school today. In light of American law schools' virtually ubiquitous claims to promote diversity and to train students for practice in a globalized society, such disregard of the language dimension is nothing short of embarrassing.

How can American law schools move towards offering instruction in foreign languages more broadly and frequently? It would probably help if the American Bar Association as their accrediting body and the Association of American Law Schools as their professional organization pushed in that direction; this would be a particularly good fit with these organizations' recent push toward more skills training in law schools.[74] Ultimately, however, offering foreign language instruction on a more regular basis is a question of every law school's institutional commitment. Such

[73] See Maxeiner (1998), pp. 35–36.

[74] See Strong (2014), p. 357 (with further references).

commitment needs to be based on a more common appreciation of the professional and educational advantages of studying law in a foreign tongue.[75]

In conclusion, it must be admitted that the current political climate in the United States is not supportive of foreign language study. Nationalism is resurgent and hostility towards immigration and immigrants appears to be on the rise. Yet, not all parts of American society are turning inward. Its universities, and especially its law schools, continue to look beyond national borders, and its legal profession is more engaged than ever with global business as well as attentive to immigration issues.

In fact, it is exactly because the wind from Washington, and more generally from the political right, is blowing in a nationalist and isolationist direction, that law schools should do what they can to counter that trend. Showing their students that law has an existence in languages other than English, promoting their foreign language skills, and especially teaching them greater sensitivity towards other cultures, keeps their minds open towards what Americans often call, with at least a touch of chauvinism, "the rest of the world."

References

Acello R (2013) Bilingual lawyers have a leg up in many niche practice groups. ABA Journal March 1, 2103, Available at http://www.abajournalcom/magazine/arcitle/bilingual_lawyers_have_a_leg-up-in_many_niche_practice_groups

Ahmed M (2007) Interpreting communities: lawyering across language difference. UCLA Law Rev 54:999–1086

American Bar Association (1983) Model rules of professional conduct. American Bar Association, Chicago

Anon (2008) Chapter Five - Making yourself marketable; Harvard Law School, Available at http://harvard.edu/content/uploads/2008/07ch5-making-yourself-marketable.pdf

Anon (2009) Bilingual attorneys find steady work. Wisconsin Law J Sept 29, 2009, Available at http://wislawjournal.com/2009/09/28/bilingual-attorneys-find-steady-work

Arzoz X (ed) (2012) Bilingual higher education in the legal context: group rights, state policies and globalization. Brill-Nijhoff, Leiden

Atiyah P, Summers R (1987) Form and substance in Anglo-American law: a comparative study of legal reasoning, legal theory, and legal institutions. Clarendon Press, Oxford

Conard A, Stein E (1957) Foreign law and foreign language. J Leg Educ 10:232–233

Cooper R (1996) A practitioner looks at globalization. J Leg Educ 46:313

Cotterrell R (2019) Comparative law and legal culture. In: Reimann M, Zimmermann R (eds) The Oxford handbook of comparative law, 2d edn. Oxford University Press, Oxford, pp. 710–733

Crank JP, Loughrin-Sacco S (2001) Foreign language across the curriculum: a model for the delivery of professional training. J Crim Just Edu 12:193–200

Curran V (1993) Developing and teaching a foreign language course for law students. J Leg Educ 43:598–605

[75] Upon the initiative of its current President, Vivian Grosswald Curran, the American Society of Comparative Law held a bilingual (French-English) conference before its annual meeting in October of 2017. The Society will include a foreign-language panel or component at its future meetings, beginning in 2019.

Curran V (2005) The role of foreign languages in education lawyers for transnational challenges. Penn State Int Law Rev 23:779–783
Curran V (2019) Comparative law and language. In: Reimann M, Zimmermann R (eds) The Oxford handbook of comparative law, 2d edn. Oxford University Press, Oxford, pp. 681–709
Dutton G, Lyon B, Rathod J, Weissmann D (2013) Promoting language access in the legal academy. Univ Maryl J Race Religion Gender Class 13:6–48
Goethe JW (1907) Maximen und Reflexionen (orig. 1833). Goethe Gesellschaft, Weimar
Herder JG (1784–1790) Ideen zur Philosophie der Geschichte der Menschheit (Zweiter Teil. Neuntes Buch. Menschenbildung. Sprache, Tradition, Kultur, Staat, Religion 1785) Hartknoch, Riga and Leipzig
Lacey F, Garcia Reyes J (1981) Training in foreign language for students of transnational law: advanced legal and business Spanish at Vanderbilt law school. J Leg Educ 31:657–663
Lakoff G (1987) Women, fire, and dangerous things: what categories reveal about the mind. University of Chicago Press, Chicago
Maxeiner J (1998) International legal careers: paths and directions. Syracuse J Int Law Commer 21:35–44
Montesqieu C-LS (1748) De l'esprit des lois. Barrillot et fils, Geneva
Rathod J (2013) The transformative potential of attorney bilingualism. Mich J Law Reform 46:863–920
Reimann M (2014) The American advantage in global lawyering. Rabels Zeitschrift 78:1–36
Sanchez G (1997) A paradigm shift in legal education: preparing law students for the twenty-first century: teaching foreign law, culture and legal language of major U.S. American trading partners. San Diego Law Rev 34:635–679
Slaughter AM (2004) The international dimension of the law school curriculum. Pa State Int Law Rev 22:417–419
Standing Committee on Legal Aid & Indigent Defendants (2012) ABA standards for access in courts. American Bar Association, Chicago
Strong SI (2014) Bilingual legal education in the United States: an idea whose time has come. J Leg Educ 64:354–362
Strong SI, Fach Gomez K, Carballo Pineiro L (2016) Comparative law for Spanish speaking laywers. Routledge, Northampton
Uyehara P (2003) Opening our doors to language-minority clients. Clear Rev 2003:544–557
Volkert CA (2013) Foreign language skills see rising demand in legal market (Nov. 6, 2013), Available at http://horberthalf.com/legal/blog/foreign-language-skills-see-high-demand-in-legal-market
von Savigny FC (1814) Vom Beruf unserer Zeit für Gesetzgebung und Rechtswissenschaft. Mohr und Zimmer, Heidelberg
von Savigny FC (1831) On the vocation of our age for legislation and jurisprudence (trans: Hayward A). Littlewood & Co. Old Bailey, London
Ward R (1996) The French language in Louisiana law and legal education: a requiem. Louisiana Law Rev 57:1283–1324